THE JEWELRY BOOK

Edited by
Melanie Grant

Introduction	4
Featured Entries	12
Directory	312
Index	315
Credits & Acknowledgments	325

The Freedom of Jewelry
—Melanie Grant

"The function of freedom is to free someone else."
—Toni Morrison

Jewelry is perhaps the most enduring expression of freedom that exists in material culture. It is currency, art, and history, reaching far back to the ancient world, and in this book, we celebrate the power of jewelry through three hundred of its most ardent innovators, including significant artists, designers, luxury houses, gem carvers, goldsmiths, dealers, galleries, and the icons and collectors who have adorned themselves through the ages. Spanning more than two centuries, those featured have been curated with the help of a panel of international experts, and their stories told by a selection of the foremost writers in the world of jewelry today. In choosing the final list of subjects for inclusion, a variety of elements were taken into account: the relevance of a subject during its time as well as its lasting impact on the jewelry landscape, wider cultural influence through specific aesthetic trends, the implementation of pioneering techniques, recognition for those previously overlooked, and an eye toward emerging designers who are moving jewelry in new directions, among many other considerations. The antique, vintage, and contemporary are examined with equal fascination; costume and fine jewelry share pages with high and artist jewelry. This is a modern encyclopedia dedicated to artistry, and it starts with the idea that pleasure is everything.

In the ancient world, when living a long life was far from guaranteed, this was especially the case. The average life expectancy during the Bronze and Iron Ages was around twenty-six years old, in ancient Greece it was twenty-eight, and in ancient Rome it was the grand old age of thirty-three, which meant that pleasure was an absolute priority. Hedonism as a life goal juxtaposed constant war, and because of the intensity of daily life, emotion was electrified. Jewelry came to mark achievements on the battlefield, passion in the bedroom, and true love fortified with deep spiritual meaning. As an empire, Rome was built on the assimilation of other cultures with trade and commerce as its backbone. In jewelry, the Romans absorbed styles from North Africa, Asia Minor, and Europe, employing casting techniques that enabled them to disperse a single design to the masses, and with that, the early "brand" was born.

Solid gold bangles studded with jasper, emeralds, and garnets imported from Egypt adorned the rich, while bronze peppered with amber, moonstone, and onyx beautified the lower echelons of society. Natural pearls from the Persian Gulf were, even then, incredibly rare and so highly valued that pearl beads were crafted as an alternative to the real thing and worn as clustered earrings called *crotalia* or "rattles." Senators wore huge gold rings set with gobstopper gemstones and, lower down the ranks, plebeians wore more conservative rings of iron. Freeborn Roman women had complete control over their own jewelry—buying and selling at will, independent of spousal control—and this, in time, resulted in a jewelry-wearing bonanza so extreme that during an economic crisis in the third century BCE, after the Second Punic War, the authorities decided to crack down.

Complex sumptuary laws were created in Rome in 215 BCE to dampen wildly extravagant living. Censors were tasked with listing offenders' crimes of excessive luxury, issuing *nota censoria* ("censorial marks") that resulted in social or legal penalties. The wearing of silk was restricted due to its high import costs from China and its heavy toll on state coffers, as was the wearing of Tyrian purple, which, if flouted by lay citizens, was punishable by death. The Roman laws of the Twelve Tables even warned against luxurious funerals and "excessive" mourning. Jewelry was an instant marker of one's station, education, and, ultimately, freedom. As merchant classes everywhere became richer, the aristocracy used sumptuary laws to curtail their social powers and to keep the best jewels for themselves, using moral and religious grounds to reinforce the status quo. In ancient Greece, centuries beforehand, the Spartans were not permitted to own gold or silver and instead had to use iron money. Iron is still the material symbol of subjugation in many cultures to this day.

As more people flocked to cities, sumptuary laws set boundaries using class as a mechanism for social order, but it was devilishly difficult to enforce them because consumption compels people to break the rules. In a consumer society, then as today, jewelry represents more than simple supply and demand. It is about the fulfillment of one's wildest dreams by reaching a peak of desire before being willingly overwhelmed by the commercial object at hand. Desire often intensifies over time alongside the knowledge required to build an important collection. The more you know, the deeper you go. The more you have, the more you want—wine, watches, cars, houses, couture clothing, and, of course, jewelry.

Diamonds, gold, platinum, rubies, emeralds, and sapphires may be the precious materials of modern society, but the idea of luxury has evolved over time. Once, exotic food and spices were the ultimate prizes. For the Aztecs, cacao beans were more precious than gold, and were traded as a currency. In the sixth century CE, the people of the Kingdom of Ghana traded an ounce of gold, which was an abundant natural resource, for an ounce of salt, which was exquisitely rare. The relationship between luxury and necessity is ever changing, and jewelry, long considered a luxury, in time also became acknowledged as a necessity within the happiness economy: when our basic needs are met, our psychological and emotional needs become paramount.

The late fourteenth century saw the rising merchant middle classes—who traded and traveled extensively between Europe, Asia, Africa, and, later, the Americas, and who were inevitably influenced by foreign tastes—often flouted sumptuary laws. They were also freer to wear unorthodox fashions, unlike the aristocracy, who were bound by strict conventions of historic protocol. During the reign of Louis XIV in France (1643–1715), the upper classes flocked to the theater and opera in their bejeweled finery, parures glittering in the evening light. Night watchmen lined the boulevards and ensured that the bourgeoisie and their huge jewels were safe as they strolled around dimly lit Paris streets. They were still subject to sumptuary laws, but historically there were always exceptions: In the thirteenth century, Louis IX had banned all women from wearing diamonds, considering only the Virgin Mary worthy of such a privilege. In the 1440s, Agnès Sorel, the low-born mistress of King Charles VII, openly defied the law by flaunting a diamond pendant given to her by the king. Because she was in his favor, she got away with it, inciting scandal and new court trends in equal measure. For those less wily, connected, or powerful, falling afoul of the sumptuary laws could be a dangerous business.

The onset of the Industrial Revolution in 1760 saw factories mass-produce "product" for the first time, empowering whole economies with stable growth and leading to the free markets enjoyed today. Consumerism, as a democratically attainable display of power, flourished, and in a capitalist secular society, woe betide any king, queen, politician, or priest who attempted to reinstate a sumptuary law in more modern times. The only thing, in theory, standing between each member of society and the jewelry of their dreams was money and desire, but as we know, life is never quite that simple. Hierarchies in place for centuries in societies across the globe, whether they be religious, tribal, caste, or class, still dictated what most people could buy or wear—until society thought otherwise.

Nearly a century earlier, in 1675, Native Americans who were captured during the First Indian War in New England—led by Wampanoag chief Metacom as he fought the invasion of their ancestral lands by English colonists—were enslaved by the English and sent to the plantations of Jamaica, Bermuda, and Barbados, taking with them a spiritual connection to silver, shell, and turquoise. In the 1770s, the enslaved populations on Caribbean plantations were restricted and forbidden to wear jewelry except for small gold hoop earrings. Those taken from Africa already had a deep heritage connected to gold, so when the gold hoop, or Creole earring, crossed continents, it endured as a symbol of beauty and then rebellion in Black culture. Having begun life in Nubia (modern-day Sudan), gold hoops appeared around 2500 BCE before surfacing later in Egypt, ancient Greece and Rome, Renaissance Europe, then in Latin America and the Caribbean, and finally found a more contemporary home in 1980s hip-hop culture worn by artists such as Salt-N-Pepa and MC Lyte.

As a coterie of freed slaves eventually grew in size and wealth in the Caribbean, sumptuary laws based on race rather than class were created to suppress and separate them from whites by restricting their access to jewelry, inheritance, and jobs. Merchants were threatened with enslavement for selling them items considered above their station, and when that didn't work, other measures were taken. On the Dutch Caribbean island of St. Maarten, for example, an ordinance adopted in 1860 ordered all free people of color to wear a red ribbon, combining race and social rank into one ominous non-jewelry wearing symbol.

In Japan in the twelfth century CE, rank was all-important, with the samurai at the top of society, followed by artisans, farmers, and merchants who languished at the bottom. During the Edo period (1603–1867), a shogunate military rule provided an era of peace and prosperity. The merchants capitalized on the economic boom and surpassed the samurai financially, and so stringent sumptuary laws were enacted to bring them back into line. A particular focus was placed on gold—banning gold thread, gold and silver leaf, and even gold lacquer on riding saddles to force the merchants to show some decorum. Elaborate hairpins were the jewelry of the day, and as the "new money" gathered pace, the virtue associated with humble attire by the samurai was eclipsed. In time, as the country opened its doors to the world, Japanese society became accustomed to wearing jewelry on the body as well. Then in 1893, Kokichi Mikimoto (see p.195) crafted the first cultured pearl, bringing jewelry democracy to the millions who had previously never had a chance of owning a natural pearl and overcoming the very notion of the sumptuary laws with a single invention.

It could be argued perhaps that no culture takes jewelry quite as seriously or delves into the complexity of class quite so profoundly as that of India. The country's three-thousand-year-old caste system may be separated into four main groups, but within those there are around three thousand castes and around twenty-five thousand subcastes. Outside and beneath these divisions sit the Dalits, or "untouchables," and as the lowest tier of society, they traditionally wear jewels made of iron, tin, or glass. Even brass was thought too extravagant for them, and if they possessed or were gifted gold or silver, it was considered too dangerous or uncouth to wear. The irony is that the humble materials the untouchables were allowed to wear have now, in the West, become the symbols for art jewelry. Iron, tin, and glass allow the transference of meaning without being overwhelmed by intrinsic value. There is still pressure for Dalits not to wear bright colors or gold jewelry, but some are flouting the rules. Much like many in the African diaspora who survived slavery only to face ongoing social and economic discrimination in the West, many Dalits today make a point of being flamboyantly dressed and of choosing their own style.

At the other end of the privilege scale is the monarchy, with access to the finest couturiers and jewelers but only within the constraints of royal protocol. With huge amounts of gold and precious stones acquired and secured in the throne rooms around the world, queens could revel in their wealth, layering eye-watering diamonds and pearls as Marie Antoinette did, woven into her wigs and stitched into her gowns (see p.183), while the lowest classes were lucky to wear jewelry at all. Historically, royal duties within European dynasties have demanded a queen, depending on her engagements, change up to five times a day, requiring matching parures or sets of lavish jewelry. Queen Mary (1867–1953) liked to pair a grand tiara with a seven-strand diamond choker, stomacher, matching brooches, medals, earrings, bracelets, rings, and the odd strand of pearls. As the grandmother of Elizabeth II, she assembled much of what is now the British Crown Jewels. She was given hundreds of extravagant gemstones during her time as queen consort, and she layered herself in them to dramatic effect (see pp.97, 187). On her coronation in 1967, Empress Farah of Iran was crowned with a tiara created by Van Cleef & Arpels from gemstones taken from the Treasury of National Jewels, delivered from their resting place in the vault at the Iranian Central Bank (see pp.218, 291). Pierre Arpels made twenty-four trips to visit the stones in Tehran before setting up residence in the bank's underground treasure chamber and working from a temporary workshop. The Iranian National Jewels still act as a reserve for the national currency.

In precolonial West Africa, the kingdom of Benin, located east of Lagos in what is now southern Nigeria, was a wealthy nation admired for its stylized gold, brass, and ivory sculpture. Sumptuary laws in Benin restricted *agbadas*, the flowing robes for men, to the upper echelons of society and enforced import restrictions on many items, including jewelry, through a series of specially created administrative posts that funneled the best jewels and clothing directly to the royal court. Access to coral was reserved for the king, who would issue a royal warrant to others he thought worthy of its significance. He would appear like a flame on the horizon during the annual royal festivities, bedecked in coral and riding sidesaddle to dazzle his subjects.

Despite its obvious intrinsic value, and even though it is brandished by the world's privileged, jewelry cannot be constrained by economics and social position alone. If that were the case, we would abandon it altogether in the face of unyielding sumptuary laws and difficult times. Instead, the baseline materials simply evolve. In Prussia, iron replaced gold from 1813 to 1815 when the royal family requested the donation of gold and silver jewelry to fund the War of Liberation to fight Napoleon. Berlin iron jewelry, which had originated in the Royal Prussian Iron Foundry a decade earlier, caught on and went from being an emblem of mourning to one of patriotism and resistance. Early pieces were even proudly stamped with the phrase "I gave gold for iron," in German. Still today the German style is darker, with design houses such as Hemmerle incorporating iron into their work (see p.133). In the 1890s, Cartier introduced their garland-style jewelry in platinum because of the density and durability of the metal (see p.54). Delicate platinum bows holding important diamonds were as strong as they were beautiful, but due to the metal's limited availability (all the platinum ever mined could fit into one room), only the most celebrated jewelers could afford to use it. During both World Wars, when platinum was banned in jewelry and reserved for machine parts, white gold was used as a substitute, and in time it became the metal of choice for most fine jewelers globally.

Though not a basic need like food and shelter, the consumption of jewelry endures, whether in precious metals and stones or in iron, tin, and glass. As a luxury good and an art form, jewelry has developed over time into an emotional need linked to happiness, creativity, and self-expression rather than physical survival. Spanish artist Pablo Picasso viewed jewelry as his most intimate form of expression—fashioned in shell, ceramic, gold—and gave his pieces away to those he loved most (see p.223). Excited by working in a new medium and exploring new elements of scale and dimension, he created his wearable sculptures with enthusiasm. In the 1910s and early '20s, Picasso was also commissioned by the Parisian avant-garde dance company Ballets Russes, which promoted lavish collaborations between musical composers, choreographers, and designers—including such luminaries as Gabrielle "Coco" Chanel (see p.60)—to make extravagant sets and costumes, dazzling all in attendance. Ever the rebel, Chanel famously mixed and wore costume jewelry with precious jewels at a time when to do so was shocking. Collaborating with Goossens, and later Gripoix in the 1950s, on costume jewels featuring both semiprecious and faux stones, Chanel brought this sensibility to the masses and forever changed the jewelry landscape and paved the way for other costume jewelry creators such as Trifari and Alexis Bittar (see pp.33, 126, 129, 287).

Theater eventually gave way to the talkies in the late 1920s and '30s, and a new tier of aspirational icons evolved. Ropes of pearls, Art Deco designs, and big diamond jewels worn by the likes of Marlene Dietrich, Greta Garbo, and Ginger Rogers flashed across the screen (see pp.88, 116). As Hollywood rose to prominence, the glitz and glamour of the red carpet as a concept followed. (Harry Winston set a high bar in 1943 when he became the first jeweler to loan pieces to a celebrity for the Academy Awards, see p.132.) At the same time, in 1925, a nineteen-year-old Josephine Baker was twirling onstage in Paris in little more than a skirt of rubber bananas and long strands of pearls. As a civil rights activist, she joined the French Resistance, smuggling messages in her music sheets during World War II, and was rarely seen without lashings of jewelry—a reminder to herself and others that she was never going back to her impoverished beginnings in Missouri (see p.27).

In the most troubled of times, jewelry has evolved and expanded in new and interesting ways. In ancient Rome when war, famine, or pestilence threatened, jewelry became more outrageous, more seductive, and more important. More recently, during the COVID-19 pandemic, beauty and pleasure became vital currencies, with literature, film, and art keeping the world sane, and jewelry lovers dancing in all their collectibles alone at home as a mode of self-preservation. According to Sotheby's, their online sales of jewelry skyrocketed in 2020 and were seven times higher than in 2019, leaping by 667 percent, compared with a more moderate increase of 13 percent from 2020 to 2021 year on year (see p.267). When life is at its most challenging, we surround ourselves with objects imbued with emotion that bring us happiness.

Yet the style and significance of what we choose to wear in modern society—when we can have almost anything now that the rules of even feudal serfdom have been largely challenged—still often align with social hierarchy and expectations. Power pearls originating in Japan, for example, have been worn by public figures such as Jacqueline Kennedy Onassis and Michelle Obama, who wished to appear feminine yet conservatively dressed (see pp.150, 214). If a woman in politics were to wear massive Creole hoops or a towering tiara as an expression of identity, she would be met with shock and, likely, outrage. The unspoken rules of jewelry etiquette still exist in the public eye regardless of budget and perceived social freedom. But even in the face of such rules (unwritten or otherwise), when people wear jewelry, they inspire others to do the same—whether in 3100 BCE when the Egyptians first mined gold, in the Golden Age of Hollywood, or in the 1980s, when women first entered the corporate jungle wearing shoulder pads and chunky gold statement jewels in search of equality. Chasing the outer trappings of a better life or as a means of defiant self-expression, whatever the consequences, is contagious. The fact that no one needs jewelry and yet so many have scaled the walls of ferocious class systems with little more than a burning desire and a purse full of hard-earned cash makes it all the more profound.

But even capitalism has its limits. Sustainability movements advocated by millennials, Gen Z, and a growing number of activists are fighting fast fashion and environmental pressures around waste. Transparency in the supply chain—where the materials used in jewelry-making come from and their entire journey from mine to market—now matters to many as much as the design, the maker, and the price. Greg Valerio, an early supporter and pioneer of ethical gold and mercury-free mining, is now working with ex-militia in the Democratic Republic of the Congo to integrate them into small-scale gold mining operations (see p.289). Ute Decker crafts her modernist jewels exclusively in Fairmined gold, of which she was one of the earliest adopters (see p.84). Younger customers especially want to know more about the ethical credentials of the creations they're wearing. Lab-grown diamonds are increasing their share of the market using alternative forms of energy but also have an environmental impact; blockchain technology is tracking each time a diamond changes hands; and a growing number of companies are embracing sustainability standards spurred by a need to protect the planet and abide by ever-evolving legislation.

According to the World Gold Council, 238,391 tons (216,265 tonnes) of gold have been mined since the beginning of human history, with two-thirds of that since 1950 alone. Of all the gold in existence today, about 45 percent goes into the jewelry industry and 55 percent goes to gold bars, coins, central banks, and reserves. If the art and application of jewelry chart the course of societal evolution both figuratively and literally, then the nature of accessibility to resources such as these represents the future power in society. And in the end, all fine jewelry is preserved or recycled—no one is throwing away a gold bar or a pocketful of diamonds. Our own time with our favorite pieces also might be fleeting, but the permanence of these materials dictates that beloved heirlooms are passed down through generations. Despite our ardent desire to acquire jewelry, the ownership of it is an illusion. As one of the great jewelry collectors, Elizabeth Taylor, once wrote in her autobiography *My Love Affair with Jewelry*, "I'm here to take care of it and to love it, for we are only temporary custodians of beauty."

And yet our collective desire to bedazzle is unquenchable. A new generation of designers has taken up the call, just as likely to break the rules as to pay homage to jewelry traditions. That manifests in a range of unusual materials appearing in high jewelry, such as Claire Choisne at Boucheron compacting black sand in her *Sable Noir* necklace, which uses 3D printing with a polymer binder in a technique borrowed from the aeronautical industry (see p.39). Or John Moore creating gargantuan neckpieces out of his newly invented material called Morphit—clay mixed with recycled paper but that contains no ceramic and air-dries rather than needing to be fired (see p.200). The way we make and wear jewelry is itself a cycle. Harry Styles in a drop-pearl Gucci earring at the Met Gala goes back to Charles I's penchant for a single baroque pearl dangling from one ear. A$AP Rocky and his gold grillz (see p.112) are connected to Mayan royalty drilling holes in their teeth and filling them with jade or to rich Etruscan women replacing their front teeth with new ones banded together with gold. Gender is now irrelevant, with sales of tiaras at Chaumet as likely to go to a man buying for himself as a woman (see pp.41, 63).

This new freedom for jewelry across class, gender, and race is now absolute, defying carefully constructed rules built over thousands of years to suppress and control. The eighteenth-century economist Adam Smith viewed collecting "baubles and trinkets" as an irresponsible and frivolous utility that would lead disastrously to insatiable desire. To defer personal pleasure in his view was to be strong, and to avoid it altogether was advisable. But time and again jewelry has disproven that theory, bringing uncontrollable joy into our lives. The concept of pleasure may not have changed much since ancient Rome, but now everyone (budget permitting) is able to indulge in wearing jewelry previously denied them by birth and by law—jewelry that speaks of freedom and at times defiance. That makes me very happy indeed.

Adler

Adler
est. Istanbul, Turkey, 1886

Electric Titanium earrings in titanium and 18-karat white gold set with diamonds and two pear-shaped tanzanites.

Classic white diamonds in grand parures may be the staple of Swiss jeweler Adler, created from their atelier nestled in Geneva, but their story began in 1886 in the ancient city of Constantinople, now Istanbul. With the maxim that true luxury is human connection, founder Jacques Adler originally trained as a goldsmith in Vienna before traveling to Istanbul and opening a small boutique. He forged a design aesthetic across East and West, before passing the company down four generations to its current custodians, Allen, Karen, and Daisy Adler. Their "classics with a twist" aesthetic includes collections such as *Evdokia*, a golden ode to olive trees from Corfu, and *Papagayo*, inspired by the lush greens of the Amazon. Since the 1980s, baguette diamonds have been a frequent feature, as have large diamonds and colored gems arranged asymmetrically. Added to this is the use of unexpected materials, such as wood, carbon, and titanium, seen in the folded, pavé-encrusted *Sail* earrings or the twisted, gem-set *Electric Titanium* line, and Adler continues to surprise and innovate. As part of its legacy, the family also supports artists in other disciplines and, beginning in 2014, young jewelers at Geneva's Haute École d'Art et de Design.

Salimah Aga Khan

Salimah Aga Khan (Sarah Frances Croker-Poole)
b. New Delhi, India, 1940

Sarah Frances Croker-Poole models for a magazine shoot, 1969.

Photograph by Clive Arrowsmith.

The extraordinary collection of jewels accumulated by Salimah Aga Khan is a reflection of an equally extraordinary life. Born Sarah Frances Croker-Poole in New Delhi, she was raised in England from early childhood. Following a brief first marriage, Poole found success in the 1960s as a fashion model in London and beyond, photographed by the likes of Cecil Beaton, Richard Avedon, and Norman Parkinson. It was in London where she met the Aga Khan IV, Prince Karim Al-Husseini. The couple married in 1969, and Poole became Begum Salimah Aga Khan. Over the years, she put together an impressive collection, made up of antique gems from both her grandmothers and pieces newly commissioned from Boucheron, Cartier, and Harry Winston, among others (see pp.39, 54, 132). After divorcing in 1995, the princess auctioned off pieces at Christie's in Geneva for charity, realizing a staggering $27 million. Headline lots included a Boucheron two-row yellow and white diamond necklace; the Begum Blue heart-shaped 13.78-carat diamond; and a 1970s Cartier necklace set with two 50-carat emeralds. The standout, though, was a 1971 Van Cleef & Arpels commission from the Aga Khan: a necklace that can be transformed into a choker with two matching bracelets and a clip, set with 44 engraved emeralds and more than 745 diamonds (see p.291).

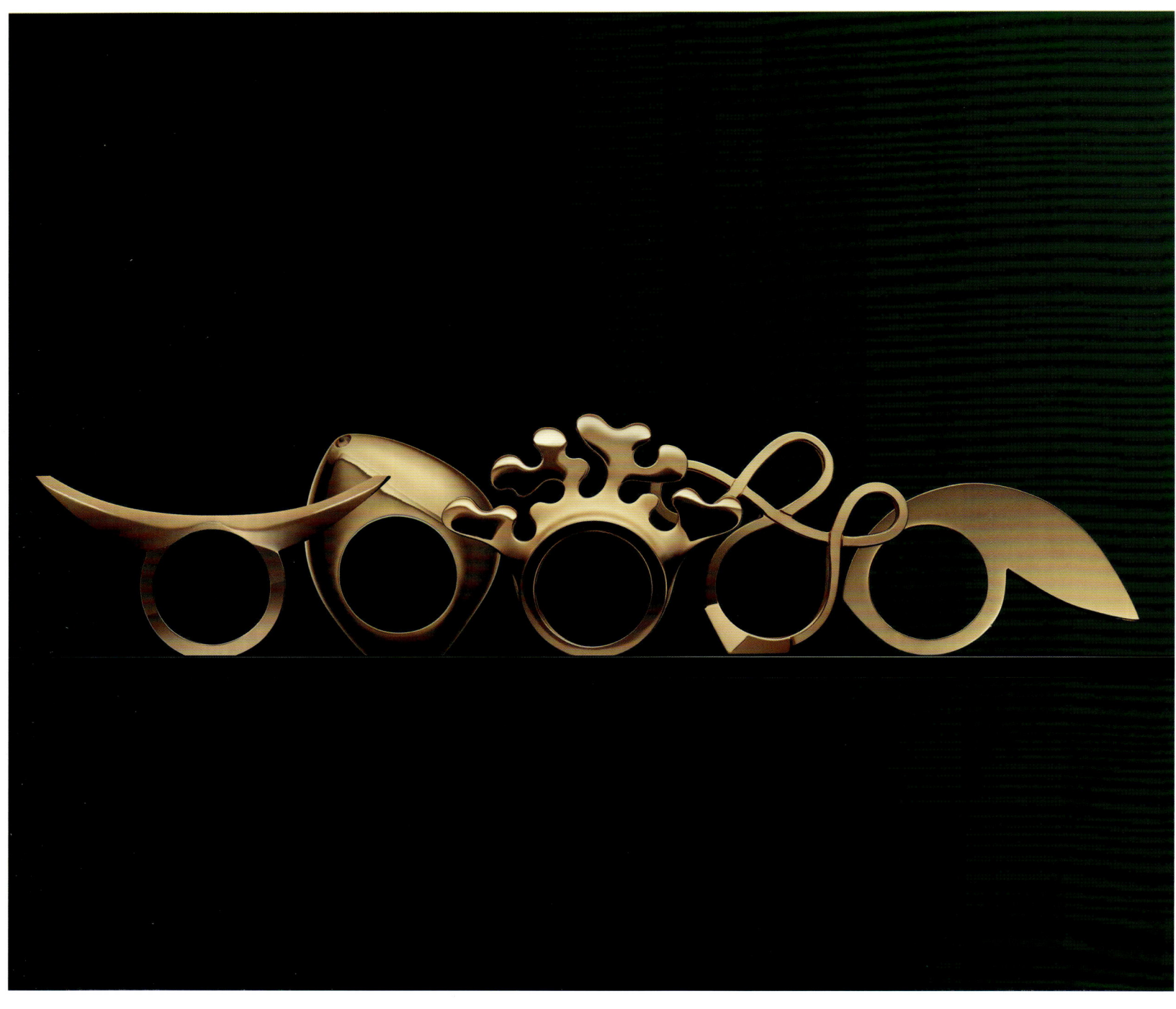

Walid Akkad

Walid Akkad
b. Beirut, Lebanon, 1965

Rings from the *Bestiaire* collection in 18-karat red gold, representing the forms of a bull, hedgehog, moose, serpent, and rabbit.

Photograph by Jeremy Zenou.

As a teenager, Beirut-born Walid Akkad moved with his family to Paris, where he went on to study jewelry design at the prestigious École de la Chambre Syndicale de Bijouterie et de Horlogerie. Since the inception of his eponymous brand in 1999, Akkad has been weaving natural beauty into his striking, modern jewels, inspired by renowned English landscape designer Russell Page's fantastical gardens, as well as his deep appreciation for Italian, French, and English gardens. Approaching each piece with reverence, Akkad analyzes his inspirations, sketches detailed concepts, and evaluates form and function before carefully constructing wax models and prototypes. Harmony and balance—cornerstones of his design philosophy—are evident alongside a minimalist aesthetic, where gold and silver are gently twisted and sculpted into sinuous earrings and bracelets. In his *Bestiaire* collection, twenty-one creatures—including a chicken, moose, moth, and octopus—are imagined in their most elemental forms in 18-karat red gold. Guided by the principles of light, Akkad also frequently incorporates gemstones and diamonds into the asymmetrical recesses and hidden surfaces of his jewels. For more than three decades, working from his Paris Atelier, Akkad has masterfully orchestrated simplicity and elegance in his limited-edition and one-of-a-kind creations.

The Al Thani Collection

The Al Thani Collection est. London, England, and Paris, France, 2014

Tiger's Eye Turban Ornament in platinum and diamonds created by Cartier London in 1937, part of the Al Thani Collection.

Photograph by Laziz Hamani.

Passionate about art and history since his first visit to the Louvre at the age of six, Sheikh Hamad bin Abdullah Al Thani has grown into a discerning collector and patron of the arts. Over the past twenty years, he has amassed around five thousand pieces of artwork, jewelry, and precious objects spanning millennia and diverse cultures, forming what is now known as the Al Thani Collection. Seemingly simple items, such as a gold pendant recognized as one of the earliest examples of goldsmithing, dating back to at least 3500 BCE, sit alongside elaborate Mughal gem-set decorative objects. Among the collection's rarities are a lavishly ornate Hellenistic golden clasp that mimics a knot from 300 BCE, and a large sixteenth-century pendant that features an intaglio on carnelian, framed in a diamond-and-ruby-studded golden circle with three drop pearls. The collection also features ornate sabers, Byzantine coins, embroidered textiles, sculptures, and illuminated manuscripts of the Quran. First shared publicly in 2014 with an exhibition of Mughal jewels held at the Metropolitan Museum of Art in New York, the collection has been shown widely at institutions around the world. Since 2021, it has found a home at the Hôtel de la Marine on Place de la Concorde in Paris, where a dedicated museum space offers visitors a wonder-filled journey through objects across time and cultures.

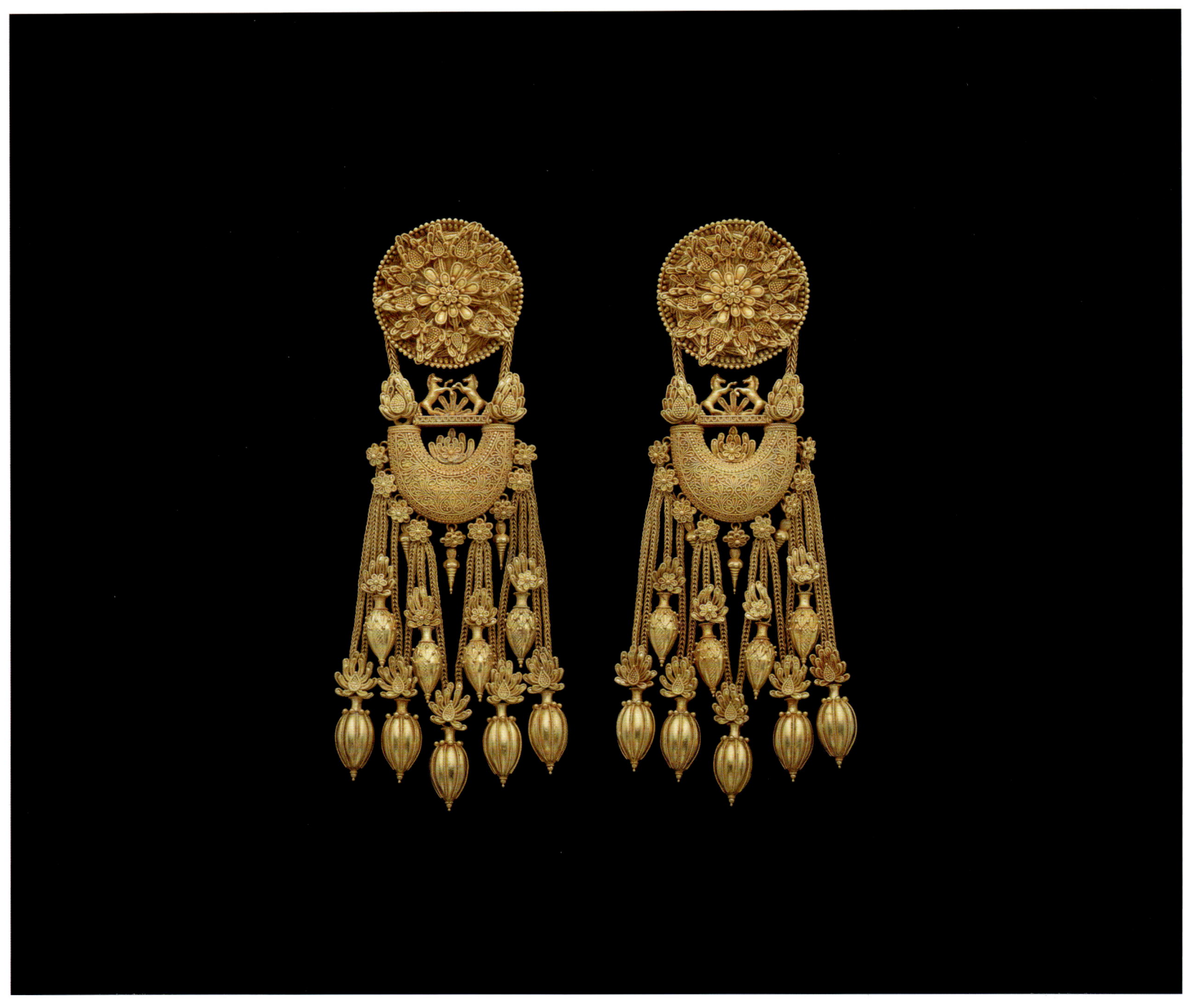

Albion Art

Albion Art
est. Tokyo, Japan, 1985

Hellenistic granulation and filigree gold earrings from ancient Greece, 4th century BCE, part of the Albion Art collection.

Renowned for its vast array of historic Western jewelry, spanning from ancient times to the twentieth century, Albion Art was founded by Japanese collector Kazumi Arikawa in 1985. Arikawa's belief in the power of beauty as a beacon of spiritual enlightenment underpins Albion Art's collecting philosophy. The distinctive approach is the result of both his background as a Buddhist monk and his early career working in his mother's jewelry business. However, it was not until he saw masterpieces of historic jewelry at the Victoria and Albert Museum during a visit to London in 1982 that he decided to abandon the commercial jewelry market and focus instead on handling only the finest and rarest historic pieces. Arikawa seeks to showcase the talismanic, purifying, and uplifting properties of jewels across generations of owners. The collection is particularly known for cameos and dynastic jewelry—especially tiaras and parures associated with the royal houses of Europe. With such an expansive collection, Albion Art is also an institute for learning, and the pieces have been exhibited in museums around the world. Albion Art's store in the Modernist Okura Tokyo hotel and a nearby showroom where a Romanesque cloister, extensive library, and Japanese tearoom combine, only amplify the inspirational power of the exceptional historic jewelry creations on display.

Madeleine Albright

Madeleine Albright
b. Prague, Czechoslovakia, 1937
d. Washington, DC,
United States, 2022

Madeleine Albright, 2000.

Photograph by Deborah Feingold.

Diplomat, professor, author, US ambassador to the United Nations, Madame Secretary. Madeleine Korbel Albright was the sixty-fourth secretary of state of the United States—the first woman ever to hold the position, appointed by President Bill Clinton in January 1997 and serving through January 2001. A renowned and skilled political leader, Dr. Albright—who immigrated to the United States from war-torn Czechoslovakia in November 1948—was a champion of freedom, democracy, and human rights. Throughout her public service and beyond, she was an avid lover of decorative and fine jewelry, namely brooches, selecting from her collection of more than two hundred pieces to express her stance on various issues. She subtly deployed an 18-karat yellow gold snake coiled around a branch with a drop diamond hanging from its mouth while meeting with Iraqi officials at the UN Security Council in response to Saddam Hussein's poet in residence calling Albright "an unparalleled serpent." During Secretary of State Hillary Clinton's receipt of the Lantos Human Rights Prize in 2013, Albright wore a fused, shattered-glass pin by artist Vivian Shimoyama with 22-karat-gold trim to honor "breaking the glass ceiling." Her approach to jewelry was both innovative and symbolic, turning accessories into powerful tools of personal expression and diplomacy.

Alexandra of Denmark

Alexandra of Denmark,
Queen Consort of Great Britain
b. Copenhagen, Denmark, 1844
d. Norfolk, England, 1925

Queen Alexandra, 1889.

In 1863 the young Alexandra, daughter of Christian IX of Denmark, married Albert "Bertie" Edward, the Prince of Wales. Alexandra had been raised in modest circumstances in the Danish royal household, but a wedding gift from the prince of a suite of pearl and diamond jewels made by Garrard (see p.117)—still worn by the Royal Family today—was a sign that her status had improved considerably. Notwithstanding the austerity of Queen Victoria's reign (see p.301), Alexandra dazzled the court with pearl and diamond chokers—said to cover up a small childhood scar on her slender neck—layered with Golconda diamond rivières, chains, and garlands of pearls with fabric chokers to match her gowns, as well as an array of brooches and a gold serpent bracelet. It was a look that set a trend society ladies followed for fifty years. Both as a princess and later as queen consort, Alexandra often refashioned old jewelry as tastes changed, just as she did for her clothes. However, she had a particular fondness for tiaras. She inherited Victoria's *Oriental Circlet* made by Garrard and had the house replace the opals with Burmese rubies from the royal collection. Garrard also created the *Kokoshnik* tiara for Alexandra, a halo design borrowed from her sister, Empress Maria Feodorovna of Russia, inspired by traditional Russian headdress.

Francesca Amfitheatrof

Francesca Amfitheatrof
b. Tokyo, Japan, 1968

Victoire necklace in platinum, white gold, and diamonds, designed by Francesca Amfitheatrof for Louis Vuitton's *Awakened Minds* high jewelry collection, 2024.

Photograph by Nathaniel Goldberg.

Few designers' careers have been so much in the public eye as that of Francesca Amfitheatrof. Her first show of silver jewelry and objets in 1993 was at the iconic White Cube gallery, where Karl Lagerfeld and Giorgio Armani bought pieces, elevating her to the pinnacle of the art and fashion worlds almost instantaneously. Since then, Amfitheatrof has worked with the likes of Chanel, Giovanni Corvaja (see pp.60, 73), Wedgwood, and the Gucci Museo. In 2001 jewelers Asprey & Garrard recruited her to lead their design teams, but becoming Tiffany & Co.'s first woman design director in 2013 was her big break (see pp.117, 283). Her two iconic collections, *Tiffany T* and *City HardWear*, revealed a minimalist, urban style, though her revival of *Blue Book* high jewelry was mainly based on designer Jean Schlumberger's mid-century Tiffany archive (see p.251). Amfitheatrof joined Louis Vuitton as artistic director of jewelry and watches in 2018, where she developed a strong image with bold metalwork and standout stones. She has favored grand themes, including heroic medieval women (*Riders of the Knights*) and the evolution of life on Earth (*Deep Time*). While continuing her work as artistic director until 2025, Amfitheatrof also became the head of creative at Codognato (see p.71).

Iris Apfel

Iris Apfel
b. New York, New York, United States, 1921
d. Palm Beach, Florida, United States, 2024

Iris Apfel on her 100th birthday, New York, 2021.

Photograph by Noam Galai.

A self-professed "accidental" style icon, Iris Apfel was a renowned interior designer immediately identifiable by her bold and maximalist aesthetic. Her signature style of "more is more and less is a bore" was characterized by a mix-and-match eclecticism that featured oversize statement jewelry—chunky beaded necklaces, large bangles, ornate earrings, and vintage accessories across various cultures and eras—coupled with an irreverent embrace of vivid colors and layered textures. Apfel grew up in New York scouring flea markets for costume jewelry, later was a copywriter for *Women's Wear Daily*, and then, shortly after marrying in 1948, she and her husband, Carl Apfel, began Old World Weavers, a textiles business that produced antiquelike fabrics; she also worked with nine presidential administrations at the White House as a restoration consultant. Later in life, throughout her nineties, she became a jewelry icon and symbol of joy, inspiration, and individuality for her millions of Instagram followers, dispensing with fashion norms and conformity. Her late-onset fame and collaborations were far-reaching—from the Metropolitan Museum of Art's 2005 Costume Institute exhibit *Rara Avis*, which featured more than three hundred of Apfel's accessories, to appearing on the cover of *Dazed* at ninety-one and signing up with IMG as a model at ninety-seven.

Assael

Assael
est. New York, New York,
United States, 1947

A pair of Fijian natural color cultured pearl earrings set on Willow Creek jasper and finished with lavender spinels set in 18-karat rose gold, from the *NatureScapes* collection, 2023.

Founded more than seventy-five years ago by Italian-born magnate Salvador Assael, the iconic New York company Assael is credited with bringing cultivated South Sea pearls to the jewelry marketplace as early as the 1950s. The company then successfully introduced cultivated Tahitian black pearls to the North American market in the late 1970s. Assael not only created a modern market for black pearls but was also known as someone who deeply valued his relationships with pearl farmers, paying them out of pocket when they had poor harvests. Because of his generosity, his eponymous company was always the first to receive rights to the latest pearls from these farms, even after his death in 2011. Assael's wife, Christina Lang Assael, took over the company and brought in master goldsmith Sean Gilson, who paired pearls with materials such as sustainably sourced coral, colored gems, and diamonds. It was Gilson who created Assael's popular *Bubble* collection, a playful jewelry line with a sophisticated mix of Akoya and South Sea pearls and natural Sardinian coral beads that appear to float around an 18-karat-gold setting. These latest innovations have transformed Assael from a wholesale pioneer to a full-fledged jewelry company, specializing in enhancing the natural beauty of pearls.

Joseph Asscher

Joseph Asscher
b. Amsterdam, Netherlands, 1871
d. Deauville, France, 1937

A feature on the cutting of the Royal Cullinan diamond, *The African World*, 1908.

Dutch-born gem dealer and diamond cutter Joseph Asscher is renowned today for his namesake Asscher cut, and contributed significant innovative techniques to jewelry-making. His family's multigenerational business—today's Royal Asscher Diamond Company—was founded in 1854 in Amsterdam, and its fame rose in parallel with the importance of the city as the heart of the global diamond industry. A leading *diamantaire*, Asscher introduced his now-iconic cut in 1902, after perfecting the distinctive step-cut faceting or steep, square shape. It was the world's first patented stone cut and became a hallmark synonymous with elegance and sophistication popular throughout the Art Deco era.

The cut features on the Cullinan II diamond on England's Imperial State Crown—one of nine stones cut by Asscher in 1908 from the world's largest rough diamond at that time, weighing 3,106 carats—and the famous Krupp diamond Richard Burton gave Elizabeth Taylor (see p.280). The Asscher cut's unique combination of geometry and symmetry allows diamonds to exhibit exceptional sparkle and depth, enhancing the stones' natural beauty and brilliance. Asscher was a pioneer in advancing diamond appraisal and grading, elevating the diamond's status as a symbol of luxury, rarity, and refinement, and influencing the industry's diamond standards for craft and artistry.

Ateliers Hugo

Ateliers Hugo
est. Paris, France, 1933

The workshop of Ateliers Hugo, 2022.

Photograph by Maxime Souyri.

From a small workshop in Aix-en-Provence, France, Ateliers Hugo was instrumental to the genre of artist's jewelry, thanks to collaborations with the likes of Jean Arp, Dorothea Tanning, Max Ernst, and Pablo Picasso (see pp.98, 223). Founded in Paris in 1933 by François Hugo, after World War II the house created enameled gilt buttons and costume jewelry for fashion houses such as Chanel and Schiaparelli (see pp.60, 250). But its place in history was cemented in 1956, when Picasso enlisted Hugo to cast gold and silver bowls and medallions he had designed for his close friends. Throughout the 1960s and '70s, Ateliers Hugo collaborated with the era's leading artists. François's son Pierre continued his father's tradition when he took the reins in 1975, partnering with luminaries including Salvador Dalí (see p.77). Today, the house is helmed by Pierre's son Nicolas, who maintains his family's legacy, working with contemporary artists such as Josh Sperling. The techniques remain unchanged since his grandfather's day, including the use of 23.91-karat gold, an alloy developed by François and his chemist wife, Monique, to achieve what they considered the ultimate color and intensity, with the strength that pure 24-karat gold lacks. The precious metal is hammered into shape, resulting in a weathered, almost ancient feeling—an aesthetic Nicolas describes as "sculptures to wear."

Solange Azagury-Partridge

Solange Azagury-Partridge
b. London, England, 1961

Cara Delevingne wears enameled *Hotlips* rings and diamond, yellow gold, and semiprecious-stone *Posie* rings by Solange Azagury-Partridge.

Photograph by Nick Knight.

For Solange Azagury-Partridge, becoming a jewelry designer was accidental. She studied linguistics at the University of Westminster and later joined London antiques dealer Gordon Watson, where she discovered her love for antique jewelry. In 1987 she designed her first piece, her own engagement ring—featuring a single uncut octahedral diamond mounted off-center in a domed gold band—because she couldn't find an existing ring she loved enough. "Finding a maker was hard, but I have never taken no for an answer," she said. By 1995 her clients included Madonna, and she had opened her first shop in Notting Hill, its padded red interior making "the neighbors mistake it for a brothel."

That same year, she released her iconic (and affordable) *Hotlips* ring series in a range of lipstick-inspired hues. In 2001 Tom Ford invited her to design for Boucheron as creative director (see p.39). Her first collection, filled with glowing, single-color gemstone pavé jewels, generated Place Vendôme–shaking headlines, and her four-golds *Quatre* ring remains an enduring design for the house long after her departure in 2004 to focus on her own brand. Working out of her London boutique, her collections channel everything from geology and mathematics to scribbles and the written word, using materials in a riot of colors, from rough stones to high-precision geometric cuts and intricate enamel.

Giampaolo Babetto

Giampaolo Babetto
b. Padua, Italy, 1947

From left: *Anello* in 18-karat white gold and niello, 1981; *Anello* in 18-karat yellow gold, 1983; and *Anello* in 18-karat white gold, 1981.

Photograph by Ali Emre Göloğlu.

A veteran goldsmith, Giampaolo Babetto is recognized as one of the world's most influential creators of avant-garde jewelry. He studied at Padua's Istituto Statale d'Arte Pietro Selvatico and later at the Accademia di Belle Arti di Venezia. Working with great sensitivity and precision, his pieces since the late 1960s have been characterized by pure and essential geometric forms, finding inspiration in the Palladian architecture of his homeland and modern art movements such as Constructivism, Minimalism, and kinetic or op art. His elegant jewels resemble miniature sculptures or architectural models, and at times individual elements are hinged together to allow movement, as in his cuboidal necklaces. His preference for working in gold owes to its malleability and warm luster, occasionally combining it with materials, such as plastic and glass. Babetto introduces color by coating select surfaces with velvety pigments or enamel in luminous green, blue, red, and yellow hues. He also uses the ancient niello inlay technique—where a black metallic alloy composed of sulfur mixed with silver, copper, or lead fills in engraved designs—to achieve arresting contrasts and highlights with the polished base metal. While Babetto is a great advocate of experimentation, he is always mindful of the functional demands of jewelry and strives to create objects that are expressive yet practical to wear.

Erykah Badu

Erykah Badu (Erica Abi Wright)
b. Dallas, Texas, United States, 1971

Erykah Badu walks the runway for Vogue World: New York wearing jewelry from her Badu World collection, 2022.

Photograph by JP Yim.

Neo-soul musician Erykah Badu has emerged as one of the most distinctive and original tastemakers of modern times. She uses jewelry to tell her story, choosing from independent brands, showcasing jewels picked up on her travels around the world, and commissioning one-of-a-kind pieces often made in collaboration with artists. When she emerged in 1997 with the album *Baduizm*, her jewelry choices honored her African American heritage with statement silver necklaces, thick cuffs, and rings. More recently, Badu has been seen gilded in custom full-finger rings and hand pieces in gold-dipped brass by Rome-based independent jeweler Angostura, or sporting tribal-inspired feather and metal face jewelry by Malakai in an eclectic mash-up of world cultures. Grillz have also become a signature for the singer, worn like armor as she strides through life, including her *Opal Grillz* made by Iranian American designer Lillian Shalom. In 2024 Badu was honored with the Fashion Icon Award by the Council of Fashion Designers of America (CFDA). To accept the award, she wore a custom headpiece and septum ring created by silver jeweler Chris Habana based on an AI-generated rendering by digital artist Parallel. The pieces melded nonspecific tribal and modern elements to create a vision of a global traveler in space and time, mirroring Badu's own philosophy in life and style.

Josephine Baker

Josephine Baker
b. St. Louis, Missouri,
United States, 1906
d. Paris, France, 1975

Josephine Baker performs in *La Folie du Jour* revue at Folies Bergère music hall, Paris, 1926.

Josephine Baker epitomized the Jazz Age flapper aesthetic on and off the stage of the Folies Bergère. After relocating from humble origins in St. Louis, Missouri, to Paris in 1925, the nineteen-year-old captivated audiences in the grandest theaters across the city. Baker made waves with her *Danse Sauvage*, a knowing play on stereotypes associated with Blackness. The strands of beads and oversize earrings she wore with her famous banana skirt tempered her near nudity, while their movement amplified her frenetic choreography. By contrast, Baker's offstage allure was sheer sophistication. Dressed in gowns by Poiret and Lanvin, she often wore ropes of pearls, earning her the epithet the Black Pearl of Paris. And she reveled in luxury, even adorning her pet cheetah with a diamond collar. One of Baker's most iconic looks features three *Giraffe* necklaces of red and black lacquer and *oréum* designed by Jean Dunand, for whom she was a muse. Dunand's famous designs, with a French interpretation of African aesthetics—geometric patterns borrowed from textiles as well as the layering found in the fashion of some groups—were cross-cultural inventions, just like the woman wearing them. Baker also rebelled against tyranny, joining the French resistance during World War II, where she sold pieces from her collection to fund food and coal supplies for the neediest citizens.

Suzanne Belperron

Suzanne Belperron
b. Saint-Claude, France, 1900
d. Paris, France, 1983

Suzanne Belperron designed the *Yin et Yang* ring in 1923 as her own engagement ring. The cushion-shaped diamond was given to her by her soon-to-be-husband, Jean Belperron, and set into hammered yellow gold in an avant-garde crossover design.

Famed for never signing her work, often stating that her style was her signature, jewelry designer Suzanne Belperron made her name in Paris in 1919 when she was first employed by the Parisian firm of Boivin (see p.35). In 1932 she transferred to Boivin's rival, gemstone dealer Bernard Herz and designed her own models there. In 1941, due to the Nazi occupation of Paris, Herz convinced Belperron to purchase the business and put it under her name. Herz did not survive the war, but his son, Jean, and Belperron held equal partnership from 1945 until Belperron's retirement and the closure of the business in 1974. Avant-garde for its time, Belperron's work deftly translated the prevailing Art Deco aesthetic into a new, modern style, replete with generous curves hewn from rock crystal and chalcedony, organic forms inspired by shells and foliage, and bold color combinations, such as citrine and gold. Her devoted clientele included Daisy Fellowes, Wallis Simpson, and Diana Vreeland—the sale of Simpson's personal collection in 1987 propelled a somewhat-forgotten Belperron back into the public's imagination (see pp.260, 267, 306). In 2015 the Belperron business was relaunched by former head of Sotheby's jewelry Ward Landrigan, and his son, Nico, now president of the company, using some 9,300 of Suzanne's archival drawings to create new collections of her timeless jewelry.

Beyoncé

Beyoncé (Beyoncé Knowles-Carter)
b. Houston, Texas,
United States, 1981

Beyoncé performs at the 59th Grammy Awards wearing a headdress, choker, and body jewelry by House of Malakai, Los Angeles, 2017.

Photograph by Kevork Djansezian.

One of the most decorated vocalists of her generation, Beyoncé Knowles-Carter rose to prominence in the late 1990s as the lead singer of R&B group Destiny's Child. Since then, her phenomenally successful solo career has encompassed eight best-selling albums, roles in films such as 2006's *Dreamgirls* and 2019's adaptation of *The Lion King*, and hundreds of accolades. To date, Knowles-Carter is the most honored female artist in Grammy Awards history. She is similarly celebrated for her glamorous red-carpet style, which usually includes spectacular diamond jewels. She is a frequent collaborator of designer Lorraine Schwartz and of Tiffany & Co., with whom she entered a commercial partnership in 2021 (see pp.252, 283). For the brand's Fall campaign that year, she became the fourth person ever to wear the 128.54-carat Tiffany Diamond. The house also provided an array of custom jewels for her 2023 Renaissance World Tour, including an Elsa Peretti metallic mesh dress and a bejeweled hat by milliner Stephen Jones (see p.221). Together with her stylist, Zerina Akers, Knowles-Carter used her visual album of 2020, *Black Is King*, to promote the work of independent Black jewelry makers such as L'Enchanteur, Mona Assemi, and Lorraine West (see p.309). That same year, she was named one of the 100 Women of the Year by *Time* magazine.

Bhagat

Bhagat
est. Mumbai, India, 1991

Earrings handmade in platinum with specially cut emeralds and opals, 2020.

Photograph by Jignesh Jhaveri.

Operating from a single showroom in Mumbai, Viren Bhagat has given contemporary Indian jewelry a new identity. Born into a fourth-generation Gujarati jewelry family, Bhagat learned from his father, an accomplished artist and art-school teacher. In the late 1980s, just when his family business was in need of fresh inspiration, he met Italian designer Gianni Bulgari (see p.46), who encouraged him to pursue new directions. Working first with his brothers, Bharat and Rajan, and then his sons, Varun and Jay, Bhagat makes pieces inspired by both Mughal designs and by traditional Indian jewelry types, such as forehead, turban, and hair ornaments. In Bhagat's creations, these traditional elements—floral forms, crescents, tassels of pearls and diamonds—are interpreted in a refined, abstracted way using specially calibrated gems, most often flat diamonds. The frequent use of old stones with irregular shapes and patina lends a softness to his often architectural creations. Unlike the rich polychromy of traditional jewelry, Bhagat works with a reduced palette, sometimes using solely diamonds and pearls complemented by a single type of colored gem, with minimal platinum and gold mounts. While his pieces might recall the European Art Deco and modernist jewelry crafted for Indian princes in the 1920s and '30s, Bhagat has created a new tradition entirely his own.

Sevan Bıçakçı

Sevan Bıçakçı
b. Istanbul, Turkey, 1972

Blue Mosque Ring crafted from gold and silver, featuring a diverse array of diamond cuts and an amethyst with a reverse intaglio engraving of a mosque.

Photograph by Serdan Salman.

Since founding his eponymous house in Istanbul in 2002, Sevan Bıçakçı has shaken up the jewelry panorama with his ingenious adaptation of ancient techniques that give his jewels an otherworldly air. Ranging from dramatic scimitar pendants extravagantly pavéd with gemstones to rings featuring tender, hand-painted, and carved miniature scenes in faceted gemstones, Bıçakçı has created a new type of medieval modernism. Of Armenian descent, Bıçakçı—whose surname means "knife maker"—was apprenticed at the age of twelve to a relative who was a goldsmith in Istanbul's old quarter. Frustrated by the loss of ancient skills, Bıçakçı rescued archaic techniques while also developing new ones. These include a patented version of reverse intaglio engraving into the underside of gemstones that he fills with a hybrid of enamel and layered painting. Bıçakçı has evolved the use of painted eggshell mosaics, crushed gemstone paving, metal-chasing, and engraving, often enhanced with foil-backed diamonds. Like a miniature snow globe, one ring re-creates a flock of spiraling seagulls inside a rock crystal sky flying over a micromosaic sea, atop which floats a gold *kaiki* boat. Beloved by collectors such as Cate Blanchett and Lady Gaga, these eye-catching jewels exude an attitude born of Bıçakçı's idiosyncratic mix of rock-and-roll irreverence with a deep respect for the past.

Gail Bird and Yazzie Johnson

Gail Bird
b. Oakland, California,
United States, 1949

Yazzie Johnson
b. Winslow, Arizona,
United States, 1946

Earrings in 18-karat gold with Picasso ammonite and Old Morenci turquoise, 2024.

Photograph by James Hart.

Considered to be among the foremost American Indian jewelry artists, known for both material and design innovation, Gail Bird and Yazzie Johnson have been creating jewelry together since 1972. Friends since they were children, both artists are self-taught, and they work collaboratively in northern New Mexico, with Bird designing and Johnson focusing on fabrication and metalwork. Their contemporary Southwestern American Indian style developed over decades, informed by their research into traditional Native American jewelry—an expansion of the symbols and narratives of Johnson's Navajo and Bird's Laguna and Santo Domingo Pueblo heritages. Explorations of prehistoric art are another source of inspiration, with petroglyph-style motifs adding character to a distinctive body of work. Moving beyond the turquoise and coral associated with traditional Native American jewelry, Bird and Johnson use more diverse stones, with a particular focus on unusual-looking gems in surprising colors and textures. A slice of landscape jasper could be juxtaposed with petrified wood; copper in agate mounted in tufa-cast gold might be hung on a simple leather thong. The duo pays particular attention to the backs of their jewels, decorating them with intricate overlay and slivers of colored stones, customizing the stones and motifs of each piece to tell a story unique to its wearer.

Alexis Bittar

Alexis Bittar
b. Brooklyn, New York,
United States, 1968

Amam Abit wears the *Liquid Lucite Ripple Collar* with hand-sculpted Lucite and 14-karat gold-plated brass, 2024.

Born in Brooklyn in 1968, designer Alexis Bittar often credits the start of his career with his discovery, at a very young age, of the outlandish fashion trends in the 1980s New York club scene. As a teenager, he sold thrifted clothes and trinkets in the East Village before teaching himself how to carve accessories from Lucite, a clear acrylic material. With these, he established his eponymous costume jewelry brand in 1990, taking inspiration from organic forms and antiques from the Bauhaus, Art Nouveau, and Art Deco movements. The sensuous, fashion-forward appeal of his sculptural designs—such as his signature wave-shaped bangles and gold-dipped cuffs—led to collaborations with Burberry, Michael Kors, and the costume designer Patricia Field on the HBO television series *Sex and the City*. Bittar was lauded by the Council of Fashion Designers of America (CFDA) as Accessory Designer of the Year in 2010 and widely praised for casting characterful women such as Joan Collins, Jennifer Saunders, and Joanna Lumley in his media campaigns. Following the sale of his brand to Brooks Brothers in 2015, Bittar took a five-year hiatus from the industry but reacquired his label in 2020, relaunching it a year later with a collection of handbags alongside his statement jewelry in liquid Lucite, gold plate, and crystal.

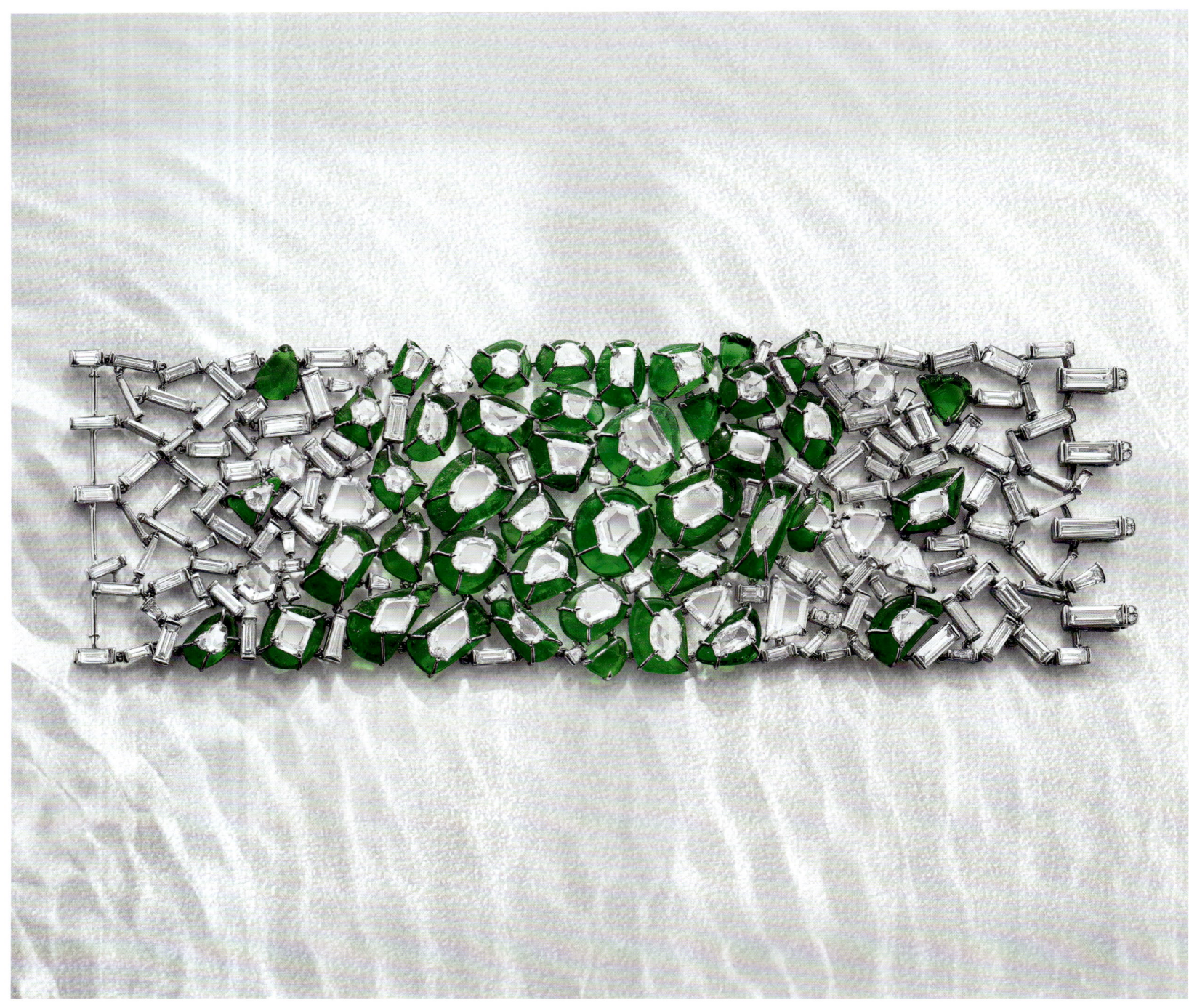

Boghossian

Boghossian
est. Mardin, Armenia (Turkey), 1868

Kissing bracelet in 18-karat white gold with emeralds and fancy-cut diamonds, 2021.

Photograph by Pedro Aguilar.

Since 1868 the Boghossian family, now led by fifth-generation Albert Boghossian, have traded gems along the Silk Road and produced gem-set high jewelry. Having emigrated from Mardin in Armenia (now part of Turkey) to Syria, then Lebanon, the Boghossians finally settled in Switzerland in the 1980s. Their designs possess a contemporary Western flair threaded with an Eastern spirit. Inspired by the Silk Road, it is woven into collections with glorious patterns, motifs, and mosaic-work, as well as special cuts and setting techniques resulting in strikingly modern pieces. Some techniques have since become house signatures, such as the Mughal art of inlay and the Kissing technique developed by Edmond Chin, who was named creative director in 2015 after partnering with Boghossian for many years. Devised in 2009, this technique sets a gemstone directly on top of a larger base stone and forms a fundamental part of their signature style. Merveilles is a more recent, now patented, addition to the family's repertoire, in which gemstones are packed so closely together that the setting disappears, making a diamond necklace appear as a stream of light. Fascinated with the creative dialogue between East and West, in 1992 the family established a foundation, with a mix of exhibitions, residences, and performances, in an effort to to bridge the cultural divide.

Boivin

Boivin
est. Paris, France, 1890

A model wears a Boivin bracelet and chameleon brooch, which was set with emeralds and rubies and could transform colors by pressing a small lever disguised as its tongue, *Vogue Paris*, April 1940.

Photograph by André Durst.

For centuries, the business of creating jewelry—from sourcing stones to designing the pieces—had primarily been a man's affair. But disrupting that tradition was goldsmith René Boivin and the eponymous Parisian maison he opened in 1890. Obsessed with ensuring comfort for the wearer, Boivin sought the insight of his wife, Jeanne Poiret Boivin, who ran all the house's business affairs. Upon René's death in 1917, Jeanne took over—becoming the first woman to direct a French jewelry house—strengthening her husband's pioneering, woman-led vision by bringing on talents such as Suzanne Belperron and Juliette Moutard (see pp.28, 204). The House of Boivin became renowned for its avant-garde approach and daring use of carved gemstones—quartz, amethyst, and rock crystal—alongside unconventional materials such as sandalwood and ebony. The *Starfish* brooch, designed in 1935 by Moutard, dazzles with its asymmetrical design and vibrant rubies and amethysts. Another standout piece is the *Sandalwood* cuff, designed by Belperron, a striking combination of rich sandalwood, gold, and diamonds, famously worn by Marlene Dietrich (see p.88). Boivin's joyful and unconventional aesthetic resonated with an eclectic and distinguished clientele, ranging from Sigmund Freud to socialite Daisy Fellowes, who were drawn to the intriguing originality of Boivin's artistry.

Joy Bonfield-Colombara

Joy Bonfield-Colombara
b. London, England, 1989

Goddess, 2024, featuring the *Gaze (hazel)* brooch in bronze with Japanese patina, recycled sterling silver, recycled 18-karat yellow gold, and natural hazel brown diamonds (top); and *Gaze (green)* brooch in bronze with verdigris patina, recycled sterling silver, recycled 18-karat yellow gold, and natural emeralds (bottom).

Photograph by Olivia Rose.

Italian-British artist and goldsmith Joy Bonfield-Colombara deconstructs classical Western notions of beauty, using patinaed bronze, platinum, silver, and gold to make miniature body sculptures that challenge the perceived value of women in society. Her series devoted to Hypatia—an ancient Greek philosopher and mathematician murdered by a mob in 415 CE for being a woman who dared to pursue intellectual interests—and her more recent *Gaze* pieces, where she carves a selection of rings and brooches with genderless, gem-set eyes, speak to the growing power of female authority beyond the male gaze. The mythological being Medusa, who was turned into a serpent-headed monster by the goddess Athena as a punishment, is honored with combs and a tiara peppered with peridot. When Medusa was beheaded, a Pegasus flew from her body, symbolizing the birth of beauty, and in Bonfield-Colombara's hands, beauty is born again. Her painter mother, Annalisa Colombara, and sculptor father, Michael Bonfield, embedded art into the fabric of her childhood, and it became her future. Bonfield-Colombara, who graduated from the Royal College of Art in 2019, infuses the Padua school, Arte Povera, modern Surrealism, and ancient modernism into every jewel with a freedom and bravery that suit her growing prominence in the world of one-of-a-kind art jewelry.

Isabelle Bonjean

Isabelle Bonjean
b. Paris, France, 1965

Editorial photoshoot for *Citizen K* magazine, March 2021.

Photograph by Isabelle Bonjean.

Photography and, later, jewelry came to Parisian Isabelle Bonjean in a seemingly random series of events. She had first wanted to be a writer but realized she was more of a visual storyteller. Then she considered becoming a war photographer, but she discovered fashion magazines while at university, and the depth of beauty portrayed therein moved her profoundly. At twenty-eight, with no connections and very little money, she brought her portfolio to *Madame Figaro* magazine looking for freelance work. Accessories and jewelry stylist Sophie Vigié was tasked with guiding Bonjean through a flurry of jewelry shoots, which led to Cartier campaigns and editorials for Italian *Vogue* (see p.54). Then digital photography arrived, and with it the freedom to shoot high jewelry without Polaroids and lab fees. Bonjean was free to experiment and push the boundaries of still life. With the advent of social media, the highly polished jewelry aesthetic gave way to a more natural look, and her work followed suit. Campaigns for major houses, including Boghossian, Chopard, and Messika (see pp.34, 66, 194), were captured with the same elegant image-making as jewelry from independent designers, such as Emmanuel Tarpin—every shoot featuring her smooth lyrical style like it is the first.

Boodles

Boodles
est. Liverpool, England, 1798

Wonderland Peacock Earrings
with yellow pear-shaped diamonds
and brilliant-cut diamonds
set in platinum.

Photograph by Rachell Smith.

For the past six generations, British jeweler Boodles has remained in the same family's hands, supplying some customers' lineages for decades. The firm originated in 1798 in Liverpool, making marine chronometers and aristocratic jewelry. A century later its then-manager, Henry Wainwright, bought the business and in 1910 his sons merged with antiquarian jewelers Boodle and Dunthorne. A new store in 1921, Boodles's head office today, expanded its reach, bringing in commissions from dignitaries, including King George V in the 1930s. In the late 1980s, a London store near Harrods changed its fortunes, while sponsorship in sports and the arts raised Boodles's profile.

Today, under head of design Rebecca Hawkins, the family team pursues sustainable methods, traceable gemstones, and single-mine-origin gold, and continues partnerships with firms such as the Cullinan Diamond Mine and the Goldberg family in New York, who cut the elegantly elongated, rectangular Ashoka diamond with 62 facets. Fine jewelry, such as the *Raindance* collection with droplike, bezel-set gems, is diamond-based, particularly the brand's signature pink diamonds. Boodles's high jewelry collections, from *A Family Journey* to *National Gallery*, are rich with colored stones and enamel details, often with hints of Art Nouveau style.

Boucheron

Boucheron
est. Paris, France, 1858

Vague asymmetrical earrings, that can be worn as a brooch, in 18-karat white gold set with 851 round diamonds, from the *Carte Blanche* high jewelry collection, 2024.

By the time he was just fourteen years old, Frédéric Boucheron had already turned to jewelry. Not content with continuing the family fabric business, he made his way through an apprenticeship, then became a clerk, a salesman, and finally a jeweler, registering his hallmark and opening an atelier in 1866 before unveiling a grand boutique on Place Vendôme in 1893. His first great creation, the *Question Mark* necklace in 1879, elegantly flowed from collarbone to décolletage and had no clasp, allowing a woman to don it herself without help and challenging the idea that a magnificent jewel was a trophy to be placed on a trophy. A revolution at the time, it won him the Grand Prix at the 1889 Exposition Universelle in Paris. This questioning of power and preciousness is sustained today by Boucheron's longtime creative director Claire Choisne, appointed in 2011, who uses materials with little intrinsic value, such as aerogel, black sand, and flower petals, to draw value back to art and emotion. "Innovation is a state of mind," she says, and that philosophy has rippled through the history of Boucheron, from the *Question Mark* collection to the recent groundbreaking *Carte Blanche* collection. The techniques and materials are a "toolbox" for a transformational vision that enables Boucheron to sit within a small coterie of master jewelers who are changing the course of jewelry design.

Louise Bourgeois

Louise Bourgeois
b. Paris, France, 1911
d. New York, New York, United States, 2010

A silver choker by Louise Bourgeois in the form of a shackle, designed in 1948 and made in 2001.

Photograph by Jordan Doner.

One of the most versatile visual artists of the twentieth century, Louise Bourgeois used diverse media and techniques, from printmaking to jewelry, to invoke and process her own experiences and memories. Born in Paris, Bourgeois moved to New York in 1938, and for the next seven decades, she created prolifically, from paintings to giant sculptures of spiders, using a variety of materials, including marble, bronze, latex, plaster, and fabric. Personal and revelatory, her art touches on topics of love, fear, family, the body, and the unconscious. Her jewelry mirrors the foreboding, dreamlike qualities of her art, evident in a striking silver choker from 1948. Made in the shape of a metal shackle, Bourgeois conceived it as a statement against both the violence she saw during the Spanish Civil War and the constraints imposed on women by society. The artist originally created the piece to wear around her own neck but returned to the design at the turn of the millennium, when she was introduced to Madrid-based jewelry designer Chus Burés, who proposed the idea of a limited series. Issued as a small edition of thirty-nine pieces, the resulting necklaces were cast from silver. Ten special examples were further adorned with a string of fourteen sparkling crystals, which could then be hung seductively from the choker, resulting in an art object that is both beautiful and unsettling.

Hamish Bowles

Hamish Bowles
b. London, England, 1963

Hamish Bowles wears a Verdura tiara and brooch at the 2022 Met Gala celebrating *In America: An Anthology of Fashion* at the Metropolitan Museum of Art, New York.

Photograph by Mike Coppola.

A curator, collector, and editor with more than three decades at Condé Nast, Hamish Bowles is a multifaceted figure in the world of fashion. With a deep knowledge of vintage, Bowles has brought a unique perspective to his reportage, matching current fashion and editorial style with an understanding of historical context. That perspective has applied as much to jewelry as sartorial concerns. Beginning as a young fashion editor at *Harpers & Queen*, Bowles was responsible for fine jewelry accounts, a role that would inform a lifelong interest. His influence extends to men's jewelry, where he plays a key role in highlighting an underexposed category. Bowles's daring choices at the annual Met Gala have not only brought attention to the possibilities of jewelry for men but also to vintage. In 2022 he graced the red carpet crowned in a Fulco di Verdura gold and platinum feather tiara set with 1,223 diamonds (see p.298). The headdress had not been worn since its debut in 1957, commissioned by American socialite Betsey Cushing Whitney for a visit to Buckingham Palace. As both a journalist and a curator, Bowles has highlighted unique jewels and collections from around the world, including his work on the *India in Fashion* exhibition at the Nita Mukesh Ambani Cultural Centre in Mumbai, which showcased the artistry of Indian jewelry and its influence on Western design.

Latoya Boyd

Latoya Boyd
b. Los Angeles, California, United States, 1983

Mermaid Cuff made with air-chased recycled copper pipe, 2018.

Latoya Boyd did not take a traditional route into the world of jewelry. Stationed in Kandahar, Afghanistan, while serving in the US Army, she came across a shop filled with eye-catching lapis lazuli, and her creative curiosity was piqued. After being honorably discharged from the army in March 2014, she completed a degree in jewelry design and metalsmithing arts from the Fashion Institute of Design & Merchandising in Los Angeles before training at the Gemological Institute of America. Since establishing her eponymous company in San Diego, California, in early 2015, Boyd has fashioned an array of unique pieces with an eye for ethical design, using salvaged copper, gold, and silver, combined with Montana sapphires cut by Jenna Sloane and Brazilian green tourmalines from the Cruzeiro mine. Her signature flame-painted copper creations span from oversize floral cocktail rings to a strand of interconnecting petals that can be converted from a statement necklace into a crown. For Sotheby's *Brilliant & Black* exhibition in 2022, Boyd hammered sterling silver into gently undulating sails, each with a suspended briolette diamond. Boyd injects her own experiences into her jewelry as well. "It embodies my strength and resilience from my military experience and life's challenges, while also showcasing my soft, feminine side and the gems of wisdom I have gained," says Boyd.

Georges Braque

Georges Braque
b. Argenteuil, France, 1882
d. Paris, France, 1963

The *Poseidon* necklace in 18-karat yellow gold, platinum, and diamonds, created in 1962, alongside Georges Braque's original gouache.

Regarded as one of the most important artists of the twentieth century, Georges Braque is best known for inventing Cubism alongside Pablo Picasso around 1908 (see p.223). In 1961, after a distinguished career as a painter, printmaker, and sculptor, he turned his attention to jewelry, initially designing a cameo ring featuring the head of Greek goddess Hecate for his wife's eightieth birthday. Collaborating with master jeweler Heger de Löwenfeld, Braque subsequently produced 113 pieces based on a series of gouaches he created on mythological subjects. Themes of flight and metamorphosis characterize the collection, and many pieces incorporate bird motifs, which for him symbolized space and time, as in his *Eosphoros* brooch and his *Mounichos* cameo ring. Fish also appeared in several of Braque's jewelry works, such as his *Scamander* brooch, a simplified piscine form of textured 18-karat gold set with tiny cut diamonds. Incorporating high-quality gold and carefully selected precious stones, Braque's jewels represent a synthesis of artistic vision and fine craftsmanship—so much so that Braque described de Löwenfeld as the "extension of [his] hands." After Braque's death, their jewelry collection was widely exhibited between 1963 and 1971 to great acclaim at thirty-four locations around the world, including at the Musée des Arts Décoratifs in Paris.

Daniel Brush

Daniel Brush
b. Cleveland, Ohio, United States, 1947
d. New York, New York, United States, 2022

Works in steel and 24-karat gold.

Photograph by Takaaki Matsumoto.

Daniel Brush was one of the most celebrated goldsmiths in the world. Fans of his are as enthralled with the exceptional craftsmanship behind his breathtaking bejeweled artworks as they are enchanted by the reclusive lifestyle in which he chose to create his work. Brush was known to sweep the floor of his workspace for hours each day to get himself in the frame of mind to create, and for keeping his personal and creative life largely guarded from the commercial art world. As an artist, he worked in many mediums, but it was his gold objets d'art that gained him the most recognition. He is best known for his gold granulation technique, an antiquated, painstaking process in which he used a single-haired sable brush to place thousands of minuscule gold beads into a specific design. Considered the most complex goldsmithing technique, he learned it by traveling to Europe and studying ancient Etruscan granulation techniques with master goldsmiths during a fifteen-year period of seclusion and study. At the time of his passing, Brush had created an unparalleled body of work that continues to be collected and exhibited at esteemed institutions such as the Metropolitan Museum of Art, the Phillips Collection, and the Smithsonian.

Buccellati

Buccellati
est. Milan, Italy, 1919

Lee Sung-kyung wears Buccellati's *Macri* bracelets, *Eternelle* rings, and pendant earrings, *Vogue Korea*, September 2021.

Photograph by Kim Young-jun.

Jewelry connoisseurs can spot a Buccellati creation in a split second: the satiny sheen of *rigato* engraved gold, the opulence of *ornato* decor, the lacelike intricacy of tulle openwork. These specialist techniques date back to the Renaissance but were developed and perfected in the workshops of the Italian jewelry house, founded in 1919 by the visionary Milanese goldsmith Mario Buccellati. The jeweler was dubbed the Prince of Goldsmiths by a client, influential Italian poet and aristocrat Gabriele D'Annunzio, who introduced him to the upper echelons of Italian society. A renowned Casanova, the poet commissioned hundreds of precious objects from Buccellati, including ornately engraved silver matchboxes and long, beaded necklaces that he gifted to his lovers. A hundred years after its founding, the house remains family-run and inextricably linked to the highest level of craftsmanship: Mario's grandson Andrea is creative director, working alongside his own daughter, Lucrezia, and other family members. In Buccellati's Italian ateliers, goldsmiths train for up to a year on brass before they make a single mark on gold. Many of these artisans spend a lifetime with the house, like their parents and grandparents before them, passing down an almost-lost art form that creates objects of mesmerizing beauty.

Bulgari

Bulgari
est. Rome, Italy, 1884

A model wears the *Tribute to Paris* necklace in platinum with 461 buff-top emeralds, 317 fancy-shaped diamonds, more than 50 pear-shaped diamonds, and pavé-set diamonds, around a central 35.53-carat cabochon emerald, from the *Eden, The Garden of Wonders* high jewelry collection, 2022.

Photograph by Cho Gi-Seok.

Founded in Rome in 1884, the renowned house of Bulgari is now synonymous with elegant but bold jewelry design. Initially, Sotirio Bulgari—originally Sotiris Bulgaris, from a Greek Epirote silversmith family—sold silver artifacts and antiques, but by the 1920s, his offerings included precious jewels, heavily influenced by the fashionable Art Deco Parisian style. Upon his death in 1932, his sons Giorgio and Costantino took over, and by the 1950s, the business was thriving. In the 1960s, Bulgari began to develop its distinctive style, characterized by big gold, three-dimensional designs adorned with colorful gemstones. The house style evolved to feature ancient coins encased in sculptural gold settings from the 1960s onward, leading to the *Monete* collection in 2013. Stylized serpents wrapped around the wrist as a key motif, immortalized in their *Serpenti* collections for both jewelry and watches. The third generation, led by Giorgio's sons, Gianni, Paolo, and Nicola, and his nephew, Francesco Trapani, guided the company from the 1970s, expanding the brand globally. Bulgari became part of the LVMH luxury group in 2011, but members of the family continue to work independently, namely Marina Bulgari, who founded Marina B in 1978, and Gianni's son Giorgio Bulgari, who founded Giorgio B in 2017 and who is the only living family member still designing jewelry.

Haroldo Burle Marx

Haroldo Burle Marx
b. São Paulo, Brazil, 1911
d. Brazil, 1991

Forma livre ring in 18-karat gold with a hand-carved tourmaline, 1970s.

Born in São Paulo, Brazil, to one of the country's most distinguished families, Haroldo Burle Marx was known for setting gemstones into elegant, symmetrical pieces with unusually patinaed gold. His clients included Queen Margrethe of Denmark, Queen Elizabeth II of England, and the Empress Pahlavi of Iran (see pp.97, 218). After studying gemology and lapidary in the German gem-cutting center of Idar-Oberstein, Burle Marx opened his own jewelry workshop in Copacabana, Rio de Janeiro, in 1945. Inspired by the ancient materiality of gemstones, which he described as "a product of nature as clouds or trees," Burle Marx used an array of colorful stones—amethyst, aquamarine, chalcedony, emerald, opal, and topaz, among others—which, through attentive cutting, were transformed into curvaceous, one-of-a-kind sculptures that stood out from their high-karat gold settings. A defining aspect of Burle Marx's jewelry is its *forma livre*, a free-form style of sculptural carving he pioneered with his brother, landscape architect Roberto Burle Marx, in the late 1940s and continued to develop after their estrangement in the 1970s. Created entirely by hand without molds, each jewel is unique, and although they recall the riches of the ancient civilizations, they are executed with a thoroughly modern approach.

Pol Bury

Pol Bury
b. La Louvière, Belgium, 1922
d. Paris, France, 2005

Bicolored bangle in
18-karat gold, c. 1966.

Fascinated by movement, Belgian artist Pol Bury was both a poet and a painter before he began making sculptures in 1952. He is best remembered for his ingenious kinetic sculptures, which are set into motion by means of water, magnets, or motors. His famous fountains, such as *L'Octagon* in San Francisco, typically feature polished steel elements that gently oscillate as water flows in, through, and around them. In the late 1960s, Bury began collaborating with GEM Montebello in Milan to translate his sculptural ideas into a series of jewelry editions in 18-karat gold (see p.199), many of which were exhibited at Cartier in New York in 1971 (see p.54). One of his most famous pieces is the *Kinetic Ring*, whose square surface is punctuated on the top and bottom by orbs connected to each other by filaments that move dynamically when the ring is worn. As with his full-size sculptures, the movement of mobile parts—usually arrangements of tiny filaments or rolling balls animated by the motion of the wearer's body and glistening as they catch the light—dazzled collectors. Bury thought of his jewelry as miniature sculptures and wanted them to be sold with their own pedestals, so that they could be mounted as art when not worn.

Carmen Busquets

Carmen Busquets
b. Caracas, Venezuela, 1965

Carmen Busquets wears 18-karat Fairmined gold earrings with green tourmalines and white diamonds and a diamond *Phillipa* ear cuff by Ana Khouri, 2024.

Photograph by Scott Archibald.

A fashion technology pioneer and philanthropist, Carmen Busquets was the cofounding investor of Net-a-Porter in 2000, with other investments such as Moda Operandi, Cult Beauty, and demi-fine jewelry brand Astley Clarke. In 2006 the Venezuelan entrepreneur opened CoutureLab in London, a fashion boutique and e-commerce platform promoting bespoke pieces from jewelers such as Silvia Furmanovich and Fernando Jorge (see pp.111, 143). Busquets's eclectic taste has made her a major collector of artist and talismanic designs—audacious statement pieces that she describes as her calling card. She's been drawn to distinctive designs by Claude Lalanne (see p.160), Anish Kapoor, and Ron Arad—for her, jewelry must have a story, an emotional connection that is about artistic rather than material value. She has added wildly imaginative pieces from Castro NYC and Lydia Courteille (see pp.56, 74) and regularly commissions unique designs from artisans such as Ana Khouri, Rosa de la Cruz, and Cora Sheibani (see p.256), as well as symbolic charm bracelets from Clarissa Bronfman and engraved gold bangles with spiritual messages from Aurora Lopez Mejia. Busquets is a believer in the power of healing stones, citing opals and moonstones as her favorites, especially those transformed by Daniela Villegas into jewelry imbued with profound meaning (see p.303).

Alexander Calder

Alexander Calder
b. Lawnton, Pennsylvania, United States, 1898
d. New York, New York, United States, 1976

Angelica Huston wears *The Jealous Husband* brass wire necklace by Alexander Calder (c. 1940), New York, 1976.

Photograph by Evelyn Hofer.

American sculptor Alexander Calder was enthralled by the possibilities of movement from an early age. Born in 1898 to artist parents in Pennsylvania, Calder spent time in Paris before settling in the United States, where his love of moving forms became intricate kinetic sculptures, or mobiles, as Marcel Duchamp christened them. Friendships with seminal artists in the 1930s—including Jean Arp, Fernand Léger, and Piet Mondrian—energized his pioneering vision. After experiencing the space of Mondrian's Parisian studio, Calder began to form his distinctive abstract aesthetic, and by 1931 he translated colored shapes into moving works powered only by the air's undercurrents. Calder brought these sculptural sensibilities to his jewelry design and was a key figure at the start of the artist jewelry movement. Central to his style was a focus on organic forms, creating fluid pieces from spirals, circles, and discs that embraced or hung from the body. From early jewelry Calder created for his sister's dolls to the later pieces for his wife, Louisa James, he tended to eschew precious materials for more quotidian items. Drawn to wire and found objects such as glass, stone, and porcelain, he created sculpted pieces that cast hypnotizing whorls around the curves of the body. His oversize brooches and roughly hammered necklaces were popular with fans, including Peggy Guggenheim and Anjelica Huston.

Maria Callas

Maria Callas (Maria Kalogeropoulos)
b. New York, New York, United States, 1923
d. Paris, France, 1977

Maria Callas in pearls, 1957.

Photograph by Cecil Beaton.

"I lived for art, I lived for love"—this aria from Puccini's *Tosca* that Maria Callas famously sang could well sum up her own life. Born in New York to Greek immigrants, Callas trained as an opera singer after moving to Greece with her mother and sister when she was thirteen. Her uniquely timbred, lyrical voice soon propelled her onto the world's most prestigious stages, transforming her into a diva. And there is no diva without jewels. Callas delighted in wearing high jewelry and often borrowed pieces from esteemed houses for her performances. Her love affair with Van Cleef & Arpels began with a diamond parure featuring important pear-shaped stones (see p.291). The 2004 Sotheby's sale of her collection revealed a dazzling array of pieces, including an unsigned wavy ruby and emerald necklace from the 1950s, her beloved Van Cleef *Cinq Feuilles* diamond and ruby brooch, and dramatic diamond earrings with baroque drop pearls. Also among her prized possessions were two Cartier brooches, one featuring a panther and the other a rose (see p.54). Many of Callas's treasures came after she left her husband, Giovanni Battista Meneghini, in 1959 for the shipping magnate Aristotle Onassis, whose understanding of women, Callas quipped, came "out of a Van Cleef & Arpels catalog." Callas's jewelry brimmed with joyful colors—a contrast to the struggles and dramas she often portrayed onstage.

Luz Camino

Luz Camino
b. Chevy Chase, Maryland, United States, 1944

Luz Camino holds her butterfly brooch, made in 2018 in shell, diamonds, and smoky quartz. She wears her white Christmas orchid earring and brooch, made of resin with enamel and peridot, and two butterflies from the 1990s made of tourmaline with pearls, diamonds, and gold, *Classpaper*, 2023.

Photograph by Javier Salas.

Jeweler Luz Camino has been dreaming up sculptural pieces that reflect the beauty of the botanical world and hyperrealistic jewels that bring nature to life for more than five decades. Blossoms and birds' wings emerge in exquisite detail, achieved through her mastery of plique-à-jour enameling and lost-wax casting. Born in the United States and raised in Spain, Camino's first pieces debuted in 1973 after she enrolled in Madrid's Escuela Sindical de Joyería, becoming the first woman in Spain to earn the master goldsmith title of Sacador de Fuego. With unbridled creativity and a reverence for craftsmanship, she designs her jewels with a meticulous eye, from the choice of materials to the enamel flourishes and patinated finishes. Bronze, silver, gold, platinum, titanium, copper, resin, wood, shells, pearls, and a vibrant array of colored stones are all part of her repertoire. Celebrating imperfection, she deftly captures the intricacies in nature—veins on leaves, delicate magnolia petals, butterfly wings—and elevates humble, everyday objects, from pencil shavings rendered in gold and edged with red spinels to rubber bands in sterling silver and pavé diamonds. In her hands, stones become vibrant and witty, whether using amethysts to add a luminous touch to thistles, wisteria, and irises, or whiskey quartz and caramel sphalerite to form an asymmetrical geometric ear pendant.

Susannah Carson

Susannah Carson
b. Napa Valley, California,
United States, 1975

An assortment of hand-painted *Lover's Eyes* with antique jewelry settings on a print of the portrait *Clarissa Had, with Difficulty, Whittled Her Suitors Down to Only Seven*, 2024.

The European tradition of gifting a miniature portrait of a lover's eye as a sign of devotion is one that dates back to the late eighteenth and early nineteenth centuries. In contrast to grander paintings, which spoke publicly of love, family, status, and power, these intimate depictions—painted with watercolors onto ivory or opaque gouaches on card—were personal celebrations of clandestine affairs small enough to be secreted into pendants, pins, matchboxes, or lockets and kept close to the heart. Having studied philosophy and literature, Carson—a California-based artist, author, and collector—revived this amorous practice in her work, using it as a means through which to explore the concept of human connection and the identities of her imagined historical sitters. Alongside vintage china plates and picture frames, Carson's unique canvases include antique lockets, studs, charm brooches, girandoles, and minimalist rings—all jewelry settings that hark back to the origins of this historical romantic custom. She creates her collections with oil paint, carefully sealing each tiny eye beneath protective resin or quartz crystal, to unite the past with the present, the known and the mysterious, and the mortal with the spiritual.

Cartier

Cartier
est. Paris, France, 1847

Panthère Chatoyante necklace in rose gold with rubellites, chrysoprases, emeralds, onyx, black lacquer, and diamonds, from the *Nature Sauvage* high jewelry collection, 2024.

Photograph by Kate Jackling.

"The jeweler of kings and the king of jewelers" is how King Edward VII of Britain once described the esteemed house of Cartier. Founded in Paris by Louis-François Cartier in 1847, the maison was elevated to global prominence by his three grandsons, Louis, Pierre, and Jacques, and a roster of trailblazing designers, such as Jeanne Toussaint, head of creation from 1933 to 1970. Cartier's creations have adorned society elites from Barbara Hutton and the Duke and Duchess of Windsor to the Maharaja of Patiala (see pp.140, 260, 261). Elizabeth Taylor turned to Cartier to design new settings for her La Peregrina pearl and the 69.42-carat Taylor-Burton diamond (see p.280) and, more recently, Catherine, Princess of Wales, chose a Cartier tiara for her marriage to Prince William. From the original Guirlande style, with its intertwined patterns of flora and ribbons, to the colorful, gem-studded Tutti Frutti creations, the pioneering approach and geometric precision of Art Deco, and the iconic Panthère, Cartier has consistently impressed its distinctive signature on a variety of designs. It is a style that has always been open to novel influences, be it the opulence of the Indian Mughal period or the abstract patterns of Islamic art. Yet Cartier's creations remain unmistakably recognizable, even in streamlined contemporary pieces—a telling sign of the jeweler's global reach and staying power.

Carvin French

Carvin French
est. New York, New York,
United States, 1954

Coiled snake necklace with yellow diamonds, rubies, and emeralds, including a 14.03-carat suspended pear-shaped emerald, set in 18-karat gold.

From Black Starr & Frost, Cartier, and Harry Winston to Tiffany & Co., Raymond Yard, Van Cleef & Arpels, and Verdura, Carvin French has made expertly crafted jewelry for America's and Europe's leading houses for more than fifty years (see pp.132, 283, 291, 298). And yet, in the tradition of a jeweler's jeweler, Carvin French is relatively anonymous to the public, instead working behind the scenes and signing its work with the names of those who conceived of the designs. Carvin French was founded in 1954 by jewelers André Chervin and Serge Carponcy, who, having arrived in New York from Paris, worked side by side in the Manhattan workshop of French sculptor and metalsmith Louis Féron before founding their own atelier at 16 East 52nd Street in Manhattan. For the company name, they combined portions of their surnames to create *Carvin* and added *French* as a nod to their heritage and training. Known for superior handcrafted jewels, Carvin French's expert goldsmiths, enamelists, and lapidary artists translated designs on paper into some of the most illustrious American-made jewels. After Carponcy's retirement in 1983, Carvin French has been led by Chervin and his family, most notably his nephew, Sylvain, and daughter, Carole. Today the workshop still produces gem-set jewelry in gold and platinum, continuing the founders' legacy.

Castro NYC

Castro NYC
est. New York, New York,
United States, 2006

Falcon Crest Pendant & Chain, 2021, featuring a 19th-century porcelain bisque doll surrounded by cultured pearls, emeralds, rubies, diamonds, brown diamonds, 18-karat yellow gold, sterling silver, and enamel.

Photograph by Castro NYC.

The turn of the millennium represented a profound shift in the life of Terry Castro, the outré co-owner of C & C Jewelers in Toledo, Ohio. His son Sir King had just been born, and to secure a regular income, Castro had turned to retail, but there was a wild creativity within him that would not be satiated with making repairs or sitting behind a counter. At night, he would sneak into the local junkyard and collect rusty car components and other metal scrap, take them to his mother's house, and reimagine their faded beauty into repurposed brutalist Gothic jewelry. Death masks, skulls, and bejeweled winged miniature antique dolls unfurled. He moved to Chicago and then in 2006 to New York, where he sold his work from a table on Prince Street in SoHo. He moved again to Istanbul ten years later, working with the artisanal masters of the Grand Bazaar, en route to his planned destination of Africa, which is where his heart belonged. Castro's work was exceptional, employing a type of ancient talismanic Futurism that attracted serious collectors. In 2022, at the age of fifty, he died in Istanbul at the peak of his creative powers, leaving his son to continue his legacy, but not before making his indelible mark on the history of design.

Catherine the Great

Catherine the Great (Sophie von Anhalt-Zerbst), Empress of Russia
b. Stettin, Kingdom of Prussia (Poland), 1729
d. St. Petersburg, Russia, 1796

Portrait of Catherine II of Russia (Catherine the Great) by an anonymous painter, c. 1780–90.

As she did with works of art, Catherine the Great used jewels to articulate her power and taste and to reinforce her claim to the Russian throne. Upon deposing her husband, Peter III, and seizing power in 1762, she commissioned court jewelers George Friedrich Ekart and Jérémie Pauzié to produce what Pauzié called "one of the richest objects [that has] ever existed in Europe": an imperial crown studded with pearls, 4,936 diamonds, and a spinel of 398.72 carats, alongside a golden orb featuring a 46.92-carat diamond mounted at the center of diamond bands. An imperial scepter mounted with a 189.62-carat Golconda diamond—presented to the empress by her lover Count Grigory Orlov—complemented this new regalia a few years later. From 1764 the empress displayed these crown jewels—as well as her personal jewelry collections and jeweled *objets de vertu*—in a gallery converted from the imperial bedchamber of the Winter Palace. Under Bolshevik rule, most of the jewels that constituted this imperial treasury were redistributed in the 1920s and '30s by Soviet authorities either directly to collectors, such as Armand Hammer and Marjorie Merriweather Post (see p.229), or by auction; 124 lots from the crown jewels were sold in 1927 at Christie's London. What remains of Catherine the Great's collection in Russia is on view at the Diamond Fund in the Kremlin.

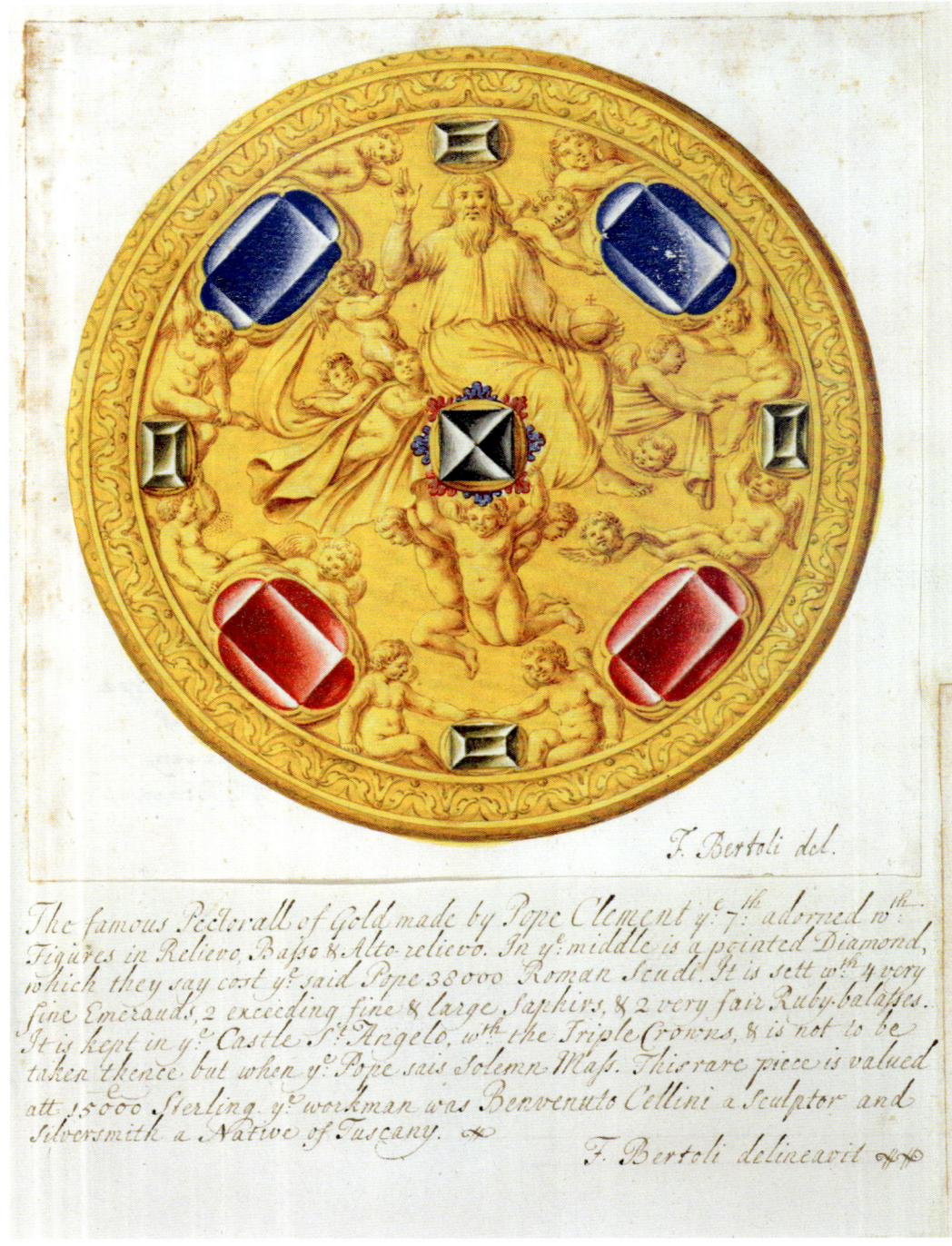

Benvenuto Cellini

Benvenuto Cellini
b. Florence, Italy, 1500
d. Florence, Italy, 1571

A drawing of a gold pectoral made c. 1523–34 for Pope Clement VII set with rubies, sapphires, emeralds, and a central diamond.

Widely considered one of the greatest goldsmiths and sculptors of the Italian Renaissance, Florentine artist Benvenuto Cellini is best known for the magnificent gold salt cellar he made for King Francis I of France (see p.110), and for his bronze statue of Perseus holding the head of Medusa, housed in Loggia dei Lanzi on the Piazza della Signoria in Florence since 1554. He was, however, not a man to mess with, as famed for his impulsive and often violent personality as he was for his superlative skill set. During his lifetime, he was repeatedly imprisoned for assault, theft, and even murder, having done away with his brother's killer, who was a rival goldsmith. His strong papal connections—Cellini produced a number of pieces for Pope Clement VII, including lavish, gem-set gold pectorals—however, got him off the hook. A flamboyant and egotistical talent who chronicled his scandalous adventures in an autobiography, Cellini was nonetheless devoted to his art and sought to instill perfectionism in others. Keen to pass on his knowledge, he wrote various treatises on metalwork and sculpture that outlined many of his masterful techniques, including how to set a ruby, cut a diamond, and create intricate filigree work. His influence stretched through the ages: a "Cellini pattern" or "Cellini style" are Victorian terms used to describe an ornate and highly decorative piece of silverware.

Wallace Chan

Wallace Chan
b. Fuzhou, China, 1956

The *Cosmos* brooch depicts two intertwined carps with a dragon in flight above and a suspended, free-moving pendulum below. The brooch is comprised of titanium set with diamonds, sapphires, rubies, tsavorite garnets, and jadeite slices, with a 5.84-carat irregularly shaped diamond at the center of the pendulum, 2021.

A renowned contemporary high jewelry artist, Wallace Chan is adept at creating pieces that combine the color-changing attributes of lightweight titanium with exceptional colored gems, diamonds, and pearls. His bejeweled creations replicate flora and fauna with mind-boggling detail, resulting in large-scale pieces that combine Eastern philosophies, traditional Western themes, and his outsize imagination. In Chan's world of creativity, the physical and spiritual; life and death; and the past, present, and future are one. A self-taught master craftsman, Chan has produced multiple innovations over his fifty-year career, including the Wallace Cut gem-faceting technique that results in a 360-degree intaglio image inside a gemstone, a patented jade refining and brightening technique, and Wallace Chan Porcelain, which is five times stronger than steel. One of his most famous creations is *A Heritage in Bloom*, a necklace created with twenty-four D-color internally flawless diamonds cut from the Cullinan Heritage, an exceptionally rare 507.55-carat diamond. Commissioned by Chow Tai Fook (see p.67), the jewel used many of Chan's artisan techniques and can be worn twenty-seven different ways. This magnum opus took more than forty-seven thousand hours to create and became the most expensive diamond necklace in the world when it was unveiled in 2015.

Chanel

Chanel
est. Paris, France, 1910

Helena Christensen wears Chanel's 1990 Spring/Summer Ready-to-Wear collection.

Photograph by Karl Lagerfeld.

Much like the tweed jacket or a spritz of N°5 perfume, jewelry has long been intrinsic to Chanel, the Parisian luxury house established by Gabrielle "Coco" Chanel in 1910. Chanel herself accessorized with rows of creamy pearls—some real, some faux—and wore gems created by her friends, including Fulco di Verdura (see p.298). In the 1920s, she irrevocably disrupted the jewelry world by making costume jewelry *en vogue*. The house embarked on partnerships with famed jewelry makers Goossens and Gripoix (see pp.126, 129), which have endured through the decades, from statement CC drop earrings to Byzantine-inspired Maltese crosses and the chunky gold jewelry of the 1990s. Chanel herself designed just one high jewelry collection, *Bijoux de Diamants* in 1932. The fifty or so pieces were strikingly modern in their focus on the purity of noble materials, including platinum, yellow gold, and diamonds. Motifs included celestial bodies, feathers, circles, and ribbons, all of which appear today within the brand's high jewelry offerings, particularly those designed by Patrice Leguéreau. The director of the Chanel Fine Jewelry Creation Studio from 2009 until his death in 2024, Leguéreau translated chapters from both Coco's biography and the Maison's visual history into precious materials, striving for the modernity in design that has remained Chanel's calling card.

Cindy Chao

Cindy Chao
b. 1974

Sara Grace Wallerstedt wears a Cindy Chao butterfly brooch with rubies, sapphires, and white and yellow diamonds, British *Vogue*, April 2020.

Photograph by Paolo Roversi.

Cindy Chao's maximalist, color-strewn, head-turning high jewelry has in just two decades propelled her to a position of global prominence. Thanks to a signature style that was influenced by her sculptor father and architect grandfather, Chao's work has a notable three-dimensional quality that fuses Eastern and Western design sensibilities. She was one of the early jewelers to use titanium in her pieces, enabling her jewels to embrace large-scale dimensions and oversize, ultra-rare gemstones. Her creations come to life thanks to her use of wax casting, a traditional jewelry-making technique, and Chao's designs often recall nature in intricate detail. A butterfly peers out as if it is about to take flight, and a floral brooch looks almost coquettish in a light breeze, pulsing with an incredible 49.12-carat Sri Lanka star sapphire. Throughout her career, Chao's pieces have repeatedly broken records at auction for contemporary Asian jewels, such as her *Ruby Ribbon* ring set with an 8.3-carat Burmese ruby that sold for $3.8 million in 2013. Her pieces are in the permanent collections of the likes of the Smithsonian and Paris's Musée des Arts Décoratifs, and in 2021 Chao was awarded France's prestigious Chevalier de l'Ordre des Arts et des Lettres. Pioneering a unique style that combines jewelry, sculpture, and architecture, she has been at the forefront of inspiring a new style of jewelry in Asia.

Charlotte of Mecklenburg-Strelitz

Charlotte of Mecklenburg-Strelitz, Queen of Great Britain and Ireland
b. Mirow, Duchy of Mecklenburg-Strelitz, Holy Roman Empire (Germany), 1744
d. London, England, 1818

Portrait of Charlotte of Mecklenburg-Strelitz by Georg David Matthieu, 1762.

Born a princess of the relatively modest German state of Mecklenburg-Strelitz, Queen Charlotte developed a seemingly insatiable appetite for jewels, which she received in abundance. First came the rich gifts upon marrying George III, king of Great Britain and Ireland, in 1761. Then, during her tenure, she added her own purchases and official gifts. She received offerings of diamonds from India, notably five remarkable stones between 23 and 38 carats from Muhammad Ali Wallajah, Nawab of Arcot. Splendidly bejeweled, the queen was vilified in popular cartoons for having accepted such extravagances, particularly from nabobs, East India Company officials who returned to Britain enriched and in search of social standing and political power. The queen's questionable approach toward such gifts is evident from her will, in which she instructed that her own jewels—including the Arcot diamonds—be sold, and the proceeds used to support her four unmarried daughters. On her death the prince regent (later George IV) refused to execute the will since the jewels were the property of the crown and she had no right to dispose of them. The scandal of Queen Charlotte using official gifts for her own purposes was comparable to the allegations made against her contemporary Marie Antoinette, who was accused of attempting to defraud the royal jewelers (see p.183).

Chaumet

Chaumet
est. Paris, France, 1780

Chaumet *Trompe-l'œil* necklace in 18-karat white gold with diamonds and pearls, from the *En Scène* high jewelry collection, 2024. The necklace was inspired by the *Indore Pears* necklace created by Chaumet for the Maharaja Tukoji Rao Holkar III of Indore in 1913.

Photograph by Thomas Deschamps.

The jewelry maison that would become Chaumet was established in 1780 by Marie-Étienne Nitot, an apprentice and then collaborator of Ange-Joseph Aubert, Marie Antoinette's jeweler in Versailles (see p.183). In 1804 Nitot supplied a coronation sword—set with a 140.5-carat diamond at the hilt—for the newly crowned Napoleon I and was appointed official court jeweler by Empress Joséphine. She had been struck by the workmanship Nitot and his son, François-Regnault, had lavished on a unique tiara, and soon Nitot's naturalistic designs were in demand throughout Europe. Joséphine reintroduced a classical style to early nineteenth-century fashion, which included tiaras and intaglios carved into colorful gemstones, with many of Nitot's commissions for her continuing to provide inspiration for Chaumet's designs today. With the fall of the empire in 1815, François-Regnault Nitot sold the company to his colleague, Jean-Baptiste Fossin, who, along with his son, Jules, continued to craft romantic jewels under the name Fossin et Fils. This became Chaumet in 1889, when Joseph Chaumet, the son-in-law of Jules Fossin's business partner, bought the firm. Owned by luxury group LVMH since 1999, Chaumet remains one of the most highly esteemed French maisons, still revered for its tiaras and naturalistic forms more than two centuries since its founding.

Richard Chavez

Richard Chavez
b. San Felipe Pueblo, New Mexico, United States, 1949

A lapis lazuli, coral, turquoise, and 14-karat gold ring, 1997.

Known for a refined aesthetic that blends contemporary design with traditional Pueblo craftsmanship, Richard Chavez is credited with evolving public perceptions of American Indian jewelry. A trained architect, Chavez carries a modernist design sense and architectural precision into his jewelry work, influenced by the sparse, balanced approach of the Bauhaus design philosophy. After making jewelry as a side job to supplement his architectural studies and part-time work, he took to the bench full-time in 1976. Chavez's signature is the precise, geometric inlay that showcases his extraordinary lapidary skills, shaping and polishing tiny shards of bright coral, speckled turquoise, milky jade, and inky lapis before setting them, primarily, in 14- or 18-karat gold. Chavez executes every step himself, from start to finish. Working from his hometown of San Felipe Pueblo, New Mexico, Chavez has trained his son, Jared, in the art and craft of jewelry to develop a creative practice focusing on silver, metal stamping, and colored gems. With a background in digital arts and printmaking, Jared brings a fresh approach to Chavez Studio that complements his father's, with them both bearing witness to their Native American heritage in a modern age.

Winifred Mason Chenet

Winifred Mason Chenet
b. New York, New York, United States, 1918
d. United States, 1993

A model wears a copper cuff and ring by Winifred Mason Chenet, 1946.

Widely considered to be the first Black commercial jeweler in the United States, Winifred Mason Chenet indelibly shaped the American jewelry landscape with her one-of-a-kind pieces expertly crafted in copper, bronze, and silver. Born in New York to West Indian parents, Chenet was influenced by the cultural traditions of her heritage and surrounded by the Greenwich Village arts scene. After studying at New York University, she began teaching and training young people in metalsmithing, through which she met Art Smith, her future assistant and mentee (see p.265). Chenet created her first piece, a pendant, in 1940, and within a decade she had her own shop, her unique jewels were being sold at stores on Fifth Avenue, and her pieces were being worn by the likes of Billie Holiday. In December 1946 her swirling, S-shaped modernist cuff embellished with two orbs and a matching circular cocktail ring graced the cover of *Ebony* magazine. After receiving a grant from the Rosenwald Fund in 1945, Chenet traveled back and forth to Haiti, where she met her husband, incorporating the rich cultural influences into her work, particularly with voodoo-inspired pieces. Chenet never repeated the same design twice, continuously exploring new motifs in her metalwork and fabricating new tools to allow her to accomplish her artistic vision.

Chopard

Chopard
est. Sonvilier, Switzerland, 1860

Orchid Earrings in gold and titanium set with yellow sapphires, garnets, opals, and 4,800 tsavorites, from the *Red Carpet Collection*, 2018.

Established in 1860 by watchmaker Louis-Ulysse Chopard, the eponymous Swiss luxury house originally specialized in streamlined pocket watches for daily wear. By 1885 the company had expanded sufficiently to count Tsar Nicholas II of Russia among its clientele, and nearly a century later the firm had passed to the Scheufele family. Caroline Scheufele introduced the company's first fine jewelry collection in 1985, when she created the *Happy Clown*—a pendant of a clown with a stomach full of diamonds and colored stones—and ushered in a glamorous new era in which spectacular gemstones were increasingly featured in Chopard's creations. Firmly established as a luxury house, in 1998 the brand became the official partner of the Cannes Film Festival after Scheufele redesigned the festival's Palme d'Or trophy by creating a single piece of hand-cut crystal with a 24-karat-gold palm branch. First introduced in 2007 to celebrate the festival's sixtieth anniversary, every year since Chopard has unveiled a new set of themed high jewelry pieces at Cannes as part of their *Red Carpet Collection*. A ring in their 2024 collection, which featured two green frogs with emerald bellies guarding a crown encrusted with clear and yellow diamonds and a 17.7-carat round-cut rubellite—a nod to the clown pendant—became one of their most coveted pieces of the season.

Chow Tai Fook

Chow Tai Fook
est. Guangzhou, China, 1929

Diamond bangle from the Chow Tai Fook high jewelry collection, 2025.

The most powerful jewelry brand in China, Chow Tai Fook began in 1929 with a single store in Guangzhou. The mega-jeweler's roots run deep into Chinese culture and, in particular, the traditional gold jewelry that is highly prized in the Asian market and remains a cornerstone of the business. In 1972 the house launched buttercup yellow solid 999.9 gold jewelry, and in 1990 they became the first Asian retailer to introduce fixed pricing, negating the need for traditional haggling. Many of Chow Tai Fook's designs are infused with Chinese symbolism. The *Rouge* core collection, for example, features the Chinese character that represents blessings and good fortune—a character that is also part of the house's name, reworked as a geometric motif recalling the gold bricks that underpin the house. In addition to fine gold jewelry, Chow Tai Fook is known for its diverse collection of stones, including the Aurora Green diamond and CTF Pink Star. The Cullinan Heritage diamond, acquired rough in 2010, produced twenty-four separate stones, which were used in the *A Heritage in Bloom* necklace by jewelry artist Wallace Chan (see p.59). In 2025 Chow Tai Fook launched 100-percent recycled gold collections and, under the creative direction of Nicholas Lieou (see p.170), a high jewelry line using heritage materials such as pure gold and precious jade with a modern aesthetic designed for everyday wear.

Christie's

Christie's
est. London, England, 1766

The Aga Khan Emerald brooch in platinum and 18-karat gold with a 37-carat square-shaped emerald and marquise-shaped diamonds. The brooch was commissioned from Cartier Paris by Prince Aga Khan as a gift to his wife, Nina Dyer. The brooch was first sold by Christie's in 1969 in Geneva to Van Cleef & Arpels. In 2024 it was sold again, for $8.86 million, setting an all-time record for an emerald sold at auction.

The first jewelry sale of renowned London auction house Christie's dates back to the French Revolution, when the collection of Madame du Barry, Louis XV's mistress, went under the hammer in 1795. This historic sale set the stage for some of the most magnificent and important royal jewels to cross the block. In recent history, notable auctions include Princess Margaret's private collection in 2006 and the 2008 sale of the hypnotic gray-blue, 35.56-carat Wittelsbach diamond, which dates back to 1666 through three royal lines. Some truly beguiling jewels have notably been sold multiple times by Christie's, such as the sapphire and diamond suite worn by Marie-Louise, Archduchess of Austria and niece of Marie Antoinette (see p.183), which Christie's hammered down in 1894, 1959, and 1961. The house has also notably influenced the market with sales of rare gemstones such as the Oppenheimer Blue diamond. Sold in 2016 for a staggering $57.5 million, its record-breaking price reinforced the idea that rare and exceptional diamonds were highly sought-after assets by collectors in both the jewelry space and the luxury market overall. Also with a lasting impact was the sale of Elizabeth Taylor's private collection in 2011, which elevated the status of fine jewelry thanks to celebrity association, alongside historical significance and record-breaking auction results (see p.280).

Aldo Cipullo

Aldo Cipullo
b. Naples, Italy, 1935
d. New York, New York, United States, 1984

Cartier *Love Bracelet* in white gold with black ceramic and diamonds launched in 2006 and based on Aldo Cipullo's original design created for Cartier New York in 1969.

Photograph by Toby McFarlan Pond.

In the late 1960s and '70s, designer Aldo Cipullo created pieces for Cartier New York that have remained bestsellers to this day (see p.54). The eldest of five, Cipullo was born in Naples, Italy, in 1935 and largely grew up in Rome. He immigrated to New York City in 1959 and studied at the School of Visual Arts before joining David Webb as a bench jeweler (see p.78). After three years with Webb, Cipullo joined Tiffany & Co., where he worked with notable designer and window dresser Gene Moore (see p.283). In 1969 Cipullo began working with Cartier New York and presented his first design for the firm, the *Love Bracelet*. A simple gold band of two halves dotted with golden screws, two of which could be locked with a special screwdriver, it became a runaway success. Seeking to ennoble the everyday and inspired by the industrial undercurrent of Manhattan as well as Cartier's own heritage, Cipullo created more jewelry with hardware at its core, chiefly among them his *Juste un Clou* bent nail designs. He also created enamel pendants with graphic patterns borrowed from backgammon boards and hamsa hand pendants. Cipullo departed Cartier in 1974 to establish his own atelier. He went on to create many notable pieces, including, in 1978, a thirty-one-piece set of jewelry commissioned by the American Gem Society that featured only gemstones and metals from the United States.

Kevin Coates

Kevin Coates
b. Kingston upon Thames, England, 1950

A *Snake for Casati* mounted brooch in 18-karat gold with carved and inlaid opal, emeralds, and silver, from *A Bestiary of Jewels*, 2014.

Contemporary British artist Kevin Coates captures both the wonder of nature as well as an inner dreamy, fantastical world using finely crafted objects. Goldsmith, jeweler, virtuoso craftsman, musician, mathematician, and philosopher, Coates embodies the spirit of the Renaissance man. Described as visual poetry, his style is derived from a singular dedication to making obscure, Gongoresque connections that travel across time and genre to reveal the invisible threads that unite and bind us. Coates handmakes each piece in his studio—using a range of techniques from casting, stone carving, and painting to inlay, mosaic, and enameling—often while listening to Proust or the music of his hero, Mozart. His ability to encapsulate profound artistic and literary ideas in his work is evident in the *A Crow for Ted Hughes* brooch from his *Bestiary of Jewels* (2014), exhibited at the Ashmolean Museum in Oxford, England, in 2014. From *A Fly for Virgil* or *A Starling for Mozart* to *A Snake for Casati*, Coates paired each historical or mythological figure to a bejeweled animal, held in an intricately painted resin wall mount that contextualizes the story, as well as a book that enriches the narrative. Coates's unique approach is celebrated in museums worldwide, including the Victoria and Albert Museum and the Wallace Collection in London and the Museum of Fine Arts Boston.

Codognato

Codognato
est. Venice, Italy, 1866

A necklace by Attilio Codognato photographed inside the jeweler's Venice shop, 2016.

Photograph by James Mollison.

The Venetian jeweler Codognato has become an institution as integral to La Serenissima's identity as the nearby St. Mark's Square. Founded in 1866 by Simeone Codognato, a dealer in paintings, objets d'art, and antiquities, the business quickly turned to producing and selling unique handcrafted jewelry. This legacy was carried forward by Simeone's son Attilio, who forged a new Gothic aesthetic centered around snakes, crosses, and skulls laden with symbolism and influenced by the archaeological discoveries of the late 1800s. Attilio's arcane art prompted reflections on the brevity of human existence and the impossible dream of eternal life, drawing clients from Gabrielle "Coco" Chanel to Andy Warhol (see pp.60, 307). But Codognato's jewelry is intrinsically linked to and reflective of Venice's unique soul. Among the jeweler's most renowned signature items is the *Moretto*, a brooch depicting a Moor's bust in carved ebony, adorned with a gem-set turban—a nod to Venice's past as a powerful commercial empire stretching beyond Europe. The most iconic motif, though, is the memento mori, a hollow skull serving as a reminder of death. Yet Codognato's skulls always wear a glistening crown, for a memento mori is also a memento vivere—a reminder to live, much like the city of Venice itself, forever on the verge of sinking yet inspiring endless joie de vivre.

Sylvie Corbelin

Sylvie Corbelin
b. Bourg-en-Bresse, France, 1958

Lucky Lucane scarab rings in gold, moonstone, diamond, and abalone with pink sapphires (left), yellow sapphires (center), and rubies (right).

Growing up in the rural French countryside, Sylvie Corbelin still draws inspiration from her childhood experience for her dreamlike fine jewelry collections today. Having first studied law and philosophy—developing a love of literature, history, and storytelling long before she discovered her passion for jewelry-making—she became an antiques dealer at age thirty-five, following in her mother's footsteps, but it was not until 2000 that she made her first piece of jewelry. Her eponymous brand followed in 2004, with a boutique at the Paul Bert Market, nestled in Saint-Ouen in northern Paris, that is a treasure trove of eclectic and fanciful jewels riffing on quirky flora and fauna themes. Corbelin's menagerie bursts with butterflies and bugs, farmyard animals, and mythical creatures, while blooms erupt with an *Alice's Adventures in Wonderland*–esque flamboyance. Now a certified gemologist, Corbelin seeks out unusual gemstones from every corner of the globe, often setting antique gemstones into her fantastical designs. Refusing to use industrial production methods or computer-aided design, Corbelin makes pieces that showcase a charmingly imperfect flair, with a brutalist, raw, and organic feel. Almost every jewel is one-of-a-kind, and Corbelin only produces around fifty pieces per year, their Surrealist aesthetic and rarity making them a jewelry collector's dream.

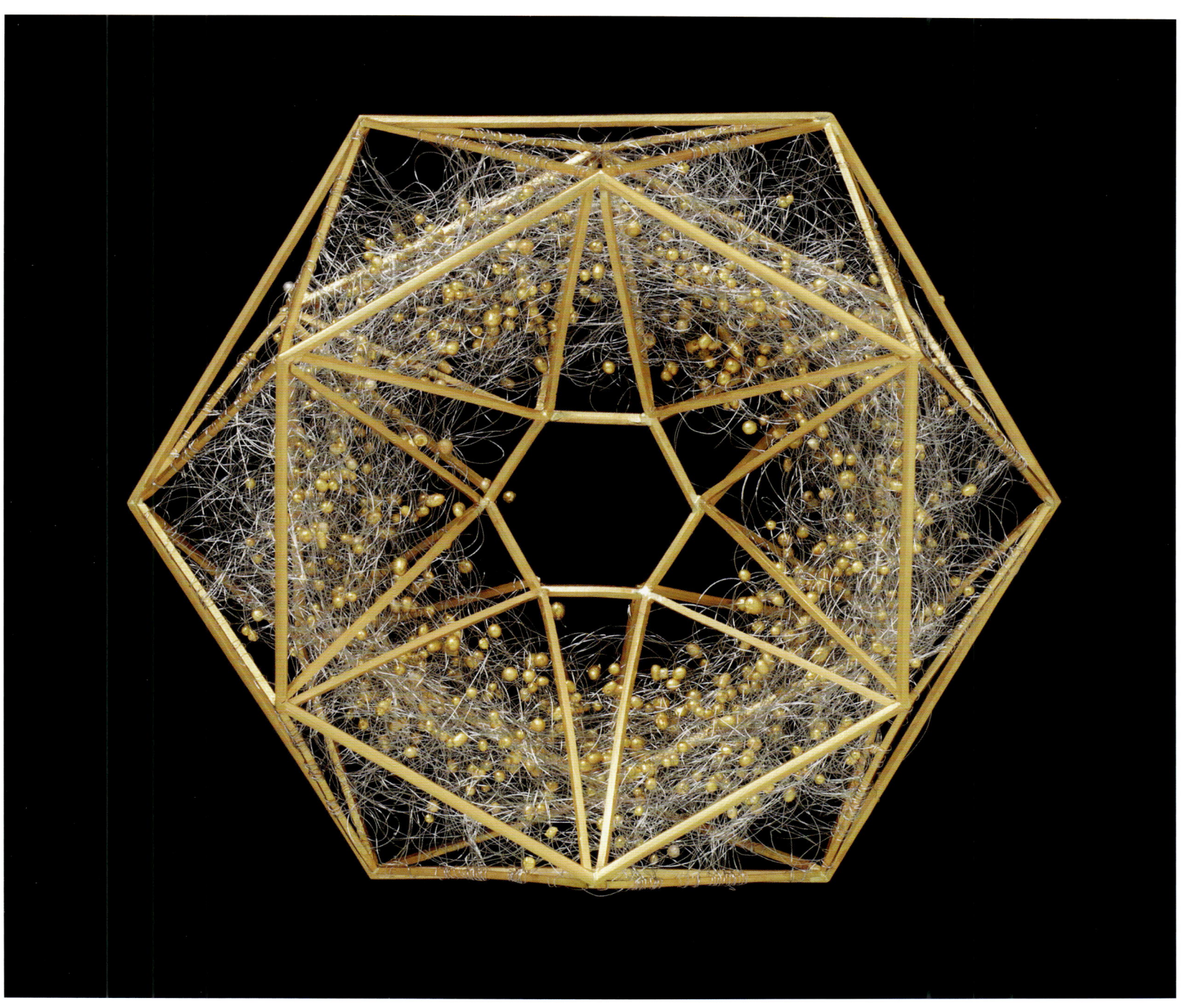

Giovanni Corvaja

Giovanni Corvaja
b. Padua, Italy, 1971

Hexagonal brooch in gold and platinum with a geometric framework containing a swirling mass of fine platinum wire decorated with granules of gold, 2000.

Anyone who has encountered a diaphanous brooch or furred jewel from Giovanni Corvaja has likely found themselves questioning their senses of sight and touch. Yet those threads forming cuffs or swirling around inside a geometric cage are indeed made of solid gold and have been meticulously woven, maintaining their fluidity and suppleness. This is not otherworldly magic but the result of relentless research and determination. Born in Padua, Italy, to two professors of chemistry, Corvaja began training as a jeweler at age thirteen. For Corvaja jewelry would be a medium for experimenting with materials and textures rather than simply crafting mundane accessories. Fascinated by golden threads, he first acquired special diamond dies to create ultra-thin gold strands and then learned from the textile industry how to transform them into objects comfortable enough to wear, some taking upward of two thousand hours to complete. His *Knitted Necklace* is formed from long ombre gold mesh tubes handwoven with custom-crafted bobbins, while a gold cage bracelet envelops thousands of hair-thin wires topped with colorful enamel accents. With his series of fur-covered jewels, Corvaja turned the mythical Golden Fleece—symbolizing an elusive, bliss-bearing prize, as well as power and prestige—into a reality, making him into the first jeweler-alchemist-artist of our time.

Lydia Courteille

Lydia Courteille
b. Paris, France

Aouatif Saadi wears the Lydia Courteille *Four-Leaf Clover Ring* with a 4-carat Ethiopian opal and displays the *Salamander Brooch* with 19 Mexican fire opals, weighing 44.05 carats in total, *Vogue Arabia*, April 2023.

Photograph by Desiree Mattsson.

An insatiable voyager to remote areas and cultures, jeweler Lydia Courteille firmly believes that "nothing beats immersion in a country to build a creative collection." Her jewelry travels across time, steeped in ancient stories and legends, especially rituals around death, expressed as memento mori pieces. Every one of Courteille's inspirations is filtered through an analytical mind honed by scientific training—she studied biochemistry and spent a decade in research before becoming an antiques dealer and launching her first jewelry collection in 1998. Immediately recognizable, her colossal pieces are often centered around outrageously large and rare minerals, such as landscape agate or rhodochrosite. She surrounds them with mixed-stone toning pavé, faceted gemstones, enamel, and gold worked to depict anything from a Zoroastrian temple to delicate leaf patterns from Islamic tiles in Samarkand. The resulting pieces are often symbolic, even political—in Courteille's *Rosa del Inca* collection, a rose gold, black diamond, and pink sapphire profile of the Emperor Atahualpa stares into a rock crystal ball carved with the face of Francisco Pizarro. Karl Lagerfeld was a fan of Courteille's work, as are Catherine Deneuve, Daphne Guinness, and Beyoncé (see p.29), drawn in by pieces that are mysteriously dark yet full of joyful color with a style that sets fire to the imagination.

Dries Criel

Dries Criel
b. Ghent, Belgium, 1992

Ventura Melrose wears *Brute* earrings and the *Lotus* bracelet in 18-karat yellow gold with 5 carats of natural white diamonds and enamel, 2023.

Photograph by Frédéric Bastin.

Entirely dedicated to his art form, Dries Criel spent his formative years as a modern and classical dancer who rarely left the ballet studio. Based in Antwerp for his dance studies, Criel took a summer job in the city's famous diamond district and everything changed. A passion for diamonds took hold and he began to develop a unique, genderless design style steeped in symbolism. Deeply inspired by the enigmatic motifs of Ancient Egypt—such as the lotus, scarab, pyramid, and sphinx—Criel blends these references with a natural dynamism he previously harnessed through dance, creating kinetic jewels that showcase strong, graphic lines and sequential silhouettes.

His pieces have an almost architectural quality, with artful angles effortlessly executed in white and yellow gold, occasionally emboldened with a streak of colorful enamel to emphasize their sleek outline. Criel collaborates with artisans across Belgium, as well as in Italy, to bring his pieces to life, with each jewel designed to give strength and power to its wearer. Since founding his eponymous brand in 2017, Criel has indeed seen his designs worn by some of the most powerful names on the red carpet, including Lady Gaga, Dua Lipa, and Beyoncé (see p.29).

Angela Cummings

Angela Cummings
b. Klagenfurt, Austria, 1944

Necklace and earring set with free-form opal plaques set in 18-karat gold, designed by Angela Cummings for Tiffany & Co., 1983.

Born in Austria and educated in Italy, Angela Cummings first made her mark when she joined Tiffany & Co. as an in-house designer in 1967 (see p.283). She became one of Tiffany's few named jewelry designers, alongside the likes of Elsa Peretti, Paloma Picasso, and Jean Schlumberger (see pp.221, 224, 251). Her pieces were notable for their intricate 18-karat-gold designs complemented with a variety of colored gems such as black opals, South Sea pearls, and black jade. However, Cummings was best known for her inlaid pieces, where she set cuts of gems and other materials into recesses carved into the surface of the metal, creating a unique pattern with a smooth finish. Several of her better-known inlaid pieces combine black gems with yellow gold in various patterns. In 1984 Cummings and her husband, Bruce—a gemologist who also worked for Tiffany—formed their own business under the Angela Cummings name. They opened branded boutiques in Bergdorf Goodman, Saks Fifth Avenue, Bloomingdale's, and Neiman Marcus, where they sold jewelry that ranged in price from one hundred to ten thousand dollars, making her pieces more accessible to a wider audience. Cummings retired in 2003 but reactivated her practice in 2013 to create a twenty-five-piece collection with distinguished jeweler Assael (see p.21).

Salvador Dalí

Salvador Dalí
b. Figueres, Spain, 1904
d. Figueres, Spain, 1989

A model dons Salvador Dalí's *Eye of Time* brooch, comprised of platinum, diamonds, blue enamel, and a Movado timepiece, with a diamond tear dropping from a ruby lacrimal sac, 1950.

A celebration of the uncanny and the power of the unconscious mind, Surrealism argued against rationality as the only means of making sense of the world. Alongside pioneers such as André Breton, Joan Miró, and Méret Oppenheim (see p.217), Salvador Dalí was one of its most famous practitioners, both in art and jewelry. His Surrealist paintings were replete with nonrational motifs, such as his distinctive melting clocks and distorted bodies, exploring his fascination with the subconscious and the imagination. In 1941 Dalí expanded these themes, creating his first collection of Surrealist jewelry with the then up-and-coming Italian designer Duke Fulco di Verdura (see p.298). Together, the duo translated everyday items—a brooch, a pillbox, a cigarette case—into otherworldly objets d'art, encircling miniature paintings and drawings by Dalí with Verdura's jeweled settings. Dalí continued to craft jewelry over the next three decades, personally selecting a rainbow of precious stones for his designs. He converted symbolic images, such as the cross, the heart, and crowns, into abstract representations drawn in diamonds, rubies, sapphires, and emeralds. Interwoven throughout is a playfulness and quirky sensuality, from brooches of ruby-studded lips revealing pearl teeth to a deliciously pulsing ruby heart.

David Webb

David Webb
est. New York, New York,
United States, 1948

Model Veronica Hamel wears a David Webb domed zebra ring, *Vogue*, September 1964.

Photograph by Irving Penn.

The epitome of American ingenuity, the sculptural power of David Webb jewelry challenged traditional notions of adornment and became instant classics within design history. In 1942, at only seventeen, Webb moved from North Carolina to New York, where he established his workshop just six years later in 1948. Drawing inspiration from ancient civilizations—particularly Greek, Egyptian, and Etruscan—he created opulent, figurative pieces recognizable for their use of textured gold, enamel, and vibrant gemstones. Eye-catching animal motifs were a recurring theme, such as his famous enameled zebra and lion bracelets, reflecting a free-spirited approach to combining naturalistic forms with intricate patterns. Webb's work, possessing both grandeur and craftsmanship, appealed to collectors who sought jewelry that made a statement. By the 1960s, he had become the jeweler of choice for cultural icons such as Jacqueline Kennedy Onassis, the Duchess of Windsor, Elizabeth Taylor, and Diana Vreeland, who famously wore her Zebra bracelet and earrings to dramatic effect (see pp.150, 260, 280, 306). In 1963 he opened his flagship store on Madison Avenue, cementing his place in the New York scene. Half a century after his death in 1975, the brand continues to honor his legacy, offering striking, original designs that remain as distinctive today as when they were first created.

David Yurman

David Yurman
est. New York, New York,
United States, 1980

Dante necklace in direct-welded bronze, 1969.

Photograph by Emil Larsson.

For the past five decades, the partnership of Sybil and David Yurman has resulted in one of America's most successful jewelry brands. Sybil, a painter, and David, a bronze sculptor, met in Greenwich Village in 1969, sparking a lifelong creative connection. Enamored with David's sculptures, Sybil voiced her desire to be able to wear one—the result was the *Dante* necklace, which would pave the way for their hugely popular global business in fine jewelry. Initially selling through craft galleries under Putnam Art Works, they soon pivoted to create luxury jewelry that embodied their ethos of merging art and craftsmanship. The brand's breakthrough came in 1978 when David twisted together solid and hollow wire tubes to create their first *Cable* bracelet. A year later, finial caps set with colorful pink tourmaline and emeralds were added in what would become David Yurman's signature design, transforming the American jewelry market when it was first released in 1983. Throughout the 1990s and 2000s, the company continued to innovate and expand its offerings, notably captured in stunning black-and-white campaigns by photographer Peter Lindbergh. With Sybil and David's son, Evan, joining in 2003, the brand came early to a growing movement around men's jewelry, further evolving their sculptural aesthetic with high jewelry in 2010 in a range of unexpected stones and materials.

De Beers

De Beers
est. Kimberley, South Africa, 1888

De Beers *Magnetism* choker, part of the *Forces of Nature* collection, featuring two 1.5-carat marquise-shaped diamonds with a jacket of green and white diamonds, 2024.

Founded in 1888 by English mining magnate and South African politician Cecil John Rhodes, De Beers has become synonymous with diamonds. The world's largest producer by value, its history traverses colonialism and two world wars, not to mention diamond deregulation and environmentalism. Despite its long, complicated, and sometimes controversial history, De Beers has been behind some of the most important stones ever discovered. To mark its centenary in 1988, the company revealed a 599-carat rough stone that was cut into the 273.85-carat Centenary Diamond, featuring 247 perfectly aligned facets. Also with an illustrious history is the 203.04-carat Millennium Star, the world's second-largest top-color internally and externally flawless pear-shaped diamond. The diamond was selected to ring in the millennium in 2000, displayed at midnight before Queen Elizabeth II in London's Millennium Dome and 8.5 million television viewers. Backed by the household slogan "Diamonds are Forever," coined in 1947, De Beers irrevocably influenced the popularity of diamond engagement rings in the public's imagination. Since its founding, the company has continuously evolved, establishing De Beers Jewellers in 2001, offering collections of natural diamond jewelry and, more recently, Lightbox, which produced jewelry featuring lab-grown diamonds from 2018 to 2024.

Victoire de Castellane

Buisson Couture Émeraude necklace in white gold and yellow gold with diamonds, pink sapphires, emeralds, tsavorite garnets, purple garnets, pink spinels, and rubies, by Victoire de Castellane for Christian Dior's *Les Jardins de la Couture* high jewelry collection, 2023.

Victoire de Castellane says her aim as a jewelry designer is never to get bored—and there's certainly nothing staid about her fantastical creations. When she was just twenty-two, she joined Karl Lagerfeld at Chanel designing costume jewelry (see p.60). So once she became creative director for Dior in 1999 and established the high jewelry division, it was with a free and creative approach to conventions (see p.89). Her aesthetic in both her personal work and for Dior Joaillerie is one of joyous abandon: a vibrant explosion of color and texture in which rare diamonds, sapphires, emeralds, and rubies are valued just like all other precious stones. De Castellane's vision is one of Surrealism, fantasy, and fun: full of flowers, nature, and the couture codes of the Maison Dior, expressed through jewels that surprise with their volume and asymmetry. She introduced mismatching earrings and multifinger rings to the high jewelry lexicon. And although de Castellane's creations are decidedly modern, they are influenced by Dior's history, from Christian Dior's beloved gardens to the house's signature toile de Jouy fabric. Dior's in-house craftspeople bring de Castellane's wildest dreams to fruition through feats of goldsmithing, which make solid gold and gemstones appear as fluid and delicate as ribbons or petals.

Loulou de La Falaise

Loulou de La Falaise
(Louise de La Falaise)
b. London, England, 1947
d. Gisors, France, 2011

Loulou de La Falaise, 1983.

Photograph by Guy Marineau.

Before English designer and fashion muse Loulou de La Falaise's tenure at Yves Saint Laurent, ladylike pearls and jeweled brooches were the dominant jewelry look in haute couture (see p.245). Together with Saint Laurent, she swept that all away. Part of the late 1960s bohemian scenes of New York and London, de La Falaise modeled for *Vogue*, designed fabrics for Halston, and turned heads with her nonconformist, vintage style, layering inexpensive bracelets to the elbow. She was introduced to Saint Laurent in 1968 by artist Fernando Sánchez, beginning a decades-long friendship and collaborative partnership. In 1972 Saint Laurent wanted to match the bigger, bolder accessory aesthetics of the 1970s. Although de La Falaise had no formal training, Saint Laurent tapped her for the job. Her approach played with bright colors, scale, and materials, and she worked with such artisans as Goossens and Gripoix to make her flamboyant designs (see pp.126, 129). She introduced leather, ceramic, velvet, plastic, shells, coral, and colorful crystals into haute couture jewelry, and could wear them better than anyone. Saint Laurent's retirement in 2002 gave de La Falaise the freedom to set up La Maison de Loulou the same year and sell her own style. Her legacy has been rekindled on the catwalk in the bold 1980s-style jewelry by Saint Laurent's latest creative director, Anthony Vaccarello.

Charlotte De Syllas

Charlotte De Syllas
b. Bridgetown, Barbados, 1946

Flight Necklace with white nephrite jade and 18-karat white gold, 2014.

Photograph by Simon B. Armitt.

British jeweler Charlotte De Syllas's journey toward stone carving began at Hornsey College of Art in the 1960s, when renowned jeweler Gerda Flöckinger taught her how to cut a cabochon. Since then, De Syllas has been honing her skills in the medium, creating pieces as varied as a gold ring with a gray chalcedony head and a necklace of black jade and labradorite depicting magpie wings, now in the collection of the Victoria and Albert Museum in London. Swirls of pink tourmaline might be encased in a ribbon of gold on a ring, or a necklace may feature whimsical, masklike faces carved from tourmaline and amethyst. Part of De Syllas's mastery comes from her experience working with materials as diverse as ebony, opal, abalone, and both black and white jade. She works strictly on commission, adapting her work to each client's personality, and has taught in Nigeria, Finland, and India. Since 2010, she has run intimate, intensive carving workshops from her Norfolk, England, studio, considered a rite of passage by jewelers all over the world. De Syllas was made a Liveryman of the Goldsmiths' Company in 2007 and was awarded the Award for Excellence from the Queen Elizabeth Scholarship Trust in 2022.

Ute Decker

Ute Decker
b. Worms, Germany, 1969

Islands Surrounded by Waves neck sculpture in 100 percent recycled sterling silver, 2017–22.

Photograph by Xavier Young.

A background in political economics and a passion for Zen philosophy might seem like an unusual path to jewelry, yet these diverse interests profoundly shape the work of London-based German designer Ute Decker. Her creations, often described as "geometric poetry," are characterized by their imposing, three-dimensional sculptural presence, defined by tubes or bands of gold or silver. Increasingly large-scale jewelry extending beyond the body challenges traditional notions of self-expression and is designed to spark conversation. In her *Islands Surrounded by Waves* neck sculpture, delicate circles are spaced between undulating curls of sterling sliver, evoking the movement of the ocean, at once serene and tumultuous. Decker's body sculpture is not meant to accessorize but to stand out, much like a provocative work of art. Behind the scenes, Decker's in-depth knowledge of the gold trade led her to become one of the pioneering designers working exclusively with certified Fairmined gold, sourced from artisanal small-scale mines that adhere to strict standards for environmental and labor concerns. Ever conscious of where her raw materials come from, combined with the meditative power of Zen teachings, Decker's approach to jewelry-making favors contemplative practices that manifest in her pieces' organic shapes and matte finishes to sublime effect.

Delfina Delettrez Fendi

Delfina Delettrez Fendi
b. Rome, Italy, 1987

Delfina Delettrez wears a pearl earring in gold with diamonds and the *Portrait Brooch* in gold and silver with rubies, pearls, and black, white, gray, and cognac diamonds, both of her own design, 2015.

Photograph by Liz Collins.

Delfina Delettrez Fendi is fond of saying she was raised on "fashion and milk." As the fourth generation of the Fendi fashion dynasty, her childhood was one of high glamour and creativity: she walked in her first catwalk show at age five and spent most afternoons in her mother's design studio. But in 2007, at just nineteen years old, she decided to follow in the footsteps of her jeweler father, Bernard Delettrez, and establish her own fine jewelry brand. Crafted by expert goldsmiths in Rome, Delettrez Fendi's designs are tinged with a gothic surrealism and a hefty dose of wit. In the *Anatomic* range, gem-set eyes and lips appear in earrings that recall the shape of a navel piercing, a theme further explored in *Two in One*, where diamonds and pearls themselves appear pierced with tiny barbells. Her quietly subversive aesthetic champions mismatching earrings and open rings—the type of jewelry, Delettrez Fendi says, women want to buy for themselves. In 2020 Delettrez Fendi joined the family business as artistic director of jewelry at Fendi. The house's first high jewelry collection debuted on the catwalk in 2022, featuring the double-F logo stretched and distorted in a contemporary, graphic exploration of the ultraprecious iconography.

Enrico and Sandra di Portanova

Enrico di Portanova
b. Los Angeles, California, United States, 1933
d. Houston, Texas, United States, 2000

Sandra di Portanova (Sandra Hovas)
b. Houston, Texas, United States, 1943
d. Houston, Texas, United States, 2000

Sandra and Enrico di Portanova in the Pleasure Dome of their home, Villa Arabesque, Acapulco, Mexico, *Town & Country* magazine, October 1982.

Photograph by Norman Parkinson.

The legendary Baron Enrico Apuzzo di Portanova, aka Ricky, was born in Los Angeles and raised in Italy. Ricky's extravagant lifestyle epitomized the opulence of la dolce vita and, later, the excesses and flamboyance of the jet set. Before becoming heir to the Texan Cullen family's oil fortune (via his grandfather), Ricky followed his father's footsteps into acting and later founded Portanuova Gioielli, a jewelry boutique in Rome. His style of jewels reflected his globe-trotting existence. He traveled the world collecting impressive gemstones that he set into finely crafted jewels perfectly pitched to the taste of his glamorous clients. In 1957, upon receiving his colossal inheritance—which by the 1980s included a monthly stipend of $1.2 million—he left Rome and bought up gemstones with the zeal of a maharaja. His third and final wife was Houston-born Sandra Hovas, who was magnificently bedecked in jewels bestowed upon her by Ricky. Ricky set the scene for epic parties at Arabesque, his Acapulco mansion, where his friends, including Joan Collins, Roger Moore, and a selection of Mexican presidents, could indulge in displaying their fabulous jewels. In 2000 Christie's New York raised $4,773,658 from the auction of the Di Portanova collection of jewels, which included nearly two hundred pieces by Bulgari, Cartier, Marina B, and Lalaounis (see pp. 46, 54).

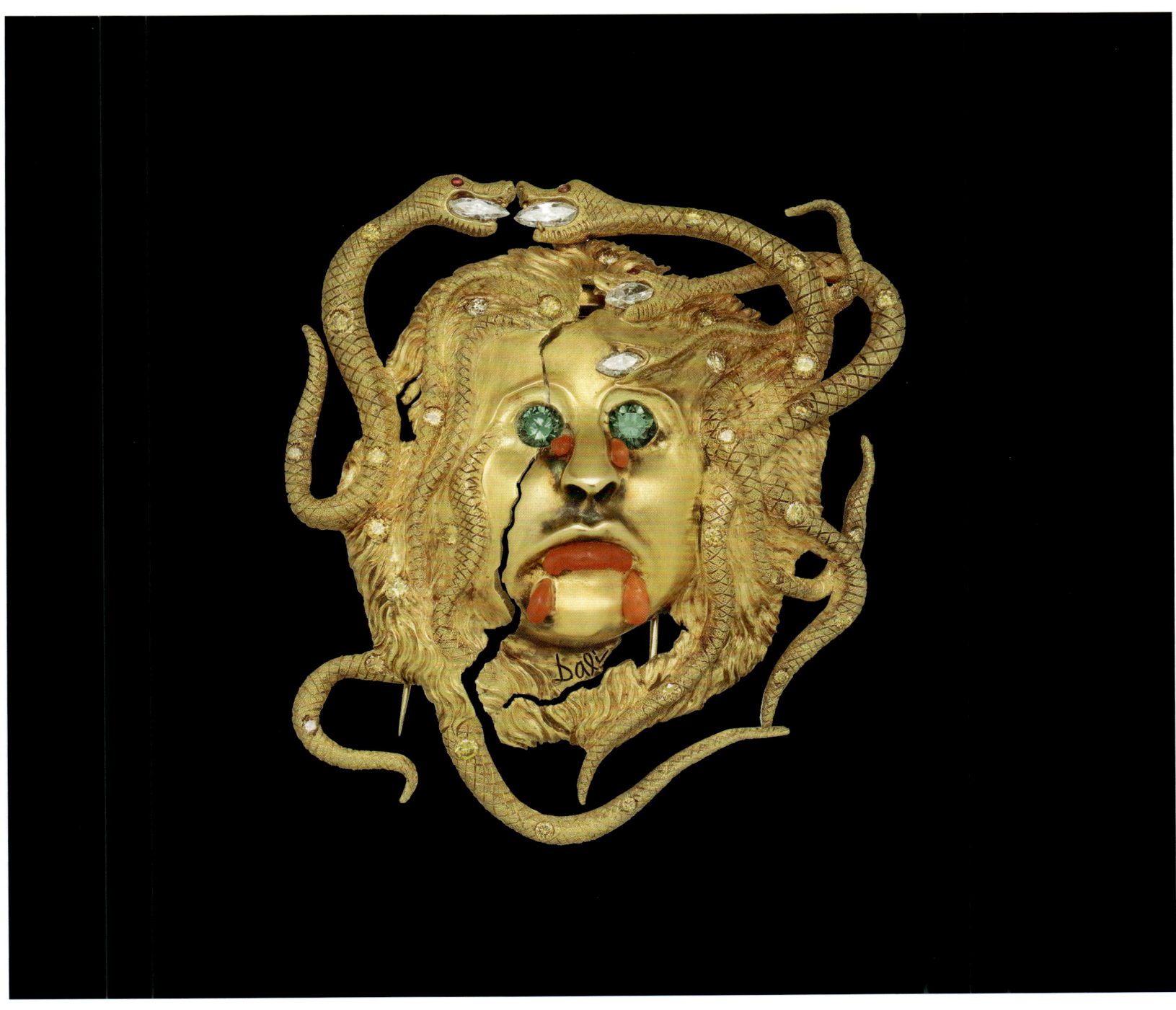

Didier Ltd

Didier Ltd
est. London, England, 2006

A unique *Medusa* brooch created by Salvador Dalí in 1955, composed of 18-karat gold with red coral and white and green diamonds, that was once part of the Didier Ltd inventory.

Founded in London by Didier and Martine Haspeslagh, Didier Ltd has become one of the foremost authorities on artistic jewels designed by mid to late twentieth century artists, architects, and designers. Nearly all the works in the Didier collection are acquired from the secondary art market and include pieces by Alexander Calder, Salvador Dalí, Alberto Giacometti, Man Ray, and Pablo Picasso, among many other fine artists (see pp.50, 77, 122, 180, 223). In recent years Didier has featured jewels by important Italian and American designers and artists at some of the world's most respected art and antique fairs, such as TEFAF Maastricht in the Netherlands, the Winter Show, and Salon Art + Design in New York. The couple dedicated their 2023 exhibition space at TEFAF to Italian artists of the Padua School, a 1950s movement that focused on antiquated goldsmith techniques in jewelry art. A highly anticipated piece from that exhibition was an 18-karat-gold brutalist cuff made by Nino Franchina, an Italian artist from Sicily; it was created with the use of an acetylene torch, which produced fissures throughout the jagged piece. The niche that Didier has pioneered has gained in popularity over the years, with both the industry and collectors now seeing these artist-created pieces as art in their own right.

Marlene Dietrich

Marlene Dietrich
b. Berlin, Germany, 1901
d. Paris, France, 1992

Marlene Dietrich, c. 1950.

Known for breaking the rules and defying norms on and off the silver screen, Marlene Dietrich always maintained her über-glamorous femme fatale allure, which made her one of the most celebrated and influential style icons of all time. The German-born American actress approached both her professional and personal lives with boldness, possessing a keen understanding of the value of her image and the clothes and jewels she wore. Born into a family in the jewelry and clock-making trade, Dietrich began honing a discerning eye for fine objects from a young age. From the time of her breakout role in *The Blue Angel* in 1930, Dietrich was rarely seen without jewelry. Even while on a tour selling war bonds during World War II, she was seen waving from an open automobile wearing a Cartier cuff, gold-plated pearls, and matching domed earrings (see p.54). With a penchant for diamonds, emeralds, and rubies, a key piece in her jewelry wardrobe was an Art Deco emerald-and-diamond brooch and bracelet set by Trabert & Hoeffer-Mauboussin. Her most cherished piece, though, was a Van Cleef & Arpels *Jarretière* (garter) cuff (see p.291). Boldly sculpted in an asymmetrical loop, it was a larger-than-life bracelet illuminated by incandescent Burmese red rubies and baguette-cut diamonds set in platinum—a perfect match for Dietrich's character.

Dior

Dior
est. Paris, France, 1946

Victoire Doutreleau models the Zaire dress and accompanying jewelry in front of Christian Dior during the general rehearsal of the Autumn/Winter Haute Couture collection, 1954.

Photograph by Mark Shaw.

A year after debuting his now-iconic *New Look* couture collection in 1947, legendary French fashion designer Christian Dior made his first foray into jewelry. Like many of the couture houses at the time, it was of the costume variety, and Dior worked with the best of the best: Gripoix, which produced exquisite glass versions of the house lily of the valley symbol; Swarovski, which created the iridescent aurora borealis stone initially for Dior's sole use; Goossens; and New York–based Kramer (see pp.126, 129, 275). In the years that followed, styles changed depending on the house's head designer, with bold, logo-sporting pieces characterizing the 1980s and extravagant beaded Masai-style necklaces for John Galliano's first haute couture collection in 1997. Fine jewelry was mostly produced in French workshops, especially that of Jean-Claude Champagnat, whose nature-inspired pieces still echo through Dior high jewelry today. Since launching in 1999, its focus has kept to key symbols from Christian Dior's interests—nature, his garden, and the couture atelier—but interpretation, in the hands of longtime designer Victoire de Castellane (see p.81), is ever evolving. Bright lacquer contrasting with equally brilliant gems; mixed metalwork; the modern lines of the *Gem Dior* collection; and jeweled flora set the tone—sparkling symbols of Dior's enduring place in the world of luxury.

John Donald

John Donald
b. Surrey, England, 1928
d. East Sussex, England, 2023

A model wears 18-karat gold nugget–flake earrings with detachable melted-edge roundels and a necklace of cultured pearls on fine wire with nugget-flake roundels, set pearls, and peridot beads in a publicity photograph for the opening of John Donald at Tecla, Old Bond Street, 1971.

By the late 1950s, British jewelry design had become somewhat stagnant, but as the Swinging Sixties dawned, John Donald saw only endless possibilities for revolutionary design. Donald had studied at the Royal College of Art and created new techniques for startling ideas based on organic shapes, roughly faceted stones and crystals, and unevenly worked gold, mixing polish and texture. Gold rods and nuggets were melted into abstract shapes, contrasting with unusual materials, such as rough iron pyrite, while gems swayed on wires inside open goldwork rings, brooches, and earrings. In 1961 Donald quickly rose to prominence after presenting his works at the International Exhibition of Modern Jewellery masterminded at the Goldsmiths' Company Hall. Success and high society beckoned, with Princess Margaret becoming a friend and client in 1964. His work for her spanned decades, including a 1967 brooch featuring a large, irregularly faceted aquamarine set in radiating, round, granulated gold tubes given to the princess by the late Queen Mother (also a client). In 1968 he opened a strikingly Brutalist shop in Cheapside, and when it closed for redevelopment in 2005, it was the last practicing goldsmith in the city. By then nearly eighty, Donald spurned retirement and returned to creating bespoke work at his country studio until his death in 2023.

Dreher Carvings

Dreher Carvings
est. Idar-Oberstein,
Germany, late 1800s

Chameleon carved from a single crystal of gem-quality Brazilian green beryl.

Photograph by Robert Weldon.

Dreher Carvings, a five-generation family business based in Idar-Oberstein, Germany, is a pioneering force within the arena of carved gemstones. As master carvers, the late Gerd Dreher and his son Patrick have transformed single pieces of rough gemstone into intricate, detailed sculptures that highlight the stones' natural beauty and complexity. Heritage techniques—including holding and moving a rough gem around a fixed spindle with mounted diamond tools—have been passed down via father-son apprenticeships, pushing the boundaries of gem carving to its limits. In addition to reproducing stone models of animals for Fabergé (see p.101) and supplying exquisitely carved stones to a number of high-end jewelry designers, their oeuvre spans the natural world. Whether ruby-engraved seahorses or three-colored tourmaline starfish, the resulting work uniquely marries process with precision, elevating gem carving to a high art coveted by collectors around the world. Dreher sculptures, which require hundreds of hours to create, usually feature beryls and quartzes, though the Drehers' preferred stone is natural agate from Brazil's Rio Grande do Sul (agate mining was also native to Idar-Oberstein), which was, for example, used to fashion an exquisite lily carving with curled petals and 18-karat-gold leaf and stamen and a rubellite tourmaline toad.

Doris Duke

Doris Duke
b. New York, New York,
United States, 1912
d. Beverly Hills, California,
United States, 1993

Doris Duke at her home,
Shangri La, in Honolulu, Hawaii,
Vogue, November 1966.

Photograph by Horst P. Horst.

Born in 1912, Doris Duke inherited an estimated $100 million at just twelve years old, upon the death of her father, tobacco tycoon James Buchanan Duke. Over her lifetime, Doris Duke became an early collector of Islamic art, enjoyed competitive surfing, and sang in a gospel choir—activities that appealed to her more than mingling in society. Above all, she was an art connoisseur and philanthropist who left her $1.2 billion wealth to charity and, controversially, to her butler, Bernard Lafferty. Among Duke's many interests, though, jewelry was a constant. She owned an unparalleled collection and yet regarded its assembly as accidental. There were pieces by Cartier from the Belle Époque that she inherited from her mother and grandmother, jewels from Tiffany & Co., and many precious pieces that she picked up as souvenirs on her travels in India and Southeast Asia (see pp.54, 283). She shared a love of Asian art with jeweler David Webb, from whom she commissioned several pieces in the 1950s and '60s (see p.78). Duke was an important client, always meeting Webb personally, and was very closely involved in the design process, often supplying gemstones she collected on her travels and creating bold pieces that included an elaborate enamel and coral ring, carved jade earrings, and an Indian-inspired ruby fringe necklace.

Dusausoy

Dusausoy
est. Lyons, France, 1840

Platinum brooch set with diamonds, c. 1930.

French firm Dusausoy revolutionized both the business and art of modern jewelry during the 1920s and '30s through its avant-garde designs and progressive use of advertising. Founded as a dealership and appraisal firm in Lyons in 1840, the company later became an outlet for the Belle Époque jewelry of Paul-Jules Dusausoy. Around 1898 his son Justin took over the business, by then based in Paris. Justin, with his children, Jean and Janine, produced Art Deco designs in refined, geometric shapes and monochromatic color schemes. Their diamond-and-platinum pieces put them at the forefront of modern French jewelry, and their innovative range of transformable jewelry, which included clip brooches that could be worn in several ways, proved highly successful. The firm began receiving major awards at international fairs, including the 1925 Exposition Internationale des Arts Décoratifs et Industriels Modernes in Paris, where their *Stalactite* bracelet won a coveted Grand Prix. Dusausoy continued trading in vintage jewelry and even offered a "remodeling" service transforming existing accessories into more fashionable pieces. With the death of Justin in 1960, Dusausoy's light began to fade, and the firm eventually closed its doors in the early 1970s. Today, it has seen a resurgence with galleries such as Symbolic & Chase (see p.277) adding prized pieces to their collections.

Melanie Eddy

Melanie Eddy
b. Paget, Bermuda, 1979

Naomy wears the *Loquat* earrings in 18-karat gold, with a satin hand-finish, and set with fancy-cut hexagonal citrines, accented by six graduated round brilliant-cut yellow diamonds.

Photograph by DeMarcus Allen.

The abstract, faceted forms of jewelry artist Melanie Eddy have their roots in a deep fascination with geometry: how it is used in architecture to foster a sense of solace, how we understand the world, and how it has informed the work of artists since the very beginning. In the summer of 1997, a chance errand at local Bermudan jewelry shop, Gem Cellar, owned by Chet Trott, led her on the path to becoming a bench jeweler under Trott's mentorship. But the diverse interests of the Central Saint Martins graduate all have had an impact on her practice, from working as a curator to working with NGOs in Afghanistan, including Turquoise Mountain's Institute for Afghan Arts and Architecture.

In 2007 she launched her eponymous brand in London, showcasing her sculptural silver jewels, hand-crafted—some from lost-wax techniques—and hand-finished by Eddy. Her triangular facets are, she says, a "love letter" to Bermuda. Beyond the symbolic association with the Bermuda Triangle, they are a reference to the sails of the Bermuda rig, the basis of all modern sailing yachts, as well as the triangular movement of goods and enslaved people going between ports of the Atlantic slave trade. "When you work in an abstract way, people may not immediately see the influences beyond aesthetics," she says. "But not everything has to be explicit to be powerful and meaningful."

Ndidi Ekubia

Ndidi Ekubia
b. Manchester, England, 1973

River necklace in Britannia silver, 2023.

Contemporary silversmith Ndidi Ekubia pushes sheet metal to its limits, and her expert command over the material leads her to create masterworks, from oversize vessels that appear almost liquid in form to tiny beakers with gilt interiors. Most of her work is made from Britannia silver, which she says "moves softly and then holds the strength of the marks." For Ekubia's first foray into jewelry, she made bold, oversize cuffs and a necklace for the Sotheby's exhibition *Brilliant & Black: Age of Enlightenment* in September 2022 (see p.267). The Manchester, England–based artist is inspired by what surrounds her every day—cityscapes, the patterns made by a river, the leaves of a tree, shadows, and ripples of water—as well as by her African heritage. For the cuffs and necklace she made for the Sotheby's exhibit, it was her drawings of moths and butterflies that inspired her, their murmuration captured with every tiny hammer stroke. With a bachelor's degree in 3D design from the University of Wolverhampton, and an exclusive by-invitation residency at Bishopsland, a postgraduate hub for jewelers and silversmiths in Reading, England, Ekubia now has works in various collections, including at the Ashmolean Museum in Oxford and the Victoria and Albert Museum.

Elisabetta Cipriani Gallery

Elisabetta Cipriani Gallery
est. London, England, 2009

Talisman necklace by Michele Oka Doner with a pendant in bronze, 18-karat yellow gold, and diamond, and a handmade chain, from Elisabetta Cipriani Gallery, 2024.

Photograph by Ali Emre Göloğlu.

As one of the pioneers of wearable art, Elisabetta Cipriani has collaborated with more than fifty international contemporary artists in the past fifteen years who otherwise would never have considered making jewels. Her tenacious and perceptive ability to seek out artists, ranging from Enrico Castellani to Zaha Hadid, and to inspire them to create limited-edition small-scale artworks from scratch sets her apart in the art world. This is partly due to her background in contemporary art after working for three years at MACRO, the contemporary art museum in Rome, where she curated important exhibitions of contemporary artists. In 2012 she exhibited the *Foglie* project by Giuseppe Penone (see p.220) at the Pavilion of Art and Design (PAD) in Paris, a piece that was later acquired by the esteemed Musée des Arts Décoratifs. Cipriani's most significant collaboration, *Labbra* by Jannis Kounellis, a re-creation of his 1972 sculpture of gold lips, stands as a testament to her unique approach. Cipriani advises collectors, such as Diane Venet (see p.297), whose artist jewelry collection is unmatched, and shows the works of both emerging and established designers and goldsmiths in her EC Lab showcase. She can be found at the world's leading art fairs, from Design Miami to the Venice Biennale, exhibiting her collaborations with a commanding mix of artistic vigor and Italian passion.

Elizabeth II

Elizabeth II, Queen of
the United Kingdom
b. London, England, 1926
d. Balmoral Castle, Scotland, 2022

Queen Elizabeth II, wearing
the *Diamond Diadem* created
by Rundell Bridge & Rundell in
1820 (see p.242), at Buckingham
Palace, London, 1955.

Photograph by Cecil Beaton.

Only weeks after her ascension to the throne in 1952, Queen Elizabeth II posed for her first official portrait wearing the *Girls of Great Britain and Ireland Tiara*, which had been a wedding gift from her grandmother, Queen Mary (see p.187). The resulting image informed the designs of coins and bank notes throughout Elizabeth's seventy-year reign, inextricably linking the monarch to the elegant diadem. The queen's priceless personal collection encompassed hundreds of jewels, many inherited from previous monarchs or gifted by foreign dignitaries. However, she was renowned for preferring sentimental pieces such as the three-stranded pearl necklace given by her father, King George VI, or the *Granny's Chips* brooch featuring the Cullinan III and IV diamonds received from Queen Mary. The queen's innate understanding of how to use important jewels sensitively was most acutely observed during official events; she opted to wear an Asprey *Maple Leaf Brooch*—given by George VI to the Queen Mother to mark their 1939 state visit to Canada—at a 2008 commemoration for the fallen Canadian servicemen of World War I. Queen Elizabeth's considered use of decoration showcased a deep appreciation of jewelry as both a physical record of the history of the British monarchy and an art of fine craftsmanship.

Max Ernst

Max Ernst
b. Brühl, Germany, 1891
d. Paris, France, 1976

Gold *Poissons* pendant, designed in 1961.

Photograph by Joel Stans.

Mechanical creatures and apocalyptic landscapes were the subjects of Max Ernst's artworks, heavily influenced by the German artist's experience serving in World War I. The art he made after returning to Cologne, near his hometown of Brühl, in 1918 captured the chaos of war and a strained state of mind during turbulent times. Alongside artists Leonora Carrington, Salvador Dalí, and Man Ray (see pp.77, 180), Ernst became a leading figure in the Surrealist movement of the late 1910s and '20s, which led him to develop several techniques that relied on the element of chance to guide his drawings and paintings. Ernst applied a similarly free-form approach to his experiments in gold wearables, which he designed in a decades-long collaboration with the French jewelry maker François Hugo, whom he met in Paris in 1922 (see p.23). At his atelier, Hugo translated frottage—Ernst's way of creating images by rubbing pencils on paper placed over textured objects—to metal using a repoussé technique he mastered while working on a series of medallions with Pablo Picasso (see p.223). The limited-edition pendants Ernst and Hugo produced together had a hand-wrought quality reminiscent of the pre-Columbian metalwork of the Americas. Intricate scales decorate the *Poissons* talisman, for example, and three circles signal a face on the *Grande Tête* pendant, giving it the uncanny appearance of a mask.

Erté

Erté (Romain de Tirtoff)
b. St. Petersburg, Russia, 1892
d. Paris, France, 1990

Design for coral earrings, 1932.

The elegance and glamorous style of Art Deco can be invoked with a single name: Erté. Born Romain de Tirtoff, the artist and designer rejected a naval career to pursue a more creative path, leaving St. Petersburg for Paris in 1910 and adopting his pseudonym after the French pronunciation of his initials. In 1915, after working for influential fashion designer Paul Poiret, producing numerous designs for dresses and accessories, Erté's illustrations of stylish figures began gracing the covers of *Harper's Bazaar*. Throughout the first half of the twentieth century, he also designed costumes and adornments for film and stage, from ballets to Hollywood productions. Although jewelry held an important place in his stage designs, it was not until 1979, at age eighty-six, that Erté's career as a jewelry designer began in earnest. Collaborating with Jack Solomon's Circle Fine Art, his intricate pieces incorporated elements from his Art Deco designs of the 1920s and '30s and were realized by the American jeweler Natalie Kane O'Keiff. Using Brazilian emeralds and blue topaz, Japanese coral, and Thai rubies, Erté created 328 limited-edition pieces, many of which are marine inspired, while others feature Egyptian and Persian motifs. With this *Art to Wear* collection, he fulfilled his long-held desire to create a luxurious yet affordable collection of jewels to be worn every day.

Eugénie de Montijo

Eugénie, Empress of the French
(Eugénie de Montijo)
b. Granada, Spain, 1826
d. Madrid, Spain, 1920

Empress Eugénie, 1856.

Photograph by Gustave Le Gray.

The restoration of a brilliant court life in Paris during the Second French Empire was personified by, more than anyone, Empress Eugénie. Born a grandee of Spain, Eugénie de Montijo married Louis Napoléon Bonaparte in 1853, just after he had become emperor. With full access to the French Crown Jewels, the empress remounted many of the historic gems into more fashionable pieces. Among these were a crown and a tiara by Alexandre-Gabriel Lemonnier, the latter using pearls worn by Empress Marie-Louise and the Duchesse d'Angoulême. Emulating Marie Antoinette (see p.183), Eugénie's tastes tended toward the cutting edge of Parisian fashions, with jewelry by François Kramer, Mellerio dits Meller, and emerging firms Boucheron and Cartier (see pp.39, 54, 193). Following the imperial family's exile in 1871, many of the empress's personal pieces were sold off. In 1887, in an attempt to erase France's royal past, the Third Republic organized a sweeping sale of the Crown Jewels. A dazzling array of pieces was auctioned off, with a large majority going to jewelers—notably Tiffany & Co. (see p.283)—for private clients around the world. Since then, some of the pieces—including the empress's Lemonnier tiara, bow brooch, and reliquary brooch made with the Mazarin 17 and 18 diamonds—have made their way back to France and are now housed at the Louvre.

Peter Carl Fabergé

Peter Carl Fabergé
b. St. Petersburg, Russia, 1846
d. Lausanne, Switzerland, 1920

Grand Duchess Alexandra of Mecklenburg-Schwerin wearing an important Fabergé tiara. Made as a wedding gift from Duke Frederick Francis IV in 1904, the tiara features nine pear-shaped aquamarines and old cushion- and rose-cut diamonds.

Born into a family of Huguenot descent, Peter Carl Fabergé took over his father's jewelry house, founded in St. Petersburg in 1842, and elevated it to new heights, making it a household name across the Russian Empire and beyond. Renowned for its bejeweled Easter eggs, the Russian court jeweler followed a tradition started by Tsar Alexander III in 1885, creating a total of fifty Imperial eggs, of which six remain missing. However, it was two iconic tiaras that cemented Fabergé's place in jewelry history: the so-called *Empress Josephine Tiara*, with Gothic diamond arches framing large pear-shaped diamonds (sold at Christie's in 2007 for one million British pounds, see p.68), and an aquamarine tiara adorned with forget-me-not flowers and pear-shaped stones in the nocks of Cupid's arrow, worn by Grand Duchess Alexandra of Mecklenburg-Schwerin. From the tiniest snuffbox in Fabergé's signature pastel hues to larger hand-carved hardstone figurines of animals, fruits, and vegetables, each Fabergé piece reflects an unparalleled devotion to beauty. Beholders are enchanted by the intricacy and delicacy of works, such as the *Mosaic* brooch, which echoes the design of the elaborate *Mosaic Egg*. In the annals of history, Fabergé is synonymous with the former splendor of the Romanov court, yet his name is also inextricably linked to its decadence and ultimate downfall.

Faerber Collection

Faerber Collection
est. Zurich, Switzerland, 1968

An antique ring from Faerber Collection with a double-layered pink agate cameo depicting a profile of Hannibal from c. 1800 within an old-cut diamond frame from c. 1900, mounted in pink gold and platinum.

Faerber Collection has earned a worldwide reputation as a prestigious dealer in exceptional jewels, many once treasured by royalty and Hollywood icons alike. Established in 1968 by Thomas Faerber, who helms the business with his children, Max and Ida, along with codirectors Alberto Corticelli and Philippe Atamian, Faerber Collection is a name inextricably linked to big-gem glamour and heritage showstoppers. It was through the company's Geneva branch in 2004 that the Louvre acquired an outstanding emerald and diamond necklace and matching earrings, both once part of a parure commissioned by Napoleon I for his second wife, the Empress Marie Louise. Rarities reach across eras and cultures, shaping an inventory full of surprises, from fanciful Renaissance brooches decorated with enamel, engravings, and gemstones to delicate nineteenth-century hardstone cameos carved by hand with vivid, lifelike details. Indeed, some of the most exuberant and complicated jewelry designs ever created have passed through the hands of Faerber Collection, including unsigned masterpieces from the Belle Époque and Art Nouveau periods and superlative gem-set treasures by the likes of Boucheron, Cartier, Chaumet, and Van Cleef & Arpels, not to mention masterpieces by contemporary talents including JAR and Othmar Zschaler (see pp.39, 54, 63, 240, 291).

Azza Fahmy

Azza Fahmy
b. Sohag, Egypt, 1945

Ansar El Yacoubi wears an Azza Fahmy pectoral collar and *Happiness* tassel earrings, *Vogue Arabia*, March 2022.

Photograph by Greg Adamski.

Bold in scale and rich in symbolism, Egyptian jeweler Azza Fahmy's designs are inspired by Middle Eastern architecture, art, and literature, with ancient motifs including scarabs, snakes, and crescent moons realized using traditional skills such as hand-piercing and filigree. Referencing pharaonic adornments and replete with Arabic calligraphy, there's a tangible sense of history to the house's designs. Championing a mix of silver and yellow gold, every piece is wrought, front and back, with intricate details. In 1969 Fahmy stumbled upon a book on jewelry designs of medieval Europe. Abandoning her training as an interior designer, she forged a new path as the first female apprentice within Khan el-Khalili, Cairo's ancient jewelry quarter. There, she trained alongside leading goldsmith Hajj Sayed, learning the traditional Ottoman jewelry-making techniques that would define her eponymous brand. With a vision to create the first Egyptian international luxury jewelry house, Fahmy founded the boutique El-Ain Gallery in 1981 with her sister Randa. While Fahmy remains as creative director, the company is now helmed by her two daughters: Fatma Ghali as CEO and Amina Ghali as head designer. The house of Azza Fahmy employs more than one hundred jewelers, who handcraft every piece, continuing to champion Egyptian creativity and craftsmanship.

Paulding Farnham

Paulding Farnham
b. New York, New York, United States, 1859
d. Santa Clara, California, United States, 1927

Iris Corsage Ornament designed by Paulding Farnham for Tiffany & Co. in gold alloys and platinum with blued steel, Montana sapphires, diamonds, demantoid garnets, and topaz, c. 1900.

A career-defining moment for Paulding Farnham, then the head designer for the quintessentially American jewelry firm Tiffany & Co. (see p.283), took place in Paris at the Exposition Universelle of 1889. Tiffany's jewelry received the gold medal—the first ever given to an American firm—mainly on the strength of twenty-four strikingly lifelike enameled and bejeweled orchid brooches conceived by Farnham. Bolstered financially and creatively by serving Gilded Age gentry, Tiffany & Co. and, by extension, its young jewelry design chief were able to surpass the historically dominant European designers on their own turf. Although Farnham became known for his botanical designs, his brilliance was not limited to any single genre. He used American vernacular and Indigenous motifs, developing a collection of copper and silver pieces modeled after pottery and baskets, while also embracing the contemporary rococo style to create diamond baubles that looked like jewels out of Marie Antoinette's coffers (see p.183). His rise ended nearly as quickly as it began: when Louis Comfort Tiffany took over the helm in 1902, Farnham exited his position. Although he is perhaps less well-known today, Farnham left an indelible legacy at Tiffany & Co., transforming the New York design studio into a powerful jewelry brand on the global stage.

María Félix

María Félix (María de los Ángeles Félix Güereña)
b. Álamos, Mexico, 1914
d. Mexico City, Mexico, 2002

María Félix with her diamond serpent necklace commissioned from Cartier in 1968.

Photograph by Ignacio Castillo.

María Félix, the larger-than-life Mexican actor and singer of the golden age of Mexican cinema, was known as La Doña for her bravura and independent spirit. Her spectacular pursuit of success and resulting jewelry collection—proudly bought with her own money—left an indelible mark on jewelry design. Not afraid to push boundaries, she inspired a flamboyant, more daring style of jewelry that suited her strong personality. Cartier was a particular favorite (see p.54). In 1968 Félix commissioned a sinuous and menacingly lifelike articulated snake necklace set with 2,473 diamonds, enticing the French house into a new look of savagely elegant jewels. But even after that undertaking, nothing could have prepared the staff at Cartier for the moment when, in 1975, La Doña swaggered into the Rue de la Paix boutique with a baby crocodile as a model for a new jewel. Cartier rose to the challenge and created a dazzling necklace composed of two interlinked crocodiles—one in 18-karat yellow gold with 1,000 yellow diamonds and emerald eyes, the other in 18-karat white gold with 1,060 emeralds and ruby eyes—which could also be worn separately as brooches. Félix's unique style inspired Cartier's *La Doña* range of jewels and watches, first released in 2006. In 2007 Christie's auctioned her estate, which showcased many of her iconic jewels, for a total sale of $7.3 million.

Feng J

Feng J (Feng Ji)
b. Hangzhou, China, 1985

A Feng J tiara in the process of being crafted with double rose-cut pink sapphires, purple sapphires, white sapphires, pink spinels, aquamarines, diamond beads, and white diamonds set with her signature floating technique in 18-karat gold, 2021.

With her work rooted in the cultural heritage of China as much as it is in French Impressionism, Feng J is leading a new wave of young Chinese high jewelry designers who are translating visual codes formed over millennia to an audience of collectors and institutions worldwide. Feng J emerged onto the global scene in 2016 when she opened her headquarters in the Place Vendôme in Paris while maintaining an atelier in Shanghai. Bringing renewed techniques to jewelry-making, such as standing mounting and the floating set—where metal settings of double rose-cut gemstones are hidden—allows her pieces to seem as if they defy gravity, possessing an ethereal softness and lightness. Named after French artist Claude Monet's masterpiece, *Les Jardins de Giverny* is a prime example—the detachable necklace can also be worn as a bracelet and a ring. With a cut-cornered rectangular step-cut fancy light pink diamond, white diamond beads, various-shaped white sapphires, pink spinels, and pastel-colored tanzanites, aquamarines, and tsavorites, all invisibly set in white gold, Feng J displays an Impressionist take on hue, light, and shadow in a painterly approach to gemstones. In November 2020 the necklace was sold at auction for $2.6 million, making Feng J the youngest Chinese jeweler to achieve such a high figure in the open market.

Paul Flato

Paul Flato
b. Flatonia, Texas,
United States, 1900
d. Fort Worth, Texas,
United States, 1999

Lisa Fonssagrives on the cover of *Vogue* wearing Paul Flato jewelry, including a choker with a pendant, brooch on a black feathered turban, and bracelets, September 1940.

Photograph by Horst P. Horst.

Often called the "jeweler to the stars," Paul Flato was best known for his flamboyant Art Deco designs. In 1928 the Texas native opened a jewelry shop on Fifth Avenue and 57th Street in Manhattan that quickly began to attract New York high society and Hollywood royalty. He opened a second store in Los Angeles in 1937, which further cemented his position as a jeweler for celebrities. Among his clients were Marlene Dietrich, Doris Duke, Greta Garbo (see pp.88, 92, 116), Mae West, Rita Hayworth, Joan Crawford, Ginger Rogers, Carmen Miranda, Katharine Hepburn, and Gloria Vanderbilt. His one-of-a-kind creations were highly complex in their design, workmanship, and use of materials. Nothing was too extravagant for Flato, which matched the fashion trends of the 1930s and '40s. In one of his pieces, a 1940 platinum Art Deco retro ribbon-shaped brooch is adorned with a floral display of 27.09 carats of colored sapphires and diamonds. In 1943 Flato was convicted of fraudulently pawning one hundred thousand dollars' worth of jewels that belonged to colleagues and clients and served sixteen months in Sing Sing Correctional Facility. Upon release, he lived in Mexico City until 1953, fighting extradition to the United States to face additional larceny and forgery charges, and in 1990 he finally moved back to Texas.

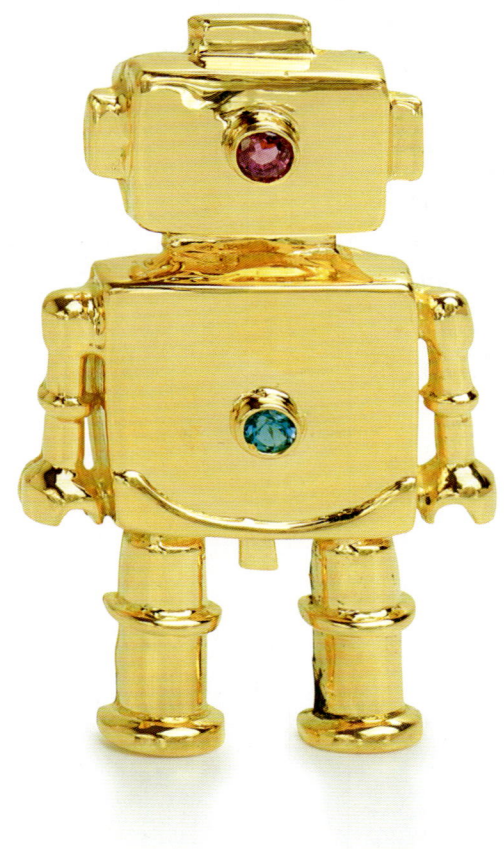

Mia Fonssagrives Solow

Mia Fonssagrives Solow
b. New York, New York,
United States, 1941

Ancestor Robot Pendant in 18-karat yellow gold with ruby and topaz, first created in 2000.

Photograph by Steve Benisty.

Jewelry has been a passion since childhood for American sculptor and designer Mia Fonssagrives Solow, who made her first brass cuff at the age of ten. The daughter of photographer Fernand Fonssagrives and supermodel Lisa Fonssagrives, as well as stepdaughter of fashion photographer Irving Penn (see p.219), Mia was destined for a life in art and design. She gained acclaim as a costume and fashion designer in the 1960s but is now recognized for her striking abstract and figurative sculptures, which include bold biomorphic forms in acrylic and fiberglass, as well as anthropomorphic animal and robot sculptures in bronze and aluminum. The sense of playfulness pervading these works is reflected in her jewelry, which typically riffs on her larger sculptures. Inspired by her ongoing series of boxy forms resembling mechanoid figures from 1950s science fiction B movies, Fonssagrives Solow's humorous robot collection includes chunky gold and silver rings resembling tiny automatons with comically large ears and pincers for hands. Each quirky character is set with rubies and diamonds that represent eyes and electronic buttons on their heavyset chests. The designer's passion for animals is also evident in her jewels: elephants and jumping horses appear as motifs on cuff bracelets, while stylized lions become gold earrings and brooches using gemstones for the majestic beast's eyes.

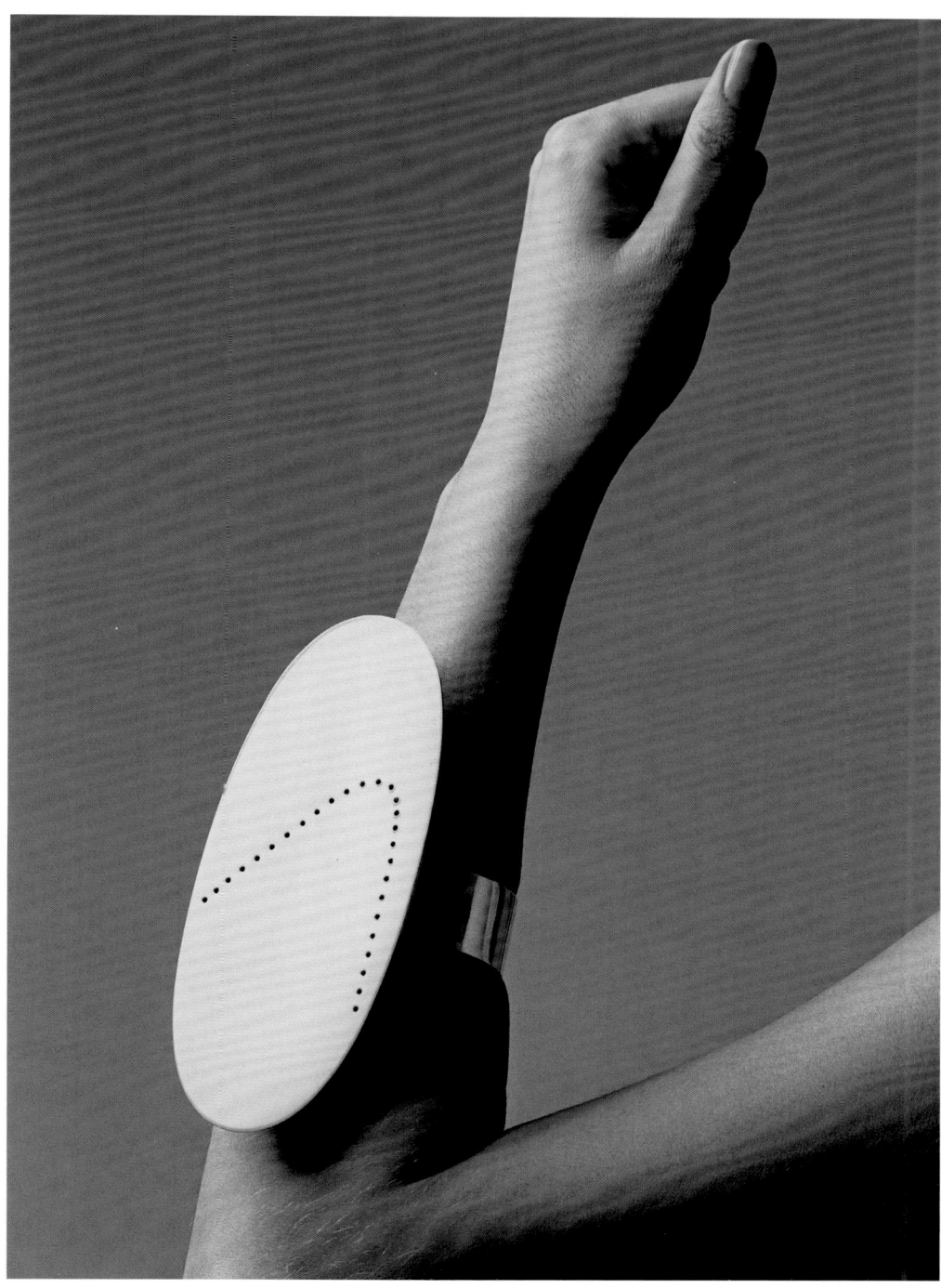

Lucio Fontana

Lucio Fontana
b. Rosario, Argentina, 1899
d. Comabbio, Italy, 1968

Elisse Concetto Spaziale LF3 bracelet in silver and lacquer, 1969.

Photograph by Ugo Mulas.

Argentine-Italian artist Lucio Fontana sought to redefine the concept of space through paintings, sculpture, and jewelry. As a founder of the modern art movement Spatialism, Fontana believed that space, movement, and time were as important to art as color, perspective, and form. He is most famous for his *Concetti Spaziali* (*Spatial Concepts*) works from the 1950s and 1960s, where he slashed and punctured his canvases and ceramics in an attempt to transcend the works' earthly limitations and connect with an infinite, immaterial, and spiritual dimension. In 1967 he collaborated with GEM Montebello, a Milan-based precious metal laboratory established by GianCarlo Montebello and his wife, Teresa Pomodoro, to produce limited-edition jewelry designed by modern artists (see p.199). Fontana created four designs: the *Anti-Sofia* necklace (LF1) and *Anti-Sofia* bracelet (LF2), along with two versions of the *Elisse Concetto Spaziale* bracelet (LF3 and LF4)—one bearing the artist's signature slash on the face of the cuff and the other perforated with a line of puncture marks. Covered with a layer of colored enamel, these thick, elliptical bracelets extended Fontana's *Concetti Spaziali* into the realm of personal adornment. The wearable artworks were famously promoted in photographs by Gianfranco Gorgoni and Ugo Mulas, with the latter's images published in *Vogue*.

Francis I

Francis I, King of France
b. Cognac, France, 1494
d. Rambouillet, France, 1547

Francis I with Eleanor, Queen of France, c. 1520–40.

Witnessing the depletion of the French Crown Jewels and the French treasury as a result of his defeat by Habsburg forces in 1525, Francis I decided to formally establish *les Diamants de la Couronne de France* and in doing so ensured their legacy for centuries to come. Consequently this group of precious jewels became constituted as an inalienable possession of the French state on June 15, 1530. The new institution created a cache of historically significant artifacts that could be used by future rulers as collateral to raise loans at time of war without risking their loss. It also meant that although queens and royal mistresses might wear the jewels, their possession and control would remain with the state. Of the initial pieces constituted by Francis I, the only one to remain is the Côte de Bretagne, a substantial spinel cut down to 107 carats during the reign of Louis XV when it was carved in the form of a dragon. Pieces were refashioned by jewelers to the crown, such as Georges-Michel Bapst and, later, Falize, and spectacular additions were made by subsequent rulers. Among these were the Mazarin diamonds, bequeathed by Cardinal Mazarin to Louis XIV in 1661, the Bleu de France bought by Louis XIV from Jean-Baptiste Tavernier in 1688 (see pp.192, 279), and the 140.64-carat Regent, acquired by French regent Philippe II, Duke of Orléans, in 1717.

Silvia Furmanovich

Silvia Furmanovich
b. São Paulo, Brazil, 1957

Botanical earrings with wood marquetry, amethysts, emeralds, and 18-karat yellow gold, 2018.

Bridging the worlds of art and adornment, Brazilian jeweler Silvia Furmanovich's one-of-a-kind creations are infused with culture and history that span continents and centuries. She comes from a long line of Italian goldsmiths, her father among them, whom she credits with teaching her that craftsmanship is of the utmost importance. Furmanovich established her own business in 1998, but it was a 2016 trip to Acre, Brazil's westernmost state, that changed the course of her career. There she met a community of artisans crafting traditional marquetry works by layering wafer-thin slivers of colored Amazonian wood. Furmanovich framed their creations with gold and gemstones, moving them into the world of high jewelry. "The intricate craftsmanship truly opened my eyes, inspiring me to explore diverse cultures, materials, and techniques that had not yet been widely utilized in jewelry design," she says. Since then, she has collaborated with miniature portrait artists in Udaipur, India, Japanese bamboo basket weavers, and silk weavers in Uzbekistan. The work of these artisans becomes the centerpiece of Furmanovich's collections inspired by Brazil's abundant flora and fauna: from marquetry butterflies to flowers adorned with Chilean woven horse mane. In each instance, she strives to safeguard and pass on centuries-old skills to the next generation.

Gabby Elan Jewelry

Gabby Elan Jewelry
est. New York, New York,
United States, 1991

A$AP Rocky wears custom gold grillz by Gabby Elan Jewelry, *WSJ Magazine*, March 2020.

Photograph by Juergen Teller.

With their company Gabby Elan Jewelry, New York–based father-son duo Gabby and Elan Pinhasov have conquered the market for custom grillz, creating sets for stars from Rihanna (see p.236), A$AP Rocky, and Marc Jacobs to Bella Hadid, Cynthia Erivo, and Tyler, the Creator. Gabby founded his eponymous company in Brooklyn in 1991 and has been hailed as the Godfather of Grillz, with more than four decades of experience as a dental and jewelry expert carving grillz. From full sets of solid gold or pavé-set diamonds to two- or three-piece sets designed with a single jeweled charm or miniature portrait, the options are endless. With requests for more individual pieces rather than full sets, clients are guided through the deeply personal process of selecting their jewels and are encouraged to tap into their creativity. Gabby mentored his son, Elan, and instilled in him the need to keep moving forward with a younger, fresher vision. "My ambition is to keep pushing the bar with designs that have yet to be seen, as well as trying to amplify each client's personality and lifestyle through their grillz," Elan says. Now located in Manhattan's Diamond District, Gabby Elan Jewelry has expanded into a wider jewelry collection, including oversize diamond-and-ruby cross pendants and skull eternity bands with diamond-set eyes.

Pratap Singh Gaekwad and Sita Devi

Pratap Singh Gaekwad,
Maharaja of Baroda
b. Baroda, India, 1908
d. London, England, 1968

Sita Devi, Maharani of Baroda
b. Madras, India, 1917
d. Paris, France, 1989

Sita Devi arranges her husband's seven-strand Baroda pearl necklace, Vadodara, Gujarat, India, 1948.

Photograph by Henri Cartier-Bresson.

In a captivating photograph by Henri Cartier-Bresson, the Maharani Sita Devi drapes strings of pearls upon her husband, Pratap Singh Gaekwad, the Maharaja of Baroda, for his fortieth birthday celebrations. Partially hidden behind him, she wears an exceptional necklace with two celebrated Brazilian diamonds, the 128.8-carat Star of the South and the 78.83-carat English Dresden. Born in 1917, the fourth child of the Maharaja of Pithapuram, Sita Devi met the Maharaja of Baroda at the Madras horse races in 1943. Entranced by her beauty, the Maharaja, already married with children, pursued her. Similarly married, Sita Devi hastily divorced her husband and remarried the Maharaja, which scandalized Indian society. As Indian Independence drew near, the Maharajas secreted their remarkable treasury of jewels—including gold ingots, pearls, rubies, diamonds, and emeralds worth millions—out of India. Chartering a private plane out of Baroda, they accompanied huge chests of gemstones and jeweled carpets, to Paris. Once settled, Sita Devi consulted Jacques Arpels, of Van Cleef & Arpels, on her private jewelry collection, which included a legendary seven-strand necklace of large Basra pearls (see p.291). Recklessly extravagant, she commissioned the jeweler to reset many of her treasures and sold pieces to maintain her lifestyle in Paris after her divorce from the Maharaja in 1956.

Galerie MiniMasterpiece

Galerie MiniMasterpiece
est. Paris, France, 2012

View of *Forms and Materials* exhibition of Sophia Vari's jewels at Galerie MiniMasterpiece, 2020.

Scenography and photograph by Yann Delacour.

On Paris's Left Bank stands Galerie MiniMasterpiece, a space dedicated to the creative possibilities of jewelry-making as a fine art practice, celebrating a fusionist approach to form, body adornment, and conceptual thinking. Established in 2012 by Esther de Beaucé, its inventory is rich in limited editions by a roster of renowned and contemporary French and international artists. Daughter of Diane Venet, one of the world's most prominent collectors of artists' jewelry (see p.297), de Beaucé grew up surrounded by conceptual art and went on to pursue a career as a gallerist for contemporary artists. Wanting to do more than just represent these artists, she explored the idea of collaborating on jewels produced in exclusive partnerships with the gallery. Among them is a collection of *Elevation* rings by late British sculptor Phillip King that riff off his large signature works in colored steel, while Argentine French artist Pablo Reinoso produced a series of golden cuffs inspired by the looping silhouettes of his monumental sculptures. More minimalist are the 18-karat white gold earrings by Korean artist Lee Ufan that hang like ribbons set with raw black diamonds. According to de Beaucé, the magic is embedded in form and fancy: "The artist-made jewel carries with it a strength, a monumentality, a poetry that takes it beyond the realm of conventional jewelry."

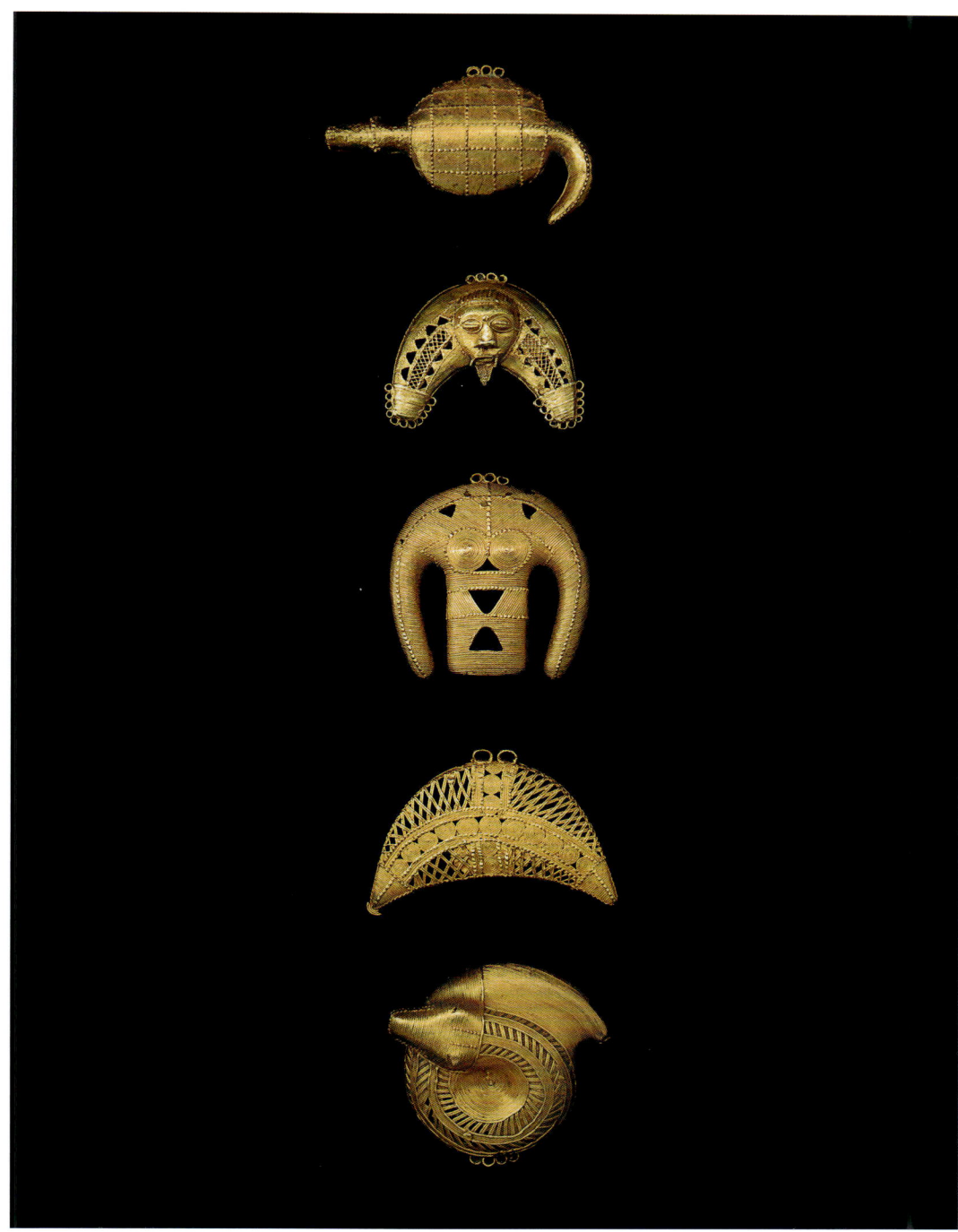

Marlène and Paolo Gallone

Marlène Gallone
b. Geneva, Switzerland, 1943

Paolo Gallone
b. Camino, Italy, 1944

Tribal ornaments from the Baule people of the Ivory Coast, crafted from gold and gold alloy using a lost-wax technique, late 19th to early 20th century.

The culmination of more than four decades of collecting across more than fifty countries, Le Monde des Arts de la Parure museum in Marrakech, Morocco, embodies the passion of its founders, Marlène and Paolo Gallone. Inaugurated in 2022, the museum displays a vast collection, ranging from jewelry to ceremonial wear, reflecting a richness of creativity and ingenuity across cultures. Housed in a building that echoes the architecture of the fifteenth-century *madrasas* at the Kasbah of Marrakech, the museum displays around three thousand of the Gallones' seven thousand artifacts gathered from their extensive travels and research across Africa, Asia, and Europe. At the heart of the collection is the exploration of human adornment, and jewelry takes the main stage. From antique Bedouin jewelry and intricately carved bronze talismanic bracelets from Mauritania to gold chief ornaments from the Ivory Coast and a nineteenth-century Chinese hairpin with electric blue kingfisher feathers, the Gallones' approach to collecting is aimed at revealing the emotional power of jewels in their many different forms. Bringing together objects that have been scattered around the world, the Gallones strive to preserve ancestral knowledge and traditions in danger of disappearing, safeguarding these treasures and passing them on to the next generation.

Greta Garbo

Greta Garbo (Greta Gustafsson)
b. Stockholm, Sweden, 1905
d. New York, New York, United States, 1990

Greta Garbo in a publicity photograph for *Mata Hari*, 1931.

Actor Greta Garbo's desire for privacy gave her an air of mystery at a time when media reporting intensified around the on- and off-screen lives of Hollywood stars. Noted for playing strong-willed women in acting roles throughout the late 1920s and '30s, Garbo possessed a glamorous style that included jewelry by Joseff of Hollywood and vintage jewels with Napoleonic provenance sourced by Trabert & Hoeffer-Mauboussin. Playing the dancer-turned-spy in *Mata Hari* (1931), Garbo wore a dress designed by Gilbert Adrian that glittered, as did her dazzling headdress and long shoulder-duster earrings by Joseff of Hollywood. The extravagance continued in Adrian's costumes for Garbo's role as the title character in *Queen Christina* (1933), with spectacular designs that blurred and combined the realms of fashion and jewelry. In a promotional still for her final film, the romantic comedy *Two-Faced Woman* (1941), Garbo wore a gold-and-diamond *Curb-Link* watch bracelet designed by Fulco di Verdura (see p.298). The piece became part of Garbo's signature look, and she continued to wear the bracelet and a similarly designed watch throughout her life. Enduringly iconic, both pieces are still produced by Verdura today, with Garbo's style a valued part of its history. Despite the high glamour Garbo often portrayed in films, she favored simpler jewels in her private life.

Garrard

Garrard
est. London, England, 1735

Hand-painted gouache of Princess Diana's iconic Garrard engagement ring with a 12-carat oval Ceylon sapphire surrounded by diamonds and set in 18-karat white gold, 1981.

Garrard became Britain's first official Crown Jeweler when it was appointed by Queen Victoria in 1843 and served six monarchs, making magnificent historic creations that are now synonymous with grand state occasions (see p.301). The firm traces its origins to master silversmith George Wickes, who registered his maker's mark in 1722 and founded his own business on London's Panton Street in 1735. Within a year, Wickes's reputation as a skilled craftsman ensured that he received commissions including a royal order from Frederick, Prince of Wales. In 1782 Robert Garrard joined the business and assumed sole control in 1802. With the company's reputation as one of the country's finest jewelers and silversmiths firmly established, Garrard presented at the 1851 Great Exhibition organized by Prince Albert, who would commission the company to recut the infamous Koh-i-Noor diamond for Queen Victoria the following year. Significant royal commissions followed, including Queen Victoria's *Small Diamond Crown*, the *Girls of Great Britain and Ireland Tiara*, the *Imperial State Crown*, Queen Mary's *Fringe Tiara* (see p.187), and the sapphire-and-diamond engagement ring worn by Diana, Princess of Wales. Today, Garrard places a sapphire inside the band of every engagement ring as the "something blue" for brides on their wedding day in homage to its royal history.

Judy Geib

Judy Geib
b. Reading, Pennsylvania, United States, 1958

Spring Flower brooch with dendritic agate, amethysts, and green tourmalines set in 18-karat gold, 2024.

Photograph by Dirk Vandenberk.

Judy Geib's naturalistic, luminous jewelry joyfully pushes against the established rules surrounding fine jewelry. Without any formal training, Geib has created sumptuous opal-set floral rings, steampunk sterling silver eyeglasses, and curlicuing earrings from her *Studio Sweep* series crafted from metal remnants left on her workbench. Her first piece, in 1997, was a spur-of-the-moment set of crude opal earrings, and since then Geib has gradually put together a body of work that springs directly from her imagination. As part of her process, she forgoes sketching, instead going right to the raw materials in her New York studio. This unique approach endows every jewel with the intimacy and immediacy of her distinct touch. She forges gold and solders combinations of gems to create rivières of Colombian emeralds, brooches with harlequin-colored palettes of precious stones, and Peter Pan collars in lacy 18-karat gold. Perhaps best known for her voluptuous dendritic agate brooches and earrings with pops of color at the edges, the result is that every element is distinctive, sometimes endearingly off-kilter, and always brimming with her unique brand of easygoing levity. She's a creative person even beyond jewelry, evident in the custom crocheted pouches and carved wooden boxes she makes to house her eclectic pieces.

Gem Palace

Gem Palace
est. Jaipur, India, 1852

Sumit Singh wears a traditional groom's *sherwani mala* pearl necklace by Gem Palace, 2020.

Photograph by Hormis Antony Tharakan.

As one of India's oldest jewelry houses, the Gem Palace is an iconic institution, based in Jaipur, with a history spanning nine generations since the atelier's founding by the Kasliwal family in 1852. The Kasliwals, who were the crown jewelers for maharajas and maharanis in the City Palace since 1725, are synonymous with extraordinary handcraftsmanship, heritage, and innovation, blending traditional Indian techniques passed down among *karigars* (or artisans)—such as *meenakari* enameling inspired by Jaipur frescoes—with modern aesthetics. Brothers Munnu and Sanjay Kasliwal modernized today's Gem Palace, frequented by India's prime ministers, British royals, including Princess Diana, and Hollywood celebrities from Gwyneth Paltrow to Angelina Jolie. Statement pieces abound, such as the *Raaja* necklace from its *Royal* collection, composed of 55 carats of rose-cut diamonds, 65 carats of emeralds, and pearls in a latticelike *jaali* design—or the house's famed poison rings featuring a hero gemstone and a hidden box encrusted with diamonds. Traditional *kundan* jewelry made of highly refined 22- or 24-karat pure gold dating back to the Mughal and Rajput eras also feature in the *Raj* collection. This bridges centuries-old techniques and contemporary designs with multicolored enamel decor and precious stones, highlighting the timeless spirit of the Pink City, and its indelible heritage.

Georg Jensen

Georg Jensen
est. Copenhagen, Denmark, 1904

Sterling silver pansy brooch designed by Georg Jensen (no. 113), 1912.

The distinguished Danish design house Georg Jensen was established in Copenhagen in 1904 by its namesake, silversmith Georg Jensen. Known for quality craftsmanship and timeless appeal, Jensen fused function with flowing forms, creating accessible designs that featured Art Nouveau shapes and platforming talent at his silversmithy—a philosophy continued today by the global house's contemporary collaborations and its creative director, Ragnar Hjartarson. Inspired by nature, Jensen used organic silhouettes in his designs, creating silver hollowware, metalwork, and cutlery, and inspiring iconic jewelry forms such as the beaded *Moonlight Grapes* motif in sterling silver and diamond-studded 18-karat gold. Helping to define twentieth-century Scandinavian design, Jensen's focus on pared-back, craft-forward innovations earned him a reputation as one of the most reputable silversmiths of his time. Following Jensen's death in 1935, this high bar attracted such designers as Henning Koppel (see p.154), Arne Jacobsen, Patricia Urquiola, and Zaha Hadid. The house debuted its jewelry collection in 2000, with the modular, interlocking *Fusion* ring designed by Danish textile artist Nina Koppel; and the *Offspring* and *Mercy* collections by American jeweler Jacqueline Rabun (see p.233), two of the house's bestsellers that further combine geometric forms with soft curves.

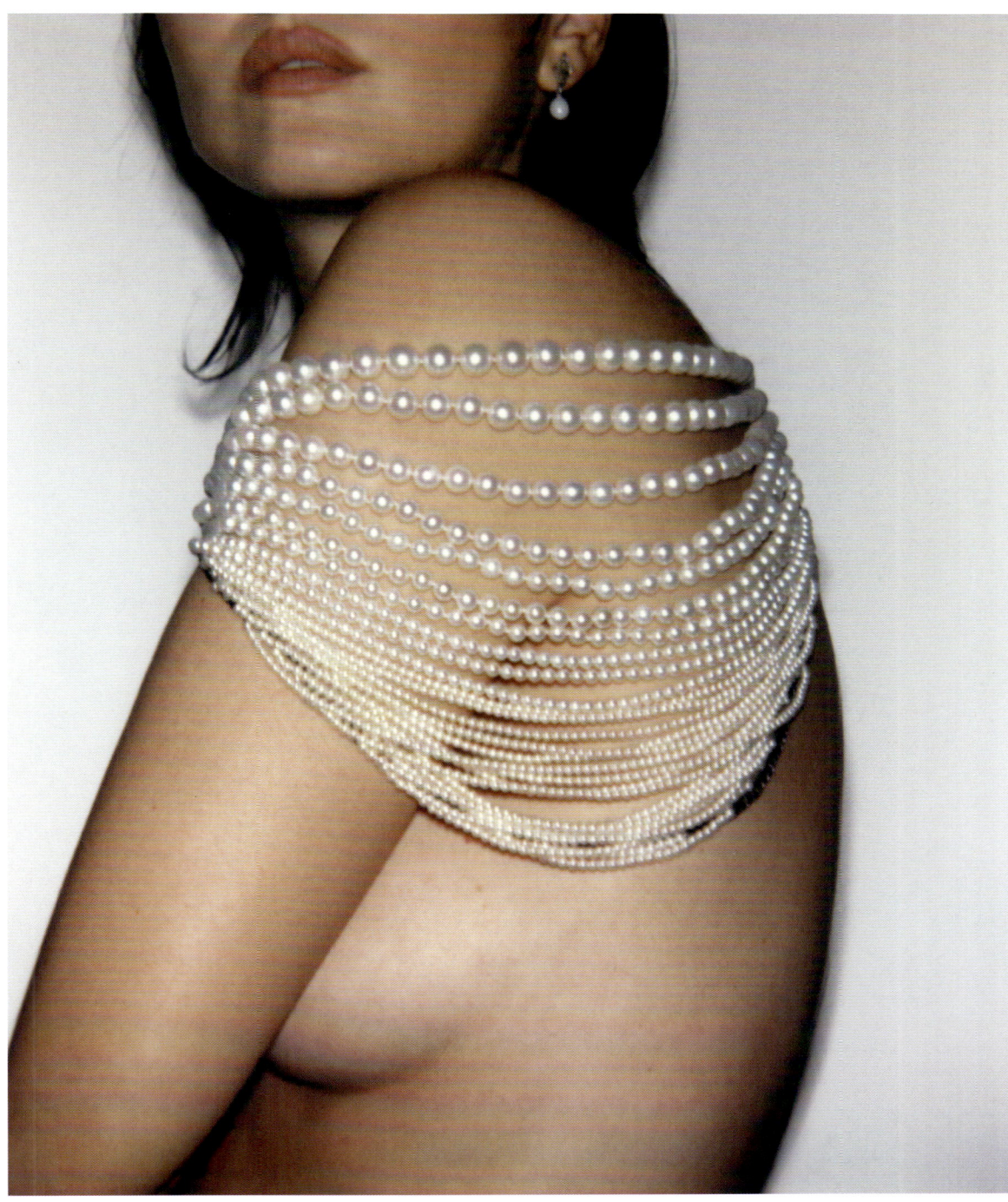

Melanie Georgacopoulos

Melanie Georgacopoulos
b. Athens, Greece, 1979

Full Circle Necklace in oxidized sterling silver with graduated 3–12 mm white freshwater pearls, 2022.

Photograph by Iga Drobisz.

Whatever you may think about pearls, designer Melanie Georgacopoulos is on a mission to challenge that. Her first real encounter with the marine gem as a potential medium came in 2007 while studying at the Royal College of Art. With training in sculpture and with a limited knowledge about pearls, the first thing Georgacopoulos did was slice one in half. To her astonishment, the cultured pearl revealed a ring pattern similar to that found in a tree trunk. From that revelatory moment, Georgacopoulos embarked on a near-obsessive experimentation with pearls. She has placed them in golden cages as centerpieces for necklaces or rings, nestled them together to create ear cuffs, coated them in gold, faceted them like diamonds, and woven them with silver threads to craft versatile bibs that can be worn as necklaces or capes. Pearls have been flaunted by royalty and worn with a twinset by suburban princesses, but Georgacopoulos has reclaimed pearls as a symbol of avant-garde design that spans the globe thanks to her collaboration with the Japanese brand and pearl producer Tasaki (see p.278). From a glossy collar of peacock freshwater pearls overlaid on mother-of-pearl to a single baroque pearl set in sterling silver to dramatic effect, Georgacopoulos goes well beyond traditional strands of white pearls.

Alberto Giacometti

Alberto Giacometti
b. Borgonovo, Switzerland, 1901
d. Chur, Switzerland, 1966

Brooch as a Draped Female Figure, gilt bronze, 1937–38.

While the spindly human forms Swiss sculptor Alberto Giacometti made in postwar Paris have come to define his practice, he also designed decorative objects and fine jewelry, becoming one of the first modernists to experiment in the craft of wearable art. After studying at the École des Arts Industriels in Geneva he moved to Paris, where he embraced sculpture. In the late 1920s, Giacometti's innovative sculptural forms led him to join the Surrealists, but despite exhibiting to critical acclaim, he struggled financially. To diversify his income, he produced decorative lamps, vases, and wall reliefs for interior designer Jean-Michel Frank and was assisted by his brother Diego.

Around 1935 he created bronze jewelry to accompany the Surrealist fashions of couturier Elsa Schiaparelli: brooches, bracelets, rings, and buttons, all featuring mythological and ancient Egyptian motifs, reflecting his long-standing love for the art of this period (see p.250). Poised between the archaic and the modern, they include a striking gilt bronze brooch in the form of a sphinx, and another resembling an ethereal female silhouette. One bracelet features a naiad, or water nymph, whose long, undulating hair forms the circle of the bracelet. All of the extant jewels preserved by the Giacometti Foundation are dated between just 1935 and 1939, after which no more were apparently made.

James de Givenchy

James de Givenchy
b. Beauvais, France, 1963

Taffin ring designed by James de Givenchy with button coral, multicolor ceramic, and 18-karat rose gold, 2024.

Under the name Taffin, Paris-born jeweler James de Givenchy—nephew of the famed haute couture designer Hubert de Givenchy—creates singular jewels that dance elegantly between modernism and minimalism. His creations have been lauded as a symphony of color and unorthodox materials, focusing attention away from intrinsic material value and firmly onto the art. Launched in New York City in 1996 and operating from an exquisitely designed private Manhattan salon, Taffin jewels range from lusciously striped ceramic and gold rings (the former material is a trademark) to necklaces of enormous Brazilian citrines and amethysts set in beautiful ceramic bezels. Unusually elongated pear-cut diamonds form the heads of ceramic and gold spears that dangle from the wearer's earlobes, while a 40.5-carat diamond plays the bud in a flower of humble pebbles worn as a necklace. Neolithic beads, leather, agates, and porcelain are just a few of the more quotidian materials Taffin explores, providing a contrast to serious gemstones, such as fancy blue diamonds, rare blue sapphires, and blood red spinels. Givenchy's ability to condense a lifetime of ideas into a simple selective design makes him a master, recognizable by all who truly know and love jewelry.

Lauren Harwell Godfrey

Lauren Harwell Godfrey
b. Los Angeles, California,
United States, 1975

One-of-a-kind *Totem* necklace in 18-karat gold with Muzo emeralds, black onyx, and diamonds, part of the *Cleopatra's Vault* collection.

Photograph by Josephine Löchen.

After an eye-opening trip to the Tucson Gem Fair in 2016, Lauren Harwell Godfrey traded in her fifteen-year career as an advertising art director to focus on establishing her own fine jewelry brand. Teaching herself how to craft accessories from tooled leather and unpolished stones, such as druzy quartz and amethyst, the Californian designer debuted her eponymous label, Harwell Godfrey, at Paris Fashion Week in 2018. Godfrey's richly textured pieces—which owe their geometric patterns to ancient textiles of the African diaspora—are crafted with 18-karat gold, precious gemstones, vibrant inlay, and ethically sourced diamonds, and are collected by luminaries such as Kamala Harris, Cynthia Erivo, and Rihanna (see p.236). Her *Cleopatra's Vault* collection, introduced in 2020, sought to bring the strong, seductive power of the ancient Egyptian queen to life through large gemstones in saturated colors that nodded to popular Macedonian stones. In creating them, Godfrey imagined "what might be found in the jewelry-adoring ruler's private stash." She used her signature triangle inlay—a nod to the pyramids—for a capsule of unique pieces set with sustainably sourced Muzo emeralds from Colombia, lapis lazuli, turquoise, black onyx, and malachite. Social causes are also high on the designer's agenda, and since 2020 her *Charity Heart* pendant has raised more than $315,000 for philanthropic organizations.

Bina Goenka

Bina Goenka
b. Mumbai, India, 1963

Butterfly necklace, made entirely by hand over a period of 4.5 years, in 18-karat gold and platinum with more than 2,900 diamonds and 5,900 natural white clam pearls, and *Clam Ear Creepers*, in 18-karat gold with 4 unique natural white clam pearls surrounded by more than 130 natural pearls and 800 diamonds, 2024.

Photograph by Jatin Kampani.

Shaping the modern jewelry landscape of India, Bina Goenka's fine collections and high jewelry are informed by her immaculate eye for detail and texture. Although she designed and created bespoke jewels for nearly a decade, it was not until 2007 that the lawyer-turned-jeweler founded her eponymous brand. A collector of stunning gems, as well as antique corals and rare conch and clam pearls, she draws on her penchant for the ornate to transform these vivid materials into intensely naturalistic forms. Conch pearl buds form a canopy for diamonds in a gold cuff, a hibiscus and its entwined stem transform into a vibrant neckpiece, and a pair of bejeweled pelicans strike a dainty pose on an ornate bracelet. Her pieces are thoroughly contemporary with hints of the past, incorporating a diverse range of influences from the Mughal Empire to celestial realms. Untreated precious stones cut to perfection are added to stunning effect. Eschewing creative constraints, she has perfected the art of hand-enameling and electrocoating, utilizing myriad techniques to embellish her creations and in some cases even camouflage the prongs holding the gems. Collaborations with select gem suppliers have yielded extraordinary, oversize jewels dripping with rubies and emeralds. Her daughter Avanti works alongside her, helping push their maximalist high jewelry forward into the future.

Goossens

Goossens
est. Paris, France, 1950

Chen Xinyue wears classic signature pieces by Goossens, including the *Stones Cross Necklace* with emerald-cut natural rock crystal, *Marie Claire México*, 2024.

Photograph by Álvaro Gracia.

Balanced at the intersection of fashion and jewelry, Goossens approaches goldsmithing and jewelry-making with the spirit of haute couture. Robert Goossens, its founder and the son of a metal foundry worker, honed his casting, engraving, and embossing skills and in the 1950s opened a workshop in Paris. His readiness to push technical boundaries, combine artificial and semiprecious stones in avant-garde sculptural designs, and reimagine the very concept of costume jewelry quickly caught the attention of leading lights such as Cristóbal Balenciaga, Madame Grès, Gabrielle "Coco" Chanel, Christian Dior, and Yves Saint Laurent (see pp.60, 89, 245). With Chanel, Goossens used unconventional materials, such as rock crystal and bronze, often mixed with precious metals, including gold and silver, creating signatures of accessible opulence. The house of Goossens continues to uphold their founder's legacy, employing artisans who preserve his trademark hand-hammering and -texturing, as well as his intricate motifs inspired by ancient artifacts, nature, and Byzantine influence, which extend also to home interior objects. Goossens maintains both a jewelry studio and a decoration atelier under the same roof since opening more than seven decades ago. In 2005 Chanel acquired the workshop as a part of its Métiers d'Art initiative to preserve heritage brands.

Graff

Graff
est. London, England, 1960

Johanna Feldmeier displays a Graff diamond ring, 2021.

Photograph by Baard Lunde.

From impoverished beginnings in London's East End, English jeweler and businessman Laurence Graff built an international brand renowned for its record-breaking diamonds. Having left school by age fifteen, Graff was let go from his first jewelry-making apprenticeship, but his love of diamonds and a steely determination saw him climb to the industry's upper echelons. Since establishing the house in 1960, he has traded some of history's most famous stones, including the 1,109-carat Lesedi La Rona and the historic Wittelsbach-Graff blue diamond, which he controversially recut in 2010 for enhanced color and clarity. Now helmed by his son François Graff, the house has more than sixty stores worldwide and continues to specialize in extraordinary diamonds, the majority of which are procured, cut, and polished in-house thanks to the company's manufacturing partner in Johannesburg. The vertical integration affords Graff's designers unmatched access to diamonds, which are often custom-cut to fit opulent creations that might be inspired by nature or modern and contemporary art—of which Laurence Graff is an avid collector. Dozens of craftspeople work in the atelier beneath the house's Mayfair headquarters in London, using computer-aided design (CAD) and 3D-printing technology to achieve the precision and perfection that are hallmarks of the Graff style.

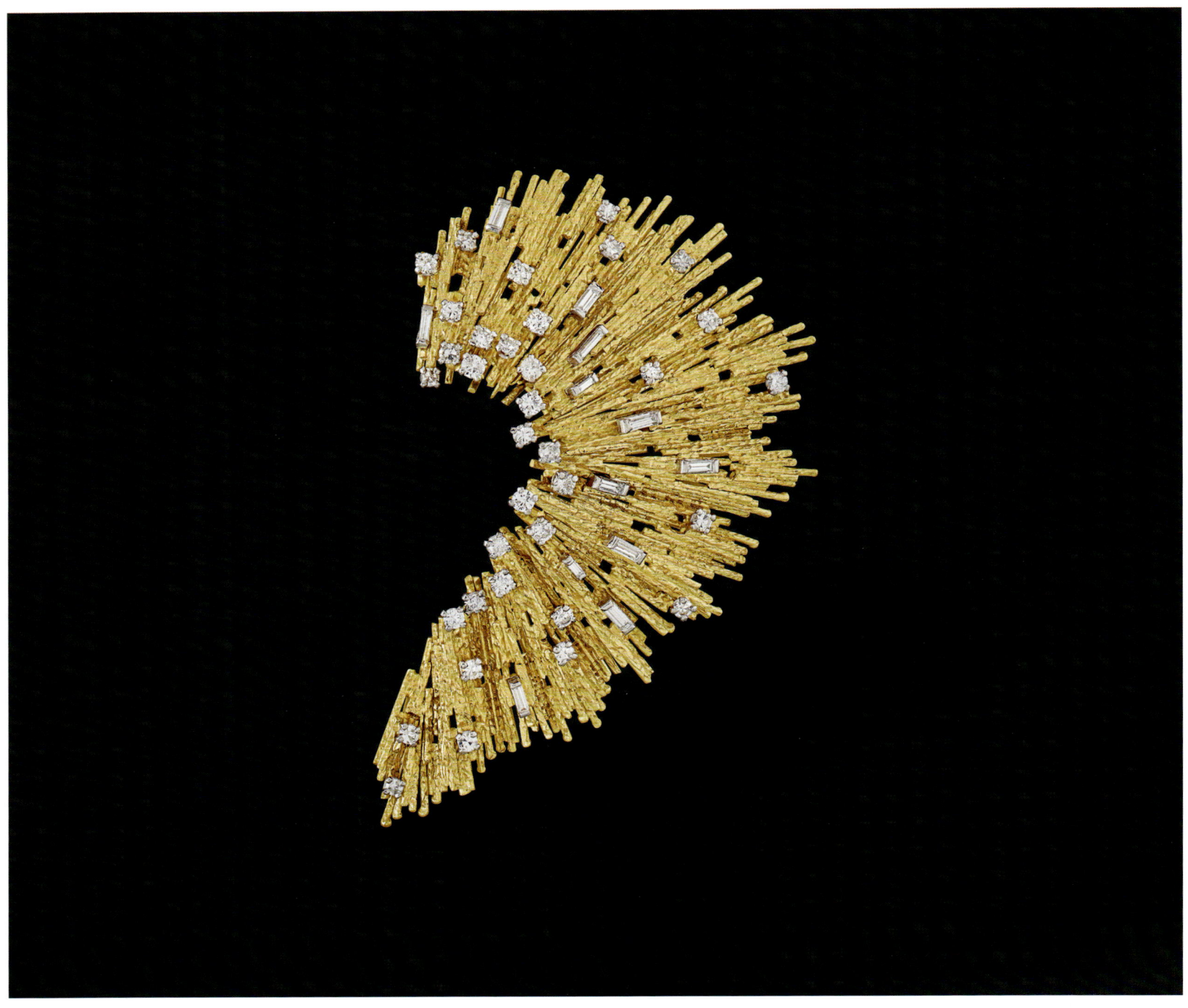

Andrew Grima

Andrew Grima
b. Rome, Italy, 1921
d. Gstaad, Switzerland, 2007

Textured yellow gold wire brooch in the form of a fan, with baguette and brilliant-cut diamonds, 1973.

Deeply enmeshed in the creative scene of the Swinging Sixties in London, Andrew Grima revolutionized postwar British jewelry design. Celebrated for his use of textured gold, large colored stones, and abstract, organic forms, his innovative wearable sculptures resulted in a type of British modernism that quickly caught the eye of Princess Margaret, Jean Shrimpton, Sharon Tate, and Jackie O (see p.150). Entirely self-taught, Grima experienced a golden era that also spanned the 1970s, with his genius recognized via numerous awards and honors, including a record eleven De Beers Diamonds International Awards. His influence expanded well beyond Britain, and he undertook a number of high-profile brand collaborations, such as the fifty-five-piece *About Time* collection with Omega, in which dials peeped out from under chunks of colored gemstone, showing time in a more beautiful way, and with Pulsar, pioneers of LED watches in the 1970s. Today, Grima's legacy is evolving in the hands of his wife, Jojo, and daughter, Francesca, who continue to mine the archive, rereleasing iconic and new future-facing designs.

Gripoix

Gripoix
est. Paris, France, 1869

Christy Turlington models Gripoix jewelry for Chanel, Autumn/Winter 1992.

Photograph by Karl Lagerfeld.

When French glassworker Augustine Gripoix opened her eponymous shop on Rue Tiquetonne in Paris in 1869, she was already a pioneer in the field of fashion jewelry, making *bijoux de couture* using glass paste, crystal, and faux pearls. More accessible than rarefied pieces in diamonds and platinum, she created *pâte de verre* jewelry from ground glass, which was then melted and poured into molds to create vibrant sculptural "gems" resembling the bold scale of Baroque jewels. Many were created in collaboration with costume and fashion designers, such Charles Frederick Worth and Paul Poiret. In the 1920s, led by Augustine's daughter Suzanne, Gripoix began working with Jeanne Lanvin and Gabrielle "Coco" Chanel to make couture jewelry (see p.60). Borrowing from Gabrielle's own jewelry and symbols of the Chanel lexicon, Gripoix produced chunky necklaces with translucent glass "gems," vibrant camellia flower brooches, and ropes of luminous Baroque pearls—from afar it was hard to discern what was real and what was fake. While the collaboration with Chanel is among the most storied, reaching the height of its popularity with Karl Lagerfeld in the 1980s and '90s, Gripoix also produced jewelry for other haute couture houses, including Pierre Balmain, Christian Dior, Givenchy, Christian Lacroix, Nina Ricci, and Yves Saint Laurent (see pp.89, 245).

Gloria Guinness

Gloria Guinness
(Gloria Rubio y Alatorre)
b. Guadalajara, Mexico, 1912
d. Épalinges, Switzerland, 1980

Gloria Guinness at her estate in Palm Beach, Florida, *Sports Illustrated*, December 1954.

Photograph by Toni Frissell.

One of fashion's most inspiring muses, beloved by the likes of Hubert de Givenchy, Christian Dior, and Cristóbal Balenciaga, Gloria Guinness was adamant that good style could not be taught, claiming that her own sartorial expression of chic was "absolutely innate." The four-times-married Mexican socialite and fashion editor, who was also one of Truman Capote's appointed Swans, was deliberately vague about her origins, amplifying a sense of mystique and regal self-possession. A fixture on "best dressed" lists throughout the 1960s and '70s, she was not so reserved when it came to her jewelry. Although famously photographed for *Vogue* in black with her signature three-strand pearl necklace, Guinness rebelled against the set monochromatic dress code. In 1966 she notably wore a 170-carat diamond and Burmese ruby collar-shaped Cartier necklace—originally commissioned by the maharaja of Nawanagar in 1937—to Capote's Black and White Ball (see p.54). Even aboard her yacht at the height of summer, Guinness could be seen dripping in jewels. A controversial figure, she made no bones about her high-society status and reliance on marital wealth. "I've never worn costume jewelry in my life," she declared to *W* magazine in 1976, adding, "It's really very self-defeating. Why should a man buy a woman real jewelry when she wears false pieces?"

Hancocks

Hancocks
est. London, England, 1849

The *Anglesey Tiara* with detachable rivière necklace from the Hancocks archives. Previously belonging to the Marquess of Anglesey, the Victorian tiara from c. 1890 features 106.8 carats of old European and old-mine-cut diamonds set in silver on gold.

Established in 1849, Hancocks is synonymous with craftsmanship, heritage, and exclusivity. Owned and run by the Burton family since 1992, it has held four royal warrants, the first received from Queen Victoria (see p.301), who also appointed the jeweler as the sole maker of the Victoria Cross, Britain's highest military honor for valor, a privilege the house upholds to this day. Fairy-tale pieces that have featured in Hancocks's inventory include the seven-piece *Devonshire Parure*, commissioned by the sixth Duke of Devonshire for his wife the Countess of Granville to wear at Tsar Alexander II's coronation in Moscow, and the Cartier diamond rose brooch worn by Princess Margaret to the coronation of Queen Elizabeth II (see pp.54, 97). Located in a renovated Georgian townhouse in the heart of London's Mayfair, Hancocks has a reputation for cherry-picking vintage masterpieces that are rich in artistry from the Victorian period through the Art Deco era and the mid-century age of glamour, with pieces signed by the likes of Bulgari and Van Cleef & Arpels (see pp.46, 291). Antique tiaras are a niche specialty, as is decorative silverware, but the jeweler's raison d'être are exceptional old-mine-cut diamonds and gemstones found in the rarest heritage wonders or freshly set in custom-made pieces noted for their daring contemporary silhouettes.

Harry Winston

Harry Winston
est. New York, New York,
United States, 1932

Arizona Muse wears a Harry Winston necklace in platinum with pear- and brilliant-cut diamonds and a 58-carat cushion-cut emerald, and platinum earrings with oval-cut diamonds, *Vogue Paris*, October 2011.

Photograph by Inez & Vinoodh.

The son of owners of a local jewelry shop, Harry Winston had from an early age both an eye for precious stones and a remarkable business sense. By age twenty-four, he had set up his own diamond jewelry company and begun to acquire important stones and clients alike. In 1947 *Cosmopolitan* magazine crowned him the King of Diamonds, a moniker that stuck throughout his life. Winston's exceptional collection of historic stones—named by *Life* magazine in 1952 as second only to that belonging to the British royal family—attracted the world's most famous jewelry aficionados, including Wallis Simpson and Elizabeth Taylor (see pp.260, 280). The latter owned the house's 69.42-carat pear-shaped diamond—purchased by her then-husband, actor Richard Burton (now the Taylor-Burton Diamond). But the stone that Winston is perhaps most associated with is the Hope Diamond—a 45.52-carat Golconda diamond that dates back to seventeenth-century India (see pp.192, 279). Among the house's most celebrated designs is the Winston Cluster—first inspired in the late 1940s by a holly wreath in winter—which mixes a host of cuts, including pear, marquise, and round brilliants, for maximum brilliance and beauty. Mixed cuts were extended to the house's floral designs, using colored stones accented by rare gemstones that speak to Harry Winston's legacy as the undisputed King of Diamonds.

Hemmerle

Hemmerle
est. Munich, Germany, 1893

One-of-a-kind bracelet in iron and white gold set with a diamond weighing more than 16 carats, 2023.

The German high jeweler Hemmerle is renowned for its many artisan techniques combining rare artifacts and stones with unorthodox materials such as wood, aluminum, iron, and steel that have been a mainstay of the brand since its founding in Munich more than 130 years ago. The company began as a goldsmith house with a specialty of providing medals of honor and gem-set adornments for the Bavarian court, and over the years its focus evolved into one of highly stylized modernist minimalism. Their signature approach requires that each Hemmerle creation is made by a single skilled craftsman who will often devote hundreds of hours to producing one piece. Their collections are frequently inspired by the natural world, as can be seen in the jeweler's master craftsmanship of their hallmark *Echinacea* earrings. The petals and stamen of the flower are made of aluminum polished to a smooth finish, with a subtle gradation of color accomplished through a detailed anodization process. Another pair of earrings in their Spring 2024 collection features Hemmerle's signature technique of reverse-setting with sapphires in tones from blood orange to mandarin. Under the fourth-generation stewardship of Christian and Yasmin Hemmerle, the company now produces about two hundred art-inspired pieces every year.

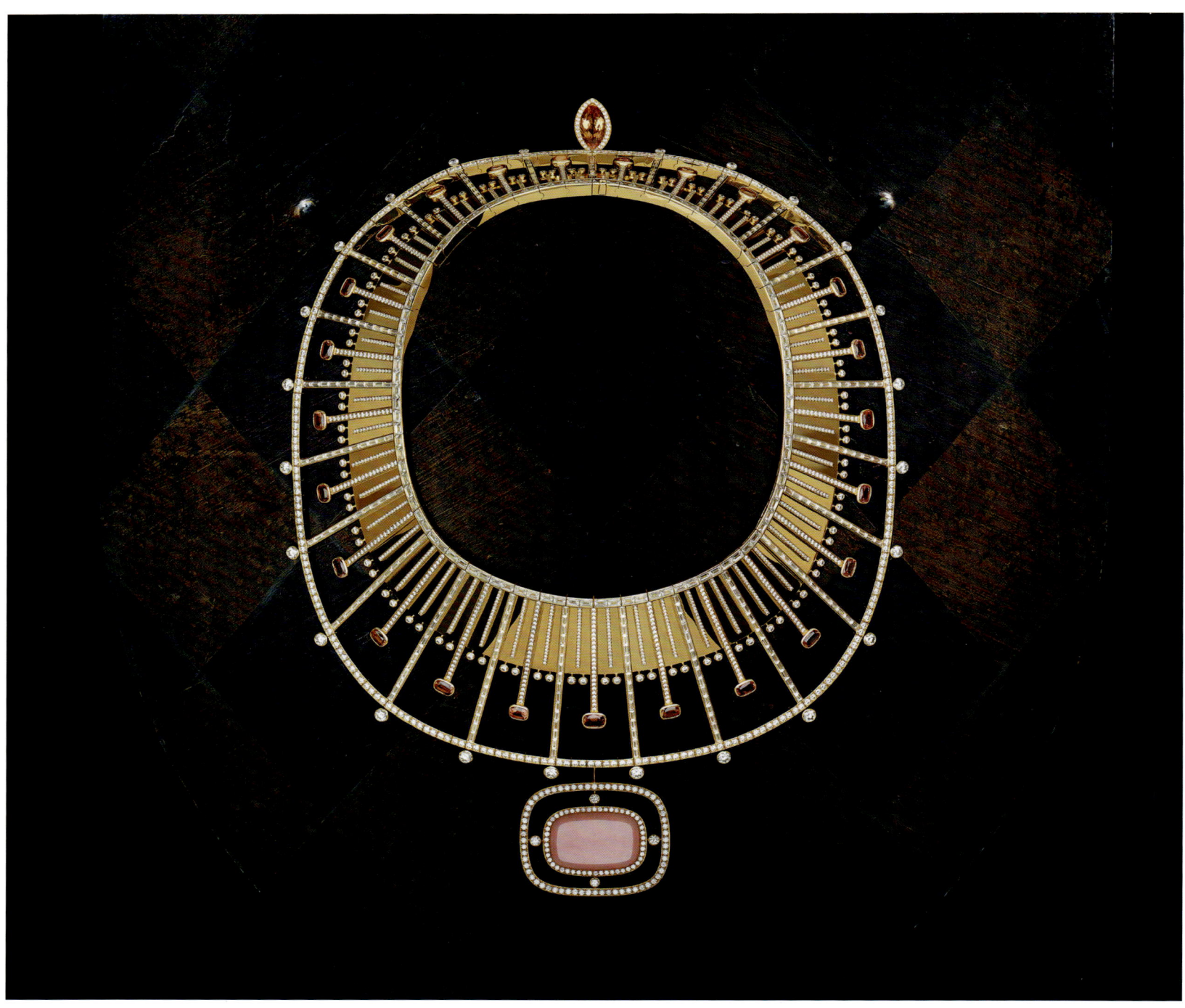

Hermès

Hermès
est. Paris, France, 1837

A high jewelry necklace designed by Pierre Hardy for the Hermès Spring/Summer 2017 collection, *Numéro Magazine* (France), February 2017.

Photograph by Toby McFarlan Pond.

The luxury house Hermès, founded in 1837, has been creating jewelry for nearly a hundred years, unveiling its first pieces as early as 1927. Primarily crafted from silver and leather, these early collections reflected the house's equestrian heritage by featuring horse bits, stirrups, and saddles. In the 1960s, the *Chaîne d'ancre* bracelet (initially designed by Robert Dumas in the 1930s)—with its interlocking oval links inspired by an anchor chain—gained new life under the Midas touch of the Georges Lenfant workshop (see p.166), becoming a hallmark of Hermès jewelry. The appointment of Pierre Hardy as artistic director in 2001 marked an ambitious new chapter for Hermès jewelry. Hardy's imaginative, colorful, and boundary-pushing creations are informed by Hermès's most celebrated and recognizable motifs. Hardy reimagined the house's codes with contemporary twists in his first *Haute Bijouterie* collection in 2010, with unconventional materials such as black jade, pink quartz, and aventurine. Innovation continued in 2021 with the collection *Lignes Sensibles*, which crafted structured lines, blending metals and gemstones. Hardy's 2024 opus, *Les Formes de la Couleur*, took Hermès jewelry to new heights, exploring a dialogue between organic shape and a kaleidoscope of color. For Hermès, jewelry is not just an accessory—it is a creative world of singular expression.

Hiro

Hiro (Yasuhiro Wakabayashi)
b. Shanghai, China, 1930
d. Erwinna, Pennsylvania, United States, 2021

Iman in gold, New York, 2005.

Photograph by Hiro.

Japanese American photographer Hiro captured his subjects in meticulously planned-out compositions colored with visual effects and a taste for the surreal. After growing up in China and Japan, Hiro arrived in New York in 1954 to study at the School of Modern Photography, eventually leaving to become an apprentice to Richard Avedon in 1956. It was Avedon who introduced Hiro to Alexey Brodovitch, the seminal art director of *Harper's Bazaar*, who hired him as a staff photographer. In still-life shoots, fashion editorials, and portrait sittings, Hiro photographed subjects as diverse as the Rolling Stones, haute couture gowns by Cristóbal Balenciaga, and Apollo spaceflight training suits. But it is jewelry that features in some of his most unforgettable pictures. Hiro disrupted traditional ways of wearing and photographing jewelry: a Harry Winston ruby-and-emerald necklace adorned the hoof of a Black Angus steer and a bird-shaped brooch, designed by Jean Schlumberger for Tiffany & Co., rested between the lips of supermodel Wilhelmina Cooper (see pp.132, 251, 283). Hiro's photographs of Elsa Peretti's iconic gold *Bone Cuff* for Tiffany & Co., placed on a clean white bone accompanied by two ladybugs, and his still life of glossy lacquer bangles floating across a dreamlike seascape are especially representative of his penchant for the uncanny (see p.221).

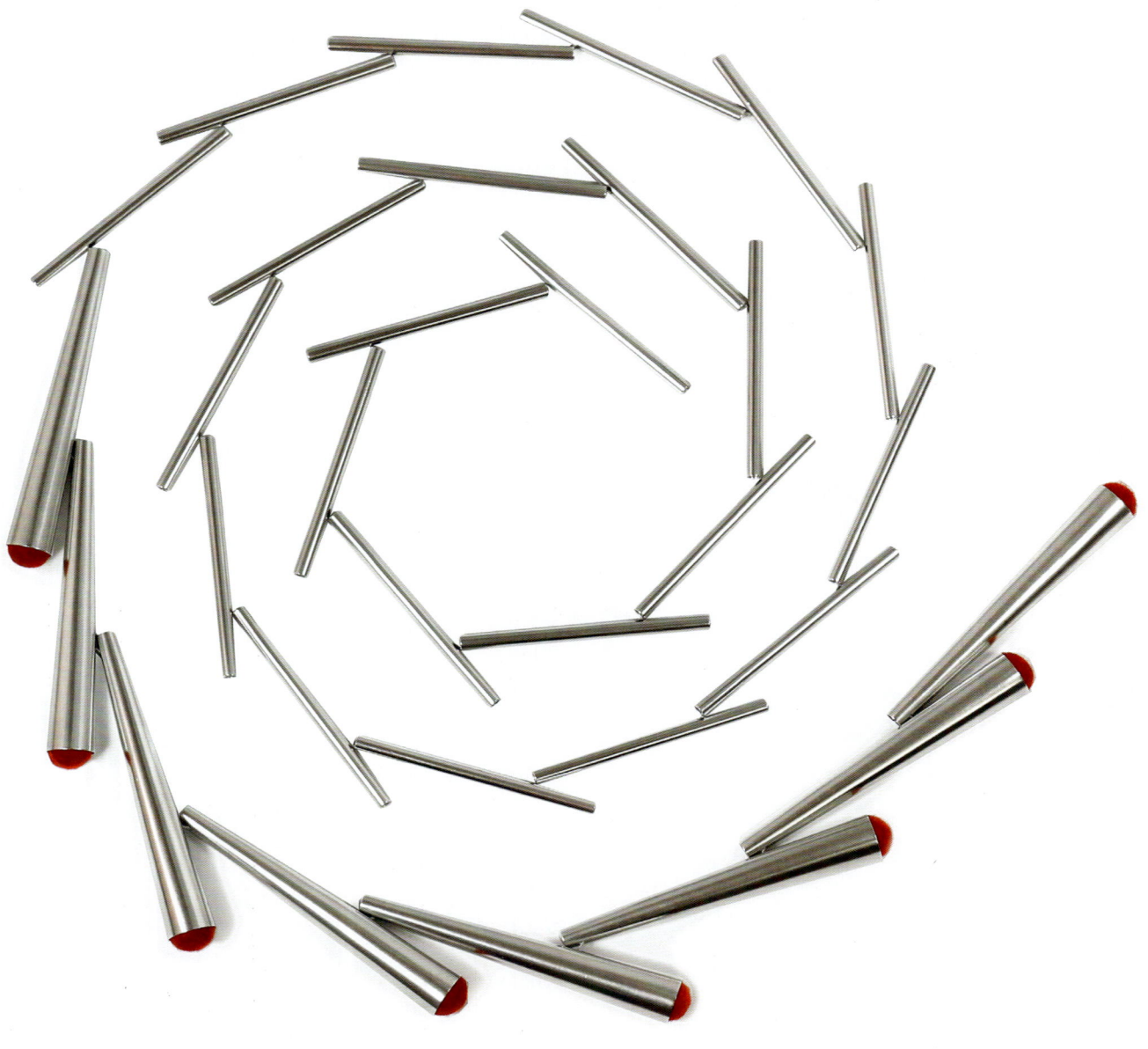

Dorothy Hogg

Dorothy Hogg
b. Troon, Scotland, 1945
d. Edinburgh, Scotland, 2022

Silver and red felt necklace, from the *Artery Series*, 2005.

Spearheading new material combinations with sophisticated techniques, Dorothy Hogg created elegant and understated jewelry that belied its complexity. Her work, both as a creator and an educator, altered the design landscape and left an indelible mark on the field of jewelry and silversmithing. Experimenting with old and new crafts, Hogg placed plique-à-jour enamel in sculptural angular forms, seamlessly married titanium and silver to create futuristic looks, and incorporated textile-making techniques into metalwork. Fraught with emotion and a testament to her meticulous yet soulful craftsmanship, starkly angled rings sit comfortably on the finger, and necklaces drape around the body with casual ease. The daughter of an Ayrshire jeweler on the west coast of Scotland, Hogg was set on her path from an early age. From 1985 to 2007, she was head of the Jewellery and Silversmithing program at Edinburgh College of Art, pioneering courses with a diverse curriculum and creating one of the first artist-in-residence programs. Seeking to inspire her students, she scoured the world for leading makers, including Onno Boekhoudt and Giovanni Corvaja (see p.73). Her dedication to her students is evident in the thousands who continue to work today, carrying forward the innovative spirit and technical excellence she instilled in them.

Nevin Holmes

Nevin Holmes
b. Ioannina, Greece, 1919
d. London, England, 1990

Brooch in 14-karat gold with emeralds and rubies, 1961.

Jewelers such as John Donald and Andrew Grima may have been heralded as leaders of modern British design in the 1960s (see pp.90, 128), but flying under the radar in London was the wildly talented designer Nevin Holmes, who set hunks of Afghan lapis lazuli, coral, and opal into textured gold. Holmes was born in Ioannina, Greece, and her father was a financier-turned-diplomat who worked for the Turkish government, while her mother spent much of her adult life in an insane asylum. At nineteen, Nevin moved to London, and after a short-lived marriage she moved to Rome, where she worked as a translator and a painter during World War II. After the war she married William Frederick Holmes and moved back to London, where her magnificent design talent was unearthed while studying at Central Saint Martins. As rebellious in her jewelry as she was in life, Holmes crafted beautifully strange surrealist brooches alongside soft emerald cabochons rising out of textured gold bangles and moonstones and natural pearls peeping out of gargantuan rings. In her studio just behind the Victoria and Albert Museum in South Kensington, she also worked with silver and bronze, but her statuesque gold work became her legacy, finding a resting place in the renowned archive of the Goldsmiths' Company, where she famously exhibited in 1972.

Anna Hu

Anna Hu
b. 1977

Mirage Butterfly brooch, handcrafted in black platinum, rose gold, sterling silver, and red lacquer, inlaid with mother-of-pearl, brilliant diamonds, and a line of five cushion-shaped pigeon blood rubies, which can be detached and worn as a ring, 2022.

A trailblazing haute jeweler, Anna Hu is celebrated for a style uniquely blending Eastern and Western philosophies and artistry, underpinned by unparalleled craftsmanship. Hu was born to a family of gemstone dealers, and her passion for jewelry began at an early age. She trained as a cellist before studying jewelry design at the Parsons School of Design and, later, the Gemological Institute of America. Honing her artistic and technical expertise, she worked for Harry Winston and Van Cleef & Arpels (see pp.132, 291) before charting her own course in 2007. Often inspired by classical music, nature (think butterflies, birds, and blooming flowers), Impressionism, Art Nouveau, and her own Chinese heritage, Hu's pieces are characterized by fluidity, rare gemstones, and intricate craft. Commissioned by Sotheby's, the scrolled *Dunhuang Pipa Necklace*, inspired by an ancient Chinese lute features a 100-carat intense yellow diamond and can be transformed into a brooch and earring set. Her inimitable *Côte d'Azur Brooch*—a 58-carat cushion-shaped Burmese sapphire alongside a floral, multi-gem branch—was another masterpiece that broke auction records for contemporary jewelry, selling for more than $4.5 million. Hu's designs have been worn by the likes of Natalie Portman, Uma Thurman, and Madonna (see p.176), and her pieces have been exhibited in museums worldwide.

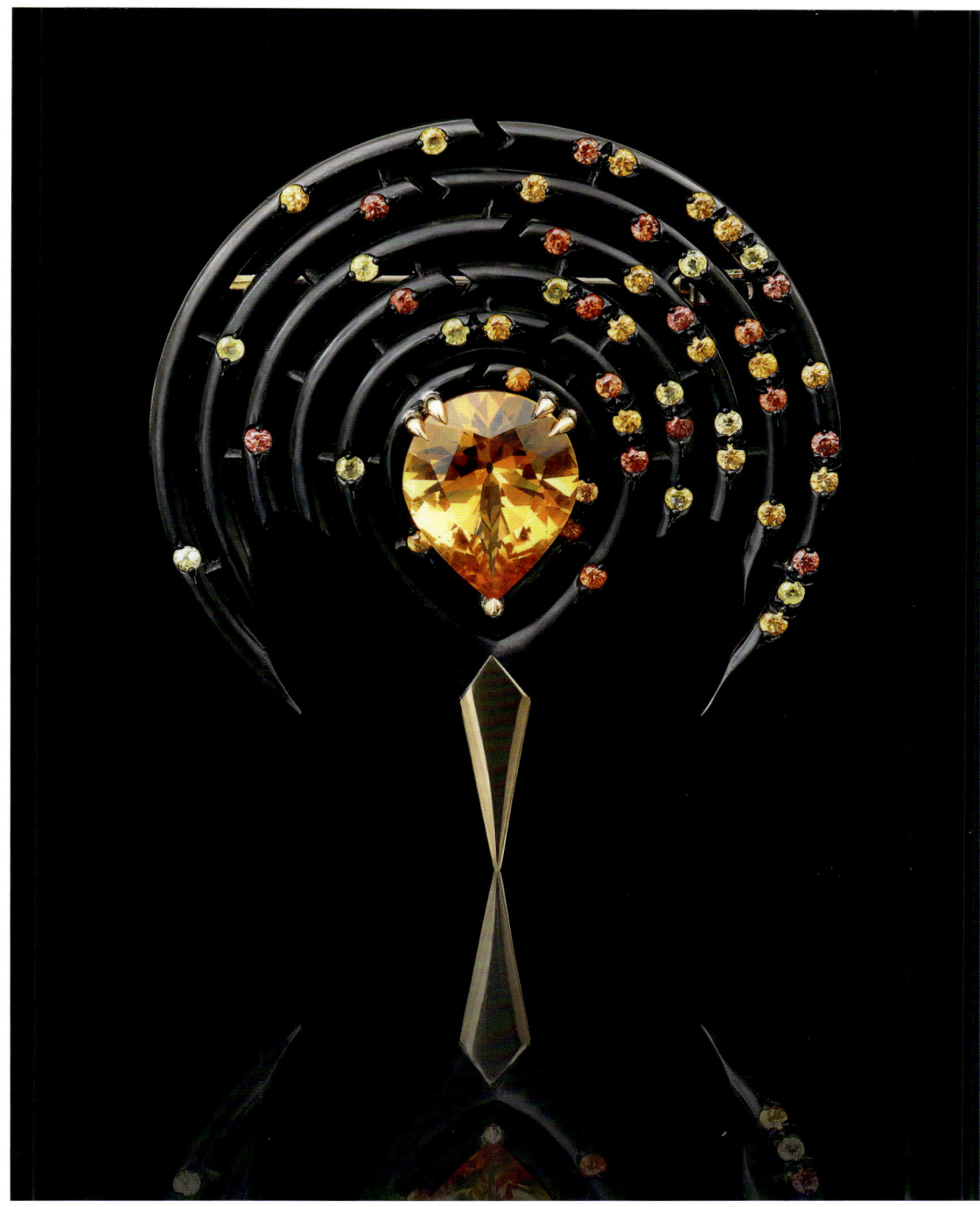

Capucine Huguet

Capucine Huguet
b. Paris, France, 1996

Foraminifera brooch, from the *Tethys* collection, in 18-karat recycled gold and chrome-plated recycled silver set with a 9.7-carat custom-cut citrine and fifty yellow and orange sapphires. The piece is inspired by a marine plankton whose rates of survival are decreasing due to ocean acidification as a result of global warming.

Photograph by Di Messina.

For French designer Capucine Huguet, the jewels she creates are inextricably entwined with stories about the planet and the interconnectedness of all life on Earth. From photosynthesis and climate change to biodiversity in rainforests and conservation of nature, Huguet weaves inspiration into her collections, working primarily in recycled 18-karat gold and silver with repurposed diamonds and ethically mined colored stones. "I love understanding how the world works, from how snowflakes form to how tornadoes come to life," says Huguet. Through detailed experimentation with engraving, color, and texture, her one-of-a-kind jewels take shape. In her first collection in 2021, *Wahlenbergbreen Mementos*, earrings, cuffs, and pendants evoked the titular Arctic glacier, with melted stalactites and ice crystals set with diamonds and gray gems. For *Tethys*—named after a Greek goddess of water—she collaborated with Chanel's Métiers d'Art arm to reinterpret marine organisms such as phytoplankton into brooches and rings using gold lacquered in vibrant hues to conjure their complex and varied organic forms. Building upon her training at the Haute École de Joaillerie in Paris and Central Saint Martins in London, Huguet is constantly honing her craft and exploring new inspirations with each jewel created in her Parisian atelier.

Barbara Hutton

Barbara Hutton
b. New York, New York,
United States, 1912
d. Beverly Hills, California,
United States, 1979

Barbara Hutton at her villa in Tangier, wearing the Pasha of Egypt 38.19-carat diamond ring, a bracelet of Golconda diamonds, and a tiara composed of the seven Vladimir Emeralds set, alongside diamonds, into yellow gold by Cartier, 1970.

Photograph by Cecil Beaton.

Eternally remembered as the Million Dollar Baby, Barbara Hutton was born in New York in 1912 as an only child and the heiress to one-third of an immense fortune amassed by her grandfather, the Gilded Age tycoon Frank W. Woolworth. By her twenty-first birthday, Hutton's inheritance stood at more than $40 million (almost $1 billion in today's currency), which she spent on an unrivaled collection of jeweled masterpieces. A set of emeralds in her possession once belonged to the Grand Duchess Vladimir of Russia, which Hutton entrusted to Cartier in 1947 to incorporate into a tiara (see p.54). For her marriage to Prince Alexis Mdivani of Georgia in 1933, Hutton's father presented her with a single-strand natural pearl necklace thought to have been worn by Marie Antoinette (see p.183). Another incredible gift, the *Hutton-Mdivani Jadeite Necklace*, later became known as one of the most significant jadeite jewels in history. A passionate jadeite enthusiast, Hutton commissioned Cartier to replace the necklace's original clasp with one of yellow gold, diamonds, and rubies to complement the exceptional vibrancy and translucence of its twenty-seven perfectly matched beads. The necklace went on to set a world record in 2014 when Sotheby's sold it back to Cartier for more than $27 million—the highest amount ever paid for any jadeite jewel at auction (see p.267).

Otto Jakob

Otto Jakob
b. Bad Säckingen, Germany, 1951

Lale X earrings in yellow and white gold, with diamonds, vitreous enamel, and painted gold, 2022.

Photograph by Volker Kirschner.

A self-taught goldsmith specializing in old-world techniques, Otto Jakob first studied painting with German artist Georg Baselitz before choosing jewelry-making as a full-time profession in 1980. His work is influenced by Etruscan, Celtic, and Hellenic art, and he learned complex, anachronistic techniques by studying the works and writings of experts such as Pliny the Elder and sixteenth-century goldsmith Benvenuto Cellini (see p.58). Jakob's craft is unique in that it combines ancient gold-making and enameling techniques with new technologies such as 3D printing. In one instance, he used a 3D printer to scan an actual flower petal, then hand-carved the wax before casting it in gold and applying colorful vitreous enamel. For a pair of his signature earrings, Jakob avoided the casting process altogether to craft the pieces directly in white gold, which reduced their thickness, making them lighter to wear. He then applied "brute force" to fold the metal and finished it with strokes of painted gold that stand out against the background of cobalt blue vitreous enamel. Jakob's complex jewels are equal parts miniature sculptures and adornment. Artistic details and artisan techniques result in creations ranging from lifelike flora and fauna and enduring geometric shapes to intricate depictions of tools and weapons from the Renaissance and Middle Ages.

Grace Jones

Grace Jones
b. Spanish Town, Jamaica, 1948

Grace Jones at Studio 54, New York, 1981.

Photograph by Adrian Boot.

Grace Jones—singer and performer, former model and actress—is the ultimate style icon. To this day, her influence in the realms of fashion and jewelry remains as singular as her persona. While Jones may not have worn as much jewelry as some of her peers, her approach to jewelry has been a fearless exploration of self-expression, and every piece she has chosen helped define a period in music, fashion, and popular culture. Although she has collaborated with established creatives, such as photographer Jean-Paul Goude and fashion designer Azzedine Alaïa, the jewels she wears often come from unexpected sources, sidestepping designs featuring diamonds and gold usually favored by celebrities. Artists, including Maripol and the late David Spada, created custom pieces that became integral elements of Jones's stage performances. A close friend of Jones's as well as a photographer, Maripol designed and created the rubber bracelets that, four decades later, remain synonymous with Jones's iconic image. Worn stacked up by the dozen, the bracelets referenced African tribal adornment and, at the same time, hinted at Western industrial components. Maripol wanted them to be "junk jewelry," mass-market and affordable so that every fan could own a piece of their heroine.

Fernando Jorge

Fernando Jorge
b. Campinas, Brazil, 1979

Galaxy earrings in 18-karat gold set with brilliant-cut diamonds in hand-carved milky aquamarine, 2018.

There is a subliminal sensuality to the jewelry of Fernando Jorge that has won the Brazil-born, London-based designer nearly universal critical and commercial success. Having studied engineering and product design in São Paulo, he soon moved into jewelry and launched his own brand upon graduating from Central Saint Martins in 2010. His designs are characterized by an abstract, rhythmic ease: voluptuous curves of colored gemstones appear alongside diamonds carefully graduated in size so as to flatter the contours of the face and body. Balancing boldness and exuberance with fluidity and refinement, his creations are made to move in harmony with the wearer.

"My aesthetic is rooted in the casual, effortless sensuality I associate with Brazil," he says. The minimalist language of Brazilian artists and designers is a source of inspiration, as are the country's rich natural colors and materials. He champions Brazilian gemstones such as tourmaline, citrine, and amethyst, alongside petrified wood, tagua nut, and pebbles. In 2022 Jorge relocated his by-appointment-only showroom from East London to Mayfair, a move that reflected his focus on elevated, high jewelry creations—the likes of which have been worn by clientele from Beyoncé to Michelle Obama (see pp.29, 214).

Judicael Sacred Skulls

Judicael Sacred Skulls
est. Pushkar, Rajasthan, India, 2003

The Great King in fossil mammoth ivory, 22-karat gold, and diamonds, with a graphite spinel crowning the top, a fire agate at the base, and a fire opal adorning the back, where a meteorite blade hangs as a dagger. The skull features a hidden chamber containing a Stanhope lens that reveals a secret image, 2018.

French-born jeweler and tattooist Judicael Vales made his first pendant at the age of twenty-three while on a solo trip to Pushkar in Rajasthan, India. He carved a miniature head from bovine bone using a pocketknife and embellished it with a silver helmet cast by a local silversmith. Enthralled by this process, he began goldsmithing, using his nomadic lifestyle to gain a deeper understanding of different workbench practices. What began as a hobby soon became a profession when, in 2010, he settled in the former gold rush locale of Nevada City in Northern California. With Judicael Sacred Skulls he focused on the human skull, and the self-taught maker developed his unique style with painstaking precision—the golden ratio is a key inspiration—growing a dedicated following of collectors, including actor Jason Momoa. Vales's one-of-a-kind pieces can take up to three years to complete, and combine high-purity 18-, 22-, and 24-karat gold with sterling silver, along with unexpected materials such as Italian brass, padauk wood, and mammoth ivory. Vales's highly decorative metalworking is inspired by the symbols of ancient Greece and China. He also likes to add a playful edge to some of his gothic designs too, or what he calls "an Indiana Jones" touch: a secret compartment that opens with a bespoke jewelry key, enhancing the skull's significance as an emblem of individuality.

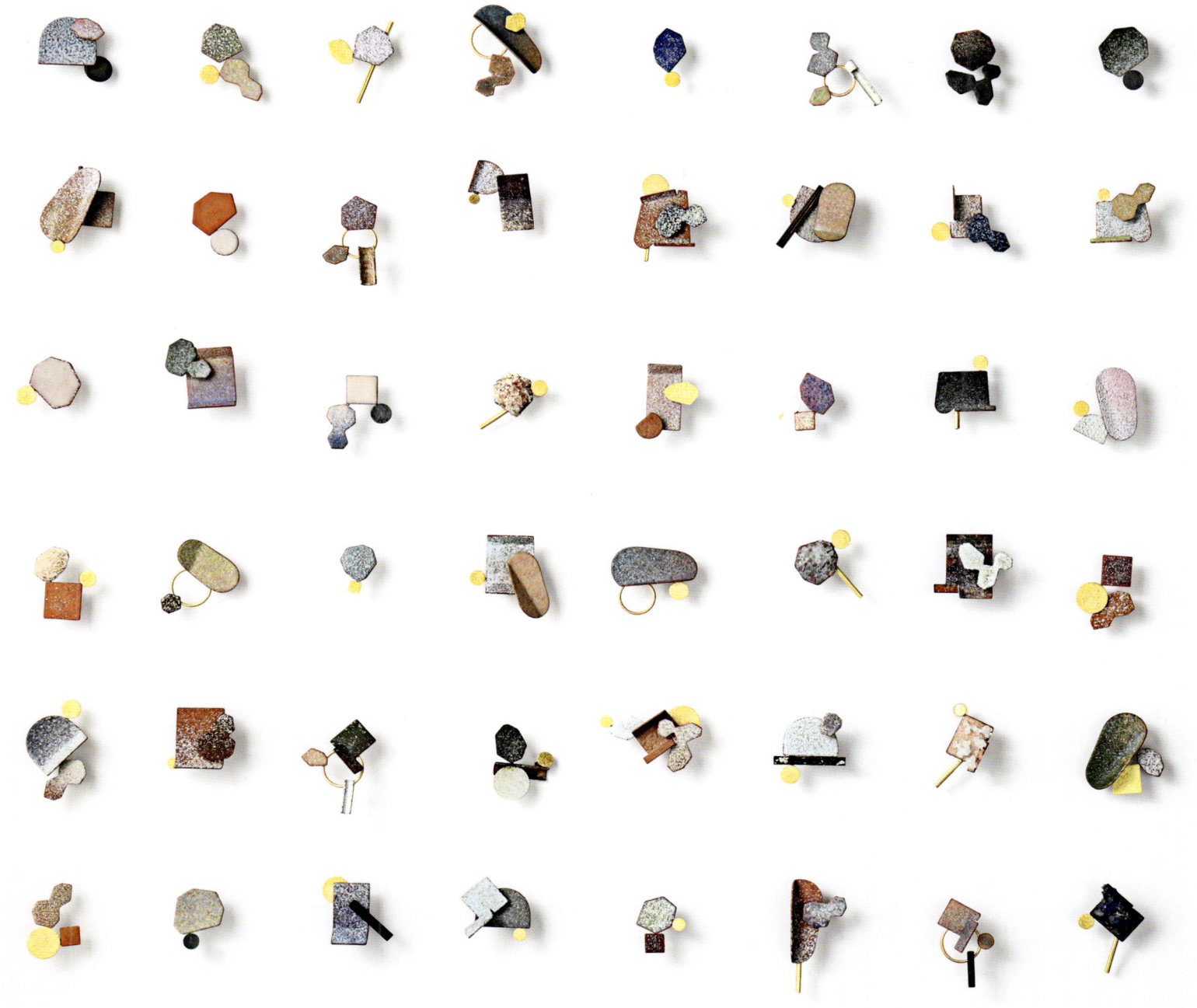

Kaori Juzu

Kaori Juzu
b. Fukuoka, Japan, 1978

108 Points of View (detail), featuring jewels in enamel, glass, copper, patinated *shakudo*, 18-karat gold, bicolor metal, and silver, 2021.

Photograph by Anders Beier.

Creating her designs by hand, contemporary goldsmith and jeweler Kaori Juzu blends Japanese craft with minimal Danish aesthetics, harnessing thirteenth-century enameling techniques. Based in Bornholm, Denmark, Juzu completed an apprenticeship with Danish jeweler Per Suntum in 2008. Juzu is known for her innovative, sculptural approach—which she refers to as *klenodie*, a Danish word meaning jewel or treasure—and her unique creations are imbued with a rhythmic quality, whether a brooch in enamel, copper, steel, bicolor metal, and silver or a patinated *shakudo* pin. Juzu's creative process is open and spontaneous, forging copper sheets to sculpt organic shapes and applying powdered-glass enamel mixtures by sifting thin layers to create color patterns and speckled textures on the work's surface. Her tableau *108 Points of View* features 108 pieces in her requisite style inspired by Eastern Buddhist rituals and fashioned from leftover materials. Her designs are also versatile and can be worn in multiple ways—for example, doubling as earrings or pins—and combined with different pieces for an asymmetrical yet complementary effect. The incongruent shapes of her designs, whether an oblong circle or asymmetrical hexagon, are further manipulated for a matte finish, layered, and fused together—a sharp contrast to traditional, glossy enamel jewelry.

Frida Kahlo

Frida Kahlo
b. Coyoacán, Mexico, 1907
d. Coyoacán, Mexico, 1954

Frida Kahlo, 1939.

Photograph by Nickolas Muray.

Renowned for her striking paintings, Mexican artist Frida Kahlo has become an enduring fashion icon thanks to the dozens of self-portraits in which she styled herself with the same care for composition, color, and symbolism as her works of art. Disdainful of convention, Kahlo challenged stereotypes and expressed herself through clothing and jewelry. A crucial feature of her self-portraits, jewelry was her passion. In paintings that vividly chronicled her emotional and physical state, as well as in her daily life, jewelry served as a distraction from a body disfigured by polio and, later, a traffic accident. The sound of her layered necklaces or bracelets jangling together often preceded Kahlo's arrival, and she created stunning clashes of colors, styles, and materials with irreverence. Mexican jewels—particularly those of the Tehuantepec region, characterized by thick gold twisted rope chains (*torzales*) strung with gold coins and religious medallions—were paired with surreal hand-shaped earrings given to her by Pablo Picasso (see p.223) or Spanish-style filigree pieces. She made necklaces with chunky Aztec jade beads, wore ancient shell bracelets, and adorned her hands with a kaleidoscope of rings. Kahlo had several gold teeth and favored yellow gold jewelry to match. More than half a century after her death, her dramatic look and quirky jewelry combinations continue to inspire a global Frida-mania.

Dina Kamal

Dina Kamal
b. Beirut, Lebanon, 1966

RA Pinky Rings, inspired by the Egyptian sun god Ra, in 18-karat polished and brushed yellow gold, 2018; and the *Flat Plate Big Ring* in 18-karat brushed gold, part of the *DK Revival of the PNKYRNG*, 2010.

Photograph by Benjamin Pexton.

The design lexicon of London-based Lebanese jeweler Dina Kamal is rich in dualities: masculinity and femininity, boldness and discretion, structure and sensuality. A trained architect, Kamal launched her eponymous jewelry line in 2010, and her design process is informed by her architectural approach. "I always consider form, proportion, context, structure, and beauty in everything I do. Most of all I consider how a piece or design can impact us emotionally," she says. Broad conceptual themes informed by history, culture, and architecture are refined and distilled into their purest, most potent form, resulting in seemingly minimalist jewels that are meticulously crafted and perfectly proportioned. Her understated aesthetic is characterized by her use of "beige gold": raw 18-karat white gold without copper, which she describes as "powerful yet neutral. It allows me to give true expression to the structure and the design." The concept of fascination—with an idea or an aesthetic detail—is what drives her designs, alongside a deep inquisitiveness about the role of jewelry throughout humanity. From traditional signet rings to tribal torques to eighteenth-century ruffs, a multitude of influences can be found within quietly confident designs that signal the wearer as the most interesting person in the room.

Grace Kelly

Grace Kelly
b. Philadelphia, Pennsylvania, United States, 1929
d. La Colle, Monaco, 1982

Grace Kelly, Hollywood Hills, California, 1955.

Photograph by Howell Conant.

Like something out of one of her Hollywood films, American actor Grace Kelly became a real-life princess, with a fairy-tale wedding and jewels to match. After being awarded the Academy Award for Best Actress for her role in *The Country Girl* (1954), she met Prince Rainier III of Monaco while at the Cannes Film Festival in 1955. Rainier gave Kelly *two* engagement rings. The first was a Cartier eternity band of heirloom diamonds and rubies, reflecting the red and white in Monaco's flag (see p.54). But it was Kelly's second ring that cemented her status as a jewelry tastemaker. Kelly wore the 10.48-carat emerald-cut diamond engagement ring, also by Cartier, on-screen in her final film, *High Society* (1956), and the style sparked many copies, with similar styles having been worn by icons from Elizabeth Taylor to Beyoncé (see pp.29, 280). Kelly is also remembered for her love of pearls, wearing a luminous pearl necklace in Alfred Hitchcock's *Rear Window* (1954). In an ode to Kelly's favorite gem, Rainier gave her an exceptional three-strand pearl-and-diamond necklace, along with matching earrings and bracelet, all by Van Cleef & Arpels, as a wedding gift (see p.291). Kelly's legendary style endures in fashion and jewelry: the Hermès Kelly bag is named for her, and her daughter, Princess Caroline, and granddaughter, Camille Gottlieb, continue to wear jewels from her collection.

Nan Kempner

Nan Kempner
b. San Francisco, California, United States, 1930
d. New York, New York, United States, 2005

Nan Kempner in her home on Park Avenue, New York, 2005.

Photograph by Mark Peterson.

American socialite Nan Kempner's recipe for a good life was to dress fabulously for every occasion, preferably in haute couture. A fixture in elite social circles in Manhattan and beyond, she was philanthropic, refreshingly frank, and full of joie de vivre. Of her famous wardrobe, she once declared, "I spend more money than I should and less than I'd like to, much less." These tendencies extended to jewelry, and especially bold pieces with avant-garde flair, crafted by the likes of David Webb, JAR, and Verdura (see pp.78, 240, 298). In the early 1970s, Kempner worked as a design consultant at Tiffany & Co., which at the time was under the tenure of Harry Platt, who engaged other young talents, including Angela Cummings, Elsa Peretti, and Paloma Picasso (see pp.76, 221, 224, 283). A true fashion maven, Kempner curated her look with precision, never gilding the lily but capturing attention in every room. For costume jewelry, she championed Chanel, Kenneth Jay Lane, and her favorite couturier, Yves Saint Laurent, who supplied her with audacious pieces, including a bib necklace made of rose quartz and rough-cut amethysts (see pp.60, 162, 245). Not one to shy away from single statement pieces—sautoirs, multistrand chokers, and earrings the size of gobstoppers—Kempner is remembered as a fearless fashion icon who turned dressing up into an art form.

Jacqueline Kennedy Onassis

Jacqueline Kennedy Onassis
b. Southampton, New York,
United States, 1929
d. New York, New York,
United States, 1994

Jackie Kennedy Onassis,
West Palm Beach, Florida, 1973.

One of the twentieth century's most influential tastemakers, Jacqueline Kennedy Onassis had a famously refined sense of style, which included jewelry ranging from an Ancient Egyptian gold snake bracelet to a ruby berry brooch by Jean Schlumberger at Tiffany & Co. (see pp.251, 283) to the golden orbs of the *Apollo* earrings by Lalaounis. She emerged into the public eye in 1953 as the fiancée of Senator John F. Kennedy wearing an Art Deco emerald and diamond *toi et moi* engagement ring worth more than $1 million. Fifteen years later, her engagement ring from Aristotle Onassis featured the 40.42-carat Lesotho III marquise diamond. Throughout her life, Kennedy Onassis made careful jewelry choices to accent the striking simplicity of her wardrobe, choosing pieces by favored houses including Cartier, David Webb, and Van Cleef & Arpels (see pp.54, 78, 291). Judiciously chosen jewels—pearl button earrings or a diamond statement necklace as first lady, or in her later "Jackie O" years, a gold rope chain—finished her outfits. At the sale of her estate at Sotheby's in 1996 (see p.267), alongside jewels worth hundreds of thousands of dollars, was a triple-row faux pearl necklace made famous in a photograph taken with her young son John. Although it was only worth a few dollars, it had become emblematic of her style and sold for more than two hundred thousand dollars.

Sharon Khazzam

Sharon Khazzam
b. Tehran, Iran, 1965

Pandora Bracelet handmade in 18-karat yellow, rose, and white gold with 185.21 carats of natural amethysts alongside diamonds, peridots, pink tourmalines, spessartite garnets, Mexican fire opals, rubies, rhodonites, and morganites, 2008.

Unbridled glee is the precise sensation Sharon Khazzam strives to elicit with her fine jewelry. Her candy-colored compositions suggest a sense of freewheeling play involving the full spectrum of rare gems, from luminous tsavorite to honey-colored fire opal and blazing rubellite. Khazzam, who often first designs a piece by creating a true-to-size watercolor painting of it, has thousands of sketches decorating the inside of her studio. Her craft is closely tied to the Persian tradition of organic metalwork, as she hand-selects and hand-sets each precious stone "to live together in harmony." After graduating with a degree in jewelry design from the Fashion Institute of Technology, Khazzam joined the iconic British brand Asprey as an in-house designer when she was just twenty-one years old, before launching her first namesake collection in 1993. Following the traditions of fine heritage jewelry, her pieces often offer multiple opportunities for wear: a bracelet might also serve as a pendant, complete with secret caches within, while drops from dangling earrings can slide onto gold wires to become necklaces. Her studio in a quiet Long Island community just outside of New York City allows her to easily collaborate with the Manhattan-based artisans who realize her work. They are guided by her direct instructions and intricate sketches of her designs—each one a work of art in itself.

Arthur King

Arthur King
b. New York, United States, 1921
d. United States, 1991

Bangle and ear clips in 18-karat gold with baroque cultured pearls and brilliant-cut diamonds, 1970s.

American jeweler Arthur King was acclaimed for his strikingly original swirling, free-form gold mounts that seem as if they have naturally grown around a flamboyant range of gemstones. King was self-taught—he began fashioning pieces out of scrap metal and other found materials while serving as a Merchant Marine during World War II—and his style of intricate, branchlike textured settings using both faceted and rough gemstones defined the sea change of postwar modernism that dared to defy convention. King opened his first shop in Manhattan's Greenwich Village in the late 1940s, where his offbeat approach appealed to the neighborhood's avant-garde artists. He soon went on to garner international success with a client list of collectors, including Clare Boothe Luce, Barbara Hutton, and Elizabeth Taylor (see pp.140, 280). Sealing his reputation, in 1961 he was invited to show his work at the *International Exhibition of Modern Jewellery* at London's Goldsmiths' Hall, a seminal event for modernist art jewelry. Ever the pioneer, King was among the first jewelers of the era to turn his attention to men's pieces, starting with shoe buckles and chunky chains in hefty, rugged gold. Today, collectors of vintage jewels avidly hunt down his signature bulging baroque pearls set in flowing tentacles of molten gold or his iconic avant-garde cuffs encrusted with rough gemstones.

Gabriella Kiss

Gabriella Kiss
b. Toronto, Ontario, Canada, 1959

Butterfly Branch hair comb in horn, oxidized bronze, and 22- and 14-karat gold, c. 1994.

Photograph by Dirk Vandenberk.

Whether the delicate, tapered form of a hazelnut or the elegant, attenuated anatomy of a wasp, it is the often overlooked and underappreciated elements of nature that are the heroes of Gabriella Kiss's jewelry. Capturing her wonder at the purposeful beauty of insects, seed pods, antlers, and fungi, she hand-carves their forms—a skill she cultivated studying sculpture at Pratt Institute in Brooklyn, New York. These carvings are then cast in silver or gold and sometimes dotted with diamonds and gemstones. In a tribute to the senses inspired by Victorian-era love tokens, hands, noses, eyes, lips, and ears carved in relief appear to be literally clipped in metal before adorning her pieces.

Kiss's work invites a grounding sense of personal interpretation and meaning, something she witnessed in the pieces of Ted Muehling, the jeweler she apprenticed with for eight years after college before she started her own collection. It is fitting that her studio is located in New York's Hudson Valley, removed from the harried pace of a metropolis and surrounded by fresh opportunities for inspiration from flora and fauna just beyond her front door. Like Kiss's creative process, the production of her pieces is thoughtful and unhurried, and the pieces themselves are only available in a select few stores that make an art of selling jewelry.

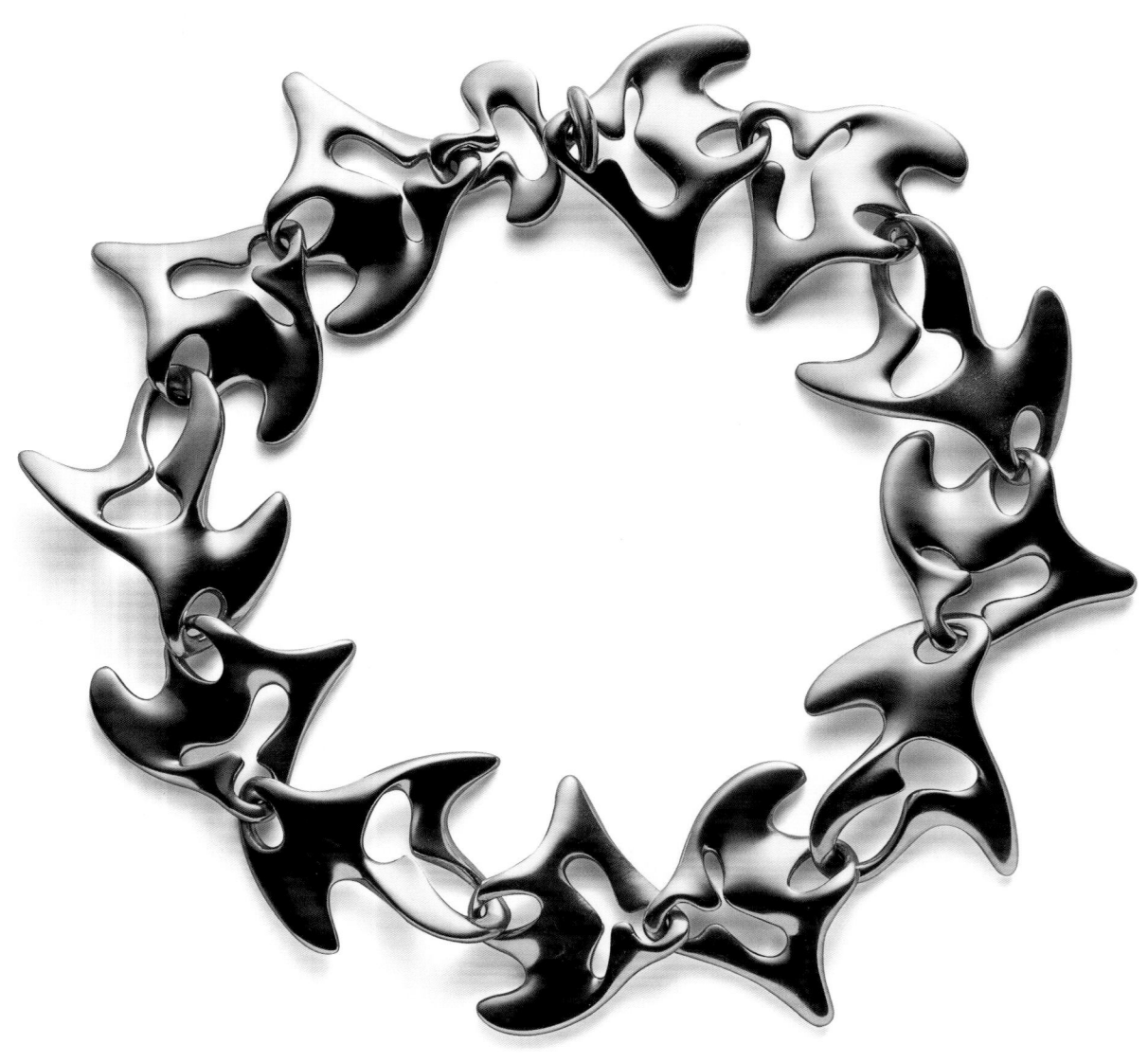

Henning Koppel

Henning Koppel
b. Copenhagen, Denmark, 1918
d. Copenhagen, Denmark, 1981

Amoeba necklace in sterling silver, designed by Henning Koppel for Georg Jensen (no. 89), 1947.

An innovative artist and designer, Copenhagen-born Henning Koppel is largely responsible for the Danish design aesthetic. In 1943, due to his Jewish identity, he fled Nazi-occupied Denmark for Sweden, and though he had first studied sculpture, he also began work as an artist for hire, eventually finding success as a jewelry designer for the Stockholm luxury goods store Svenskt Tenn. Returning home in 1945, he secured a contract with renowned silversmith Georg Jensen (see p.120), where he produced some of the most celebrated designs of modern Scandinavian jewelry. His strongly three-dimensional pieces in silver and gold were typified by fluid, organic shapes and clean lines, reflecting his training in sculpture and the influence of abstract artists such as Jean Arp and Constantin Brâncuși, whose biomorphic forms he much admired. Designs such as his *Splash* brooch (1946) and *Amoeba* bracelet (1947) exemplify his approach, resulting in pieces unlike anything Georg Jensen had produced before. The complexity of Koppel's jewelry pushed the envelope of what was possible with silver, and he often tested the patience of the silversmiths he worked with. In addition to jewelry, he designed pioneering hollowware, flatware, lighting, clocks, and furniture, ensuring his place as one of the most important and imitated Danish product designers of the period.

Nikos Koulis

Nikos Koulis
b. Athens, Greece, 1977

ME Collection one-of-a-kind necklace with 9.13 carats of pear-shaped white diamonds set in brushed yellow gold, 2024.

Photograph by Yiannis Bournias.

With boutiques in Athens, Mykonos, and Paros, Nikos Koulis's distinctive and avant-garde aesthetic heralds a new era in Greek jewelry design. Although the designer hails from a family of Greek goldsmiths, his creations bear little resemblance to traditional Hellenistic jewels. A former diamond dealer, Koulis launched his eponymous brand in 2006, growing in importance and evolving his style. "Time is a trusted companion, offering me endless inspiration through its influence on the human experience," he says—and the concept of timelessness is a constant focus. Greek mythology and classical art, architecture, and sculpture have all inspired his designs, but modernity is his modus operandi. Koulis's Athenian workshop patented the use of black enamel for his Art Deco–influenced designs, an innovation that in 2016 won him the first of four Couture Design Awards. He has suspended diamonds in translucent enamel, wound them among gold wire, and juxtaposed them with sinuous snake chains for the 2019 *Feelings* collection. His 2023 *ME* series explored the contrast between the cool, industrial masculinity of aluminum and the glamour of diamonds and gemstones. As he says, "Embracing contradictions is my way of expressing curiosity and exploring new creative boundaries."

Sam Kramer

Sam Kramer
b. Pittsburgh, Pennsylvania, United States, 1913
d. New York, New York, United States, 1964

Sterling silver cuff bracelet with applied copper domed circles, glass taxidermy eye, and peridot, c. 1950.

A provocateur, Sam Kramer advertised himself as making "fantastic jewelry for people who are slightly mad." Part of a burgeoning studio jewelry movement, Kramer was one of the first to open a studio-shop in New York's Greenwich Village neighborhood in 1939, inspiring his peers to follow suit. Making and selling silver jewelry, the artist, his bizarrely decorated studio-shop, and its wares were all unique. The studio-shop was a hangout for a Bohemian cast of characters, and to get through the door, you first needed to grasp a metal door handle, but in place of a doorknob, it featured a hand, which in winter months donned a warm woolen mitten. Inside, would-be clients were met with Kramer's biomorphic jewelry, primarily in silver, featuring taxidermy glass eyes and other unexpected "found" materials set into flowing, abstract shapes. In 1940 Kramer married Carol Enners, and the two began working together, alongside studio assistants who produced work for sale in the shop. A master at self-promotion and a lover of shock value, he was inspired by the likes of American showman P. T. Barnum and Surrealist artist Salvador Dalí (see p.77). In the 1950s he costumed women he called Space Girls in bubble helmets and sent them out into the city on mopeds or on foot handing out flyers for the shop, all while wearing his avant-garde and otherworldly jewelry.

George Frederick Kunz

George Frederick Kunz
b. New York, New York, United States, 1856
d. Shrub Oak, New York, United States, 1932

Illustration from George Frederick Kunz's *Gems and Precious Stones of North America* showing hiddenite (A), golden beryl (B), aquamarine (C), azurite and malachite (D), emerald (E, H), microcline (F), and cut aquamarine (G), 1890.

Hired by Tiffany & Co. in 1879, at the age of twenty-three, as its resident gem specialist, George Frederick Kunz, a self-taught mineralogist from New York, became one of the foremost international experts in his field. Rising through the ranks, Kunz became vice president at Tiffany in 1907 and continued to work for the company until his death in 1932 (see p.283). During his tenure at Tiffany, Kunz acquired remarkable and significant gems from around the world for inclusion in its collections. He was also tasked with overseeing the cutting of what would become one of Tiffany & Co.'s most iconic stones: the Tiffany Yellow Diamond, which he studied for a year before cutting it down by more than 150 carats. Financier J. P. Morgan, a longtime patron of Tiffany, worked closely with Kunz to assemble his incredible gem collection, which was later donated to the American Museum of Natural History in New York. It was during his time at Tiffany that Kunz first recognized a distinctive variety of the mineral spodumene—a gem that ranges in color from delicate pastel pink to intense violet purple—which was later named kunzite in his honor in 1903. Among his other pursuits, Kunz researched freshwater pearls for the United States Fish Commission and published hundreds of works on gems and minerals.

Kutchinsky

Kutchinsky
est. London, England, 1893

Hand-forged 18-karat gold and diamond ring, c. 1972.

Photograph by Chris W. Johnson.

British luxury jeweler Kutchinsky brilliantly captured the zeitgeist of London's changing moods from the 1950s to the 1980s. From small beginnings in London's East End, Polish émigré Hirsch Kutchinsky was from a family of court jewelers to King Ludwig II of Bavaria. He fled the Polish pogroms in 1893 and funded his London business with diamonds stitched into his wife's clothes. The company remained a family business with Joseph, Hirsch's son, at the helm in the 1960s and '70s, and then his son Paul in the 1980s. In this era of excess, Kutchinsky operated out of an opulent Knightsbridge showroom and counted Princess Diana and the Sultan of Brunei among its clients. Paul sashayed into the next generation with groovy outsize tiger's-eye pendants in rippling gold frames, chunky textured gold rings, and an emerald-eyed winking cat brooch. His innovative spirit was evident in an ambitious project to create the largest jeweled egg to outdo the famous Fabergé creations (see p.101). Completed in 1990, the Argyle Library Egg was just over two feet (60 cm) tall, set with twenty-four thousand pink Australian Argyle diamonds, and crafted from more than thirty pounds (15 kg) of gold. Fate, however, was not on Paul's side, and the $11.5 million dollar egg remained unsold. The business closed in 1991, a dramatic end to what was a flamboyant turn on the jewelry stage.

Lacloche Frères

Lacloche Frères
est. Paris, France, 1901

Loelia Ponsonby, the Duchess of Westminster, wears a tiara commissioned from Lacloche Frères that includes the Arcot I and Arcot II historic pear-shaped Golconda diamonds, *Vogue*, August 1931.

Photograph by Cecil Beaton.

Brothers Leopold, Jacques, Jules, and Fernand Lacloche were daring entrepreneurs who established a network of jewelry businesses across Europe in the late nineteenth century. After Jacques died in a train crash in 1900, the remaining siblings opened a boutique on Paris's Rue de la Paix, in the heart of the city's illustrious high jewelry district. Here, their influential reputation was sealed, specializing in the finest gemstones and loved by film stars, heiresses, and international royals alike. In the 1920s, Lacloche became synonymous with the Art Deco style, boasting outposts across France as well as in London, Madrid, and New York. The brothers were revered for their ability to translate the dominant aesthetics of the period—including *japonisme*, geometrical, and architectural themes—into exquisite jewels rich in craftsmanship with high-carat diamonds and colored gemstones. Among their creations was a halo-shaped tiara commissioned by the Duke of Westminster, which was set with more than 1,400 diamonds, including the Arcot diamonds originally gifted to King George III by Nizam Ali Khan of Hyderabad in 1785. The company briefly closed in 1931 but was relaunched in 1936 by Jacques Lacloche Jr., and the firm thrived under his direction until the mid-1960s, with distinguished clients including Lady Clementine Hozier, Grace Kelly, and Elsa Schiaparelli (see pp.148, 250).

Claude Lalanne

Claude Lalanne
b. Paris, France, 1925
d. Fontainebleu, France, 2019

Gilded fingertips created by Claude Lalanne for Yves Saint Laurent's Autumn/Winter 1969 haute couture collection.

Photograph by Matthieu Lavanchy.

French artist Claude Lalanne studied architecture at the École des Beaux-Arts before meeting her husband and collaborator, the sculptor and installation artist François-Xavier Lalanne, in 1952. Working together as Les Lalanne, the pair created quirky sculptures and decorative objects inspired by nature. Outside of this partnership, Claude was a prolific jewelry maker, first exhibiting her pieces in Paris in 1964. Although she went on to design for GianCarlo Montebello, Yves Saint Laurent (see p.199, 245), French auction house Artcurial, and Greek firm Zolotas, most of her sculptural jewels were handcrafted privately for friends, family, and collectors. An early torque necklace featuring a golden mouth and her *Pomme Bouche* brooches of apples with expressive apertures typify her surreal and whimsical approach. For Saint Laurent's 1969 haute couture show, Lalanne famously adorned the models with gilded body parts, including fingertips, cast from their own anatomies. For Maria Grazia Chiuri's first haute couture show at Dior in 2017, Lalanne made textured metallic blooms (see p.89). Through her signature electroplating process of submerging flowers, leaves, twigs, butterflies, and other organic materials into a plating bath, Lalanne re-enchanted the wearers' experiences of the natural world using bronze, silver, and copper.

René Lalique

René Lalique
b. Aÿ-Champagne, France, 1860
d. Paris, France, 1945

Dragonfly corsage ornament in gold with wings composed of stained glass enamel accented by diamonds, a woman's bust in sculpted chrysoprase, and a cabochon-cut chalcedony along the body, c. 1897–98.

The undisputed master glassmaker of the Art Deco age, René Lalique was also a revolutionary jeweler who broke new ground with his daring creations that helped define the avant-garde spirit of the Art Nouveau movement. At the age of sixteen, Lalique moved to London, where he honed his drawing skills at the Sydenham Art College, immersing himself in the British Arts & Crafts style before returning to his native France, where he worked in the ateliers of prominent houses such as Boucheron and Cartier (see pp.39, 54). In 1885 he established his own Parisian workshop and became the talk of the town thanks to his shimmering designs inspired by the natural world. Infused with a sense of romance and mysticism, their fluid lines, openwork detail, and delicate enameling were combined with the use of unorthodox materials such as ivory, horn, coral, and molded glass, along with unexpected semiprecious stones from corundum and carnelian to agate, jasper, and opal. Lalique's intricate silhouettes—exotic insects, Japanesque florals, fairy-tale nymphs, tumbling vines—were beloved by the intellectual and artistic elite. Actor Sarah Bernhardt wore his most elaborate creations onstage and glassmaker Émile Gallé christened Lalique "the inventor of modern jewelry."

Kenneth Jay Lane

Kenneth Jay Lane
b. Detroit, Michigan, United States, 1932
d. New York, New York, United States, 2017

Audrey Hepburn as Holly Golightly wearing a Kenneth Jay Lane pearl necklace on the set of *Breakfast at Tiffany's*, 1961.

American costume jeweler Kenneth Jay Lane was best known for his "fabulous fake" jewelry designs, among the first faux pieces to be worn by Manhattan's elite. Born in Detroit, Lane studied at the Rhode Island School of Design and moved to New York, where he briefly worked for *Vogue* magazine's art department. While designing shoes for Delman and Roger Vivier at Christian Dior, he designed jewelry on his own time—including leather-wrapped bangles for his friend, designer Bill Blass—eventually launching his own namesake collection in 1962. Expanding from private client sales, he sold to retailers and the home shopping network QVC. Striving to create costume jewelry that looked as real as possible, he imported custom stones from Germany. Whether a gunmetal-and-emerald snake collar or a glamorous geometric Art Deco hinged cuff, Lane's designs bridged the gap between couture and everyday wear. A lifelong lover of fashion, he was influenced by British royal jewels and designers such as David Webb and Jean Schlumberger (see pp.78, 251). His circle of friends both inspired and wore his jewels, and included Diana Vreeland, Babe Paley, Audrey Hepburn (famously wearing his five-strand pearl necklace in *Breakfast at Tiffany's*), and Jackie O, who gave Lane permission to replicate her iconic Van Cleef & Arpels Maharani necklace (see pp.150, 291, 306).

Shaun Leane

Shaun Leane
b. London, England, 1969

Aluminum *Coil Corset* created by Shaun Leane for Alexander McQueen's *The Overlook* collection, Autumn/Winter 1999.

Photograph by Ann Ray.

In 1992 two lads in their early twenties met in a London pub and went on to create fashion history. Jewelry was integral to the way designer Alexander McQueen presented his clothes and Shaun Leane—who collaborated with him for nearly eighteen years until McQueen's death in 2010— designed the dramatic and provocative jewelry that helped convey McQueen's hard-edged message. Fueled by reckless excitement, the two pushed the parameters of where and how jewelry can be worn. Trained in metalwork before becoming a goldsmith's apprentice at age fifteen, Leane manipulated aluminum rods into a coiled corset for the 1999 collection *The Overlook* and crafted a seductive sterling silver rose corset for McQueen's 2000 haute couture collection for Givenchy. His technical expertise contributed to the raw, emotional intensity of McQueen's catwalks: a crown of thorns for the *Dante* collection and silver tusk earrings for *The Hunger* collection (both in 1996), which would later become a signature of Leane's eponymous brand (until his exit in 2024); a ferocious tusk mouthpiece for a show in 2000; and, the following year, a spiky Tahitian pearl neckpiece that was in imminent danger of piercing model Karen Elson's cheek. Together Leane and McQueen were fearless. The hauntingly beautiful designs from Leane's archive were subsequently sold at auction in 2017 by Sotheby's New York.

Austy Lee

Austy Lee (Lee Chun Pong)
b. 1981

The Ring of Fuxi in 18-karat yellow gold with Burmese green and purple jades, black enamel, and fancy pink and yellow diamonds, from *The Jade Dynasty* collection, 2024.

Illuminating ancient legends in an artistic form, each of Austy Lee's ornate designs has a history and tells a story, pulling from religious totems or rare pieces of decorative art for inspiration. In his early years, Lee learned jade carving and the restoration of antiques from his uncle, awakening a love of jewelry craftsmanship and antique Chinese and Japanese decorative arts. Initially working as a graphic designer before graduating with a degree in product design in 2008, Lee moved into jewelry with a two-year internship at the Hong Kong boutique of Swiss jewelers Adler (see p.12). In 2011 he became chief designer at Wendy Yue, creating colorful jewels until he left in 2017 to establish his eponymous brand. Lee could now break free to explore ancient and modern design and craft techniques. From Japanese lacquerware, *Menuki* (traditionally used to decorate Samurai swords), and *Obidome* (Japanese obi clips) to jade carving and lava cameos, he combines tradition with his passion for color. Ideas are eclectic, from an Edo-style square gold bangle with Meiji era lacquerware set with rubies, yellow diamonds, and abalone shell to antique agate cameos re-set with colored sapphires to carved Imperial jade earrings in contemporary settings. Rare gemstones, meditation, his Chinese heritage, and ethnic artistry are all crucial sources of inspiration for Lee's unique vibrant designs.

Fred Leighton

Fred Leighton (Murray Mondschein)
b. New York, New York,
United States, 1932
d. New York, New York,
United States, 2017

Cate Blanchett wearing a Fred Leighton pearl necklace, 2004.

Photograph by Alan Gelati.

As jeweler to Hollywood's stars, Fred Leighton was known for curating iconic, one-of-a-kind period pieces, housed in his New York boutique. Elevating antique jewelry—whether Victorian, Art Nouveau, or Art Deco—to the silver screen and the red carpet, from the Academy Awards to the Met Gala, Leighton was among the first to lend celebrities his haute vintage pieces. His grand entrance at the Oscars was in 1996 with an Australian opal choker loaned to Nicole Kidman in collaboration with Miuccia Prada, who designed Kidman's dress. Leighton's other notable Oscar jewels included diamond dress clips for Charlize Theron's Vera Wang gown in 2000 and delicate diamond headbands worn by Natalie Portman in 2006 and Lupita Nyong'o in 2016. His list of star-studded clientele is endless: Sarah Jessica Parker, Kate Winslet, Sophia Loren (see p.174), Meryl Streep, even the ever-particular Joan Rivers. Born Murray Mondschein, he assumed the Fred Leighton name from an arts and crafts store he had purchased in Greenwich Village. He started out selling wedding dresses and Native American and Mexican silver jewelry, later evolving to sell vintage pieces. Leighton's collections contain rare jewels, including originals by Suzanne Belperron, René Boivin, and David Webb (see pp.28, 35, 78), and his team continues to create custom pieces today, inspired by past and present eras.

Georges Lenfant

Georges Lenfant
b. France, 1880s
d. France, c. late 1940s

Studies for Lenfant bracelets with fine stones, as well as *pietre dure* with inlays of semiprecious stones, 1930.

The prestigious hallmark of Georges Lenfant—a diamond shape that contains his initials—is an undeniable indication of twentieth-century goldsmithing par excellence. Founded in 1903, Lenfant's atelier near Rue de la Paix in Paris quickly gained a reputation for high-quality craftsmanship and innovation, collaborating on designs for such iconic houses as Boucheron, Bulgari, Tiffany & Co., and Van Cleef & Arpels (see pp.39, 46, 283, 291). Revered for his dexterous use of gold on chains and bracelets, Lenfant, working alongside his son Jacques, harnessed a new sense of fluidity and tactility in the world of high jewelry. Through the 1960s and '70s, Jacques took this artistry to new heights as the workshop played with different proportions and created myriad new patterns, structures, and textures by weaving, braiding, twisting, fluting, and coiling gold to create bold sculptural forms. The pieces' surfaces, as intricately formed as woven fabric, stood out immediately, some thickly knotted like rope, others more delicate and meshlike. Their iconic designs have persisted in the Tiffany optical swirl pattern panther link, Cartier's zodiac pendants, and in the Hermès anchor link (see pp.54, 134). Jacques retired in the 1980s and worked with younger jewelers in the Lenfant studios until his death in 1995, and the Lenfant trademark and atelier was closed for good in 2003.

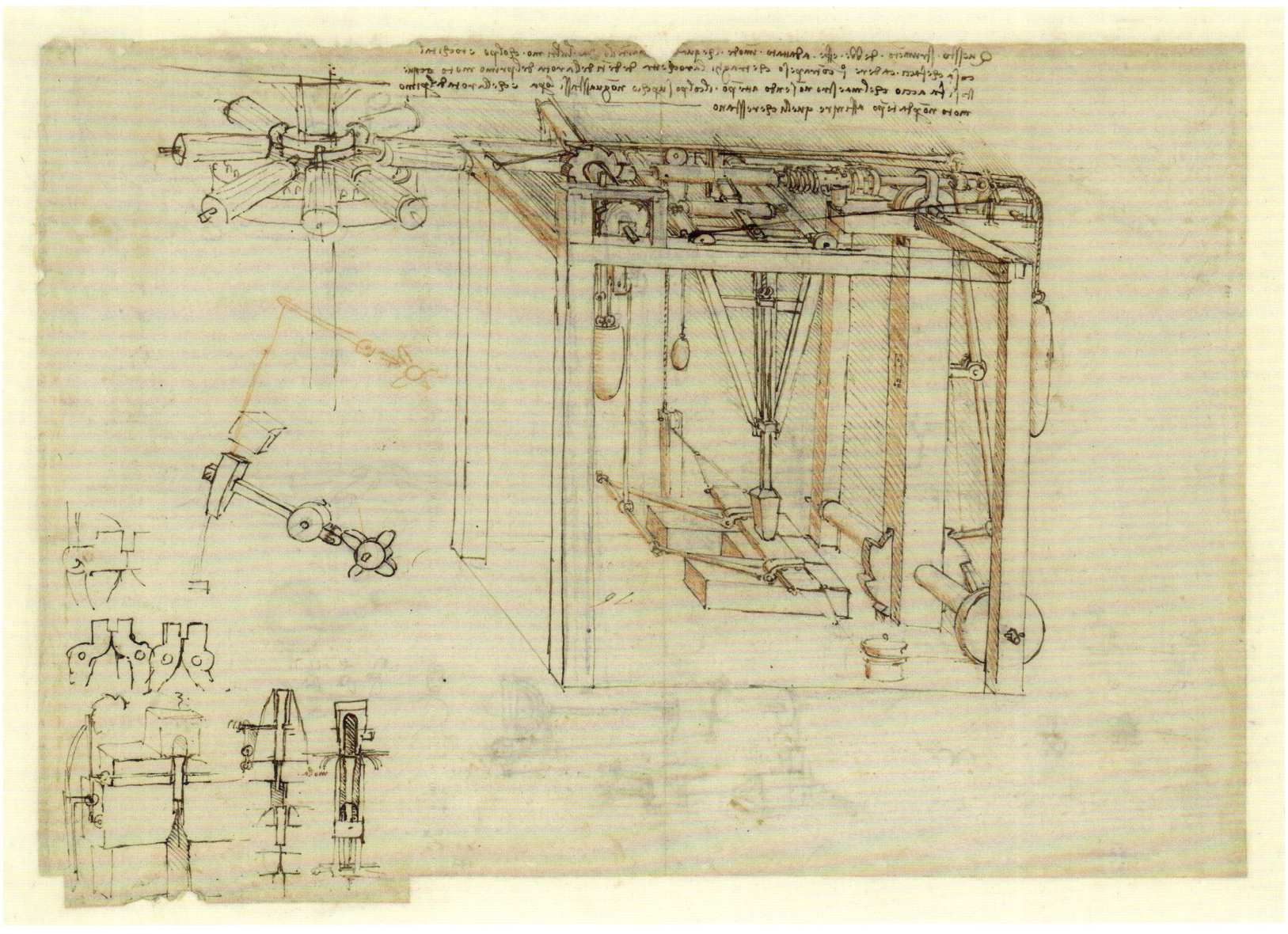

Leonardo da Vinci

Leonardo da Vinci
b. Anchiano, Italy, 1452
d. Amboise, France, 1519

Drawing for a design of a gold-beating machine by Leonardo da Vinci, *Codex Atlanticus*, sheet 29 recto, c. 1493–95.

One of history's most accomplished polymaths, Leonardo da Vinci had an insatiable appetite for knowledge that spanned disciplines as diverse as anatomy, astronomy, architecture, military defense, civil engineering, and acoustics. The Renaissance artist was also a gifted goldsmith who trained under the Florentine sculptor, painter, and metalworker Andrea del Verrocchio, known for his bronze statues, including his figure of David commissioned by the Medici family. A master at casting precious metals, Verrocchio nurtured Leonardo's eye for detail and encouraged him to apply science and logic to every creation, so much so that his young prodigy predicted developments in jewelry-making and goldsmithing centuries ahead of their time. He designed an automatic hammer operated by weights to mechanize the craft of gold-beating for the accelerated production of gold leaf and also developed a recipe for how to make artificial pearls. For this, Leonardo suggested remodeling small seed pearls into larger polished forms, dissolving them first in lemon juice to obtain a powder, which could then be reconstituted with egg whites. Today it is his artistic application of the golden ratio that continues to influence the jewelry and watch worlds, as designers seek to apply his harmonized propositions to the cut of diamonds and to the shape of luxury watches.

Liberace

Liberace (Wladziu Valentino Liberace)
b. West Milwaukee, Wisconsin, United States, 1919
d. Palm Springs, California, United States, 1987

Liberace wearing his iconic rings in his $55,000 marble bathtub, 1978.

Melding madcap piano medleys and friendly Midwestern charm with over-the-top Las Vegas glamour, American entertainer Liberace knew how to command the stage. As a teenager, he got his start playing at cocktail lounges and silent-movie theaters. In the 1950s, Liberace's nightclub act, in which he chatted with the audience and keyed breezy mixes of classical songs and popular hits, made it to television; the fifteen-minute, twice-a-week program *The Liberace Show* was an immediate success and was syndicated to hundreds of stations. Part of the appeal of his live concerts, which drew crowds throughout the 1970s and '80s, was Liberace's extravagant costumes, accented by sparkling brooches, chunky gold bracelets, and oversize rings on almost every finger. When he played the piano from behind the glow of a candelabra, his fingers shimmered with stacks of custom-made jewels, from large amethysts, sapphires, and opals set in gold to a miniature grand piano encrusted in Swarovski crystals. After Liberace's death in 1987, his estate was bequeathed to his family and friends, and some of his most iconic pieces, including a candelabra-shaped ring gifted to him by William Harrah of the Harrah's hotel chain, were consigned for auction in 2011. "People ask how I can play with all those rings," Liberace wrote in his 1986 autobiography, "and I reply, 'Very well, thank you.'"

Roy Lichtenstein

Roy Lichtenstein
b. New York, New York, United States, 1923
d. New York, New York, United States, 1997

Teardrop Pendant in cloisonné porcelain enamel with gold wire and a silver backplate, c. 1965 (fabricated c. 1966–67).

Famous for his comic strip–inspired paintings, Roy Lichtenstein brought a combination of parody, playfulness, and pluck to the 1960s Pop art genre. Using his signature Ben-Day dots in vibrant primary colors, he both celebrated and critiqued consumer culture. His style was designed to be accessible to all, which is one reason Lichtenstein applied it to jewelry in the mid-1960s that was produced by Multiples Inc., a New York–based publishing company specializing in affordable limited-edition artworks designed for home display and personal adornment. In 1968 the company issued a multicolored enamel Pop art brooch of a woman's face made in collaboration with the artist that originally retailed at just twenty-five dollars; it is now predictably a coveted collector's item, known to reach five figures at auction. But this partnership wasn't the artist's first foray into jewelry design: In the late 1940s to early 1950s, he made silver pendants and necklaces embellished with tiny abstract forms resembling the figurative works of Pablo Picasso (see p.223) and Joan Miró, whose work he admired. Surviving editions of these tiny wearable sculptures are extremely rare and serve as early examples of Lichtenstein's innovative use of metal in fine art, as evidenced by his perforated stencils made of aluminum, which helped him achieve his uniform pixel-like style and his later monumental steel sculptures.

Nicholas Lieou

Nicholas Lieou
b. 1982

Top to bottom: 3.15-carat step-cut diamond ring; 2.04-carat marquise-cut diamond ring; 2.11-carat old European–cut brown diamond ring; all set on rhodium-plated, sand-blasted matte 18-karat gold, 2023.

With distinctly minimalist forms, Nicholas Lieou's signature style blends East and West through contemporary codes. In contrast to the decorative designs emanating from many of his peers within Asia's current generation of jewelers, he presents a streamlined approach to high jewelry. Lieou's exposure to traditional Chinese craftsmanship and modern design shaped an aesthetic that is at once balanced, monochrome, and gender-fluid. Interested in the tension between strength and fragility, Lieou made it his mission to update pearl jewelry, building clean silhouettes with one side pavéd in variously sized diamonds. In 2015 he was appointed design director of high jewelry and custom design at Tiffany & Co., where he updated the brand's *haute joaillerie* offering under design director Francesca Amfitheatrof (see pp.19, 283). With a debut collection of classic pearls set on sinuous lines of gold, he launched Mr. Lieou in 2019, which primarily focuses on bespoke pieces for collectors. The following year, a ten-piece capsule collection featuring rare fancy-colored diamonds for Sotheby's Diamonds solidified his reputation as a leading voice in contemporary high jewelry. In 2024 Lieou was appointed as the creative director of high jewelry at Chow Tai Fook (see p.67), bringing his distinctive minimalist, androgynous aesthetic to a global audience via the heritage brand.

LL Cool J

LL Cool J (James Todd Smith)
b. Bay Shore, New York,
United States, 1968

LL Cool J shows off his three-finger "JAME$" ring and a gold nugget ring by Tito Caicedo of Manny's New York, Hyde Park Corner, London, 1986.

Photograph by Richard Bellia.

Trailblazing American rapper LL Cool J rose to prominence in the 1980s with his smooth style and innovative sound. He was among the first rappers to achieve commercial success with his 1985 debut album, *Radio*. His breakout single, "I Need Love" in 1987, brought him widespread recognition by introducing a love ballad into a genre not typically focused on romance. As LL Cool J's popularity soared, so did his vibrant presence onstage and in music videos, influencing future generations of musicians, athletes, entertainers, and fans. He adorned himself with oversize gold dookie rope chains, iced-out three- and four-finger rings—two memorable ones reading "JAME$" and "COOLJ"—chunky bracelets, and large diamond stud earrings, which became a hallmark of his success. One of his iconic tracks, "Jingling Baby," from the 1989 album *Walking with a Panther*, even features the unforgettable chorus line, "Let me see your earrings jingle, love." The catchy phrase refers to the large, gold Creole earrings typically worn in pairs or threes, producing a jingling sound with every movement. Accessorizing custom Dapper Dan or a B-Boy tracksuit, LL Cool J's inimitable use of jewelry was at the forefront of the growing hip-hop jewelry trend that still thrives today.

Lola Fenhirst

Lola Fenhirst
est. Paris, France, 2015

Stephany Amado wears the *Sybil 7-Point Diamond Necklace* in 18-karat yellow gold with bezel-set and pavé diamonds and the *Sybil Diamond Cocktail Ring* in 18-karat yellow and white gold with an inner cache of round brilliant-cut diamonds, 2021.

Photograph by Menelik Puryear.

Lola Oladunjoye's earliest jewelry icon was her great-uncle, Sir Adesoji Tadeniawo Aderemi, the first African to be appointed a governor in the British Commonwealth. She first met him when she was seven years old, and she was "struck by the heft and majesty of his many jewels." Many years later, memories of hand-carved gold, brass, ivory, and coral rings began to surface when Oladunjoye started designing herself. Born and raised in London by Nigerian parents, the designer emphasizes her heritage through architectural forms. She founded her brand, Lola Fenhirst, in 2015 to create handmade pieces of wearable art, blending motifs from traditional African adornment with jewelry-making styles and techniques from Europe and South Asia. She often references beads, an important motif in Yoruba culture that also play an integral part in religious rites. Exploring the interplay of these symbols of royalty, wealth, and fertility became the cornerstone of her *Beaded* series. Another iconic collection, *Pit*—with shallow circular craters set with diamonds, rubies, sapphires, or lapis lazuli—references the open-pit mines dotted across Africa and celebrates the rich mineral resources of the continent. Oladunjoye also took part in the *Brilliant & Black* exhibitions curated at Sotheby's (see p.267), celebrating Black jewelry designers from around the world.

Charles Loloma

Charles Loloma
b. Hotevilla, Arizona,
United States, 1921
d. Phoenix, Arizona,
United States, 1991

Mosaic cuff bracelet in 14-karat gold with architectural inlay of Kingman and Morenci turquoises, coral, lapis lazuli, and wood, c. 1975.

One of the first Native American jewelers to achieve international acclaim, Hopi artist Charles Loloma created jewelry with bold lines, setting turquoise, spiny oyster shell, lapis lazuli, and coral into hefts of gold and silver. Loloma experienced early success in painting and later ceramics, before shifting his attention to jewelry in 1955. He created necklaces, bracelets, and rings but also ornaments such as bolos and belt buckles that are closely associated with the American Southwest. The dynamism of his work evoked the surrounding landscape in Hotevilla, Arizona: varying heights of stones mirrored the valleys and mesas, and his color palettes brought to mind stunning desert sunsets.

There was a duality to his work, which included opaque stones inlaid inside the jewel so that the most colorful part of the art was hidden, as if a secret to be uncovered by the wearer. Balancing an active artistic practice with teaching, Loloma was among the inaugural instructors at Institute of American Indian Arts when it opened in Santa Fe in 1962. His teaching meant that his work quickly impacted the next generation of artists, including protégés such as his niece Sonwai (Verma Nequatewa) and the Algerian Moroccan artist Eveli Sabatie (see p.177). Loloma left behind an extraordinary oeuvre of jewelry and continues to be a source of inspiration among Hopi, Pueblo, and Diné artists.

Sophia Loren

Sophia Loren (Sofia Scicolone)
b. Rome, Italy, 1934

Sophia Loren photographed for *Paris Match*, May 1962.

Photograph by François Pagès.

After winning the Academy Award for Best Actress in 1960 for her role in *Two Women*, Sophia Loren went on to conquer cinema, her image permanently ingrained in popular culture worldwide. The embodiment of the Italian bombshell, she possessed an incandescent beauty and an effervescent personality that could only be paired with bold, outsize jewelry, typically in full parure, because Loren did nothing by halves. At the 1960 premiere for *Two Women*, under a fur cape she revealed a Bulgari necklace with sapphires, rubies, and diamonds in a floral setting, matched with drop-shaped sapphire earrings and a massive domed sapphire ring (see p.46). At Cannes in 1966, she dazzled again, this time with a diamond-studded floral setting by Van Cleef & Arpels, featuring a larger-than-life faceted emerald pendant paired with cluster earrings (see p.291). For the July 1965 cover of British *Vogue*, photographed by David Bailey, Loren wore a turban adorned with emeralds and beads. Never one to hide from the spotlight, at a London film premiere, Loren donned a tiara—only to discover Queen Elizabeth II was in attendance, and the monarch was the only one permitted to have a crowned head (see p.97). The queen, however, did not protest; after all, she was meeting red-carpet royalty from Hollywood's golden age, and there was more than enough room for both women to shine.

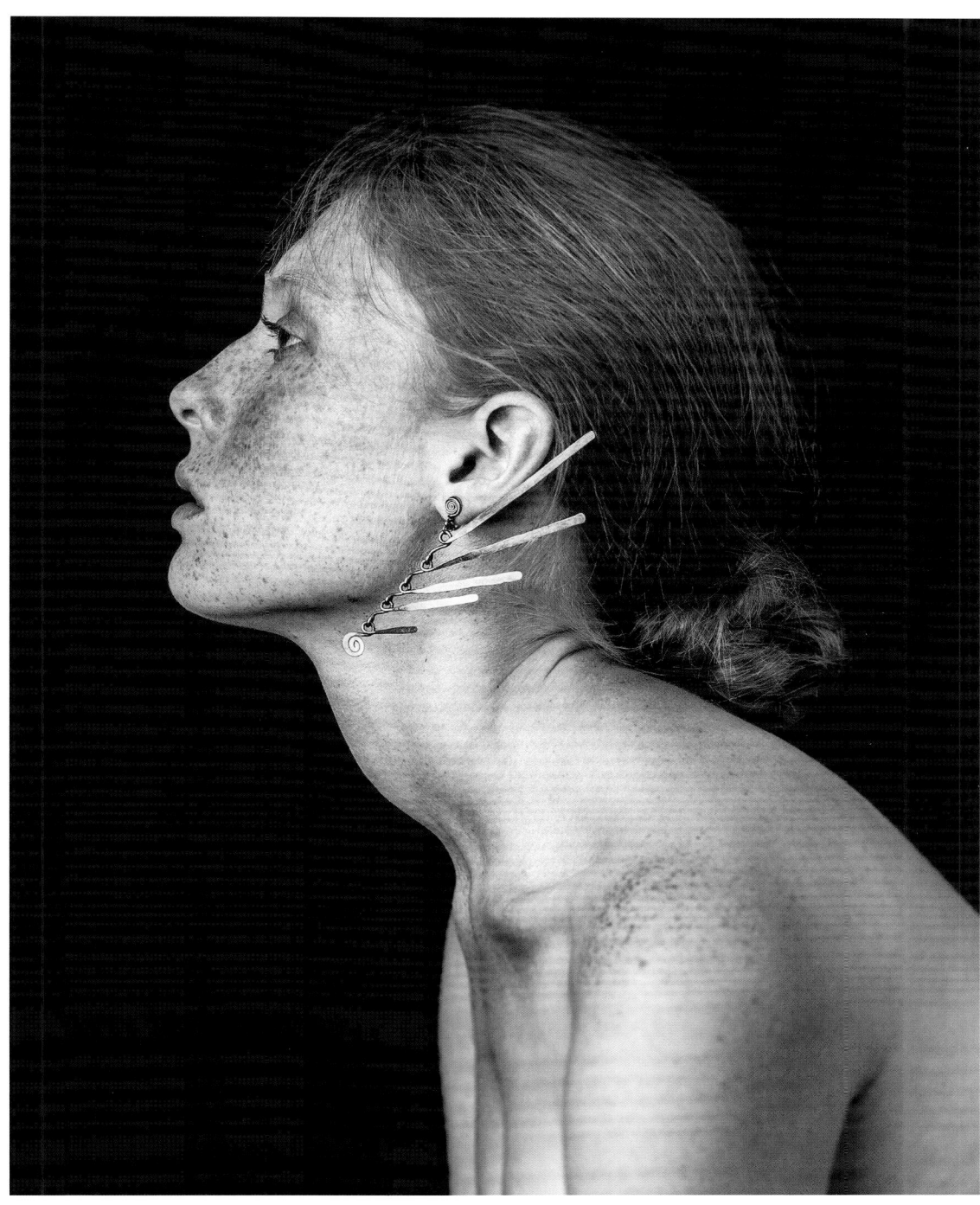

Louisa Guinness Gallery

Louisa Guinness Gallery
est. London, England, 2003

A model wears Alexander Calder's brass wire earrings made c. 1942, part of the Louisa Guinness Gallery archive.

Photograph by Alexander English.

While jewelry galleries abound across major cities worldwide, in 2003 Louisa Guinness was one of the first to open a gallery dedicated specifically to artist jewelry. Based in London, Guinness's practice focuses on historic works by such artists as Alexander Calder, Salvador Dalí, Claude Lalanne, Man Ray, and Pablo Picasso, and (see pp.50, 77, 160, 180, 223), alongside a curated selection of top-tier vintage jewels and collaborations with contemporary artists. The impressive roster of talent producing unique jewelry includes Anish Kapoor, Ron Arad, and Jeff Koons, who shrunk down his stainless steel *Rabbit* sculpture to become a platinum pendant. Guinness also offers the work of independent jewelers, in what she describes as a "curative" assembly. The selection encompasses leading designers such as Hannah Martin—her provocative, outsize *New Rebel* gold-and-malachite bangle in the form of a bolt packing a rebellious punch—and Melanie Georgacopoulos with a bangle that embeds diamonds and pearls into a creamy, glossy cushion of mother-of-pearl (see pp.121, 185). Guinness has expanded the idea that jewelry can be art by encouraging well-known fine artists from Grayson Perry to Marc Quinn (see p.232) to embrace the medium in innovative ways, offering jewelry collectors a new way to experience their passion.

Madonna

Madonna (Madonna Ciccone)
b. Bay City, Michigan,
United States, 1958

Madonna performs during the MTV Video Awards, New York, 1984.

Photograph by Richard Corkery.

As one of the most recognizable cultural icons in the world, Madonna has used jewelry as a key part of her image since she burst into the public eye in 1979. By turns a 1980s popstrel, '90s vamp, and 2000s dance maven, her jewels have always been an important tool for personal expression. In the early '80s she stacked bangles and layered long chains and bead necklaces in what became the decade's quintessential punk-pop look. A few years later, the old Hollywood glamour of the Material Girl, dripping in pearls and diamonds, peaked at the 1991 Oscars, to which she wore $20 million worth of Harry Winston diamonds (see p.132). Crucifixes and rosary beads entered the mix as an expression of her Catholic identity, which was subverted during her Like a Prayer era. In the late 1990s, she became interested in Eastern mysticism and Kabbalah and began wearing Indian and Southeast Asian–style necklaces, red silk bracelets, and stacked silver and gold bangles. In recent decades, her jewelry has become more refined. Madonna has been seen on the red carpet in pieces by Bulgari, Cartier, and Van Cleef & Arpels (see pp.46, 54, 291), as well as jewels by Loree Rodkin, Lynn Ban, Jacob & Co., and House of Emmanuele, showing the ultimate style chameleon's sharp eye for mixing heritage houses with independent designers.

Mahnaz Collection

Mahnaz Collection
est. New York, New York,
United States, 2013

Swirling Fish brooch by Eveli Sabatie in 18-karat gold and silver inset with sugilites, moonstones, spinels, and garnets, c. 1990.

Photograph by Kevin Kish.

Feeding a healthy obsession with artistic and well-crafted jewels from the 1960s to the present, the Mahnaz Collection is a gallery on Madison Avenue in New York that reflects the passion and intellect of Mahnaz Ispahani Bartos, a longtime collector of antique Mughal era *kundan* and *meenakari* jewelry. The gallery has a subspecialty in big names, such as Boucheron, Bulgari, and Chaumet (see pp.39, 46, 63). But other pieces reveal forward-looking, independent designers, goldsmiths, and artists from around the world. A textured sterling silver bracelet by Finnish artist Björn Weckström shares space with a molten 18-karat-gold pendant necklace centered with an aquamarine pendant by Canadian jewelry designer Karl Stittgen. Mahnaz also holds an 18-karat-gold *Lamellae* ring by the renowned late architect Zaha Hadid for Georg Jensen (see p.120). London creators such as George Weil, John Donald, and Andrew Grima are also part of the firm's forte (see pp.90, 128). At the core of each piece in the collection, however, is its individual story, many previously unrecognized. A small staff of jewelry professionals pores over research materials to communicate the unique cultural context, geographic significance, and historical importance of each creator, whether a Hopi artist from Arizona or a Danish silversmith, providing a foundation of intellectual substance that complements the beauty of each piece.

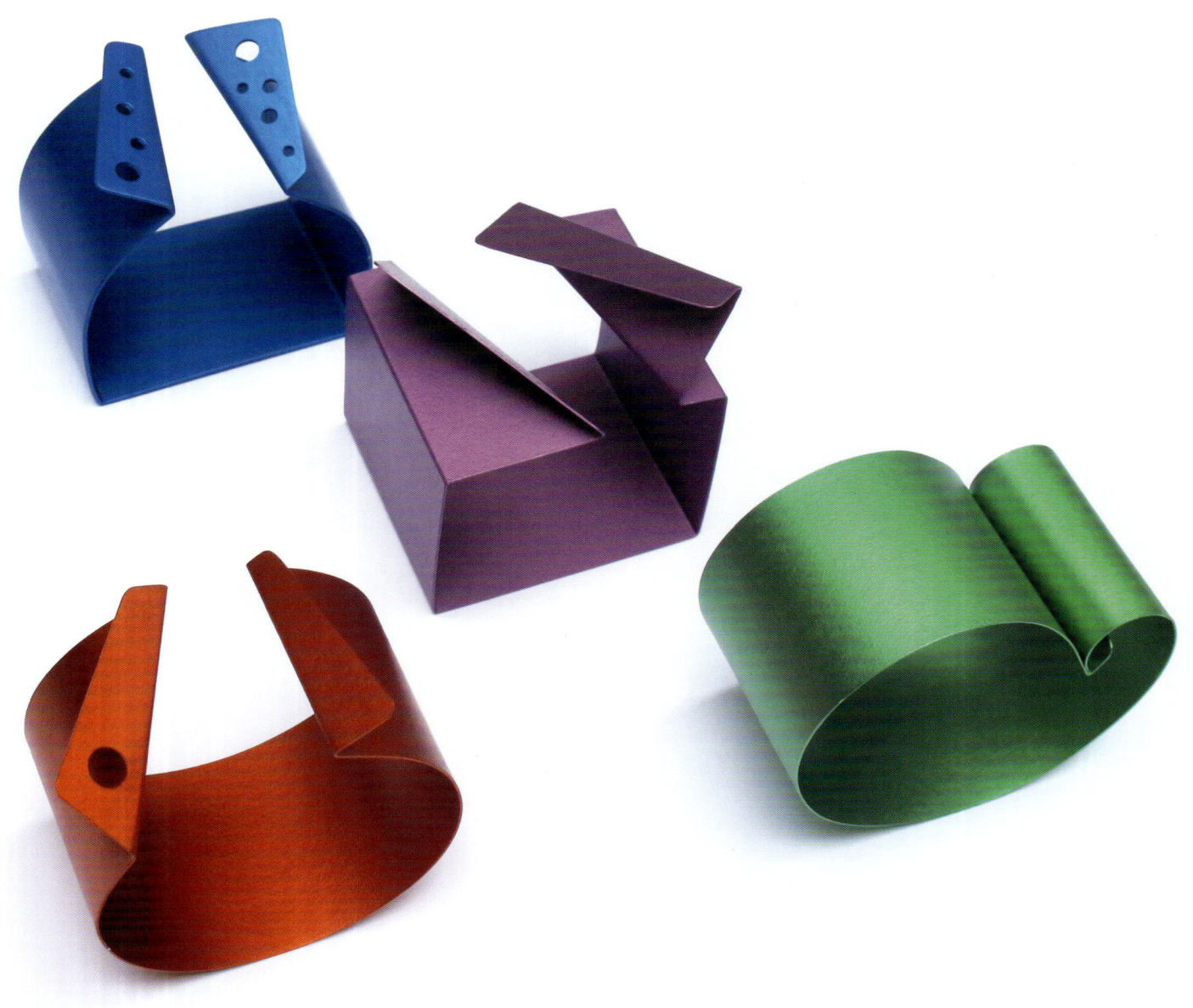

Fritz Maierhofer

Fritz Maierhofer
b. Vienna, Austria, 1941

Anodized aluminum bracelets, 2011.

Born in Vienna, Fritz Maierhofer began his jewelry journey as a goldsmith's apprentice in London under Andrew Grima in 1967 (see p.128). While working for Grima, he oversaw ornamental watches for Omega in 1969 before developing a keen interest in jewelry, inspired by artists Stella Lichtenstein, Jim Dine, and Ernest Trova, and the rich tableau and vibrant lights of London. Maierhofer reimagined jewelry as a free-form medium for visual impact, challenging traditional norms of adornment and liberating jewelry to become wearable art. He first combined high-low materials such as colorful acrylics with precious metals, whether springlike coils of aluminum brooches or striped acrylic rainbow glass rings. After returning to Austria in 1970 and purchasing a farmhouse five years later, his metalwork became quieter, expressed in soft tin and gold, seen in necklaces featuring rolled, cylindrical pendants with tapered tails. Maierhofer's jewelry is a language unto itself, characterized by bold and unique forms representing an inner, almost meditative dialogue reflective of his personal life. He also experiments with newer materials, such as Corian—a composite material of acrylic resin and natural minerals—to produce coral-like brooches and geometric rings, inspiring generations of designers to think beyond tradition and to continually push jewelry as high art.

Maison Fouquet

Maison Fouquet
est. Paris, France, 1860

Brooch/pendant by Georges Fouquet in the form of a lady comprised of 18-karat gold, carved chalcedony, enamel, rubies, rose diamonds, and natural pearl, late 19th century.

One of the great French families of jewelers from the nineteenth and twentieth centuries, Maison Fouquet was founded by Alphonse Fouquet in 1860. Creating Renaissance Revival pieces in the classically decorative tradition, he featured dragons, sphinxes, and other mythological creatures, while his son Georges would later embrace more naturalistic, Art Nouveau styles at the turn of the century, re-creating the sinuous lines of plants and flowers in gold with enamels, opals, pearls, and fine diamonds. Georges also partnered with celebrated artists, such as Alphonse Mucha, to create jewelry in unconventional and theatrical compositions, including a coiling gold serpent bracelet for the French actress Sarah Bernhardt. Later, Georges's son Jean took over the maison, eschewing Belle Époque styles and designing sleeker linear creations typical of Art Deco, whether a multicolored-gem-and-diamond bangle by painter and artist Cassandre or a gold, silver, and black lacquer necklace highlighting a singular cut-cornered aquamarine. Inspired by Cubism and Futurism, Jean preferred simple shapes: triangles, pyramids, and semicircles. He maintained the maison's illustrious legacy until the financial crisis in 1929 forced the company to file for bankruptcy; however, Jean still continued to create a small number of pieces with his father's workshop until 1960.

Man Ray

Man Ray (Emmanuel Radnitzky)
b. Philadelphia, Pennsylvania,
United States, 1890
d. Paris, France, 1976

A model wears the *Optic Topic* mask designed by Man Ray in 1974 and executed by GEM Montebello in gold-plated sterling silver in 1978.

Photograph by Alexander English.

Twisting traditional forms of beauty into the bizarre, the experimental photography of American artist Man Ray ironically made him highly sought after by the fashion industry in the mid-twentieth century. Man Ray went on to make fundamental contributions to both the Dada and Surrealist movements, and though he considered himself a painter foremost, he became known for his innovative approach to photography. He shot for Chanel, *Vogue*, and *Harper's Bazaar*, utilizing his pioneering solarization technique, where he added dark outlines to images by exposing them to sunlight when they were partially developed. In the 1960s, he began collaborating with Milan-based jeweler GianCarlo Montebello on wearable works that echoed the eerie forms of his sculptures (see p.199). The seemingly blinding *Optic Topic* mask from 1974 took its inspiration from the aluminum masks worn by race car drivers from the 1930s, while the gold, almond-shaped *Oculist* brooch appeared as an eye with a deep green malachite. His *Pendantif-Pendant* earrings borrowed their spiral motifs from an assemblage he made in 1919 by unfurling a paper lampshade around a metal post. Famously, the French movie star Catherine Deneuve modeled these earrings on the cover of the June 1968 *Sunday Times Magazine*, which Man Ray photographed himself in his small Paris atelier.

Robert Mapplethorpe

Robert Mapplethorpe
b. New York, New York,
United States, 1946
d. Boston, Massachusetts,
United States, 1989

Untitled (Necklace), Polaroid, c. 1974.

Created and photographed by
Robert Mapplethorpe.

American photographer Robert Mapplethorpe's stark, black-and-white portraits, floral pictures, and documentation of the gay BDSM community in 1970s New York are what made him famous—and infamous. Less well-known, however, is the artist's talent for jewelry-making, which he developed early in his career when he was experimenting with multiple mediums. By stringing together beads with inexpensive or found objects such as dice, crab claws, crucifixes, and rabbits' feet, Mapplethorpe fashioned striking chokers and long, talisman-like chains that he wore stacked and also gifted to his friends and collaborators. Though Mapplethorpe's life was cut short by AIDS in 1989, the primeval punk aesthetic of his handmade jewelry pieces, which were immortalized in now-iconic snapshots of the artist with the musician Patti Smith, influenced other creatives. One such maker is the Italian designer Gaia Repossi, who in collaboration with the Robert Mapplethorpe Foundation launched *Repossi / Robert Mapplethorpe* in 2021, a capsule of fine jewelry inspired by Mapplethorpe's work. Riffing on the Americana tropes found in Mapplethorpe's practice, Repossi's collection traded his plastic and common materials for precious metals and diamonds, a sparkling tribute to a visionary mind gone too soon.

Marchak

Marchak
est. Kyiv, Ukraine, 1878

Three-strand necklace with turquoise and lapis lazuli beads and a central oval lapis lazuli plaque, accented by an engraved turquoise and enamel clasp set in gold, early 20th century.

If the luminous still-life paintings of Impressionism could metamorphose into jewels, they would look rather like the vibrantly colored, nature-inspired creations of design house Marchak. Born in 1854 into a Ukrainian Jewish family, Joseph Marchak became an apprentice in a jewelry workshop at age fourteen. Ten years later, with a hundred-ruble dowry from his young wife and money earned from pawning his clothing, he handcrafted his first item—a simple gold chain so exquisitely executed that it revealed Marchak's remarkable potential. Marchak became known as the Cartier of Kyiv, and the high society of the city, then at the height of its grandeur, flocked to Joseph's workshop to commission jewels that were the talk of the glittering ballrooms of the Russian elite before the Russian Revolution in 1917 ended the house's glory. In stark contrast to the decadent style of Fabergé (see p.101), Marchak's jewels in buttery yellow gold juxtaposed refined gems with semiprecious stones, and unusual materials pulsated with the charm of the vast Ukrainian countryside. After Joseph's death, the family fled to Paris, and his youngest son, Alexander, opened a shop near the Place Vendôme in 1920. Working with designer Alexander Diringer, through 1957, and then Jacques Verger, the House of Marchak was reinvigorated, creating luxe, colorful jewels for the American market.

Marie Antoinette

Marie Antoinette, Queen of France
b. Vienna, Austria, 1755
d. Paris, France, 1793

Portrait of Queen Marie Antoinette of France by an unknown artist, after Jean-Baptiste André Gautier d'Agoty, c. 1775.

The ill-fated Austrian-born French queen Marie Antoinette was undoubtedly one of the greatest jewelry collectors of all time, so much so that it was written into her marriage contract that she was to receive 500,000 francs' worth of jewelry from the French royal family and the same amount from her Austrian family. In reality, she was given many times more than that by her husband's grandfather, King Louis XV. Portraits of the queen show her bedecked with sumptuous suites of diamonds and pearls, often woven throughout her extravagant wigs or stitched onto her court dresses. In 1785 Marie Antoinette was at the heart of the Affair of the Diamond Necklace scandal in which a comtesse impersonating the queen absconded with a lavish necklace of nearly 650 diamonds weighing almost 2,800 carats. Extraordinarily, many of Marie Antoinette's jewels survived the French Revolution, having been smuggled out of the Tuileries Palace in Paris, where she was imprisoned, and eventually being passed on to Marie Antoinette's sole surviving child, Marie-Thérèse Charlotte of France. Items that have appeared at auction since include a necklace of 331 natural pearls and an enormous drop-shaped natural pearl and diamond pendant that sold at Sotheby's in 2018 for $36 million—a new auction record for a natural pearl (see p.267).

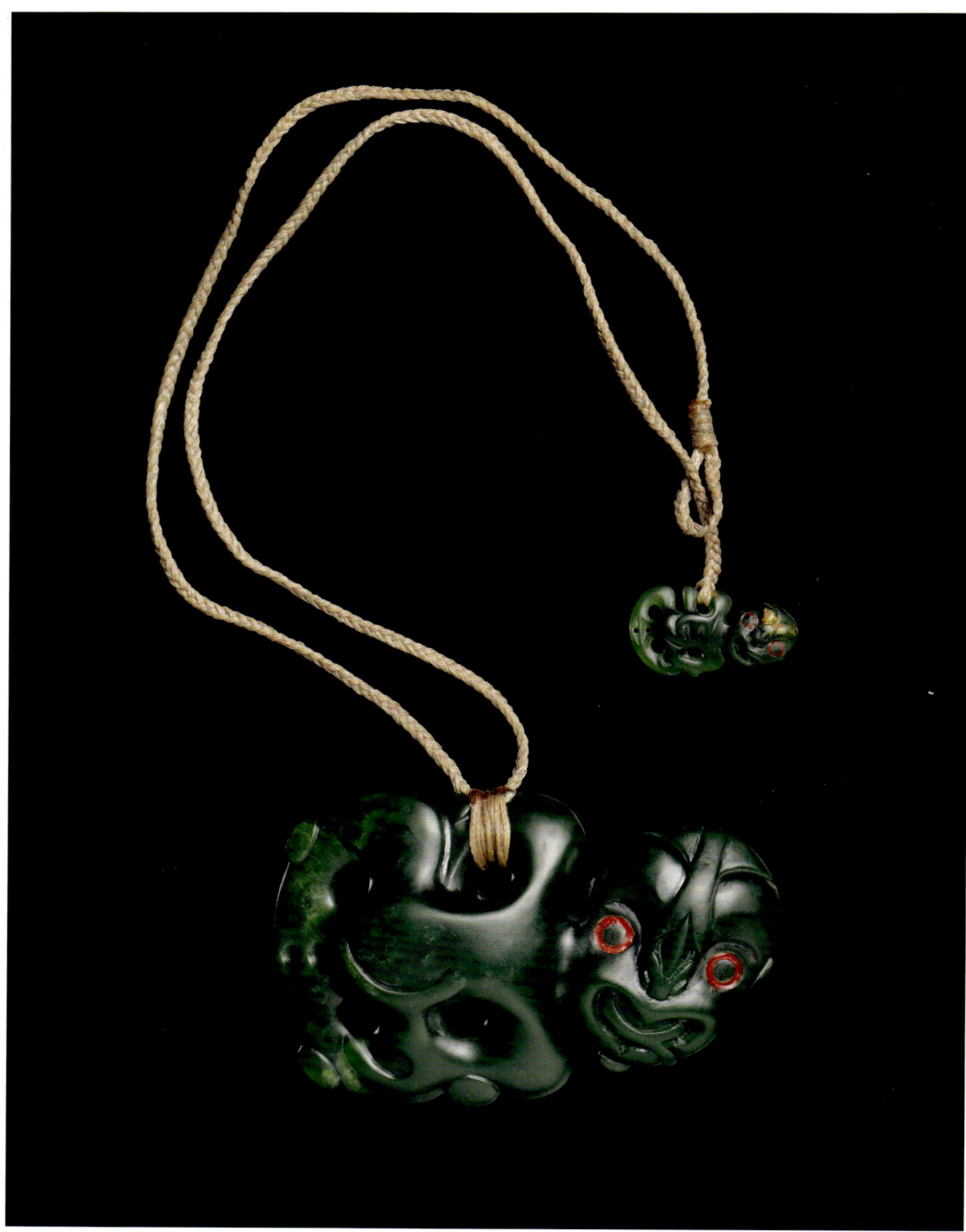

Joel Marsters

Joel Marsters
b. Rotorua, New Zealand, 1990

Makan pounamu amulet gifted to Makau Ariki Atawhai, wife of Kiingi Tuheitia, former Māori King, 2024.

Photograph by Maarten Holl, Te Papa.

Based in Rotorua, New Zealand, traditional Māori carver Joel Marsters is known globally through his social media handle @manapounamu—a variation of his grandfather's name but also a portmanteau of two Māori words meaning "prestige" or "status" and "green stone." After attending the New Zealand Māori Arts & Crafts Institute in Rotorua, Marsters studied at Te Takapū o Rotowhio (the National Stone and Bone Carving School) under master carver Lewis Gardiner, whom he works with today at Rākai Jade. Since graduating in 2013, Marsters has focused largely on *hei tiki*, the traditional form of a worn pendant considered a *taonga* (treasure) to Māori. He sees his work as a form of healing, connecting people to their spirituality, and he harbors a deep understanding and reverence for traditional forms, as well as the spiritual bond between both the *tiki* and the materials they're carved from. Marsters primarily works in pounamu—a hard, green-hued stone native to New Zealand and culturally important to Māori, also called nephrite jade—but has created pieces with other indigenous materials as well, from serpentine to whale bone and *paua* (abalone) shell. As in early times, when *hei tiki* were given names as if they were individuals, Marsters names all his carvings, and he strives to find a connection between the wearer and himself regardless of their backgrounds.

Hannah Martin

Hannah Martin
b. Yorkshire, England, 1980

Jehnny Beth wears rings from the 2020 *A New Act of Rebellion* collection (clockwise from top left): *Pierced Armor Ring* in 18-karat yellow, rose, and white gold; *Pierced Stone Ring* in 18-karat yellow gold with malachite; *Rebel Bolt Ring* in 18-karat yellow gold; and *Unchained Ring* in 18-karat yellow and white gold.

Photograph by Anthony Byrne.

"The experience of live music feeds my creative soul," proclaims the London-based jeweler Hannah Martin, who merges a punk-infused, rock 'n' roll approach with precious materials and fastidious craftsmanship. Having graduated in jewelry design from Central Saint Martins in 2005, she worked briefly at Cartier (see p.54) before launching her eponymous brand. She explores themes of sensuality, gender, and rebellion in tactile, androgynous jewelry. "My design aesthetic is highly sensual—I want you to want to touch the pieces, to feel something when you wear them," she says. There's a voluptuousness to pieces that might at first appear tough, such as the *New Rebel Bolt* bangle, whose carved malachite shackle is held in place by fluid curves of gold; or the *Spur* ring—a sharp, smooth arc of gold that's as enticing as it is menacing. In 2023 Martin launched Hannah Martin Pierced, with a range of solid-gold jewelry designed to elevate the piercing experience, informed by her own everyday look. That same year, she collaborated with Applied Art Forms, Coldplay bassist Guy Berryman's fashion label, resulting in styles from a razor wristband and dog tag pendant to safety pin and skull earrings. Her tenth collection, *The Perfect Drug*, released in 2024, is a punk riff on Constantin Brâncuși sculptures, Man Ray photography (see p.180), and the queer erotic art of Tom of Finland.

Hedy Martinelli

Hedy Martinelli
b. Zagreb, Croatia, 1931

Antique silver mesh cuff with buckle made of golden vintage element, and brown and white diamonds, 2014.

Hedy Martinelli jewelry represents three generations of women creating modern, eclectic pieces for more than fifty years. Known for organic forms, at times with a medieval touch, the company's designs combine traditional precious materials with unusual, often repurposed ones. The journey of Hedy herself began in former Yugoslavia, where her grandmother and mother were gem and jewelry dealers. After marrying Vincenzo Martinelli and settling in Rome, she opened a jewelry boutique in 1975, initially specializing in Art Deco designs. Over time, Hedy shifted from dealing in period jewels to creating unique pieces, combining vintage items with repurposed materials, such as iron mesh from ancient armor or antique silver mesh evening bags transformed into tubular chains. A pioneer in recycling and repurposing, Hedy introduced black as a key color for her mounts, using burnished iron, steel, silver, and gold to tone down her large designs, making them wearable from morning to night. Today, Hedy's daughter Francesca and granddaughter Livia Mimosa Fazioli have joined the company, which creates approximately one hundred unique pieces annually. Livia expanded the brand in 2018 with Seliti by Hedy Martinelli, a line of serial handcrafted silver and gold jewels that maintain a sculptural, organic quality while also ensuring they are light, wearable, and more accessible.

Mary of Teck

Mary of Teck, Queen
of the United Kingdom
b. London, England, 1867
d. London, England, 1953

Queen Mary wearing the *County of Surrey Tiara*, an eleven-row pearl choker with diamond spacers, a diamond stomacher given to her by the Maharaja of Kapurthala for her wedding in 1893, a diamond leaf brooch, and a floral diamond bracelet, 1901.

The British Royal Family's most forward-thinking collector, Mary of Teck wed the future King-Emperor George V in 1893. As queen of the United Kingdom and the British dominions, and also the empress of India, she amassed a trove of legendary gemstones and proved to be a visionary jewelry enthusiast, unafraid of renovating important pieces to suit contemporary tastes. Many significant stones were gifted to her, such as the 530.2-carat Cullinan I diamond and the 317.4-carat Cullinan II diamond, which were presented by the High Commissioner for Southern Africa in 1910 and were set into the *Sovereign's Crown* and *Imperial State Crown*, respectively. Both diamonds are still part of the Coronation Regalia today. She inherited other jewels also, such as the Cullinan VI diamond, which she received from her mother-in-law, Queen Alexandra (see p.18), and wore as a pendant with Cullinan VIII. Queen Mary also patronized esteemed jewelers and estate sales, exhibiting a flair for how to style jewels creatively and demanding both transformability and versatility from her pieces. Her *kokoshnik*-style *Fringe Tiara*—created in 1919 from a diamond necklace gifted to her by Queen Victoria (see p.301)—could either be worn as a headpiece or a necklace. It was bequeathed to Elizabeth II, along with the majority of Queen Mary's jewelry collection, in 1953 (see p.97).

Desiree Mattsson

Desiree Mattsson
b. Northern Norway

Leomie Anderson displays a yellow diamond ring and makeup by Pat McGrath, *British Vogue*, December 2017.

Photograph by Desiree Mattsson.

The cinematic, Gothic noir style manifested by photographer Desiree Mattsson in the photoshoot of Edward Enninful's iconic first *British Vogue* issue in December 2017 was breathtaking in its intensity. Rich in deep color, the juicy yellow diamond ring perched between lips iced in red crystals by Pat McGrath was a world apart from the windswept wilds of the Lofoten Islands in northern Norway, where Mattsson grew up. She was given her first camera at nine years old, and despite not knowing how it worked at first, she went outside into the snow, and her creative self was born. First emerged black-and-white portraits using natural light inspired by the work of Peter Lindbergh. Then a model agent nudged her into fashion and beauty, where she compiled her own team and her dramatic evolution began. *Vogue* Germany licensed one of her photos in 2015, and the late Hervé Léger asked her to shoot his 2017 *Cruise Collection* in Paris. Fashion covers for *Harper's Bazaar*, *Elle*, and numerous international editions of *Vogue* followed, and jewels by Louis Vuitton, Bulgari, and Cartier (see pp.19, 46, 54) have glistened seductively in the thousands of striking images she has produced, all in her signature style of bold contrasts whether captured in black and white or vivid color.

Satta Matturi

Satta Matturi
b. Kono, Sierra Leone, 1976

Nomoli Totem Collector's Edition earrings cast in single-mine-origin 18-karat yellow gold with carved lapis lazuli and brilliant-cut diamonds, 2024.

Photograph by Turi Lovik Kirknes.

Africa, with its myriad cultures and historic ornaments, provides endless inspiration for Sierra Leone–born and UK-raised jewelry designer Satta Matturi. She launched her brand, Matturi Fine Jewellery, in 2015 after nearly two decades working in rough diamond sales and valuations for De Beers, where her father had also been employed (see p.80). Her contemporary designs blend traditional African motifs with modernism, evident in her handcrafted *Nomoli Totem Masks*. A regular feature in her collections, the Nomoli totems combine colorful stones, such as rubellite and green onyx, with single-mine-origin gold and natural diamonds to evoke spiritual beings and function as a tribute to West African ceremonial masquerades. Adorned with custom-cut ornamental stone spikes or fringed gold headdresses, her *Whispers of Meroë* collection was created in homage to the ancient Egyptian queens of the Nubian kingdom of Kush, each piece stamped with the Eye of Horus. Matturi is part of the modern-day African Art Deco movement and continues to travel extensively between Africa and Europe. In 2022 Matturi was appointed to the executive board of the Responsible Jewellery Council, and the following year, she was lauded by the Initiatives in Art and Culture (IAC) for her outstanding contribution to the gold and diamond industries.

Jessica McCormack

Jessica McCormack
b. Christchurch, New Zealand, 1979

Zoë Kravitz wears jewels from the Jessica McCormack *Day Diamonds* collection, 2024.

Photograph by Campbell Hooper.

London-based, New Zealand–born jewelry designer Jessica McCormack developed a love for jewels thanks to her auctioneer father, but it was working in the jewelry department at Sotheby's in London that set her on the path to launch her eponymous brand in 2008. Opening her now-famous London townhouse in Mayfair's Carlos Place in 2013, McCormack has garnered a cult following of major Hollywood stars and global royalty—including Charlize Theron, Victoria Beckham, Meghan Markle, and Zendaya (see p.311)—with her antique-inspired, contemporary pieces that find the ideal balance between luxurious and wearable. Her signature use of the button-back setting, which originated in the Georgian era, encases the back of each diamond in gold to add depth and increased sparkle. Describing her in-house workshop at Carlos Place as "the beating heart of the business," McCormack champions craftsmanship, having steadily built up an atelier staffed by highly skilled goldsmiths, setters, and polishers all devoted to their craft. Hit collections have been inspired by everything from woven friendship bracelets and Barbara Hepworth sculptures to cult films such as *The Lost Boys* and the humble sailor's knot, but all are imagined in McCormack's inimitable style with diamonds, gemstones, and 18-karat gold.

Margot McKinney

Margot McKinney
b. Toowoomba, Australia, 1959

Atoll Collier, featuring thirteen Australian boulder opals weighing a total of 253.16 carats, Tahitian pistachio green pearls, green and blue tourmalines, zircons, and demantoids.

Inspired by the natural landscape of her native Australia, Margot McKinney's jewels are unapologetically voluminous. Continually drawn to the allure of big gems—boulder and black opals, as well as sumptuous baroque and round pearls—she celebrates her muses: her incredible collectors who revel in covetable pieces that pack a punch. At her atelier in Brisbane and with gem-cutters in Bangkok, Thailand, and Idar Oberstein, Germany, McKinney translates these remarkable gems into jewelry that bursts with color. She works with a variety of craftsmen and -women to experiment with endless textures and shapes, primarily worked in gold and, more recently, titanium. A fourth-generation jeweler and gemologist, she has forged relationships with the finest gem-cutters in the world, allowing her first dibs on enticing choices for the centerpieces of her works. McKinney also works closely with sustainable and independent pearl farmers, such as the fifth-generation Aji Ellies in East Arnhem Land, as well as pearl stringers in Brisbane. Executed with impeccable finesse, the jewels are often offset by carefully considered stones and vivid contrasting colors that reflect McKinney's world: the vibrant blues of the Australian coast; emerald green rainforests; and flashes of pink tourmaline, yellow sapphire, and amethyst found in the region's abundant flora and fauna.

Evalyn Walsh McLean

Evalyn Walsh McLean
b. Leadville, Colorado,
United States, 1886
d. Washington, DC,
United States, 1947

Evalyn Walsh McLean wearing the Hope Diamond on a necklace and the Star of the East in a feathered aigrette, Washington, DC, c. 1914.

Society heiress Evalyn Walsh McLean was one of the greatest jewelry collectors of the early twentieth century. The daughter of an Irish prospector who discovered one of America's largest gold mines, she was born Evalyn Walsh in 1886 and took her husband's name in 1908 after eloping with newspaper publishing heir Edward Beale McLean. A generous and well-connected hostess, she threw magnificent soirées for her powerful circle, which included presidential families such as the Hardings, Tafts, and Coolidges. She was immortalized by Cole Porter in his song "Anything Goes" (see p.228) and became a best-selling author in her thirties with her autobiography, *Father Struck It Rich*. McLean was the last and longest owner of the infamous 45.52-carat Hope Diamond, which she and her husband acquired from Pierre Cartier in 1911 for $180,000—more than $5 million today (see pp.54, 279). By that time she was already the owner of the 94.78-carat pear-shaped Star of the East diamond, also purchased from Pierre Cartier and famously smuggled back to the United States to avoid exorbitant customs fees. In perhaps her most famous portrait, taken around 1914 in Washington, DC, McLean can be seen wearing both the Star of the East in a feathered aigrette and the Hope Diamond on a chain, together with ropes of pearls.

Mellerio dits Meller

Mellerio dits Meller
est. Paris, France, 1613

Two-piece mistletoe wedding tiara in platinum with diamonds and natural pearls, 1905.

The world's oldest family-run jewelry house, Mellerio dits Meller has, for more than four hundred years and fifteen generations, supplied royalty from Europe to Asia with serious jewels that smile rather than shout. A family of Italian goldsmiths, the Mellerios migrated to Paris in the early sixteenth century, but it was in 1613 that they established their company after being granted privileges by Queen Marie de Médici to serve the court after foiling an attempt to assassinate her son Louis XIII. The jewelers thrived, and in 1777 began trading in Versailles, catching the eye of Marie Antoinette (see p.183) and, after the revolution, Empress Josephine. Presciently, in 1815 Mellerio became the first jeweler to open in the Place Vendôme, supplying royal jewels to Empress Eugénie (see p.100) and queens from Spain to Russia. The maison has remained there ever since, housing its collection of gems and its archive of hundreds of thousands of sketches and records dating back to its founding. Mellerio's characteristic ovoid diamond cut, which originated with Marie de Médici, was revitalized in the 1950s through collaborations with couturiers Balmain and Balenciaga, with gems set in abstract, hand-textured gold. Today, the company is still in family hands, mixing delicate, ornate goldwork and exemplary colored stones with a depth of seductive style still sought after in the modern world.

Messika

Messika
est. Paris, France, 2005

Rose Chalme wears the Messika *Fiery* collection in white gold with pear-shaped diamonds, 2024.

Photograph by Isabelle Bonjean.

Among the grand storied jewelry maisons of Paris sits a young disruptor, Messika. Founded in 2005 by Valérie Messika, the brand applies modern, urban, and edgy design to white diamonds. Valérie learned everything about the stones from her father, André, one of France's most respected diamond merchants. Rather than follow him into his business, Valérie knew she wanted to do something different, to fill a niche between the heritage jewelers and inexpensive brands. André gave her his blessing, albeit urging her only to work with diamonds. In Valérie's eyes, diamonds had become too sacred, and her vision was to put diamonds on the skin of women as if they were a tattoo, to make them an easy and constant companion. By nature a minimalist with a love of symmetry, Valérie introduced ideas such as the *Move* collections, where brilliant-cut diamonds playfully glide along hidden rails set in oval panels. She is agile with her ideas, able to hone in on a trend but create original jewels that are both modern and timeless. The brand moved into the high jewelry sphere in 2013, and since 2020 has straddled the worlds of art and fashion, presenting collections during Paris fashion week, as well as collaborating with supermodel-turned-entrepreneur Kate Moss. With every new creation, Messika gives the diamond a new and modern language.

Mikimoto

Mikimoto
est. Toba, Japan, 1893

Yuto Ebihara wears *The Bows* high jewelry necklace in white gold with Akoya cultured pearls, diamonds, and a 53.17-carat sea green tourmaline, 2024.

Photograph by Koichiro Doi.

The eldest son of a noodle maker, Kokichi Mikimoto was born in 1858 in the seaside town of Toba in southeastern Japan. Observing the declining supply of natural pearls brought in by local pearl divers, he and his wife, Ume, established their own oyster farm in the Shinmei Inlet of Ago Bay in 1888 and began experiments to produce cultured pearls. Despite having no scientific training, they successfully cultivated the world's first semispherical pearl in 1893, for which Mikimoto received a patent in 1896. This was followed by the arrival of the first spherical cultured pearl in 1905 and the opening of Mikimoto's debut international boutique in London in 1913. A few years later, when a London newspaper published an attack describing cultured pearls as fraudulent, Mikimoto launched a legal battle in Paris to protect his public standing. Emerging victorious, Mikimoto and his pearls gained a worldwide reputation for excellence, embellished by Mikimoto's dazzling, Art Deco–infused designs. Due to Mikimoto's efforts, Japan became renowned as the source of the finest cultured Akoya pearls, producing $16 billion worth of these nacreous gems during peak years. Mikimoto's brand remains celebrated for its elegant creations, which have earned it membership in the Fédération de la Haute Couture et de la Mode in Paris.

Monies

Monies
est. Copenhagen, Denmark, 1973

A model wears Monies copper bracelets, prehistoric ammonite bangle, and rings with rutilated quartz, garden quartz, and brown lip mother-of-pearl, 2013.

Photograph by Morten Bjarnhof.

As an avant-garde jewelry house with a five-decades-long legacy, Monies blurs the line between jewelry and fine art. Founded by the Danish husband-and-wife duo Nikolai and Gerda Monies in Copenhagen in 1973, Monies is renowned for its unconventional compositions and irreverent spirit. Traditionally trained as goldsmiths, Gerda went to work for Whiting & Davis in Boston—originators of the iconic 1920s flapper mesh purses—while Nikolai focused on design, working for Ettore Sottsass (see p.268) and Mario Bellini in Milan. Upon their return to Copenhagen, Nikolai and Gerda embarked on their first creations together, crafting bold pieces with their love for raw, unmanipulated, and often humble materials from the natural world. With handmade one-of-a-kind pieces, whether a statement necklace of pristine, jagged mountain crystal with a toggle clasp or a headpiece featuring prehistoric sharks' teeth—both made by Gerda to celebrate Monies's fiftieth anniversary—the Monies aesthetic is timeless, pure to its source material, and uncompromising in design. Monies is now led by Nikolai and Gerda's son, Karl, as the house's creative director, and each piece—including bracelets, necklaces, and earrings of baroque and freshwater pearls, amber, rare ammonites, and bog oak—continues to be procured, designed, and assembled with a deep reverence for the materials.

Jesse Monongya

Jesse Monongya
b. Phoenix, Arizona,
United States, 1952
d. Scottsdale, Arizona,
United States, 2024

Shooting Star cuff in 18-karat gold with Lander Blue turquoise, coral, lapis lazuli, and diamond, 1998.

Photograph by Hee Jin Kang.

Jesse Monongya, a master jeweler of Navajo and Hopi heritage, is celebrated for his breathtaking inlay work, which blends Native American traditions with contemporary elegance and craft. Born in Arizona in 1952, Monongya was raised by his Navajo grandmother in Two Grey Hills, New Mexico. In 1974 he began to work with his father and mentor, Preston Monongye, a legendary jewelry designer. Monongya's early education in metalworking—and the opportunity to observe artist jewelers such as Lee Yazzie, Dennis Edaakie, and Charles Loloma (see p.173)—propelled him to create jewelry that embodied the beauty of his cultural heritage and the vastness of the natural and spiritual worlds. Monongya's aesthetic drew on themes including constellations and the cosmos, and the sacred landscapes of the Southwest. His iconic pieces feature intricate inlays using materials such as turquoise, lapis lazuli, opal, and coral, often combined with sterling silver and gold. His most distinctive works feature his night sky designs inlaid into the silhouette of a bear, symbolizing strength and power, among other forms. Monongya created award-winning pendants, necklaces, bracelets, earrings, and bolo ties, with each piece telling a unique story, and honoring Indigenous artistry while pushing the boundaries of contemporary design.

Marilyn Monroe

Marilyn Monroe
(Norma Jeane Mortenson)
b. Los Angeles, California, United States, 1926
d. Los Angeles, California, United States, 1962

Marilyn Monroe at the premiere of *Some Like It Hot* in Times Square, New York, 1959.

Photograph by Bob Henriques.

Dressed in a hot pink satin gown and dripping in jewels, Marilyn Monroe sang "Diamonds Are a Girl's Best Friend" in the classic 1953 film *Gentlemen Prefer Blondes*, professing her penchant for luxury brands such as Cartier, Harry Winston, and Tiffany & Co. (see pp.54, 132, 283). In truth, the actress wore rhinestone creations for the role, many designed by Joseff of Hollywood, the industry's premier costume jeweler during cinema's Golden Era. However, one extraordinary natural stone did create its own special effects off-screen: Marilyn wore the 24-carat Moon of Baroda pear-shaped yellow diamond for the film's promotional tour, presented for the first time on a simple leather cord, marking a rebellious move in twentieth-century jewelry styling. Marilyn was not a material girl herself, opting for mainly costume jewelry in her private life. She did love pearls and was particularly fond of her Mikimoto necklace from Japan (see p.195), a gift from her second husband, the baseball legend Joe DiMaggio. Secured by a diamond clasp, the choker-style strand of forty-four Akoya cultured pearls became Marilyn's signature accessory, worn long after her brief marriage to DiMaggio ended. She claimed the necklace evoked "happier times," a bittersweet sentiment that underscores the transportive power of jewelry, be it a blockbuster gem or a timeless classic.

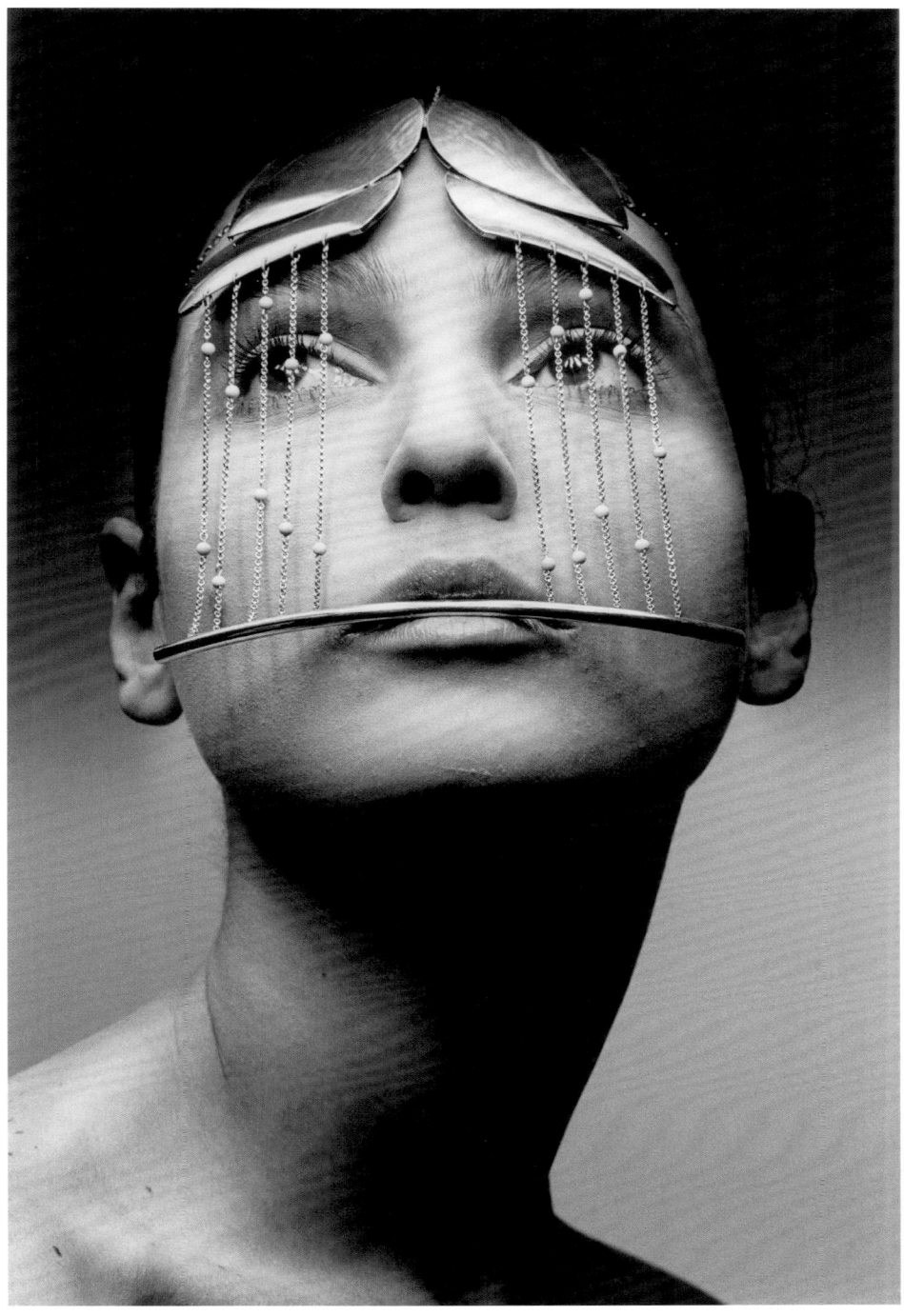

GianCarlo Montebello

GianCarlo Montebello
b. Milan, Italy, 1941
d. Milan, Italy, 2020

Jewelry by Pietro Consagra for GEM Montebello, 1969.

Photograph by Ugo Mulas.

Italian designer and craftsman GianCarlo Montebello was behind some of the most innovative artist jewelry of the late 1960s and '70s. In 1967, with his wife, Teresa Pomodoro, he founded GEM Montebello, a goldsmith workshop that produced limited-edition jewelry designed by renowned fine artists, a practice that he saw as an "informative mission" to educate the public about the art of the time. By the late 1970s, Montebello had collaborated with more than fifty artists, architects, and designers on close to two hundred editions, including Pol Bury, Lucio Fontana, Claude Lalanne, Alex Katz, Hans Richter, Niki de Saint Phalle, and Ettore Sottsass (see pp.48, 109, 160, 268). Montebello's relationship with photographer Man Ray was particularly impactful, and the two worked together until the artist's death in 1976 (see p.180). Man Ray's *Optic Topic* mask, made from gold-plated silver and inspired by the aluminum masks worn by race car drivers, was conceived in 1974 and created in a run of just one hundred pieces. Montebello shut down GEM's operations in 1978, but he continued to design jewelry under his own name throughout his life. Describing his creations as "body ornaments," Montebello largely forewent gems and instead favored highly polished stainless steel or 18-karat gold plates shaped into gauntlet-like cuffs or collars resembling delicate woven chainmail.

John Moore

John Moore
b. Leamington Spa, Warwickshire, England, 1980

Cranes Fighting in the Snow pectoral in Morphit, pigment, wood, silicone, steel, aluminum, and lacquer, 2024.

Photograph by David Myers.

John Moore's large-scale wearable sculptures dare to propel jewelry into a new dimension. Each magnificent piece is brought to life by movement on the body and in turn transforms the silhouette of the wearer. Light slides across polished surfaces, metal moves with mercurial liquidity, and color ripples with the brilliance of a butterfly wing. Echoes of primeval knowledge inform the fractal forms of natural architecture and sacred geometry in jewels reminiscent of ancient Egyptian pectorals or Amazonian tribal jewels. Ever evolving, Moore has devised multiple new techniques and pushed boundaries with his invention of Morphit. Developed over two years, Moore describes this new medium as his take on papier-mâché using acid-free, conservation-grade materials, including recycled paper fiber and adhesive—although the exact composition remains a trade secret—which he can make in a kaleidoscope of colors to be used alongside wood, resin, and metal. In recognition of his cutting-edge practice, Moore was presented with the prestigious Goldsmiths' Company Award in 2016 and 2019. In 2024 his pectoral *Cranes Fighting in the Snow* was exhibited by Didier Ltd at the Treasure House Fair in London alongside works by Salvador Dalí and Pablo Picasso (see pp.77, 87, 223), a recognition of the artistic and technical merit of a jeweler who dares to stand out and make a mark.

Alexandra Mor

Alexandra Mor
b. Haifa, Israel, 1972

One-of-a-kind curved chandelier earrings in platinum set on 18-karat yellow gold with brilliant-cut sapphires, pearls, pear-shaped Andean opals, white topaz briolettes, cushion-cut aquamarines, green-blue oval-cut cabochon tourmalines, and white diamonds.

Photograph by Russell Starr.

Crafted in New York City by master artisans, Alexandra Mor's highly sculptural gem-set designs in 18-karat gold and platinum play with shape and proportion, intensifying the subtleties that exist between form, light, and texture. Regularly captured on the red carpet worn by an A-list crowd that includes Oprah Winfrey, Lupita Nyong'o, and Naomi Watts, Mor's dynamic one-of-a-kind creations have a numinous quality that evokes a sense of vitality and strength. Juxtapositions play an important part in Mor's work: a platinum cuff composed of sinuous diamond waves is at once rhythmic and ruptured like shattered glass; a platinum ring with a 33-carat Asscher-cut amethyst is cradled by diamond-set "tendrils" that extend from the shank, contrasting intense color with a more delicate icy shimmer. Committed to craftsmanship and the preservation of the natural world, Mor uses sustainably sourced metals and conflict-free gemstones. She also pushes the boundaries of luxury design by experimenting with unexpected materials: Having moved to Bali with her family in 2016, she discovered the tagua seed, which, when carved, is almost identical to ivory. Collaborating with Balinese artisans, Mor combines this natural ivory alternative with precious stones, South Sea pearls, and traditional gold filigree to create enigmatic jewels rich in detail and ancient symbolism.

Robert Lee Morris

Robert Lee Morris
b. Nuremberg, Germany, 1947

A model wears jewelry and body armor by Robert Lee Morris, 1987.

Photograph by Susan Wood.

Artist jeweler Robert Lee Morris burst onto the New York cultural scene in 1977 when he opened his gallery, Artwear, in Manhattan, showcasing the work of more than four hundred artist jewelers and his own visionary pieces. Having been discovered by gallerist Joan Sonnabend in 1971, Morris's pieces were first displayed alongside those of Alexander Calder, Man Ray, and Pablo Picasso (see pp.50, 180, 223). However, it was the opening of his own space that led Morris to collaborate with Donna Karan, for whom he designed thirty-seven collections. He also created pieces for Karl Lagerfeld, Kansai Yamamoto, Geoffrey Beene, and Michael Kors, and his work has appeared on the cover of *Vogue* magazine and on countless celebrities. Creating armorlike breastplates, warrior headdresses, metal finger talons, and surreal brass goggles, Morris's work is highly sculptural and often figure-hugging, acting as an oversize extension of the body itself. Working with silver, gold-plated brass, onyx, carnelian, copper, and other materials, Morris creates everything from belts and pins to large-scale chandeliers and verdigris sculptures. His virtual studio gallery today sells his own impressive body sculpture alongside that of other artist jewelers, and Morris continues to tell his extraordinary story through his vast archives and ongoing passion for the medium.

Moussaieff

Moussaieff
est. Bukhara, Uzbekistan, c. 1850s

High-jewelry bangle with 130.05 carats of white diamonds, including 105 carats that are D color and internally flawless, and 17.07 carats of pink diamonds.

With a family name that has become synonymous with outrageously large and high-quality diamonds, Moussaieff can trace its legacy as gem dealers back to mid-nineteenth-century Bukhara, in what is now Uzbekistan. Here, they began as pearl and stone merchants along the Silk Road, a network of trading routes that bridged the Eastern and Western worlds for roughly 1,500 years. Shlomo Moussaieff, the family's forebear, who had a deep passion for gemstones, ventured into the Persian Gulf to source natural pearls directly from divers, which he traded for gemstones from India. The next generation saw his son, Remo, establish himself as a gem dealer in Paris, supplying the master jewelers of the Belle Époque throughout the 1920s. The modern House of Moussaieff took form in 1963 when the founder's grandson, also called Shlomo, and his wife, Alisa, opened a boutique at the exclusive Hilton hotel on Park Lane in London. The couple solidified the brand's reputation as the go-to *haute joaillerie* powerhouse, drawing customers from red-carpet Hollywood to Middle Eastern royalty. Moussaieff is known for dealing in rare Golconda diamonds, significant natural pearls, and magnificent colored gemstones, and the house's own collection famously includes the legendary Moussaieff Red—at 5.11 carats, it is the largest natural fancy red diamond recorded.

Juliette Moutard

Juliette Moutard
b. Maisons-Laffitte, France, 1900
d. Oise, France, 1990

Starfish brooch designed by Juliette Moutard for Boivin in 18-karat gold with 71 collet-set cabochon rubies, 665 pavé-set amethysts, and fully articulated arms, 1935 (fabricated 1937).

Succeeding jewelry designer Suzanne Belperron at the maison of René Boivin in 1933, Juliette Moutard worked closely with René's widow, Jeanne Boivin, in translating her daring ideas into jewelry (see pp.28, 35). While most of their peers were working in the Art Deco style, Boivin produced abstract, figurative, and naturalistic designs. Botany was a passion for Moutard, who in 1944 created one of Boivin's famous floral designs, the foxgloves. She also proved adept at animals, in line with the postwar craze for big cats, producing articulated lion and tiger brooches, and adding horses, elephants, and chameleons that could rotate colors with the push of their gem tongues. Her artistry notably came to the fore with a ruby-set starfish brooch designed in 1937 for actor Claudette Colbert. Talented and highly educated, Moutard grew up outside Paris and attended both the École Nationale Supérieure des Arts Décoratifs and École de la Bijouterie. In the 1920s, after receiving her degrees, she joined Verger Frères, a clockmaker and workshop producing jewelry for the major houses—Mauboussin, Cartier, Van Cleef & Arpels—as well as designing jewels for them to sell (see pp.54, 291). While much of Moutard's decade of work there was undocumented, she was likely to have been part of Verger's creative team, which prepared her for her lifelong career at Boivin, where she remained until 1970.

Moza bint Nasser

Moza bint Nasser, Sheikha of Qatar
b. Al Khor, Qatar, 1959

Sheikha Moza bint Nasser wears a diamond brooch and earrings while attending the Bastille Day ceremony in Paris, 2007.

Photograph by Clemens Bilan.

Sheikha Moza bint Nasser has initiated a string of social reforms across Qatar in her role as chairperson of the Qatar Foundation for Education, Science, and Community Development, devoting herself to improving health and education for young people and launching Education Above All (EAA) to ensure a quality education for hard-to-reach children in poverty-stricken areas. When accompanying her husband, the former Emir of Qatar, to official functions, Sheikha Moza became celebrated for her style, encompassing modern fashion while respecting the modest codes of the region. Her sartorial flair is complemented by an extensive jewelry collection, which includes pieces from Bulgari, Chaumet, and Graff, among others (see pp.46, 63, 127). Highlights include an extensive portfolio from Cartier (see p.54), from a spectacular diamond snake *Eternity* necklace to loops of pearls, an oversize *Hamsa* necklace, and a *Tutti Frutti* necklace with a central 67.7-carat engraved ruby pendant from Mozambique. They join exceptional pieces in her archive, notably Buccellati earrings; a custom gold, diamond, and mother-of-pearl Silvia Furmanovich marquetry belt; a Van Cleef & Arpels diamond rose brooch; and a pair of Chaumet's diamond wings brooches (which also could be worn on an aigrette), closely set in diamonds and streaked with blue enamel (see pp.45, 111, 291).

Mr. T

Mr. T (Laurence Tureaud)
b. Chicago, Illinois,
United States, 1952

Mr. T at home in Los Angeles, 1991.

Photograph by Eric Robert.

Having worked as a bouncer, trained as a professional wrestler, and served in the US military, Mr. T first stepped into the limelight as boxer Clubber Lang in the 1982 film *Rocky III* and swiftly became a star and a household name thanks to cult TV series *The A Team*. As Sgt. B. A. Baracus, he stole the show with his tough-guy attitude, unforgettable catchphrases (including the much repeated "I pity the fool"), and ultra-bling aesthetic, which he carried into his personal style. Bedecked with gold jewelry—giant sovereign rings, hoop earrings, layered link bracelets, cascades of hefty necklaces—Mr. T lifted the era's hip-hop style to new heights. A form of armor as well as ornamentation, Mr. T's maximalist look was also a statement against social marginalization: his chains were a symbol of the racial oppression endured by his African ancestors, and his signature Mohawk was inspired by the Mandinka warriors of West Africa. Indeed, even his name was a form of activism. Growing up in the Robert Taylor Homes on Chicago's South Side, he had seen white people routinely address his father, uncles, and other Black men as "boy," so he chose "Mister" to force a sign of respect from those who addressed him. Unapologetically ostentatious, he challenged entrenched power structures by using gold jewelry as a proud statement of his African American identity and heritage.

Shinji Nakaba

Shinji Nakaba
b. Kanagawa, Japan, 1950

Hand-carved pearl skulls and *Vanitas* ring.

Photograph by Setsuko Nishikawa.

Best known for his delicately sculpted pearls, Japanese artist Shinji Nakaba carves these tiny organic forms into highly detailed skulls, beatific faces that evoke friendly moons, cherubic baby heads, and eyes with their lashes deftly drawn in black ink. The miniature sculptures are then placed on gold wire as solitaire rings, strung together as necklaces, or placed on hooks to be worn as pendants. Having dabbled in fashion and shoe design as well as hairdressing, Nakaba switched to jewelry in 1974 at the age of twenty-four, after taking a basic jewelry-making course in Tokyo. He then went on to develop the distinctive glyptic art—a specific technique of sculpting used in crafting jewelry—for which he is now a widely recognized expert. While Nakaba favors pearls, he works in a variety of other mediums, including stone, shell, upcycled aluminum, precious gemstones, and metals, seeing all materials as equal. Now based in Hashimoto, Japan, Nakaba has a strong tendency toward human forms, and he shapes intricate and delicate fingers, hands, lips, and faces reminiscent of the way ancient artists carved cameos. He won the Loewe Foundation Craft Prize in 2023, and his work is included in the collections of the Museum of Fine Arts Boston, the Montreal Museum of Fine Arts, and the National Museum of Western Art in Tokyo, among many others.

Johnny Nelson

Johnny Nelson (Johnel Jamison) b. Reading, England, 1988

Aurora Anthony wears the Johnny Nelson *4 Fingers of Def* and *Her Freedom* four-finger rings, 2020.

Photograph by Danita Bethea.

From Martin Luther King Jr. and Frederick Douglass to Harriet Tubman and Sojourner Truth, the faces of Black icons are expertly rendered in gold and silver on rings, pendants, and earrings by Johnny Nelson. Born in Reading, England, and raised in Brooklyn, Nelson was profoundly influenced by his artistic parents—his father was a musician, and his always-fashionable mother taught him to make jewelry. He became a touring musician and in 2014 he turned to jewelry looking for a way to enhance and amplify his stage presence. Nelson soon began crafting pieces that reflected his identity, cultural heritage, and life experiences, with his breakthrough coming in the form of his now-iconic four-finger ring in a hip-hop-inspired interpretation of Mount Rushmore. More faces followed, each a significant Black figure in history or music, sparking a collaboration with fashion brand Pyer Moss in 2019. Other collections centered around self-empowerment through precious stones and talismans, such as the *All Power Fist* motif, inspired by the Black Panther Party. "Incorporating Black history into my art is crucial because it honors the rich cultural legacy and resilience of my ancestors. I believe it's essential to celebrate and reflect on our shared histories, allowing my work to serve as a platform for storytelling and empowerment within the Black community," says Nelson.

Louise Nevelson

Louise Nevelson
b. Kyiv, Ukraine, 1899
d. New York, New York,
United States, 1988

Louise Nevelson wearing her black painted-wood jewelry, c. 1965.

Photograph by Ugo Mulas.

Renowned for her towering monochromatic sculptures crafted from found objects and scavenged wood, Louise Nevelson's Gothic-infused minimalism was in direct contrast to her unabashedly flamboyant personal style. In her later years especially, she had a predilection for patterned kaftans, long headscarves, wide-brimmed hats, and bold statement necklaces, which she often wore all at once. Nevelson began designing and making her own jewelry in the 1960s, taking her lead from her eclectic collages and epic wall assemblages by combining fragments of wood, stone, glass, and metal with slivers of yellow gold to form totemic-looking wearable sculptures. Her iconic 1974 *Pendant*, measuring just two inches wide, nevertheless evokes her larger work with its relieflike quality, raw texture, and interlocked forms in 18-karat gold and black painted wood. Around two hundred of Nevelson's jewels remain in private and museum collections today, although one archival piece was given a new lease on life in 2021 thanks to fashion designer Hedi Slimane, who, as part of Celine's Artist Jewelry Program, collaborated with the Louise Nevelson Foundation to reissue a large sculptural oak and metal pendant as an homage to the great artist. Nevelson famously said, "My work is delicate; it may look strong, but it is delicate. True strength is delicate. My whole life is in it."

Oscar Niemeyer

Oscar Niemeyer
b. Rio de Janeiro, Brazil, 1907
d. Rio de Janeiro, Brazil, 2012

Brasília Ring in 18-karat textured yellow gold from the *Oscar Niemeyer by HStern* collection, c. 2008.

Brazilian architect Oscar Niemeyer was instrumental in shaping modern architecture. In 1956 Juscelino Kubitschek, Brazil's newly elected president, asked Niemeyer to develop a visual language for Brasília, the new capital city. Here, the architect designed a number of civic buildings, among them the Roman Catholic Cathedral of Brasília, a hyperboloid structure made from sixteen concrete columns. A winner of the Pritzker Architecture Prize and the RIBA Royal Gold Medal, Niemeyer designed roughly six hundred projects over the course of his career, championing curves and abstract forms in his work. In addition to his architectural triumphs, Niemeyer is celebrated for his jewelry line with the firm HStern. The first HStern collection pieces were released in 2008, followed by eight more designs in 2014, two years after the architect's passing. The flora in the collection—represented as gold flowers dangling from earrings and necklaces—is hollow to honor Niemeyer's appreciation for underfilled areas. Concave domes are mirrored in the *Pampulha* ring, which sits like a crown on the wearer's finger. Other pieces, including zigzag diamond earrings and a yellow and white gold wave bracelet with diamond-encrusted edges, were inspired by the clean lines in Niemeyer's sketches, expressing his quintessential curves and sinuous forms through precious metals.

NN by NGHI

NN by NGHI
est. Brooklyn, New York,
United States, 2012

Web of Shadows self-replicating molecules mask, necklace, and sleeve, 2013.

Photograph by Frej Hedenberg.

The pursuit of beauty as an unknown alien force is a common thread running through the cutting-edge works of Nghi Nga for his brand NN by NGHI. Translated through a contemporary lens, Nga's experiences of displacement and escapism find resonance in his tactile and highly sensory works. Born in Vietnam, his family immigrated to Australia and his formative years were influenced by global subcultures. With the surf culture of Australia, the Harajuku street culture of Tokyo, and the art and music scene of New York City molding his mindscape, Nga worked as a multimedia artist and fashion photographer before turning to jewelry. The scale of his future-forward and experimental wearables has spanned from body armor and masks to delicate arachnoid rings. Humble materials—circuit board, molded leather, carved wood—alternate with silver, gold, platinum, and titanium, which are used sparsely to great effect. By utilizing honed techniques in silversmithing, texturing, hollow-form jewelry, and wax carving, Nga elevates these precious metals and uses semiprecious stones to add flourishes to his one-of-a-kind pieces. Beginning in 2022, he has collaborated with the Muzo emerald mine in Colombia, setting spectacular emeralds in a ring of textured silver and platinum feathers or space-age gold curves as he heads confidently into the high jewelry space.

The Notorious B.I.G.

The Notorious B.I.G. (Christopher Wallace)
b. Brooklyn, New York, United States, 1972
d. Los Angeles, California, United States, 1997

The Notorious B.I.G. at the Good Luck Bar, Los Feliz, Los Angeles, 1997.

Photograph by Shawn Mortensen.

Synonymous with the East Coast hip-hop scene and gangsta rap tradition, the Notorious B.I.G.—also known as Biggie Smalls—has been lauded as one of the greatest rappers of all time. Raised in Brooklyn, New York, by Jamaican parents, he crafted lyrics about the struggles he faced throughout his life and delivered them with a laid-back verve in hits such as "Big Poppa" and "Juicy." Though he only released one album during his lifetime, B.I.G.'s music, as well as his unique style, have helped shape the musical canon. One of the most recognizable pieces of hip-hop jewelry, his "Jesus piece" necklace, commissioned in a run of three from the jeweler Tito Caicedo, was carved in the image of Jesus Christ and finished with a diamond-studded crown of thorns. One of B.I.G.'s most iconic accessories, however, was made from a much cheaper material—it was a plastic crown that B.I.G. wore for a 1997 photoshoot with photographer Barron Claiborne that resulted in the now-famous portrait of the rapper, *King of New York*. The shoot took place only three days before B.I.G. was killed in a drive-by shooting in Los Angeles. The plastic crown was originally purchased for $6, but it resold for $594,750 in 2020 at Sotheby's first auction spotlighting hip-hop memorabilia (see p.267).

Nuun Jewels

Nuun Jewels
est. Paris, France, 2014

Large feather earrings in multi-colored titanium and gold set with Asprey-cut diamonds and rock crystal, from the *Asprey × Nuun Feather Collection*, 2024.

Photograph by Eugénie Martinez.

For Nourah Al Faisal, princess of the royal House of Saud, jewelry is a celebration of womanhood. She works under the name Nuun Jewels, and the designs she creates are an expression of freedom and identity beyond the bridal pieces she first constructed as a hobby from her home in Riyadh, Saudi Arabia. With Nuun, she combines Bedouin styles with graphic, geometric minimalism, having apprenticed under designer Thierry Martin in the workshops of the Place Vendôme before venturing into her own world of scattered diamonds, gold, and titanium. Inspired by jewelry pioneer Ibtisam Al Qusaiby and emboldened by a growing collector base, in 2024 she released a thirteen-piece capsule collection with Asprey London. The jewels are a reimagination of Asprey's heritage *Feather* collection, referencing the ostrich feathers from the coat of arms of the Prince of Wales in stylized, colored titanium. "We're at a time when we're only just beginning to see Saudi females on the world stage in terms of design," she says thoughtfully. "This kind of validation is really important to me." Growing up around strong, purposeful women, she has high, perfectionist expectations, and pushing Asprey's classical style forward in unconventional ways is part of that vision. Her work is an artistic exploration rather than a unit of creativity and, more broadly speaking, a living evolution of Arab modernity.

Michelle Obama

Michelle Obama
b. Chicago, Illinois,
United States, 1964

Michelle Obama in pearls at the Democratic National Convention in Denver, Colorado, 2008.

Photograph by Jeff Riedel.

As First Lady of the United States, Michelle Obama cultivated an elegant and accessible look that reflected a new style of leadership when her husband, Barack Obama, became president in 2009. For the inaugural ball, she commissioned a set of jewels by American designer Loree Rodkin, including the *Celestial* diamond earrings, which the jeweler later said represented hope for the future. By day, Michelle Obama can be seen in timeless pearls, brooches, or understated gold hoops; for grander occasions, she often chooses statement jewels, recently including silver puzzle earrings by Elizabeth Hooper and gemstone drops by Emily P. Wheeler. Unafraid to mix fine and fashion jewelry, she has paired a jade ring by Dickson Yewn with costume jewels by Tom Binns, and frequently eschews big houses in favor of independent designers, such as Alexis Bittar, Almasika, Jennifer Fisher, Kihry, and Grace Lee (see pp.33, 248). Pieces are also selected for their deeper meaning: At the first US-Africa Leaders Summit in 2014, Obama chose bronze-and-horn bangles that had been made in Kenya for ethical jeweler Ashley Pittman. During the 2020 Democratic National Convention, she wore a gold necklace by Los Angeles designer ByChari that spelled "Vote." Through her jewelry, as in her politics, Obama sends a message of grace, inclusivity, and empowerment.

Jariet Oloyé

Jariet Oloyé
b. Lagos, Nigeria, 1946

Monumental Cocktail Ring in recycled sterling silver, black rhodium, and gold vermeil finishing, 2021.

Photograph by Simon B. Armitt.

For Nigerian British designer and contemporary fine jeweler Jariet Oloyé, there are few artisanal crafts she has yet to explore. Many of Oloyé's works are inspired by her childhood, a precious time spent immersed among Yoruba artists in southwest Nigeria, observing them creating mixed-media artworks while narrating their folklore for the next generation. She learned the Yoruba's traditional textile-making skills, along with woven basketry, before focusing on more formal jewelry training in London. Oloyé obtained her degree in silversmithing and jewelry, developing the skills that would later enable her to create her calling card—a repetitive loop design layered and woven to create voluminous, sculptural jewels and interior accessories. Since establishing her brand in 2016, Oloyé has explored the potential of metal and glass, experimenting with manufacturing techniques to develop remarkable fusions of the two mediums, with her works often inspired by nature's organic forms. Delving into the relationship between touch, memory, and craftsmanship, Oloyé's designs riff on the power of light, color, and magic, using lost-wax casting to create kiln-cast glass pieces, including her striking signature bangles. Each of Oloyé's jewels are meticulously crafted by hand, melding her mastery of traditional basketweaving with contemporary silversmithing.

Michelle Ong

Michelle Ong
b. 1957

Oceanic Embrace brooch in platinum, 18-karat white gold, and titanium with white, yellow, and black diamonds around a central 31.41-carat cushion-shaped blue sapphire, 2022.

Michelle Ong stepped into the jewelry spotlight in 2005 as the forerunner of a new wave of jewelry artists from Asia, introducing a modern yet ethereal, feminine, nature-inspired aesthetic to her fusion of East-meets-West designs. In the eighteenth century, the decorative arts experienced an Orientalist revival in which the East was romanticized in European jewelry. Just after the 2000s, another revival occurred but this time in the hands of Chinese heritage artists such as Ong. With exhibitions in London and Glasgow, she showcased her blend of classical Chinese elements—dragons, clouds, and jade carvings—with Western motifs and patterns, such as lace and Art Deco–inspired features in vibrantly colored jewels. By pulling from her heritage, Ong introduced a new perspective on cultural references that she refined with Western standards of quality craftsmanship. Originally having studied sociology at the University of Toronto, she undertook an apprenticeship with a Hong Kong–based diamond importer in the early 1980s, setting her on the path to jewelry-making—and spawning a personal fondness for rose-cut diamonds. In 1985 Ong met precious stone expert and dealer Avi Nagar, and after many years of shared ambitions and artistic visions, they founded their brand Carnet in 1998, creating signed, limited-edition, and unique jewels.

Méret Oppenheim

Méret Oppenheim
b. Berlin, Germany, 1913
d. Basel, Switzerland, 1985

Fur Bracelet in 18-karat burnished gold with fur, first designed in 1935.

Photograph by Hans-Jörg Walter.

Leading Surrealist Méret Oppenheim established her place in art history with her famous fur-lined teacup, *Object*, in 1936. This iconic work of twentieth-century sculpture has its genesis in the fur-covered brass bracelets that the German-born Swiss artist designed for Elsa Schiaparelli in 1935 (see p.250). It was over a meal in a Parisian café with artists Pablo Picasso and Dora Maar (see p.223) that Oppenheim was challenged to consider what else she could cover with fur. The juxtaposition of contradictory elements is central to both Oppenheim's art and her jewelry. Among her intriguing pieces are fur- and snakeskin-covered brass rings, a brass necklace in which two rows of femur bones frame a pair of stylized lips, and a braided silk wristband with brass ends—a feminist critique of the ornamentalizing nature of jewelry and the expectations imposed on women in the early twentieth century. Perhaps one of her wittiest pieces is *Sugar Cube Ring*, conceived in 1936, in which a real sugar cube is set in a gilded silver ring. Juxtaposing the permanent and the impermanent, the throwaway and the precious, it allows the wearer to exchange the sugar cube for a fresh "jewel" whenever they wish.

Farah Diba Pahlavi

Farah Diba Pahlavi, Empress of Iran
b. Tehran, Iran, 1938

Empress Farah leaving Golestan Palace, Tehran, after the coronation of her husband, Shah Mohammad Reza Pahlavi, 1967.

Photograph by Carlo Bavagnoli.

From an architecture student in Paris to a young queen of Iran to the nation's first modern empress, Farah Diba came to represent the liberalization of women in her country. In 1959, at the age of twenty, Farah met Shah Mohammad Reza Pahlavi, and the couple was married within the year. In her public role as empress, Farah wore Western-style parures, conforming to the European-inspired protocol that prevailed at her husband's court. The jewelry designed for the empress drew on the peerless collection of gems in Iran's state coffers, many of which had been seized from the Mughal treasury when Nader Shah conquered Delhi in 1739. Among these was the 60-carat pink Nur-al-'Ayn diamond, which was used as the centerpiece for the empress's wedding tiara, designed in 1958 by Harry Winston (see p.132). For the coronation held in 1967, Van Cleef & Arpels designed a parure for the empress, including a crown—loosely inspired in form by the Pahlavi crown worn by her husband—a pair of earrings, and a necklace, drawing on jewels from the treasury (see p.291). A further parure of emeralds was commissioned from Cartier for the celebrations of 2,500 years of the Persian Empire in 1971 (see p.54). When the imperial couple fled Iran in 1979, such ceremonial jewels were left behind and remain today in the Central Bank of Iran.

Irving Penn

Irving Penn
b. Plainfield, New Jersey, United States, 1917
d. New York, New York, United States, 2009

A black eagle wearing a necklace of round and pear-shaped diamonds totaling 175 carats, originally presented by Napoleon Bonaparte to his wife, Marie-Louise, following the birth of their son, Napoleon II, *Vogue*, July 1961.

Photograph by Irving Penn.

One of the most influential photographers of the twentieth century, Irving Penn brought an elegant inquisitiveness to every image he captured. Penn is known for his modern, often humorous perspective, and his jewelry photography is but an extension of his work in fashion and still life. Among his most iconic jewelry images is *Faucet Dripping with Diamonds*, taken in Harry Winston's office when the diamond dealer found himself with three almost identical pear-shaped diamonds (see p.132). This impromptu shot, which shows the gems dripping one by one from a leaky faucet, revealed Penn's ability to merge technical versatility with a surreal touch. This was especially evident in his work for *Vogue* across the latter half of the twentieth century. In the 1950s Penn's portrait of a Cartier jewelry messenger humanized the brand (see p.54), adding a personal dimension to the world of luxury, while his photograph for the July 1961 issue of *Vogue* showing a black eagle wearing an antique diamond necklace brought together both Surrealism and portraiture. To show off Bulgari's enamel snake bracelets, Penn photographed them coiled around a model's hands as if alive in a 1971 image (see p.46). Over a prolific career in fashion photography, Penn's inquisitive eye injected irony and wit into the often clichéd positioning of jewelry.

Giuseppe Penone

Giuseppe Penone
b. Garessio, Italy, 1947

Foglia (Leaf) necklace in 24-karat gold, 18-karat gold, and bronze, 2011.

A key member of the Arte Povera movement that dominated the Italian art scene in the 1960s, Giuseppe Penone uses simple gestures and elemental materials to explore the relationship between humans and the natural world. In 2011 he worked with renowned gallerist Elisabetta Cipriani, who invites leading contemporary artists to create exclusive pieces of wearable sculpture for her eponymous London jewelry gallery (see p.96). The collaboration resulted in *Foglia (Leaf)*, a 24-karat-gold pendant in the shape of a leaf imprinted with the artist's palm and draped over a bronze twig. *Foglia* recalls Penone's works from the 1970s that use natural materials and images of his own body to emphasize the role of the physical senses in a person's experience of the world. Commenting about the piece, the artist said, "The imprint of the skin, the lines of the hand, nails, and veins draw, literally and metaphorically, a network that links us to the leaves and trees, water and stones, animals." In 2022 Penone again collaborated with Cipriani to create *Salvia*, a ring decorated with a highly realistic sage leaf in 18-karat gold and overlaid with a stylized musical note to poetically evoke the melodies of nature, from rustling leaves to whispering winds.

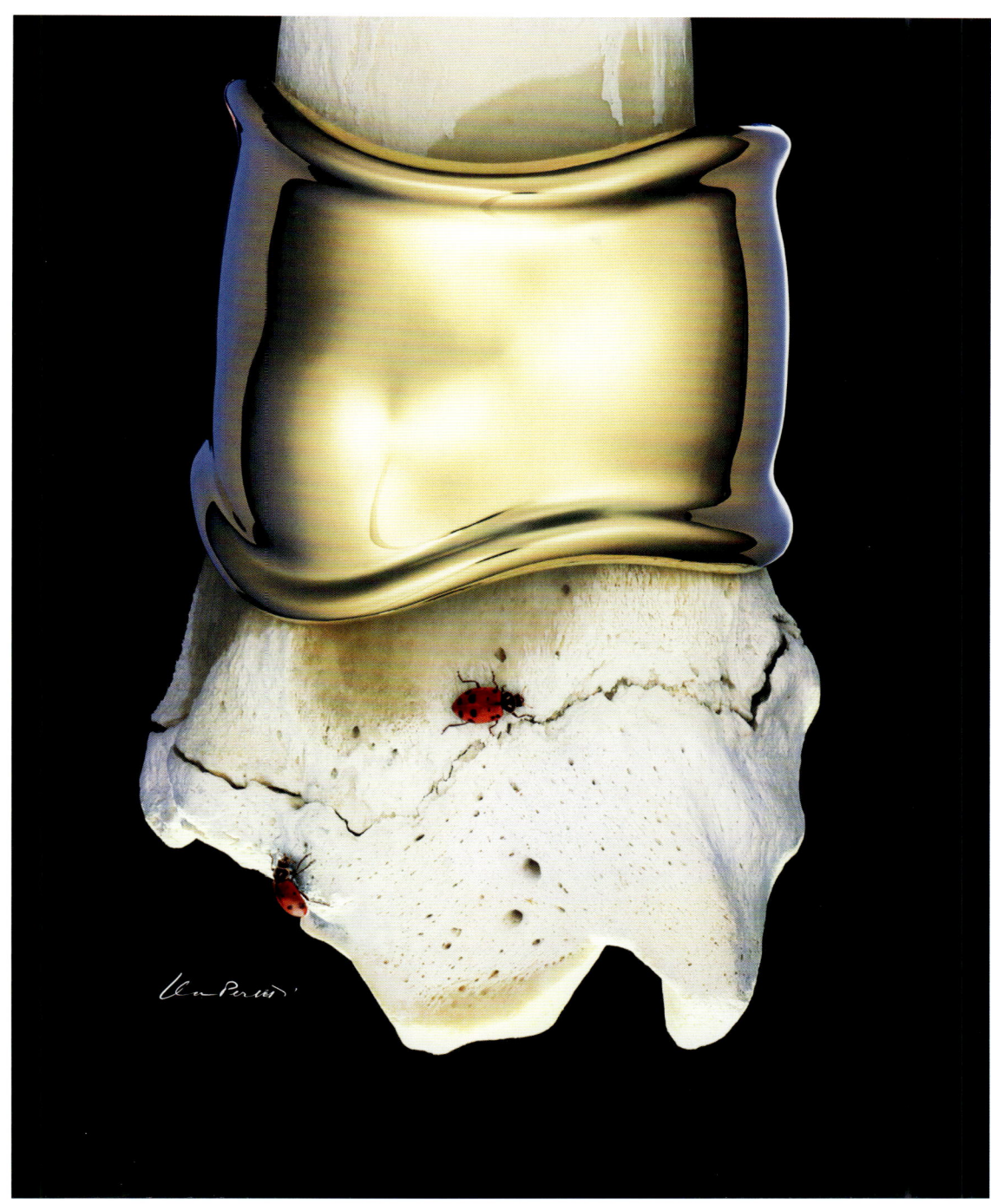

Elsa Peretti

Elsa Peretti
b. Florence, Italy, 1940
d. Sant Martí Vell, Spain, 2021

Tiffany & Co. advertisement for Elsa Peretti's *Bone Cuff*, which was first designed in 1970.

Photograph by Hiro.

Elsa Peretti's work for Tiffany & Co. forever revolutionized jewelry and object design, leading to some of the most enduring and collectible pieces of modern times. Her well-documented passion for organic forms developed early: as a child in Rome, she had a penchant for stealing bones from the crypt of a seventeenth-century Capuchin church, reveling in their forms and forbidden nature. A former model and interior design student, Peretti's sensuous and sculptural aesthetic led to collaborations with designers such as Giorgio di Sant'Angelo, for whom she created her first bud vase on a chain, and her close friend Halston, who helped her broker a contract with Tiffany & Co. in 1974 (see p.283). Her creative alliance with the company, which lasted until her death in 2021, made Peretti a household name and gave rise to collections including *Bone Cuff* (inspired by the Capuchin skeletons), *Diamonds by the Yard*, *Open Heart*, *Bean*, *Bottle*, *Snake*, and *Scorpion*—all of which remain as timeless as when they were first introduced. These designs—many of which elevated sterling silver as an affordable yet still luxurious material—broke free from traditional norms and accompanied a historic shift wherein women no longer waited to be gifted jewelry but rather purchased it for themselves.

Piaget

Piaget
est. La Côte-aux-Fées, France, 1874

Emerald and diamond earrings from the *Essence of Extraleganza* collection, 2024.

Photograph by Brigitte Niedermair.

Combining Swiss craftsmanship with flamboyant style, Piaget was founded in the village of La Côte-aux-Fées, France, in 1874 by Georges-Édouard Piaget, a farmer who built pocket watches on the side during the winter for extra income. Over the next eighty-five years, Piaget established itself as a pioneer in ultra-thin watches and lavishly embellished jewelry, and in 1959 introduced its first collection of high jewelry at the newly inaugurated Salon Piaget in Geneva, where Piaget would also establish their goldsmithing and gem-setting ateliers. Heralding a golden era of the brand, the groundbreaking *21st Century Collection* was introduced in 1969 and included timepieces set into textured gold necklaces punctuated with stone beads and dials that could also be worn as bracelets. That design history has evolved today into, among others, the 2023 nature-inspired *Metaphoria* collection showcasing cascading blue aquamarines alongside black opals, evoking flowing streams and inky oceanic depths. Roses are another frequent motif—a nod to the lifelong passion of the company's president, Yves Piaget—appearing on ear cuffs, rings, and chokers. And for its 150th anniversary in 2024, the maison created the ninety-six-piece *Essence of Extraleganza* collection—a culmination of its design prowess featuring spessartite garnets, Madagascan blue sapphires, and Colombian emeralds.

Pablo Picasso

Pablo Picasso
b. Málaga, Spain, 1881
d. Mougins, France, 1973

A ring created by Pablo Picasso for Dora Maar containing her portrait in ink and colored pencil on paper set into enameled yellow-metal composite, c. 1930s.

Although Spanish artist Pablo Picasso, one of the most influential artists of the twentieth century, is best known for his Cubist paintings and sculptures, he also extended his remarkable creativity to jewelry-making. While trapped in France during World War II, Picasso was inspired by his muse and partner, artist Dora Maar, to create a series of wearable artworks. The first pieces he designed were composed of miniature portraits of Maar, engraved on metal and enclosed in antique frames. Beginning in the 1940s, he became drawn to found objects, crafting jewelry from a wealth of materials, including stone, metal, and bones, which he then gifted to friends.

Inspiration came from eclectic sources—jewelry molded from fired clay and juxtaposed against smooth enamel stemmed from his love of pottery, while gold and silver pieces allegedly came into being after a visit to his dentist to discuss his gold teeth. Picasso evolved as a jeweler after a meeting with goldsmith François Hugo in 1956, who worked with the artist to bring his mystical world of nymphs, bulls, centaurs, and abstract faces to life in large, Renaissance-inspired platters (see p.23). These works were accompanied by a series of gold medallions, marking the beginning of Picasso's commercial jewelry operation, which Hugo's son, Pierre, continued after their deaths.

Paloma Picasso

Paloma Picasso
b. Paris, France, 1949

Paloma Picasso, 1980.

Photograph by Roxanne Lowit.

The jewelry designs of Paloma Picasso are immediately recognizable for their striking graphic forms and use of large semiprecious stones in vibrant hues. The daughter of artists Françoise Gilot and Pablo Picasso (see p.223), she initially dreamed up costumes and jewelry for avant-garde theater productions staged across late-1960s Paris, including necklaces assembled from rhinestones, which she had taken from bikinis originally made for the Folies Bergère. In the early 1970s, her close friend Yves Saint Laurent invited her to design jewelry for his runway collections (see p.245). After a brief stint at Greek jeweler Zolotas, in 1980 Picasso was approached by John Loring at Tiffany & Co. to create pieces for the firm, where she has been blurring the boundary between high and costume jewelry ever since (see p.283). Picasso initially took varied inspirations—from Moroccan culture to the graffiti tags on the streets of New York—and designed them into scribbles, zigzags, and Xs sculpted of gold. She increasingly made use of colorful humble gems, such as citrines and amethysts—stones that had previously been overlooked in high jewelry. Picasso has carried her fresh, maximalist approach into modern design: her 2016 *Anniversary Necklace* dazzles with more than fifteen vivid stones set in platinum and white gold.

Pomellato

Pomellato
est. Milan, Italy, 1967

Spinelli di Fuoco plastron necklace with 238 spinel cabochons, totaling 365 carats, arranged around a rose gold chain adorned with a line of white diamonds, from the *Dualism of Milan* high jewelry collection, 2024.

Inspired by his father's advice to "pick a winning horse" and his fascination with the natural beauty of horses in general, Milanese gold chain wholesaler Pino Rabolini chose the name Pomellato for the company he founded in 1967, after the Italian word for a dapple gray. Rabolini broke away from traditional jewelry norms, catering to the newly independent women of the era. He redefined jewelry as a form of personal expression rather than a symbol of wealth and status, introducing the concept of prêt-à-porter jewelry—wearable yet sophisticated pieces designed for everyday use and to be mixed and matched. In 1969 the original horse-head logo was replaced with the facsimile handwritten signature *Pomellato*, engraved on every piece. It became part of the iconic style of the brand, which garnered fame for its bangles with invisible hinges and chains of variously shaped links with clasps created with ingenious mechanisms. Unconventional gemstone cuts set with oversize prongs, such as the *Griffe* collection, introduced in 1990, or with no prongs at all, as in *Nudo* (2001), jostled next to the irregular diamond pavé seen in the *Sabbia* line (2003). Since 2013 Pomellato has been part of the global luxury group Kering, and the brand continues to uphold its tradition of innovation, fine craftsmanship, and a rebellious spirit rooted in Milanese design.

Arnaldo Pomodoro

Arnaldo Pomodoro
b. Morciano di Romagna, Italy, 1926

Gold brooch with circular-cut rubies, c. 1950–59.

A master at manipulating metal to engender strong emotional responses, Italian artist Arnaldo Pomodoro trained as a goldsmith and is best known for his *Sphere Within Sphere* series of monumental bronze sculptures. Futuristic and fractured, these artworks appear at once mechanical and organic. As a jewelry-maker, Pomodoro was also something of an alchemist. Working with his brother Giò, he produced gold and silver pieces using the lost-wax technique of cuttlefish bone casting, whereby molten metal is poured into hollowed-out bones to achieve pronounced ridges on the material's cooled surface, endowing jewelry with dynamic patterns and textures. Arnaldo's aesthetic soon shifted toward more architecturally informed silhouettes. He produced deconstructed abstract frameworks on gold earrings, cuffs, and pendants, and oversize orb shapes on bold gold necklaces, bangles, and rings, which the artist described as "rehearsals" for his larger sculptures. Working with his brother-in-law, the celebrated jeweler GianCarlo Montebello (see p.199), in the 1970s, Pomodoro produced a series of pieces for Montebello's GEM project, a collection of affordable limited editions made in partnership with established artists, joining an illustrious lineup of collaborators that included Lucio Fontana, Man Ray (see pp.109, 180), Niki de Saint Phalle, and Hans Richter.

Billy Porter

Billy Porter
b. Pittsburgh, Pennsylvania,
United States, 1969

Billy Porter bedecked in pearls during New York Fashion Week, 2019.

Photograph by Santiago Felipe.

Though he initially found success on the Broadway stage, American actor and singer Billy Porter was introduced to the masses as Pray Tell, the fierce yet fatherly ballroom emcee in FX's Emmy-winning drama *Pose*. Following the show's premiere in 2018, Porter became a sensation on red carpets, often appearing in daring gender-bending ensembles that pushed against the typical Hollywood dress code. Porter's signature style was a marriage of masculine and feminine elements, epitomized by the instantly iconic look he wore to host the 2019 Academy Awards preshow: a sculptural ball gown with a sharp black tuxedo jacket from designer Christian Siriano. For the 2020 Golden Globes, he donned a white feathered suit adorned with more than four thousand Swarovski crystals, an ensemble that was finished with a Tiffany & Co. 40-carat diamond pendant necklace worth more than $2 million (see pp.275, 283). And at the 2021 Emmy Awards, a pair of diamond ear cuffs and a white gold-set diamond-and-emerald necklace by Lorraine Schwartz sparkled atop Porter's ruched all-black outfit (see p.252). In a 2019 essay for *Vogue*, Porter detailed how he often uses his wardrobe to express himself and make political statements, writing, "I'm not a drag queen, I'm a man in a dress." He's shown time and time again that fashion—and jewelry—need not be limited by traditional norms.

Cole and Linda Porter

Cole Porter
b. Peru, Indiana, United States, 1891
d. Santa Monica, California, United States, 1964

Linda Lee Porter
b. Louisville, Kentucky, United States, 1883
d. New York, New York, United States, 1954

Cole and Linda Porter return from a voyage on the S.S. *Fredonia*, c. 1930s.

"I could never curl my lip, to a dazzlin' diamond clip," penned American composer and songwriter Cole Porter in his popular 1948 musical *Kiss Me Kate*. Porter and his wife, Linda Lee Thomas, were an unconventional couple at the center of café society on both sides of the Atlantic, and the couple shared a love of jewelry and precious objects. While on their honeymoon after their 1919 wedding, they met Duke Fulco di Verdura in Palermo; the three became lifelong friends, and the Porters played a formative role in the duke's burgeoning career as a jewelry designer (see p.298). In 1925 they invited him to a party, where he first met Gabrielle "Coco" Chanel (see p.60), with whom he subsequently collaborated on many jewelry designs, including the famed *Maltese Cross* cuffs, and in 1939 the Porters helped finance Verdura's eponymous retail shop on New York's Fifth Avenue. Cole also commissioned one-of-a-kind pieces for Linda from the most important jewelry designers of the time, including a scarab beetle–shaped buckle brooch from Cartier and a pair of whimsical, teardrop clip brooches encrusted with diamonds and emerald beads from Paul Flato (see pp.54, 107). After each of Cole's Broadway premieres, Linda gave him a specially designed cigarette case commemorating the occasion, with more than twenty designed by the couple's friend Verdura.

Marjorie Merriweather Post

Marjorie Merriweather Post
b. Springfield, Illinois, United States, 1887
d. Washington, DC, United States, 1973

Portrait of Marjorie Merriweather Post by Frank O. Salisbury, 1946. Post is depicted wearing a platinum Art Deco fringe necklace made by Cartier New York in 1937 with calibre-cut and channel-set sapphires, diamonds, and a 38.31-carat cushion-shaped Burmese sapphire that can be detached and worn as a brooch.

Washington, DC, is perhaps not the likeliest place to find one of the most historically significant collections of jewelry from Tsarist Russia. Yet thanks to Marjorie Merriweather Post—the well-traveled heiress of General Foods Corporation, businesswoman, and philanthropist renowned for her impeccable taste—the extraordinary assemblage she curated over her lifetime is now on display at her former home there, the Hillwood Estate, Museum & Gardens. Post began collecting in the 1920s during her second marriage, to financier Edward Francis Hutton. This era saw the acquisition of several remarkable Cartier pieces (see p.54), including a bracelet set with a velvety 58.33-carat Kashmir blue sapphire and a striking pendant brooch with more than 250 carats of carved Mughal emeralds. One of Post's first Russian acquisitions was a pair of earrings with two triangular diamonds suspending pear-shaped drops, originally from the collection of Felix Yusupov—husband of the last tsar's niece and the infamous assassin of Rasputin—who maintained the diamonds belonged to Marie Antoinette (see p.183). Post's fascination with Russian imperial jewels deepened during her time in Moscow as the wife of US ambassador Joseph E. Davies (her third husband) and added an important dimension to her phenomenal collection.

Prince Dimitri

Prince Dimitri
est. New York, New York,
United States, 2007

Emerald tree brooch, inspired by the orangerie of Versailles, in oxidized bronze and 18-karat yellow gold with 79.65 carats of emeralds and a 7.36-carat baguette brown diamond. The front panel opens to reveal tree roots and soil in cognac diamonds and a panel engraved with, "For those who listen, even the stones speak."

Photograph by Michael Oldford.

Glamorous, opulent, eclectic, and exotic, each Prince Dimitri jewel is loaded with symbolism. Some are alive with humor, but all are infused with the magnificence of the prince's family's historic jewels. Related to a sprawling web of European royalty, Prince Dimitri of Yugoslavia is the great-great-grandson of the Grand Duchess Vladimir of Russia, who amassed one of the most important jewelry collections in history. The stories of these fabulous jewels—long since dispersed—filled Dimitri's childhood, and he later cultivated an enviable knowledge as senior vice president of the jewelry department at Sotheby's New York. A wealth of culture and intellect inspires both his writing and documenting of his family history, as well as his eponymous jewelry house founded in 2007. A true original who has forged his own style, Dimitri confidently scours the world for inspiration for his own jewelry creations. He shifts from the curved paisley motifs of Mughal India to the angular medieval crosses in oxidized bronze or tribal Makassar ebony necklaces. Above all, he embraces unusual materials and vibrant, richly hued gemstones, including Siberian amethysts handed down from his great-grandmother Queen Elena of Italy that he has incorporated into his designs (see p.249).

Robert Procop

Robert Procop
b. California, United States, 1958

Toi et Moi Ring with a 3.39-carat kite-shaped Colombian emerald and 2-carat kite-shaped diamond, bordered by square, baguette, and round brilliant diamonds set in platinum.

Beverly Hills jeweler Robert Procop feels as comfortable talking to miners in remote locations as he does presenting his gems and jewels to the rich and famous. Spending much of his life in Los Angeles, Procop has launched many high-profile collaborations with celebrities and tastemakers. In 2010 he and actress Angelina Jolie began working on the *Style of Jolie* jewelry collection, in which all proceeds went to Jolie's nonprofit organization, Education Partnerships for Children of Conflicts, which builds schools for girls in impoverished countries. Many of the rare colored gems were cut into a unique tablet shape that Procop and Jolie created together. Two years later, Procop teamed up with longtime friend Brooke Shields to create the *Legacy Brooke* jewelry collection, whose proceeds went to a Los Angeles transitional housing shelter for victims of domestic violence. Procop says his most important skill is buying statement gemstones when the price is right. At the 2024 Treasure House Fair in London, the public had a chance to view the types of gems Procop has acquired; the exhibition he curated consisted of eight rare and exceptional unmounted colored gems of more than 100 carats and was a testament to his love of extraordinary gemstones.

Marc Quinn

Marc Quinn
b. London, England, 1964

Orchid Ring in 18-karat polished gold, 2011.

Photograph by Tom Carter.

Rising to prominence through his association with the Young British Artists (YBAs), who dominated the London art scene in the 1990s, Marc Quinn is best known for his provocative sculptures interrogating the human form, environmental issues, and the intersections of art and science. Embracing an array of materials, he has made art from ice, flowers, human DNA, and, most famously, his own frozen blood in the life-size self-portrait bust *Self* (1991). In the late 2000s, Quinn moved into designing jewelry, and his first pieces, commissioned by Louisa Guinness Gallery (see p.175), included a striking "frozen" strawberry pendant in white gold. Cast from a real fruit, it is set with 270 brilliant-cut diamonds in place of the fruit's seeds and a further 250 pavé-set diamonds resembling clusters of ice crystals. In 2008 he unveiled a stunning golden lip pendant with a ruby-encrusted tongue, part of a collection by Versace in collaboration with contemporary artists to celebrate the annual Whitney Gala in New York. Quinn has frequently used orchids in his artworks, and in 2011, in partnership with upscale British department store Selfridges, he created several unique white gold necklaces and rings cast from real flowers, making the ephemeral permanent.

Jacqueline Rabun

Jacqueline Rabun
b. Bitburg, Germany, 1961

Metanoia torque in 18-karat gold with rutilated quartz, created in collaboration with Carpenters Workshop Gallery, 2021.

Photograph by Oliver Beamish.

Self-taught jewelry artist Jacqueline Rabun launched her first collection in 1990, shortly after she moved from Los Angeles to London. With minimalist, organic forms that drew the focus to the materials themselves, the *Raw Elegance* collection would set the tone for the rest of her career. From carving precious metals into wearable sculpture to setting her jewels with carefully considered polished stones, her pieces are gracefully, quietly beautiful—full of smooth, tactile shapes that comfort and nourish. Through purity of design, Rabun aims to provide a sense of calm as she explores the human experience, balancing artistry and commerciality in a way that does not dilute her unique aesthetic language. Since 2000, alongside her own brand, she has collaborated with the Danish jewelry house Georg Jensen (see p.120) and is behind some of the heritage house's most successful pieces, including the *Cave* ring—a domed ring in solid silver or gold with a single concave sphere representing a private retreat for meditation. In 2023 Rabun was the subject of a retrospective at Carpenters Workshop Gallery in London, showcasing more than three decades of her designs. Part of a collection created for the occasion, Rabun designed the *Metanoia* torque and ring with golden strands of rutilated quartz revealed through fluid, circular openings as an embodiment of the journey of life.

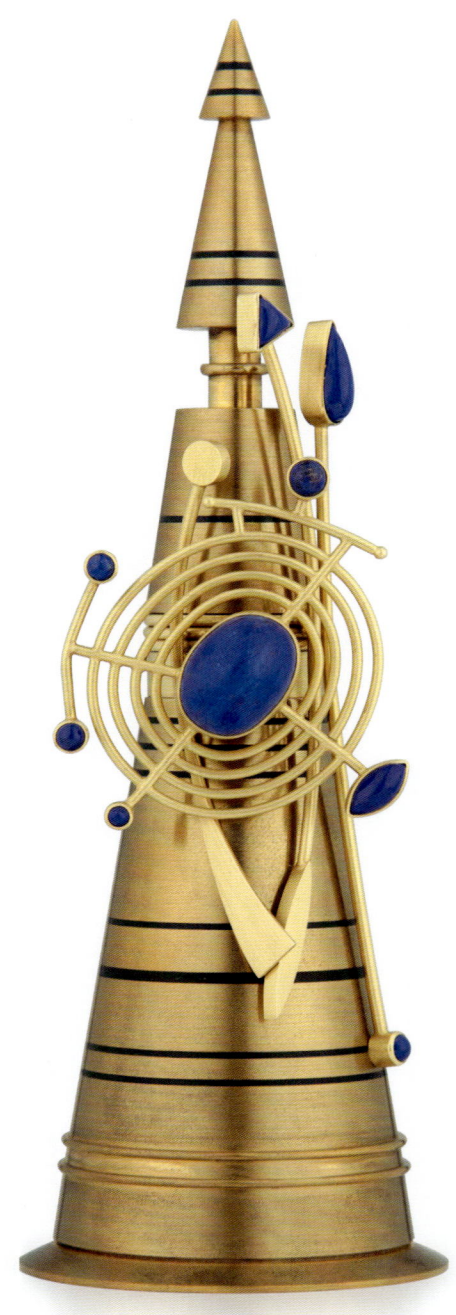

Wendy Ramshaw

Wendy Ramshaw
b. Sunderland, England, 1939
d. London, England, 2018

Midnight Two Ringset (4 Part) in 18-karat gold and lapis lazuli on a blue inlaid brass stand, c. 2010.

Blending art and craftsmanship with geometric forms and a distinctive use of color and materials, British artist Wendy Ramshaw has elevated jewelry into a form of artistic expression rather than mere adornment. A pioneering design doyenne, Ramshaw pushed the boundaries of sculpture, installation, and craft. Inspired by local art galleries, museums, and the surrounding images of old lighthouses and model ships in her native port city, she studied illustration and fabric design at Newcastle upon Tyne College of Art and Industrial Design and later at the University of Reading and the Central School of Art and Design. She was first celebrated for her 1970 solo exhibition at London's Pace Gallery, where she presented gold ring sets with gemstones—a tableau she iterated upon and deconstructed across materials and media throughout her career. As stackable "pillar" rings in silver, yellow gold, or 18-karat matte white gold, these designs incorporated silhouettes of inlaid gems—amethysts, peridots, agates, emeralds, sapphires, tourmalines—or Pop art shapes, as with 1990's *Picasso's Ladies* series with accompanying bespoke sculptural stands. For Ramshaw, rings were the most intimate and personal pieces of jewelry, and the sets were born from her natural desire for balance and proportion, marrying technological precision with ornamentation.

Reza

Reza
est. Paris, France, 1984

Eventail Cuff in 18-karat rose gold with sandblasted and polished surfaces set with 152 brilliant-cut diamonds and two pear-shaped diamonds, from the *Dune* series, 2024.

Photograph by Richard Pierce.

One of the greatest gem merchants of the twentieth century, Alexandre Reza amassed an unparalleled collection of exceptional and rare stones, both new and old, thanks to his vast knowledge and keen eye. Born into a family of jewelers, Reza briefly followed his father into business before setting out on his own at age eighteen. A fearless risk-taker, he traveled the world to source spectacular and unique stones—primarily old-mine diamonds, emeralds, rubies, and sapphires—and dared to recut high-quality stones to increase their value. By the mid-twentieth century, Reza had become a key gem supplier for Boucheron, Cartier, Harry Winston, and other major maisons (see pp.39, 54, 132). He opened his eponymous store in the Place Vendôme in 1984, with other high jewelry boutiques following in Cannes, Geneva, and Monaco. Reza offered opulent designs inspired by Renaissance art combined with a modern twist, always using his rare stones as the focal point of his jewels. He retired in 2007 and the following year Reza's son, Olivier, took the helm and infused a new energy into the company, relocating the house from the Place Vendôme to New York in 2020. He continues his father's legacy of using the finest gemstones, and has evolved the Reza style into a bold, modern aesthetic while maintaining the highest standards of design and craftsmanship.

Rihanna

Rihanna (Robyn Rihanna Fenty) b. Saint Michael, Barbados, 1988

Rihanna wears Boghossian's *Mardin* diamond-and-aquamarine choker, part of the *Silk* high jewelry collection, to the British Fashion Awards, London, 2019.

Photograph by Daniele Venturelli.

For Bajan singer and business mogul Rihanna, statement jewelry forms a key part of an iconic self-image. Her extensive collection—from chunky chains to priceless stones, antique pieces to contemporary independent designers—demonstrates an eclectic taste. Worn together in a juxtaposition of styles, from high to fine to fashion jewelry, Rihanna brings a distinctive street style to traditionally precious and traditional jewels, whether on the red carpet or in more personal moments. At the 2021 Met Gala, Rihanna paired a custom Balenciaga dress with more than 267 carats of Bulgari high jewelry in three statement necklaces (see p.46). For her Super Bowl performance in 2023, she pinned three antique brooches from Joseph Saidian & Sons to her red Loewe jumpsuit. A casual pregnancy announcement in 2022 saw the star photographed with vintage fashion jewelry from Chanel layered over her bare stomach, worn with a Rolex watch customized by Patcharavipa (see p.60). In 2024 she sported a bespoke ring from jeweler XIV Karats, spelling out "MOM" in gold underlined in diamonds. Rihanna has also designed her own pieces, launching a jewelry line under her Fenty brand and working closely in 2017 with Chopard copresident and creative director Caroline Scheufele on a nine-piece capsule high jewelry collection in rose gold, ceramic, and diamonds (see p.66).

Michael Robinson

Michael Robinson
b. Auckland, New Zealand, 1978

Jewelbot Blue rendering, 2021.

Illustration by Michael Robinson.

Robots may well inherit the earth, but for Michael Robinson—who makes fewer than ten jewels a year by hand—the human touch is a sacred, irreplaceable element of the design process. Born and raised among the dramatic and mountainous New Zealand landscape, Robinson found metalsmithing by chance and taught himself in a lifelong process of experimentation. He has no shop and there is no automation. Robinson makes every element of every jewel himself from his current base in Boston, whether that be his *Koi Pond* series or *Rain or Shine* ear pendants. At the start of each creation, meticulous watercolor renderings are a bridge from past to future. Robinson tells the story of his life through each piece, expressing deeply held emotions and capturing past moments of intense happiness. His work is bedecked in gemstones and bursting with color, but it was his attempt to tame the idiosyncrasies of titanium that made him think differently about metal and the techniques he uses to fuse his vision to reality. From his seclusion at the bench, he sees a future filled with artificially intelligent overlords attempting to understand the magic and soul of jewelry and has started designing pieces for them to wear when they take over the world.

Luz Mila Patiño Rodríguez

Luz Mila Patiño Rodríguez,
Countess du Boisrouvray
b. Oruro. Bolivia, 1906
d. New York, New York,
United States, 1958

Portrait of Luz Mila Patiño
Rodríguez by Philip de László, 1931.

Luz Mila Patiño Rodríguez, later the Countess du Boisrouvray, lived a glamorous life. The youngest daughter of a Bolivian mining millionaire, Simón Patiño, she grew up surrounded by the fruits of his labor, including a vast jewelry collection. The family moved to Paris, and later Madrid, and Rodríguez picked up an eclectic sense of style. In Paris, Luz met and married her husband, Comte Guy de Jacquelot du Boisrouvray, an acclaimed mining engineer and first cousin of Prince Rainier III of Monaco. Guy's cosmopolitan tastes shaped a passion for collecting, which he shared with Rodríguez. Early in their marriage, the couple relocated to New York and began a lasting friendship with Louis Arpels, who regularly hosted them in the Van Cleef & Arpels Fifth Avenue boutique and advised them on extraordinary pieces to collect (see p.291). Their collection was later put up for auction at Sotheby's by the couple's only daughter, Countess Albina du Boisrouvray, to benefit a number of charities—netting $31.2 million it was the largest sale of jewelry in the firm's history at the time (see p.267). Highlights included a spectacular Chaumet 32.08-carat Burmese Mogok ruby and diamond ring bought by Lily Safra, a Cartier necklace featuring twelve squared emeralds and twenty-four rounded diamonds, and a Van Cleef & Arpels necklace composed of five large sapphires and round diamonds (see pp.54, 63, 244).

Daniel Roseberry

Daniel Roseberry
b. Plano, Texas, United States, 1985

Akon Changkou wears a Schiaparelli eye earring in brass with resin and rhinestones, *Vogue* Germany, March 2021.

Photograph by Julia Noni.

As creative director of Schiaparelli, American fashion designer Daniel Roseberry has given the storied Paris couture house a contemporary voice. After a decade at Thom Browne, Roseberry was tapped in 2019 to head the newly revived Schiaparelli, which was originally established in 1927 but had been shuttered from 1954 to 2013. The brand's DNA is anchored in the pioneering spirit of its founder, Elsa Schiaparelli, and her collaborations with the vanguard of Surrealism in Paris during the 1920s and '30s, including artists Jean Cocteau and Salvador Dalí (see pp.77, 250). Instead of simply reissuing Elsa's courageous designs, Roseberry draws from the house's rich history while striving to create a modern wardrobe that captures the same sense of fearlessness. Inspired by a 1937 eyeball brooch design by Cocteau, he has crafted brass earrings set with enamel eyes, as well as rings that cover the wearer's finger entirely like a second skin, chokers with bulbous faux pearls set in tooth-shaped surrounds, and giant gold-dipped breastplates that mimic the complex bronchial network of the lungs, notably worn by Bella Hadid at the 2021 Cannes Film Festival. Roseberry made history in 2021 when Lady Gaga performed at the 2020 US presidential inauguration with a large Schiaparelli dove brooch on her lapel.

Joel Arthur Rosenthal

Joel Arthur Rosenthal (JAR)
b. New York, New York,
United States, 1943

Sheep's Head clip in silver, 18-karat gold, and aluminum with micro-pearls and star sapphire cabochons, 2006.

Just off the legendary square of the Place Vendôme is a jewelry boutique with no display window and no set opening hours. It does not advertise, and only a handful of preordained collectors are invited to view the treasures within. Despite this, Joel Arthur Rosenthal, more commonly known as JAR, has become one of the world's most influential and sought-after jewelry designers since founding his atelier in 1978. Born in New York, Rosenthal relocated to Paris in 1977 after a brief career in screenwriting and then needlepoint, which attracted luxury houses such as Hermès and Valentino. It was only when he was asked to design a mount for a gemstone that he discovered a profound talent for creating jewelry, which consumed the rest of his life. Creating around seventy to eighty pieces a year, each JAR jewel is crafted by hand—overseen by Rosenthal and his partner Pierre Jeannet—and is unique, blending artistry with technical mastery to redefine the concept of high jewelry in modern times. A camellia brooch with its open petals entirely pavéd with 173 carats of rubies is as likely as a dragonfly pin with wings of carved rock crystal or fan-shaped electric-blue titanium earrings. Whether in sapphires or spinels, platinum or gold, each jewel is infused with naturalism as a maximalist work of art in its own right.

Olivier Rousteing

Olivier Rousteing
b. Bordeaux, France, 1985

Mamuor Majeng wears Balmain Homme Fall/Winter 2024 collection as he walks the runway during Paris Fashion Week, 2024.

Photograph by Stephane Cardinale.

As a fashion designer, Olivier Rousteing has a vision that is singular, powerful, and luxe. Appointed creative director of Balmain in 2011, Rousteing designs jewelry for the house that is equally opulent and stems from the way he wears jewels himself. Rings, cuffs, and chains are used to artfully embellish his gender-fluid personal style. For him, jewelry is armor and strength, contributing to the mindset that drove him to success as one of the youngest designers ever to lead a major French brand. Infused with that same confidence, his first fine jewelry collection for the house saw Pierre Balmain's own *Labyrinth* motif from the early 1970s reworked into generously proportioned solid gold rings and cuffs, while other pieces referenced the quilting and embroidery from some of his own collections, in smooth onyx and glittering diamonds, stamped with the Balmain coat of arms. For his Spring/Summer 2022 collection, Rousteing sent models down the runway sporting tops fashioned to resemble massive gold chains, and his Fall/Winter 2024 men's collection featured gold breastplates embossed with layered chains alongside face jewelry and chunky black-and-gold cuffs. His collections—based on the personal mantra "Vida es arte" (Art is life)—draw on rams, chains, and other powerful symbols of mythology to feature spectacular pieces that sit easily alongside the Balmain monogram.

Rundell, Bridge & Rundell

Rundell, Bridge & Rundell est. London, England, 1787

The *Diamond Diadem* created by Rundell, Bridge & Rundell in 1820. The diadem features two bands of pearls and 1,333 diamonds set in silver and gold, including a 4-carat pale yellow brilliant diamond at the center of the front cross. The four sprays of roses, shamrocks, and thistles represent the national emblems of England, Ireland, and Scotland.

As Royal Goldsmiths and Jewelers from 1797 to 1843, the London firm Rundell, Bridge & Rundell served four monarchs from George III to Queen Victoria (see p.301), creating some of the most iconic jewels in British history. Established in 1787 as Rundell & Bridge, the company (whose name underwent several iterations) employed the finest metalsmiths of its time, including Paul Storr. In addition to providing regalia for coronations and state events, the firm offered jewels to the public—much in vogue, thanks to their superb design and innovative techniques executed by master craftsmen. The firm created storied pieces steeped in symbolism, including the *Sovereign's Ring* in 1831, featuring a ruby cross surrounded by sapphires and diamonds, as well as the *Queen Consort's Ring*, last used for the coronation of King Charles in 2023, alongside the elaborately gem-set *Jewelled Sword of Offering* commissioned by George IV in 1820. However, it was the famous *Diamond Diadem* that became one of the most recognizable jewels in the Royal Collection. Made in 1820 for the coronation of George IV, it was worn by the late Queen Elizabeth II on her coronation and at every State Opening of Parliament during her reign, as well as appearing on postage stamps and currency (see p.97). In 2024 Queen Camilla again donned the diadem for the State Opening of Parliament.

Sabba

Sabba
est. Paris, France, 2014

Jet and diamond earrings in titanium and yellow gold, set with two marquise-cut diamonds weighing 2.35 and 1.69 carats, 2021.

Alessandro Sabbatini is the antithesis of the traditional high jeweler: he is surprisingly young, likes to laugh, and is enthusiastically effervescent. Yet his jewels sit alongside revered names such as Wallace Chan, Taffin, Hemmerle, and JAR at New York's prestigious FD Gallery (see p.59, 123, 133, 240). At age twenty, while studying at the Richemont Creative Academy, he was sent to Hong Kong, where he worked with the esteemed jewelry house Carnet, and later moved to Cartier's Paris design team, where he worked for three years (see pp.54, 216). In 2014 he set up Sabba, which exclusively makes one-of-a-kind, eye-catching, contemporary jewels with traditional references; the pieces are often outsized and always alluringly feminine. Sabbatini's use of outré volumes in superlight titanium and adventurous color combinations, with the lightest of touches, breathes new life into classics. Girandole earrings set with gray moonstones whisper understated sophistication. A natural pearl necklace is transformed into shoulder-grazing earrings with diamond "wings" that sway like the quills of a feather in the breeze. Chubby black jet beads playfully bubble around exquisite diamonds in a pair of earrings the size of your palm. The gloriously wide arc of Sabba jewelry evokes the best of the past with a touch of the unusual.

Lily Safra

Lily Safra
b. Porto Alegre, Brazil, 1934
d. Geneva, Switzerland, 2022

An emerald-and-diamond necklace from Lily Safra's personal collection sold in the Jewels for Hope auction, featuring two strands of graduated emerald beads, weighing a total of 598.71 carats, gathered by an oval-shaped bombé clasp with emeralds and diamonds mounted in platinum and gold.

A Brazilian philanthropist, Lily Safra was a leading figure in the world of jewelry collecting, with her impeccable taste and a burning desire for exceptional jewels. Known for her discerning eye, Safra had a collection that boasted historic jewels as well as rare pieces from Cartier, Chaumet, and Van Cleef & Arpels (see pp.54, 63, 291). In 2012 Safra made headlines with the record-setting philanthropic Jewels for Hope auction at Christie's (see p.68), raising nearly $38 million from the sale of seventy of her pieces, with proceeds donated to thirty-two charities. Among the pieces—which ranged from Belle Époque and Art Deco jewels to designs from Boucheron, Bulgari, and Fred Leighton—were eighteen JAR creations, the largest selection ever seen on the market from a single owner (see pp.39, 46, 165, 240). The highest-ticket item, however, was the so-called Hope Ruby, which fetched more than $6.7 million—a world record for the sale of a ruby at the time. Crafted by Chaumet, the 32.08-carat Burmese ruby was set into a gold ring, where it was flanked by diamonds; it was formerly part of the collection of Luz Mila Patiño Rodríguez (see p.238). Beyond her private collection, Safra's early patronage and championing of certain designers—particularly JAR, whom she began collecting in the 1980s—played a pivotal role in elevating their profile.

Yves Saint Laurent

Yves Saint Laurent
b. Oran, Algeria, 1936
d. Paris, France, 2008

Yves Saint Laurent surrounded by models Iman, Rebecca Ayoko, Mounia Orosemane, Pat Cleveland, Sayoko Yamaguchi, Violeta Sanchez, and Amalia Vairelli at the end of the Saint Laurent Rive Gauche Spring/Summer 1984 fashion show, Paris, September 1983.

Photograph by Françoise Huguier.

A designer who made fashion history with his haute couture and ready-to-wear creations, Yves Saint Laurent also had a passion for jewelry. Shortly after establishing his namesake atelier with business partner Pierre Bergé in 1961, Saint Laurent, who was previously at the helm of fashion house Dior, added jewelry to his catalog (see p.89). In the ensuing decades, the designer collaborated with other creatives on jewelry design, among them his friend Paloma Picasso, artist Claude Lalanne, noted jeweler Roger Scemama, and tastemaker Loulou de La Falaise, who was also one of Saint Laurent's foremost muses (see pp.82, 160, 224). The fashion business partnered with expert workshops to make its jewelry, working with the likes of Martine Boutron, Caillol, and Gripoix (see p.129). With the atelier of Robert Goossens (see p.126), Saint Laurent created bold pieces such as gilt metal manchette cuffs festooned with white shells and cuts of rock crystals. Golden metal was among Saint Laurent's go-to materials; he also embraced faux gemstones, rhinestones, colored resins, woods, and surprising materials such as twisted silk cords and python snakeskin. Recurring motifs in his work also include tassels, hearts, and doves. In 2023 the brand launched Saint Laurent Haute Joaillerie, a collection of fine jewelry that features Saint Laurent's beloved designs in yellow gold, white gold, and diamonds.

Fabio Salini

Fabio Salini
b. Rome, Italy, 1963

A model wears Fabio Salini earrings in carbon fiber, white gold, and titanium with sapphires and diamonds.

Photograph by Martin Morrell.

An innovative jeweler with a dynamic form of modernist design, Fabio Salini regards himself as "a composed rebel," thriving on challenging traditional high-jewelry associations. In his hands, an Art Deco–like diamond-and-ruby circle at the center of a red satin collar can be transformed into an elegant body harness, while large black discs of carbon fiber are artfully converted into bold earrings thanks to fine lines of diamonds and clusters of gems. Salini studied geology at the University of Rome while gaining experience at Bulgari and Cartier (see pp.46, 54). In 1999 he launched his first collection at Petochi, one of Italy's oldest jewelry houses, followed by the opening of his own store in Rome in 2004. Salini's references are eclectic—from early inspiration by linear French Art Deco jewels and the rounded volumes of the 1980s to futuristic shapes in colored titanium in recent creations—and he explores a wide range of materials, including rock crystal, silk, leather, shagreen, and highly polished gold. His pursuit of technical innovation and refined craftsmanship is relentless, as can be seen in his earrings with invisible fittings and sautoirs with versatile magnetic clasps. Salini's understanding of line, shape, composition, and structure devoid of superfluous ornamentation make his jewels ultimately modernist in the twenty-first century.

Elsa Sarantidou

Elsa Sarantidou
b. Athens, Greece, 1967

Python ring hand-sculpted in sterling silver and 18-karat gold with yellow diamonds, from the *Animal Kingdom – Save the Planet* collection.

Photograph by Giorgos Vitsaropoulos.

When Elsa Sarantidou was five years old, at her childhood home in Athens, she began sculpting Ganesha, the Hindu god of new beginnings, from soft clay and decided then and there to become a jeweler and to live in Paris. She may have been to the City of Light dozens of times since then, but her base is now London, where she studied in 1992 and moved to in 2015, and where, as an artist, she carves her colossal, sculptural, voluminous body architecture. Sarantidou's first collection more than thirty years ago was crafted in titanium, but she then evolved, leaning into gold, silver, and warm-colored diamonds as she absorbed knowledge from a range of teachers, including Joel Degen, Brian Marshall, and Mark Lewis. "I have to like the tutor. There must be a symphony," she says. Despite forays back to Greece with work showcased at the highly acclaimed Eleni Marneri Gallery, she found the avant-garde collector base in London more attuned to the scale and substance of her Gothic modernism. The movement of the sea haunts her dreams, and the power of the natural world imbues her art. In her *Secret Garden* collection, she 3D-printed a blossom onto sheets of blackened, silverlike metallic fabric before cutting it into flowing, twisting body sculpture. Working primarily by night, she only makes around thirty pieces each year.

Catherine Sarr

Catherine Sarr
b. Paris, France, 1980

Vici earrings by Catherine Sarr for Almasika, 2021.

Photograph by DeMarcus Allen.

A fascination with universal symbols and stories underpins the striking jewelry of designer Catherine Sarr. Having lived in four countries on three continents, the designer and art collector is drawn to forms that transcend generations and cultures. The cowrie shell is one such example—a symbol of spirituality, prosperity, and fertility—while a form of concentric circles represents the universe. Sarr founded her jewelry brand Almasika in 2014, which embraces ancient motifs that are translated into sculptural, contemporary jewels whose curvilinear silhouettes echo the contours of the body. The brand's name is a fusion of *Almasi*, meaning "diamond" in Swahili, and *Sika*, meaning "gold" in the Akan languages spoken in West Africa. Sarr fabricates every design in 18-karat gold, sometimes adding pavé or bezel-set diamonds to emphasize its fluidity. While her inspirations are deep, Sarr's designs exude an effortless simplicity that she says reflects a Parisian aesthetic, an ode to her city of birth. Now based in Chicago, alongside her husband, Mamadou-Abou Sarr, she cofounded the Sarr Collection to support emerging artists. In turn, contemporary art inspires her own creativity. "My guiding philosophy has always been to find what we have in common with others," she says. "Whether the inspiration is literal or abstract, each collection aims to celebrate our shared human experiences and connections."

Royal House of Savoy

Royal House of Savoy
est. Turin, Italy, 1861

Portrait of Elena of Montenegro, Queen of Italy, 1913. The Italian crown jewels passed to Elena in 1900 upon her marriage to King Victor Emmanuel II from the Royal House of Savoy.

Shrouded in mystery, Italy's former crown jewels have remained hidden in the vaults of the national bank since 1946, when the eighty-five-year reign of the Royal House of Savoy ended. It was then that Italy voted in favor of a republic, and King Umberto II—the so-called May King who reigned briefly from May 9 to June 2, 1946—ordered the jewels to be consigned to the then-governor of the Bank of Italy, Luigi Einaudi, before going into exile. King Umberto II included a note to accompany the jewels: "Entrusted to the custody of the central cashier" to be "kept at the disposal of those who have the right." The question of who exactly "have the right" has been an ongoing debate ever since—is it the Savoy family or the Italian Republic?—with the occasional rumor of the jewels having been tampered with or disappeared arising from time to time. While they have remained unseen for nearly eight decades, among the jewels is an exceptional brooch set with a pink diamond and a double-strand chain resembling the House of Savoy's heraldic knot. The most significant piece, however, is a tiara crafted by court jeweler Musy Padre e Figli of Turin, the Savoys' hometown. Featuring diamond-studded swirls crossed by pearls, it was a favorite of Queen Margherita (who reigned alongside Umberto I from 1878 to 1900), earning her the moniker Queen of Pearls.

Elsa Schiaparelli

Elsa Schiaparelli
b. Rome, Italy, 1890
d. Paris, France, 1973

Fiona Campbell-Walter wears an oversize brooch by Schiaparelli, *Vogue*, November 1952.

Photograph by Robert Randall.

Eccentric and prone to springing fashion surprises, Elsa Schiaparelli, alongside her rival Gabrielle Chanel, dominated haute couture in the late 1920s and '30s. Her meteoric rise began with a black-and-white sweater featuring a large trompe l'oeil bow, igniting a creative dialogue between fashion and art. She surrounded herself with leading artists such as Jean Cocteau, Marcel Vertès, and Salvador Dalí (see p.77), some of the first known artist-couturier collaborations in modern European history. Their Surrealist artwork appeared on her gowns, such as Dalí's lobster dress and shoe hat. Like her outré embroideries, costume jewelry added an ornamental touch. By 1935 she had opened a couture maison in the Place Vendôme, but nevertheless she worked with *paruriers*—makers of costume jewelry—for her fantastical designs. Alberto Giacometti and Méret Oppenheim also created bijoux for her (see pp.122, 217), as did Russian-French writer Elsa Triolet, who made necklaces, including one in the form of aspirin tablets. Schiaparelli also spotted the talent of Jean Schlumberger—who would make his name at Tiffany & Co. (see pp.251, 283)—and worked with him in the late 1930s and beyond to make buttons and costume jewelry, from gilt cupid clips to sea creatures. She retired in 1954, but a reimagined Schiaparelli brand continues to push the boundaries of artist jewelry today (see p.239).

Jean Schlumberger

Jean Schlumberger
b. Mulhouse, France, 1907
d. Paris, France, 1987

Tiffany & Co. Schlumberger Starlight brooch in 18-karat yellow gold and platinum with diamonds and a tanzanite weighing more than 16 carats.

Born to a wealthy family of textile manufacturers, Jean Schlumberger cultivated deeply imaginative interpretations of nature that made him one of the most gifted jewelry artists of the modern age. A self-taught creative, Schlumberger was enlisted by Italian designer Elsa Schiaparelli in 1937 to conceive collections of buttons and costume jewels for her clothing (see p.250). His fanciful works—which evoked natural reliefs of animals, fruit, insects, and seashells—led to his discovery by *Vogue* editor Diana Vreeland (see p.306). In 1956 Schlumberger was recruited by Tiffany & Co., giving rise to an unprecedented chapter of creativity at the New York jewelry house (see p.283). Schlumberger imagined fantastical collections that captured the color and dynamism of the natural world. One of his first projects was a *Ribbon Rosette* necklace featuring the iconic Tiffany Diamond, famously worn by Audrey Hepburn in publicity photographs for *Breakfast at Tiffany's*. Other collections, such as his *paillonné* enamel bangles, the *Bird on a Rock*, and the *Sixteen Stone* diamond ring, earned Schlumberger a legion of high-profile admirers, including Greta Garbo, Jacqueline Kennedy, and Elizabeth Taylor (see pp.116, 150, 280). Today, many of Schlumberger's most repeated motifs still feature in Tiffany & Co.'s annual Blue Book Collections, reflecting the enduring power of his trailblazing ingenuity.

Lorraine Schwartz

Lorraine Schwartz
b. New York, New York,
United States

In an ode to the Statue of Liberty, Blake Lively wears a copper tiara with diamonds and Paraíba tourmalines and diamond and emerald earrings by Lorraine Schwartz at the 2022 Met Gala celebrating *In America: An Anthology of Fashion*. The tiara was featured in the *Crown to Couture* exhibition at Kensington Palace in 2023.

Photograph by Gilbert Carrasquillo.

The granddaughter of a prominent *diamantaire*, American jewelry designer Lorraine Schwartz has diamonds in her DNA. Schwartz added gemstones to her family's repertoire and established her eponymous brand in 2001, favoring glamorous designs with oversize gems in high-contrast, saturated colors. Known for her top-quality stones, she quickly became the go-to jewelry designer for royal families, heads of state, and style icons from Barbra Streisand and Elizabeth Taylor to Lady Gaga, Taylor Swift, and Beyoncé (see pp.29, 280). In addition to creating some of the most memorable red-carpet looks—and most high-profile engagement rings—of our time, Schwartz has transformed the way emeralds are perceived in high jewelry. Her innovative approach to the stones was showcased by Angelina Jolie at the 2009 Oscars with 115-carat Colombian emerald drop earrings, and by Beyoncé, who donned a 50-carat emerald ring and matching cluster earrings, weighing in at 80 carats, during her performance at Barack Obama's presidential inauguration in 2013. Beyond her influence on celebrity style, Schwartz is working to reinvigorate the jewelry industry by creating more opportunities for BIPOC designers through the Beyoncé Knowles-Carter × Lorraine Schwartz GIA Scholarship and the Emerging Designers Diamond Initiative, a partnership with the Natural Diamond Council.

Seaman Schepps

Seaman Schepps
est. New York, New York, 1934

Koi Fish Brooch with coral, turquoise, pearls, and diamonds set in 18-karat yellow gold.

In 1934 artist and entrepreneur Seaman Schepps opened a store on Madison Avenue in the heart of New York City. By the 1940s he had developed a formula for designing bold, colorful, and sculptural jewels that were popular among the rich and famous, earning him the moniker America's Court Jeweler. Schepps's clientele included US President Franklin D. Roosevelt, the Duchess of Windsor (see p.260), and members of the Du Pont, Mellon, and Rockefeller families. His first innovation was his *Turbo Shell Earrings*, adorned with touches of gold wire and precious gems, which remain a signature of the company today. Following this was the *Mousetrap Link Bracelet*, inspired by the coiled metal of a mousetrap spring, which featured links connected with gem-set gold tubing. Seaman Schepps's extravagant jewels were distinctive and fashionable. Many of the pieces were also made with unconventional materials, such as coral, ivory, rock crystal, wood, and glass. Schepps personally preferred cabochon, or irregularly cut gemstones, and often used soft-colored stones such as topaz, citrine, and quartz. The Schepps brand was acquired in 1992 by jewelry manufacturer Anthony Hopenhajm, who continues to produce pieces based on Schepps's original designs and molds while also opening stores in Palm Beach, Nantucket, and New York City.

Tupac Shakur

Tupac Shakur
b. New York, New York,
United States, 1971
d. Las Vegas, Nevada,
United States, 1996

Tupac Shakur wearing his iconic gold jewelry, *Details* magazine, 1996.

Photograph by David LaChapelle.

A musician, actor, activist, and one of the most popular hip-hop artists in history, Tupac Shakur has sold more than seventy-five million records worldwide, despite his brief career being cut tragically short with his death in 1996. A firm believer in the power of self-expression, he defined himself through both his art and his appearance, firmly establishing his own hip-hop style. Early on he favored leather cord necklaces before progressing to silver and then gold pieces as his fame grew. He was rarely pictured without a succession of heavy gold chains, rings, and jeweled watches. His collection included yellow gold Rolex watches, often studded in diamonds on the bracelet and bezel.

Gold chain necklaces featured different pendants, from an oversize cross and a crown to the logo of Death Row Records drawn in diamonds and the Makaveli *Euphanasia Chain Medallion*, featuring a Black Angel of Death. Today, Tupac's jewelry continues to make the headlines—in 2023 a gold, ruby, and diamond crown ring he designed was sold by Sotheby's at auction for $1 million to Canadian rapper Drake. In 2021 the Tupac estate announced a four-piece NFT series, the *Immortal Collection*, bringing to digital life four of Tupac's most iconic jewelry pieces, including a solitaire diamond ring and distinctive "2Pac"-emblazoned ring, which he designed in the last year of his life.

Joe Sheehan

Joe Sheehan
b. Nelson, New Zealand, 1976

Links in argillite, basalt, and graywacke, 2015.

Photograph by Sam Hartnett.

While Joe Sheehan's carvings can weigh as much as four tons, the artist has been creating wearable stone sculptures since graduating from university in Auckland, New Zealand, in the mid-1990s. For jewelry, the Wellington-based artist's preferred medium is nephrite jade, known in New Zealand as pounamu, the Māori word for the hard green stone found throughout the country. Having worked at his father's business, which mainly sold Māori-inspired pounamu pieces, Sheehan didn't want to appropriate another culture's art and so developed his own distinct design language, often using basalt, marble, granite, argillite, and other stones sourced from New Zealand. Rings are shaped as a stylized outline of a house, carved from various shades of pounamu and designed to fit snuggly on the finger, while a nephrite jade bracelet mimics a single handcuff, complete with a silver and brass key. Sheehan often plays with scale and perspective, carving stone tubes that appear as sharp angles; or rings carved in relief out of a large chunk of stone that are unliftable with a single finger, requiring the wearer to be bound, quite literally, to the ring. While his work is intrinsically tied to New Zealand, Sheehan has gained a worldwide audience for his carved jewels, and pieces are now held in museum collections, including the Victoria and Albert Museum in London.

Cora Sheibani

Cora Sheibani
b. Zurich, Switzerland, 1980

RK Fern Earrings made from green anodized aluminum and gold set with Silex jasper and spessartine garnets, 2021.

Cora Sheibani cannot recall a time in her childhood without art, history, and poignant discussions about creativity—a passion that was nurtured in a home filled with artifacts, paintings, and collectibles. Her parents, gallerists and collectors Bruno and Yoyo Bischofberger, shaped a young Sheibani's prudent eye. Since founding her eponymous brand in 2002, Sheibani's dissident approach has led to pairings of unconventional materials such as wood, bronze, copper, aluminum, and platinum that share compelling narratives. Unafraid to mix these diverse materials with traditional gems in a riot of colors, her pieces reference everyday objects—masks, tortes, clouds, cake molds, cacti, and potted plants—as unlikely muses. Reveling in the constraints that dictate the direction and conception of her pieces, she says, "I like the challenge of having to make the jewel practical, comfortable, beautiful, interesting, and different." She dismantles the seriousness of precious jewelry, anchoring each piece by a distinct inspiration that proffers its design premise. Delving into the science and history behind her medium, Sheibani's *Facets & Forms* collection explores the interior worlds of gemstones through various cuts set in a single piece. Sheibani's creations have evolved into cohesive collections, all crafted in Europe with precision and ingenuity that distill the defining features of her style.

Ambaji Shinde

Ambaji Shinde
b. Mapusa, India, 1917
d. New York, New York, United States, 2003

Scroll necklace created by Ambaji Shinde in collaboration with Nanubhai Jhaveri with elongated baguette, rectangular, and square-cut diamonds, c. 1954.

Referred to as the "jewel behind the jewel," Ambaji Shinde designed exquisite pieces for royalty and celebrities. During his almost forty-year tenure at Harry Winston, Shinde created such iconic designs as the Taylor-Burton necklace and the Star of Independence, the large pear-shaped diamonds weighing in at 59.42 and 75.52 carats, respectively (see pp.132, 280). Born in 1917 in Mapusa, India, Shinde enrolled at Bombay's Sir J.J. School of Art in 1934. Despite his training in textile art and design, Shinde opted to venture into jewelry and joined one of Bombay's leading jewelry companies, Narauttam Bhau Jhaveri. In 1938 Shinde created the coronation jewels of the Maharaja of Baroda (see p.113), laying the foundation for his successful tenure at Harry Winston. Winston and Shinde worked together to experiment with intricate stone settings, using a range of gemstones, such as white and fancy-colored diamonds in pink, blue, yellow, green, and orange tones. Moving away from bulky castings, they pioneered almost-invisible platinum settings and introduced the "cluster" diamond settings that showcased different cuts positioned at various angles and heights, creating a three-dimensional look with exceptional brilliance and play of light. Upon his death in 2003, Shinde bequeathed thousands of his sketches to the Gemological Institute of America for future students of jewelry design.

Nina Simone

Nina Simone (Eunice Kathleen Waymon)
b. Tryon, North Carolina, United States, 1933
d. Carry-le-Rouet, France, 2003

Nina Simone performs on stage at the Newport Jazz Festival in Rhode Island, 1968.

Photograph by David Redfern.

On the cover of Nina Simone's 1967 album *High Priestess of Soul*, an illustration depicts the singer-songwriter and musician in regalia that befits her self-appointed moniker, complete with a Nefertiti-style headdress, jeweled necklace, collar composed of piano keys, and sovereign's orb at hand. Her everyday attire was often no less grand. Her wardrobe was replete with hard-to-miss pieces that may not have been made of precious materials but that were valuable tools in defining her image: swinging, shoulder-dusting earrings that moved with the rhythm of her fierce piano playing; beaded bib necklaces; and crystal ornaments dangling from a gravity-defying updo. As she belted out soon-to-be classics such as "I Put a Spell on You," "To Be Young, Gifted and Black," and "Mississippi Goddam," her jewels were a silent accompaniment and a radical demand to be seen as a glamorous, accomplished, and multifaceted person in a country that still required her to fight for fundamental rights. The weight of her activism—she met with Martin Luther King Jr. during a march in Montgomery, Alabama, and was a public supporter of Malcolm X—was said to have contributed to her eventual move abroad. Jewelry distributed to radio disc jockeys to promote Simone's 1970 album *Black Gold*, which included pendants in the shape of Africa, was an outward expression of her passionate and trailblazing politics.

Maggi Simpkins

Maggi Simpkins
b. Portland, Oregon,
United States, 1988

A model wears jewels from the Maggi Simpkins capsule bridal collection in collaboration with Misfit Diamonds, 2023.

Photograph by DeMarcus Allen.

Los Angeles–based designer Maggi Simpkins serendipitously entered the jewelry industry in her early twenties, when she began making fashionable costume jewels. Her turn to precious metals, diamonds, and colored stones began in 2009 before learning the nitty-gritty of the trade while working at a diamond wholesaler in 2011. She struck out on her own in 2015, and, since then, Simpkins has made her mark as a custom designer specializing in commissioned engagement rings and fine jewelry that capture the unique narratives of each client. Her design credo leans in to craftsmanship and heritage juxtaposed with color and texture, primarily using yellow gold to create one-of-a-kind engagement rings meant to endure as future family heirlooms. Simpkins breaks away from the ubiquity of classic styles through unique arrangements and cluster assemblages of colored stones in vivid hues, particularly sapphires and emeralds. Unlike many of her contemporaries, she employs prongs in her designs to encourage a tactile exploration and resolutely handcrafts each piece. For the 2022 Sotheby's exhibition *Brilliant & Black*, Simpkins gained acclaim for her million-dollar *In Bloom* ring, which featured a central pink diamond surrounded by petals of custom-cut rubies and pink sapphires set in 18-karat rose gold, setting the stage for a bold new chapter for the designer.

Wallis Simpson

Wallis Simpson
b. Blue Ridge Summit, Pennsylvania, United States, 1896
d. Paris, France, 1986

The Duchess of Windsor wears a Vionnet dress with pearls, *Vogue*, November 1944.

Photograph by John Rawlings.

Immortalized in history as the reason King Edward VIII abdicated the British throne in 1936, Wallis Simpson is equally remembered for her impeccable taste and style. She shared a love of jewelry with her husband, who enjoyed creating bespoke pieces for her, including a nontraditional Cartier emerald engagement ring, weighing in at almost 20 carats (see p.54). The full extent of her jewelry collection was revealed in 1987, the year after her death, when it was sold at Sotheby's, fetching a total of $50 million (see p.267). She inspired Van Cleef & Arpels to create their iconic zip necklace, and from them she also acquired a sapphire and diamond *Jarretière* bracelet and *Deux Plumes* clip set with diamonds and mystery-set rubies (see p.291). Simpson and Edward frequented Cartier, and she was often seen with favorite pieces, such as the emerald-eyed *Panther* bracelet and the *Flamingo* brooch with a brilliant plume of rubies, emeralds, and sapphires. She refreshed and reconfigured her jewels regularly. In the 1960s, emerald and diamond necklaces from Harry Winston were exchanged for a pear-shaped pendant (see p.132), while Cartier reimagined an emerald Van Cleef & Arpels bracelet into a necklace. In a nod to the modern 1960s style, marquise-cut diamonds enveloped an almost 50-carat pear-shaped emerald from Harry Winston, which could be detached and worn as a brooch.

Bhupinder Singh

Bhupinder Singh,
Maharaja of Patiala
b. Patiala, India, 1891
d. Patiala, India, 1938

Maharaja Bhupinder Singh, 1911.

Photograph by Carl Vandyk.

In 1925 the head salesman of Cartier Paris was summoned to a hotel on the Champs-Élysées by Maharaja Bhupinder Singh of Patiala, one of the richest men in the world, who from the age of nine had ruled a princely state in the Punjab. The salesman was presented with chests of large loose precious gemstones, which the Maharaja wanted Cartier to reset in a modern Western style (see p.54). The commission took the jeweler three years to complete. Gemstones were transformed into sumptuous turban ornaments, bracelets, anklets, and necklaces to be worn by the maharaja, including the magnificent Patiala necklace featuring nearly three thousand diamonds and the De Beers 234.6-carat yellow diamond (see p.80). (The necklace controversially disappeared in 1948—the De Beers diamond resurfaced at auction in 1982 but without the necklace.) However, Cartier wasn't the maharaja's only commission. He returned to Paris in 1928 with a retinue of forty servants and six iron chests of precious stones for Louis Boucheron to reset in the Art Deco style, resulting in 149 pieces of jewelry (see p.39). Such magnificence did wonders for the reputations of Boucheron and Cartier. By that time, however, the maharaja was financially stretched, and he petitioned the government for a loan to settle his debts—a loan he must have received, because he went on to commission even more jewelry.

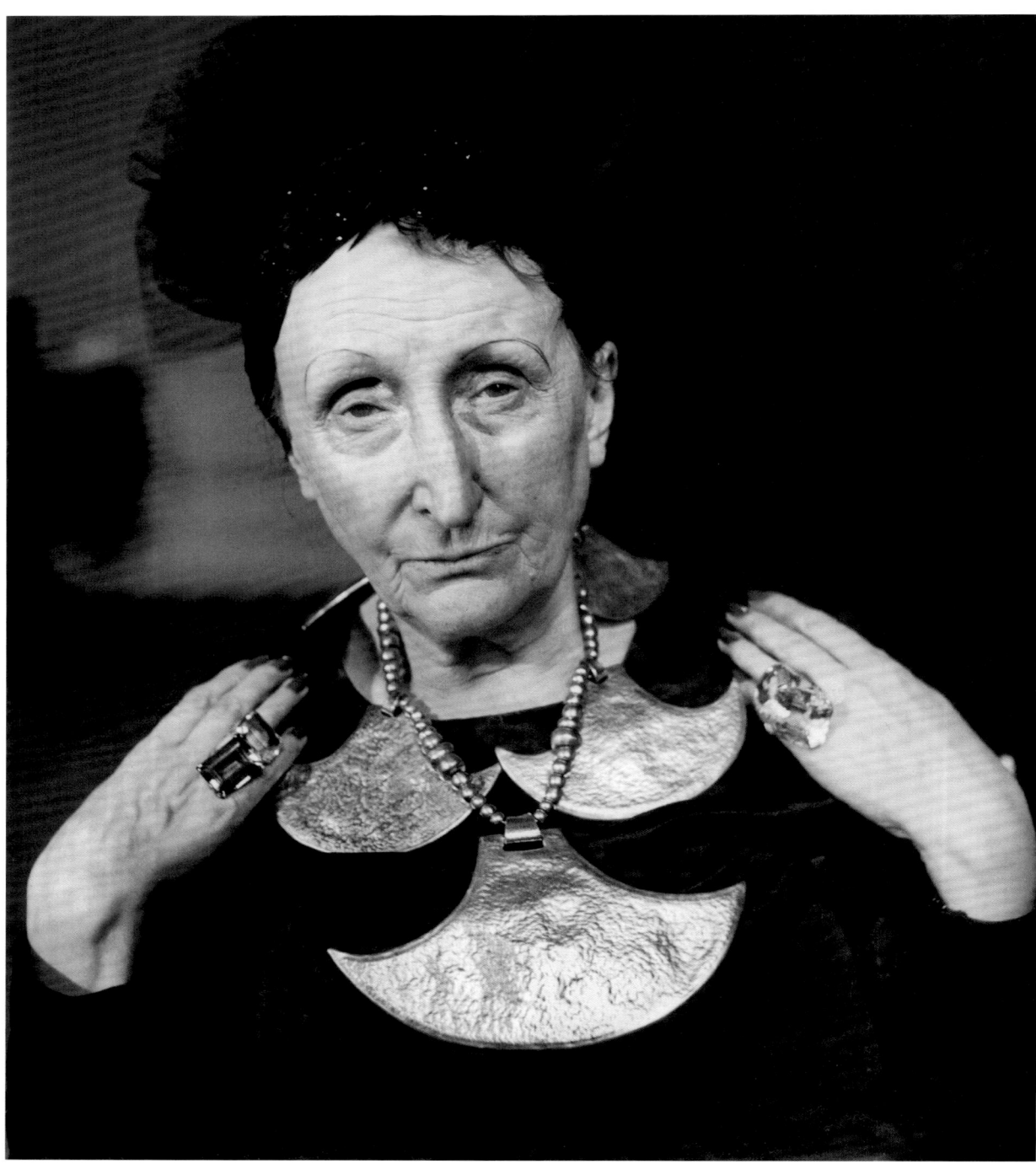

Edith Sitwell

Edith Sitwell
b. Scarborough, England, 1887
d. London, England, 1964

Edith Sitwell, 1959.

Photograph by Jane Bown.

Part of a literary dynasty, the intellectual and eccentric English poet Edith Sitwell cut an imposing figure. As well-known for her distinctive style as for her experimental poetry, Sitwell's bohemian aesthetic was characterized by rich brocade and velvet gowns, feathers, gold turbans, and bold jewelry. A vibrant member of the 1920s Bright Young Things set, she held court with writers and artists such as Cecil Beaton and Evelyn Waugh. The group encapsulated the flamboyant spirit of the time, a mood Sitwell translated into an eclectic and joyful jewelry collection. She spoke in interviews about her love for jewels, telling *Harper's Bazaar* she would feel undressed without her rings. Her favorite pieces included sizable aquamarine rings and red, green, and black amber bracelets she stacked up her arm, enjoying the clash of colors and the mix of materials. For official portraits, she chose jewelry sourced from all over the world, such as oversize brooches brought back from China by her brother and embellished silver gilt Indian bangles. In a photograph by Jane Bown, Sitwell is pictured in an large gold collar, or her "Aztec" necklace, as she referred to it. Created for her by socialite Millicent Rogers, it reportedly clinked so loudly during her reading at the Edinburgh Festival in 1959 that the audience struggled to hear her.

Slick Rick

Slick Rick (Richard Walters)
b. London, England, 1965

Slick Rick in his signature layers of gold jewelry, New York, 1991.

Photograph by Al Pereira.

As one of the most sampled hip-hop artists of all time, English American emcee Slick Rick set the standard for rap music today—and as a longtime jewelry aficionado, known to perform onstage with an eye patch and layers of thick gold chains, he has helped to define the genre's look as well. Born in London in 1965, he moved to New York with his family in 1976 and was introduced to the city's then-emerging hip-hop scene. He teamed up with the beatboxer Doug E. Fresh in 1985, and together they penned early classics of the genre such as the songs "The Show" and "La Di Da Di." When Rick began acquiring oversize necklaces and rings from dealers in New York's Chinatown, he viewed it at once as a symbol of his success and as a testament to the culture from which he came. "My jewels are my superhero suit," he wrote in 2022, "an extension of my beautiful brown skin." His pieces, including a massive pendant decorated with a Libra star sign, have become emblems of hip-hop itself, and others, such as his gem-encrusted eye patch and crown, appeared in the 2024 exhibition *Ice Cold: An Exhibition of Hip-Hop Jewelry* at the American Museum of Natural History in New York, for which Rick served as a senior curatorial advisor.

Pippa Small

Pippa Small
b. Montreal, Quebec, Canada, 1968

A New Day Greek ring in 18-karat gold set with kunzite.

Photograph by Jillian Boardman.

An ardent champion of ethical jewelry, Pippa Small has dedicated her practice to both understanding and lifting up the global communities in which she finds endless inspiration for her jewels. Deftly combining her work as an anthropologist and jewelry designer, Small is as likely to collaborate with high-fashion names—including Tom Ford at Gucci and Phoebe Philo at Chloe—as she is to work with traditional craftspeople, from the San of southern Africa to the Kuna peoples of Panama. She opened her first shop in Notting Hill, London, in 2007, but has continued to lead a semi-nomadic lifestyle, traveling widely to source ethically mined gems and to create jewelry with artisans from around the world: earrings with flowers and tiny butterflies from Myanmar; rings featuring alluvial emeralds from Colombia; and ancient Afghani motifs with rough-cut stones, such as lapis lazuli or agate, set in gold vermeil from Kabul. Small also offers a range of contemporary designs, which focuses on her love of natural gemstones, from watermelon tourmaline to rhodochrosite, bezel-set in 18-karat gold. Through it all, she continues her philanthropic initiatives and commitment to ethical practices, working with organizations, such as the Turquoise Mountain foundation in Afghanistan, to preserve traditional craftsmanship, for which she was awarded an MBE by Queen Elizabeth II in 2013.

Art Smith

Art Smith
b. Santa Lucia, Cuba, 1917
d. Brooklyn, New York, United States, 1982

Half and Half brass necklace, c. 1949.

One of the leading modernist jewelers of the twentieth century, Art Smith created pieces at a time when being a Black designer was often challenging. After graduating from Cooper Union in 1940 and working for four years with jeweler Winifred Mason Chenet—a celebrated master of copper and brass (see p.65)—he struck out on his own, eventually landing in a Greenwich Village boutique he would occupy for more than three decades. Born in Cuba to Jamaican immigrants, Smith was influenced by his father's adherence to Marcus Garvey's Pan-Africanism movement, and Afrocentric themes were a throughline in his designs. Working largely in copper, brass, and silver, his work echoed the curvaceous lines of African and West Indian art. Those inspirations merged with the influences of Alexander Calder (see p.50), Surrealist art, and Black contemporary dancers of the period, with whom he often collaborated on stage jewelry. Smith's biomorphic, abstract shapes were of an outsize scale that refused to be overlooked, even by the most vaunted fashion bibles. By the mid-1950s, *Vogue* and *Harper's Bazaar* had both featured his work, leading to notable commissions in precious metals by Eleanor Roosevelt, Duke Ellington, and Lena Horne, among others. His jewelry had a symbiotic relationship with the human form, never truly alive until worn and in motion.

Castro Smith

Castro Smith
b. Newcastle, England, 1988

Heavyweight *Heart Signet* ring in yellow gold with ceramic-plated engravings.

The intricate drawings that crowd Castro Smith's sketchbooks reveal the passion he has for his craft—engraving. Over the span of a single decade, he has become one of Britain's leading exponents of seal engraving, where the balance of light and shade gives life to deep designs that "slowly emerge from the tools." After studying painting and printmaking, Smith had planned to design computer games, but an engraving apprenticeship at Goldsmiths' Company and RH Wilkins had him discover his true calling. Smith's breakthrough came when, hurrying to finish a ring, his chisel slipped, and to cover the error, he engraved the ring's sides and shank—what is now his signature, along with the addition of color in translucent, metallic lacquer. In 2017 he won a scholarship to further his art in Japan, studying with such masters as Hiroshi Suzuki and Kenji Io and learning to make his own tools. From signet rings to charm bracelets, Smith has mastered highly detailed engravings on remarkably small canvases. Influenced by historical motifs, myths, and the natural world, his designs are incredibly varied—from a signet with a golden dancing bear and tendrils of greenery depicting the pagan Green Man to dragons, zodiac signs, and idyllic flowers sprouting from human hearts—yet all retain his elegant gift for storytelling in miniature.

Sotheby's

Sotheby's
est. London, England, 1744

A natural pearl and diamond devant-de-corsage sold by Sotheby's as part of the *Vienna 1900: An Imperial and Royal Collection* auction in November 2023. The piece, which features a floral wreath of diamonds with drop- and button-shaped pearls, was given by Philipp, the Duke of Württemberg, to his bride, Archduchess Maria Theresa of Austria-Teschen, as a wedding present in 1865.

Since its founding in London by Samuel Baker in 1744, Sotheby's has grown to become one of the world's largest players in jewelry auctions. Diamond and gem sales are often the headline attractions among jewelry auctions, and Sotheby's is at the forefront of supremely valuable and historically important gems. The CTF Pink Star, which fetched $71.2 million at a Sotheby's Hong Kong sale in 2017, was deemed the world's most valuable gem or jewel ever to sell at auction. At Sotheby's in Geneva, a single pearl pendant owned by Marie Antoinette set the world record in 2018 for the sale of a natural pearl at $36.2 million (see p.183). Geneva was also the location of "the alternative crown jewels" auction of the Wallis Simpson collection in 1987—a historic $50-million sale that broke the record for a single-owner jewelry collection and became a monumental moment for public perception of jewelry, previously seen as a product or accessory rather than as an art form (see p.260). Today, the auction house continues to hold live jewelry sales in major cities and is known for themed exhibitions, such as specialized events for Black jewelry designers, men's jewels, and for significant individual designers. Dedicated online sales are also held year-round, allowing digital bidding, which has expanded the house's global reach and attracted younger audiences to jewelry collecting.

Ettore Sottsass

Ettore Sottsass
b. Innsbruck, Austria, 1917
d. Milan, Italy, 2007

A model wears the *Double-Barreled Ring* in 18-karat gold and platinum with onyx and diamonds, created by Ettore Sottsass for Cleto Munari, c. 1984.

Photograph by Jordan Doner.

Italian architect Ettore Sottsass was a great innovator of postmodern design. The son of an architect influenced by the sleek Modernism popular in Vienna at the turn of the century, Sottsass spent much of his life railing against the movement's strict adherence to utility. His first foray into jewelry-making was in the 1960s, creating simple pieces using inexpensive materials (in lieu of precious stones) set in gold. Sottsass has said that his designs during this period were meant for "queens or Sumerian priestesses rather than for society ladies." Particularly impacted by his travels in India, Sottsass frequently used the simple, geometric shapes of ancient and premodern art in his work. In 1981 he founded the groundbreaking Memphis group, a collective of designers who challenged industry norms by creating furniture, ceramics, lighting, fabric, jewelry, and other objects using unconventional materials, especially plastic, in bright colors. Around this time, Sottsass's friend and fellow designer Cleto Munari invited him to translate his architectural mastery into a jewelry collection. Collaborating for two decades, the duo created dozens of pieces. One ring, inspired by a Florentine cathedral, adopted the shape of a church's dome, while the massive square *Tetto* ring made from gold, onyx, and diamonds evoked an architectural rendering of a building's roof in Sottsass's wholly original style.

Glenn Spiro

Glenn Spiro
b. London, England, 1962

Nuage Diamond Cuff, set with 44 old-mine, cushion-shaped white diamonds weighing a total of 49.69 carats, 452 brilliant-cut diamonds, and 1,196 single-cut diamonds, mounted in titanium.

Possessing a keen creative and aesthetic sense, British designer Glenn Spiro dreams up extraordinary jewels, mixing five-thousand-year-old stones with high-tech metals. Proud of his humble beginnings in East London, he left school at fifteen to apprentice in a goldsmith's workshop, English Art Works, producing for Cartier before setting up his own business at twenty-one (see p.54). In the early 1990s, he joined Christie's, where he saw clients gravitating toward private, artisan jewelers working with unique stones, and he aspired to join the ranks (see p.68). His work evolved into more extreme juxtapositions of style and craft: rough-hewn, not-quite-roundels of antique turquoise are mixed with modern, precision-geometry diamond cuts, or glowing, ultra-smooth cabochons with conventional halos of small diamond brilliants alternate with engraved eighteenth-century Baoulé gold from the Ivory Coast. Of the ancient stones he uses, he says, "Each has a story, often of passion or war." Carnelian and agate that date to 4000 BCE Mesopotamia are as likely to be set in geometric titanium as in gold, and humbler materials such as wood, horn, leather, bronze, and copper connect the ancient stones to the present and the future. Spiro has no qualms about his work, saying, "I've always designed things people don't want, but then someone always does."

Pierre Sterlé

Pierre Sterlé
b. Paris, France, 1905
d. Paris, France, 1978

A flying bird brooch with a body of cabochon black sapphire, a nape of gold beads, and wings in textured gold with brilliant-cut diamonds set in platinum.

Crafting gold as supple as fabric so that jeweled bows appear to flutter and foliage seems to quiver in a breeze, Pierre Sterlé was an innovative designer whose mastery of goldwork earned him the title "couturier of jewelry." Born in 1905 to a prominent Parisian financier, Sterlé was placed under the care of his uncle, a goldsmith supplying Paris's leading houses, after his father went missing in action during World War I. Displaying a natural flair for design, Sterlé secured commissions from iconic maisons such as Boucheron and Chaumet (see pp.39, 63), eventually launching his own workshop in the mid-1930s. A technical genius, Sterlé relentlessly researched and innovated new techniques to achieve daring, experimental jewels. He pioneered his *fil d'ange*, or "angel wire," knitting gold into fine ropes that formed fringes for his dramatic bird brooches. Inspired by nature—with feathers, flowers, and birds being favorite motifs—Sterlé's jewels were informed by extravagant, baroque asymmetries. Vibrant gemstones—such as coral, lapis lazuli, and peridot—set in yellow gold also became a hallmark, alongside the vivid juxtaposition of classic round diamonds with the sharp geometry of baguette cuts. Elite clients, including King Farouk of Egypt, the Maharani of Baroda (see p.113), and the Begum Aga Khan, flocked to Sterlé, drawn by his collaborations with Parisian couturiers.

Marguerite Stix

Marguerite Stix
b. Vienna, Austria, 1904
d. New York, New York, United States, 1975

Brooch with six seashells bezel-set in 14-karat gold, a central coral cabochon, a removable coral cabochon drop, and emerald accents, 1960s.

While shells have been used in jewelry-making since prehistoric times, Marguerite Stix elevated them into the realm of high jewelry in the 1960s. Born and raised in Vienna, Stix studied at the Wiener Werkstätte workshop under visionary designer Josef Hoffmann, who encouraged her to work in a variety of mediums. Stix fled to Paris at the outbreak of World War II and became a specialist maker of ceramic buttons, supplying top couture houses. In 1941 she immigrated to New York, where she met her husband, gallerist Hugh Stix. Together they traveled the world and amassed a collection of some fifteen thousand shells, eventually turning part of their Greenwich Village home into a *wunderkammer* called the Stix Rare Shell Gallery. Marguerite's passion for tropical sea treasures initially led her to creating wallpaper and lithograph patterns, but by 1964 she became fully focused on the art of transforming shells into wearable sculptures, eventually selling them through Cartier in New York and attracting celebrity collectors, such as Jacqueline Kennedy Onassis (see pp.54, 150). Among her most memorable creations are scallop-shell minaudières secured with gold frames and giant pearl clasps, iridescent cherrystone shells refashioned as brooches encrusted with glittering gems, and oversize rings crafted from open clam shells mounted in gold and resembling butterflies in flight.

Studio Renn

Studio Renn
est. Mumbai, India, 2018

Vadlo necklace and bracelet in sterling silver and gold with diamonds, 2025.

Deriving its name from the Latin for "rebirth," Studio Renn was founded in 2018 by the Mumbai-based husband-and-wife team of Rahul and Roshni Jhaveri, causing a reevaluation of contemporary Indian jewelry. They don't leverage India's decorative heritage and are open to taking risks with the unfamiliar. For their award-winning *Strangler* ring set with diamonds, the duo utilized acid-treated concrete, providing a core juxtaposition: concrete is common yet useful, and diamonds are rare and serve no practical purpose. Drawing on Rahul's family background in diamond-cutting and polishing, they began designing jewelry for friends before formalizing the business. While the design process is collaborative, Rahul is primarily in charge of production and Roshni oversees the studio and business operations. Together they create "studies," referencing shapes from nature but in an abstracted way. They use unconventional materials and finishes with a play on reflections and texture using gloss or matte to dramatic effect. Many of their designs are provocative, with names such as *Puffball Void*, which explores incompleteness with half-polished metal and unset voids, and *Crocodile*, with jagged green Zambian emeralds. They have a brutalist yet playful sensibility, experimenting with techniques in diamond polishing; processed roughs; antique cuts; and unusual, often rejected colors.

Arman Suciyan

Arman Suciyan
b. Istanbul, Turkey, 1972

Wings of Victory and *Ascending Crane* rings, 2014.

Photograph by Deniz Köylü.

From minimalist bangles sculpted in silver to highly ornate textured gold rings set with vibrant pink sapphires, Turkish jewelry designer Arman Suciyan displays his mastery over precious metals. Apprenticed at age fifteen to a goldsmith in Istanbul's Grand Bazaar, Suciyan observed the traditional skills of the trade and found a penchant for wax modeling. After four years, in 1988 he went on to work for Misak Toros, who taught him the techniques of fine jewelry-making, before moving to the UK to attend the Kent Institute of Art & Design in 1994. It was there that he was introduced to British jeweler Stephen Webster, whom he joined after graduation as a goldsmith. Over the course of a decade with Webster, Suciyan pushed the boundaries of wax modeling on elaborate figurative pieces. In 2004 Suciyan turned to his own work, embracing sculptural pieces with unexpected contrasts. A 2015 collection was inspired by Kurt Vonnegut's *The Sirens of Titan*, sparking the idea of an intergalactic winged goddess traveling through space and time to give life to nature. Suciyan translated this into a series of bird-inspired pieces in the *Odyssey* collection, such as the sleek silver *Crane* ring with outstretched, gem-studded wings. His *Hyper Baroque* collection, on the other hand, went back to unadorned metals, shaping rose and yellow gold into sleek, fluid infinity rings based on nature's own architecture.

Gearry Suen

Gearry Suen
b. Harbin, China, 1996

Orchid Calligraphy Earrings in titanium and 18-karat yellow gold with yellow, orange, pink, and purple sapphires, yellow and white diamonds, pink and purple spinels, and orange garnets, 2024.

Embracing a new concept of modern elegance, nuanced with a futuristic twist, Gearry Suen's vivacious, free-form approach to his jewels effortlessly captures the harmonious balance of nature and the cosmos. Born in Harbin, the northernmost province of China, Suen moved to London to learn jewelry design, attending Central Saint Martins and then completing his studies at the Royal College of Art in London in 2020, where he also took painting and industrial design courses. The mix of Suen's training in diverse disciplines has led to his singular style of fluid shapes composed from a tantalizing mix of materials. Whether inspired by the abstract silhouettes of ancient Chinese painting and calligraphy, Modernist architecture, or artificial intelligence, Suen seeks a seamless integration of stones and precious metals, each element appearing to fall into a comfortable embrace to tell multilayered stories through his jewels. Inspired by creatures in Hieronymus Bosch's *The Garden of Earthly Delights*, Suen's *Chimera* earrings feature a sprawling, organic form of hand-carved Hetian jade, titanium, and gold, set with a dazzling array of diamonds, Paraíba tourmalines, rare hauynes, and other multicolored stones. Designing and engraving each piece himself, Suen focuses on private commissions, often based around a client's gemstone, imbuing their character into every artful jewel.

Swarovski

Swarovski
est. Wattens, Austria, 1895

Ariana Grande wears pieces from the *Millenia* collection, 2024.

Photograph by Mert and Marcus.

"A diamond is for everyone," Daniel Swarovski pronounced, realizing his vision in 1895 to make crystals more brilliant, alluring, and accessible than ever before by founding his namesake brand in Wattens, Austria. For more than 125 years, Swarovski has been globally renowned for its crystals, later evolving to become a leading jewelry and accessories brand. Honoring a rich tradition of craftsmanship and innovation—Daniel invented an electric machine that produced Swarovski's precision-cut crystals—Swarovski's new cuts, generational know-how, and continuous refinement accentuate sparkle and brilliance across a broad array of everyday jewelry lines, from archival signatures, such as the *Nirvana* cocktail ring or *Slake* bracelet, to today's *Lucent* earrings and *Millenia* necklace. While Gabrielle "Coco" Chanel was among Swarovski's customers in the 1920s, creating brooches and embroidery using various crystals, the house has also collaborated with more than 250 designers, including Christian Dior, Alexander McQueen, Dolce & Gabbana, Jean Paul Gaultier, Karl Lagerfeld, and Versace (see pp.60, 89, 163). In 2021 style doyenne Giovanna Engelbert was appointed creative director of Swarovski, ushering in a new era for the brand, debuting *Collection One*—a range of chunky pieces in pop colors—and in 2023 introducing the *Galaxy* collection, featuring lab-grown diamonds.

Tilda Swinton

Tilda Swinton
b. London, England, 1960

Tilda Swinton wearing Fred Leighton diamond brooches, *T: The New York Times Style Magazine*, August 2005.

Photograph by Raymond Meier.

The off-screen, anti-ingenue jewelry worn by Scottish actor Tilda Swinton parallels her fearless choices on-screen. Not one for conventional, high-carat confections, Swinton gravitates toward jewelry makers and designs with an idiosyncratic point of view. Like some of the directors she has worked with repeatedly, such as Wes Anderson and Luca Guadagnino, she has a roster of creative collaborators she often turns to for her eclectic yet contemporary adornment. On the red carpet, Swinton has worn subversive pieces by Delfina Delettrez Fendi (see p.85) that emphasize the relationship between gems and negative space, such as the *Today Tomorrow* cuff made custom for her appearance at the 2018 Venice Film Festival and comprising a giant yellow morganite and diamonds that seemed to float weightlessly on her arm. Swinton has also favored architectural design via diamond earrings from Repossi and has gone to Venetian maison Codognato for ornate, old-world jewels (see p.71) that pose a striking counterpoint to her typically minimalist and androgynous clothing. Another frequent partner is Damiani: on the night of Swinton's Oscar win in 2008, she wore a torqued, weighty diamond-and-gold cuff from the Italian brand, which took on a different appearance from every angle, a most fitting jewel for the chameleonic actor.

Symbolic & Chase

Symbolic & Chase
est. London, England, 2003

A pair of Suzanne Belperron rock crystal and diamond *Éventail* clip brooches in platinum and gold, c. 1935, from the Symbolic & Chase collection.

Located in a private salon on Old Bond Street, London, Symbolic & Chase spans two floors of design and antiques. Founded in 2003 by Martin Travis, after he left Christie's jewelry department, and Sophie Jackson, who had worked at Sotheby's, the gallery presents a collection of fine jewels and objets curated with an anthropological perspective that focuses on jewelry as a form of art. While Symbolic & Chase specializes in twentieth-century European masterpieces, it also includes carefully selected treasures, such as a Bronze Age bracelet, that span much of human history. Renowned for its treasure hunter's approach to sourcing rare and exceptional pieces, Symbolic & Chase has built an extensive archive, from iconic designs by Suzanne Belperron and René Boivin to antique pieces by Harry Winston and Van Cleef & Arpels (see pp.28, 35, 132, 291). The gallery also offers contemporary jewels, introducing the work of new-generation designers such as Theodoros and Vamgard (see pp.282, 290). Travis and Jackson have developed a unique approach at Symbolic & Chase that goes above offering an exquisite selection of jewelry and places a strong emphasis on education and research. This commitment to understanding the context around each jewel's creation has cemented their international reputation among collectors, institutions, and designers.

Tasaki

Tasaki
est. Kobe, Japan, 1954

Necklaces and ear cuff from the *Danger* collection, featuring Akoya pearls adorned with yellow-gold fangs, 2022.

Photograph by Kyosuke Azuma.

Founded in 1954 by Shunsaku Tasaki, the son of humble pearl farmers, the Japanese house of Tasaki grew into a global luxury brand and retail powerhouse. With an uncompromising focus on quality and research, Tasaki is responsible for a host of innovations in their field: they were the first to farm the near-extinct winged Mabe pearl in 1970, as well as the first Japanese jeweler to become a De Beers Sightholder, allowing them to purchase rough diamonds directly from the company (see p.80). In 2009 Toshikazu Tajima, a seasoned luxury fashion executive, was appointed CEO and injected an edgier, design-forward approach to the collections. This vision was led by creative directors such as fashion designers Prabal Gurung and Thakoon Panichgul, and through collaborations with outside designers such as Greek jeweler Melanie Georgacopoulos (see p.121). Panichgul has added an exciting coolness and edginess into the brand, beginning with his debut *Balance* collection, which aligns pearls perfectly on a level bar, evoking a purist, linear beauty—a bestseller that has been revisited in subsequent designs. This line was followed by *Danger*, a collection that subverts the pearl completely, setting punk-style horns and spikes into the gem. Ever evolving, Tasaki has since launched a high jewelry collection featuring bold, one-of-a-kind statement pieces that move beyond the pearl.

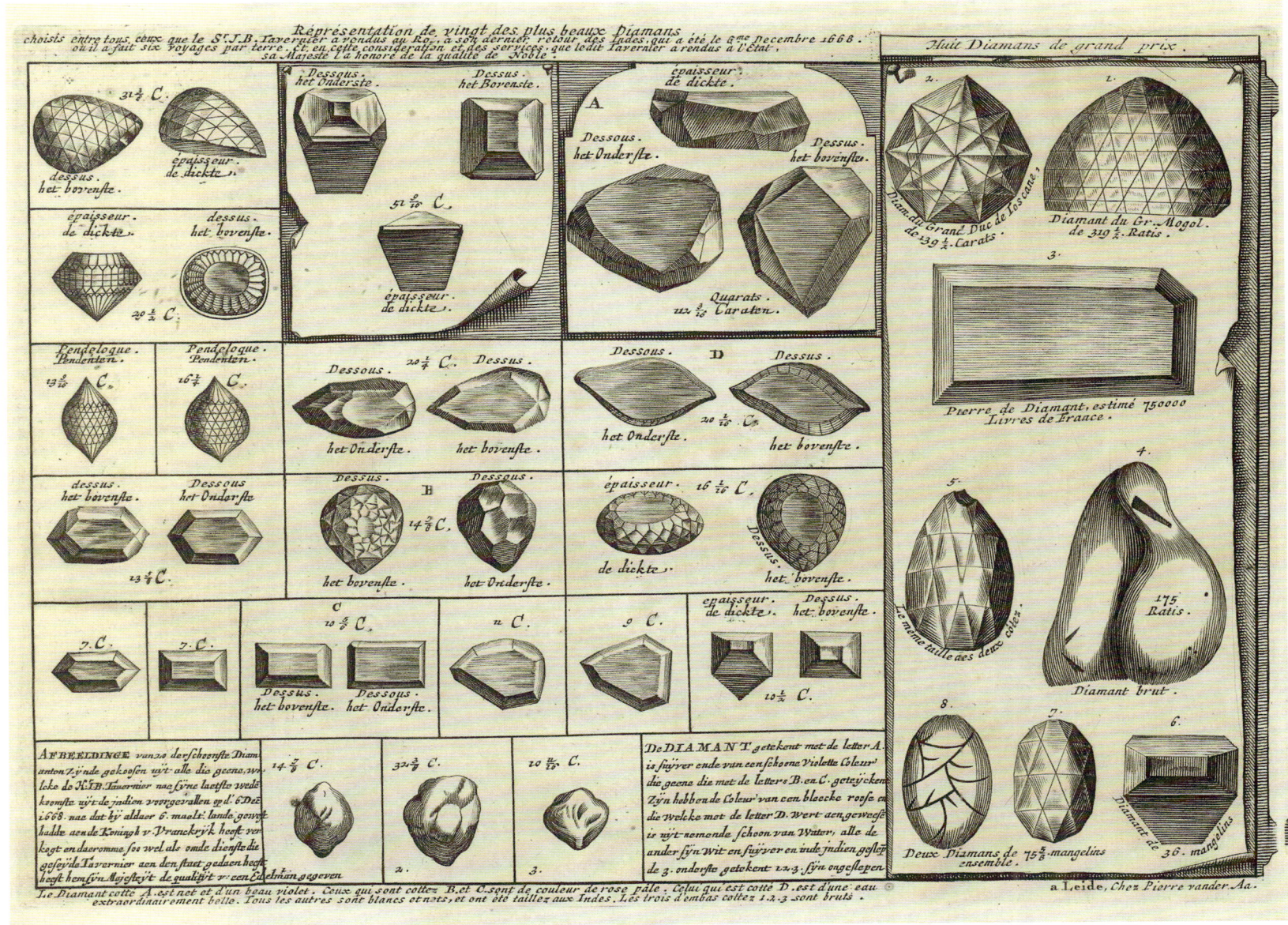

Jean-Baptiste Tavernier

Jean-Baptiste Tavernier
b. Paris, France, 1605
d. Moscow, Russia, 1689

Illustrations by Jean-Baptiste Tavernier showing "twenty of the most beautiful diamonds" from those he sold to King Louis XIV upon his return from the East Indies in December 1668, including the 280-carat Great Mogul Diamond at top right and what would become known as the Hope Diamond under label A.

Born in Paris in 1605 and raised in Antwerp, Jean-Baptiste Tavernier was possessed by an insatiable wanderlust that took him to Persia and India, where he made his fortune in the gem trade. He chronicled his six voyages to Asia between 1630 and 1668 in several books, along with maps of his travels, a skill he learned from his cartographer father. Tavernier's books recount visits to the diamond mines of Golconda, in India, and the invitation to inspect the imperial treasures owned by the Mughal emperor Aurangzeb. It included the Great Mogul Diamond that, based on Tavernier's skillful sketches of its halved-egg shape, is now identified as the Orlov Diamond. During Tavernier's travels, he acquired a 115-carat dark blue diamond, thought to be from the Kollur Mine in the Golconda region. A shrewd trader, he returned to France and sold it and other diamonds to King Louis XIV. Recut into a heart shape, it became known as the French Blue, and after the French Revolution it passed through many owners, including George IV of England, to later be renamed the Hope Diamond (see p.132, 192). In payment from Louis XIV, Tavernier received the equivalent of 172,000 ounces of gold and a letter of ennoblement to the Baron of Aubonne.

Elizabeth Taylor

Elizabeth Taylor
b. London, England, 1932
d. Los Angeles, California, United States, 2011

Elizabeth Taylor poses for *Life* magazine wearing her own earrings and a blue triangle pendant necklace, which was spontaneously borrowed for the photoshoot from the photographer's wife, Yvonne Halsman, October 1948.

Photograph by Philippe Halsman.

One of the best-known jewelry collectors in history, Elizabeth Taylor wore her splendid jewels with the same gusto with which she acquired them over her lifetime. The legacy of Taylor's collection was cemented in December 2011, when Christie's dedicated its entire Rockefeller Center headquarters to a four-day exhibition and live auction of her estate, complemented by a fifteen-day online sale, the first such sale in the history of the auction house (see p.68). The sale of Taylor's jewels, considered one of the most expensive private collections of jewelry in the world, resulted in the highest sale of jewels in auction history at the time, achieving $137.2 million (and setting seven other records for individual pieces). The auction was a fitting tribute for someone whose life embodied jewels as adornment. François Curiel, Christie's international jewelry director, first met Taylor in 1998 and was immediately impressed with her broad knowledge of jewelry, saying she possessed an expert's eye for craftsmanship, rarity, quality, and history. Taylor didn't put her valuable pieces away for special occasions, either—she regularly wore them, including her signature 33.19-carat diamond ring, a gift from Richard Burton. Taylor also owned a Cartier Ruby Suite gifted to her by her third husband, film producer Mike Todd, which she wore on many occasions until her death in 2011 (see p.54).

Ten Thousand Things

Ten Thousand Things
est. New York, New York,
United States, 1991

Hand-cut rock crystal
collar with hand-fabricated
28-karat gold links, 2022.

Photograph by Thomas Kletecka.

Founded in 1991 in New York by Ron Anderson and David Rees, Ten Thousand Things set out to create a new idiom in jewelry, its name inspired by a verse from the *I Ching* that evoked the idea of endless creativity. In direct opposition to the vogue for mass-produced statement costume jewelry, Ten Thousand Things instead turned to the shapes and forms of the natural world to offer a novel approach that stepped outside of the maelstrom of mainstream jewels. Their big break came in 1992 when Kate Moss donned a pair of Ten Thousand Things freshwater pearl earrings in her first campaign for Calvin Klein, with dozens of major fashion credits following. Self-taught and unencumbered with preconceptions, the duo handmakes everything from delicate chains threaded with small gemstone drops, reminiscent of jewelry from Ancient Rome, to large-scale sculptural silver forms inspired by Georgia O'Keeffe's orchid paintings, and sumptuous ropes of Keshi pearls with baroque undertones. The bestselling oversize *Totem* earrings are formed from four flat, gently curving pieces of hand-cut luminous stone or crystal arranged in a cascade. Layered with meaning and instinctively appealing, they have captured the attention of clients who are not afraid to express their individuality, including Julianne Moore, Susan Sarandon, and Reese Witherspoon.

Theodoros

Theodoros
est. Athens, Greece, 2008

A flexible bracelet with rhodium-plated rose gold links set with 8.53 carats of diamonds, 2022.

Something of a recluse, the elusive Greek designer Theodoros Savopoulos has cultivated a global cult following since establishing his eponymous company in 2008. His jewels are highly ornate, with elegant simplicity, often prominently featuring large flawless diamonds, invisible settings, and micro pearls, along with the occasional appearance of jadeite. Unbound by formal training, Savopoulos has created a body of work that is delightfully eclectic and transcends eras and trends. A flexible bracelet with graduated links of custom-finished gold and set with a central 3.05-carat diamond—flanked by six other diamond accents—was inspired by traditional Indian armlets, while sapphires, colored diamonds, and other stones are set into Lucite rings to dramatic effect with a modern flair. Early in his career, Savopoulos established his own workshop and selected experienced artisans to work exclusively for him, fostering a rare synergy between conception and realization. For Theodoros, materials and techniques are carefully chosen to enhance the unique beauty of gemstones rather than conforming to a predetermined aesthetic with the view of impressing a recognizable house signature. But there are some features that are quintessentially Theodoros: old-cut diamonds, unusual-colored gemstones, and natural pearls with a charming patina.

Tiffany & Co.

Tiffany & Co.
est. New York, New York,
United States, 1837

Tiffany & Co. reinterprets Jean Schlumberger's iconic *Bird on a Rock* brooch, first introduced in 1965, with a selection of rare colored gemstones, accented by diamonds, pearls, and vibrant *paillonné* enamel, from the *Rainbow Bird on a Rock* high jewelry capsule collection, 2024.

Over nearly two centuries, Tiffany & Co. has grown into the quintessential American jewelry house. The New York–based company was established in 1837 by Charles Lewis Tiffany and his business partner, J. B. Young. The firm's famous Blue Book direct-mail catalog was first offered in 1845 and in 1877 Charles sealed his status as the King of Diamonds with the purchase and cutting of the Tiffany Diamond, a 128.54-carat fancy yellow stone. With the appointment of Charles's son, Louis Comfort Tiffany, as the company's first design director in 1902, Tiffany & Co. entered a period of unrivaled creativity. Louis's colorful, naturalistic Art Nouveau aesthetic remains a major inspiration for the brand. Other extraordinary talents soon left an equally indelible mark: In the early 1900s gemologist George Frederick Kunz introduced new gemstone varieties, such as kunzite and morganite (see p.157). Appointed in 1956, Jean Schlumberger's imaginative designs, such as the famous *Bird on a Rock*, attracted a roster of high-profile collectors (see p.251). When Elsa Peretti joined in 1974, her sensuous designs revolutionized the concept of fine jewelry for every day, and in the 1980s Paloma Picasso's sculptural pieces reimagined street art as statement jewelry (see pp.221, 224). The brand was acquired by French luxury group LVMH in 2021, setting the stage for an entirely new era.

Gabriel Tolkowsky

Gabriel Tolkowsky
b. Tel Aviv, Mandatory Palestine, 1939
d. Tel Aviv, Israel, 2023

Gabriel Tolkowsky examines the Centenary Diamond, 1991.

Photograph by Richard Gardner.

A sixth-generation diamond expert, Gabriel "Gabi" Tolkowsky stamped significant marks on his family's legacy: diamonds named in his honor, knighted by the Belgian government for contributions to the diamond industry, and commissioned to cut the world's largest faceted diamond. After training with his father, Tolkowsky began working with De Beers in 1975 (see p.80). During his tenure, he was entrusted as the master cutter for the 273.85-carat Centenary Diamond, and after three years of meticulous work, De Beers unveiled the diamond in 1991 to commemorate its one hundredth anniversary. The stone gained global recognition as the largest, most perfectly colored, and most flawlessly cut diamond in modern history. This achievement led to De Beers assigning him the task of cutting the Golden Jubilee Diamond, weighing an impressive 545.67 carats. The same specialized equipment and tools developed for successfully cutting the Centenary Diamond were utilized for the Golden Jubilee Diamond due to its intricate internal structure. Tolkowsky continued to innovate and created the world's first triple-brilliant-cut diamond, the Gabrielle Diamond. The Gabrielle cut featured a round shape with 105 facets, surpassing the traditional Classic Round Brilliant cut by an impressive 48 facets.

Elie Top

Elie Top
b. Nord-Pas-de-Calais, France, 1976

Diamond Caméléon Ring in yellow gold, rose gold, and distressed silver, set with diamonds, 2021.

Photograph by Hugues Laurent.

In 2015 Elie Top debuted his namesake brand with *Mécanique Céleste*, a collection themed around Art Deco, industrial-inspired design that used a bespoke mechanism to allow his spherical jewels to be viewed both open and closed. Top wanted the focus of his work to be its design approach rather than its gemstones. Unsurprising for a designer who forged his early career at two of Paris's leading fashion houses, where he created bold, dramatic jewels that made a resounding impact on the catwalk. Having studied at the Chambre Syndicale de la Couture in Paris, Top joined Yves Saint Laurent in 1997, designing accessories and learning his craft from Loulou de La Falaise (see pp.82, 245).

When creative director Alber Elbaz arrived in 1998 to design the Rive Gauche collection, the pair instantly clicked. Together they moved to Lanvin in 2001, where Top's bold, baroque bijoux offset Elbaz's minimalist designs, helping revitalize the brand. The duo started covering eighteenth-century-inspired jewelry with fabric—using brass and pewter, there were chunky chains, cuffs, bug brooches, and heart pendants. Today, Top works primarily in gold and silver, usually combined in each jewel. He draws inspiration from seventeenth- and eighteenth-century architecture, antique jewelry, and, as in the armor-inspired *La Dame du Lac* collection, continues to allude to the mystical past.

Vivianna Torun Bülow-Hübe

Vivianna Torun Bülow-Hübe
b. Malmö, Sweden, 1927
d. Copenhagen, Denmark, 2004

Torun models a pendant necklace of her own design, c. 1950s.

Photograph by Gilles Ehrmann.

For Swedish silversmith and jeweler Vivianna Torun Bülow-Hübe—better known just as Torun—silver was the epitome of simple and stylish design. Torun was drawn to silver for its ability to be teased into sculptural shapes, and the jewelry she created was the antidote to the more ostentatious jewelry popular in the Swinging Sixties. The workshop she established in Sweden in the 1940s encapsulated her distinctive aesthetic, her swirls of silver reminiscent of the graceful loops she observed her skates making on the ice as a child. Eschewing precious stones, Torun re-created these elegant whorls in silver, embellished only with simpler materials such as moonstones, pebbles, and rock crystal. She paid careful consideration to the way jewelry moved on the body, and in tracing the lines of the wrist, neck, and décolletage, her jewelry cut sensuous silhouettes. She celebrated practicality in her pieces, with clasps becoming decorative elements in their own right, rather than something to be hidden away. In 1969 Danish jewelry company Georg Jensen began to exclusively produce her designs, including *Beans* and *Forget Me Knot* (see p.120). Georg Jensen also commissioned a wristwatch she designed with no hour hand or number, as she resented the relentless march of time. With a mirrored back and its solitary second hand, it became an enduring icon of minimalist jewelry design.

Trifari

Trifari
est. New York, New York,
United States, 1910

Twiggy wears three large, jeweled pins with matching bracelets by Trifari, *Vogue*, November 1967.

Photograph by Bert Stern.

A prominent name in vintage fashion jewelry, Trifari created costume jewels worn everywhere from Broadway to the White House. Trifari was founded in 1910, when Gustavo Trifari, the son of a Napoli goldsmith, adapted the skills learned from his father to produce elaborate yet more accessible pieces. Trifari's success was marked by shrewd collaborations in marketing, with custom designs for famous actors, and creatively by the arrival of Alfred Philippe in 1930, bringing with him skills learned at Cartier and Van Cleef & Arpels, such as invisible settings (see pp.54, 291). Hand-setting pieces, he brought a new level of craftsmanship to costume jewelry. During World War II, costume jewelry became an indulgence, and a colorful brooch livened up an otherwise austere suit. Unlike gold, silver and vermeil were freely available, and Trifari made a variety of nature-inspired and Art Deco–motif jewels. Crown pins used rhinestones, faux pearls, and colorful enamel, and Jelly Belly brooches depicted miniature animals. Rather than opting for fine jewelry, US First Lady Mamie Eisenhower commissioned a costume parure from Trifari for her husband's presidential inaugural ball in 1953, firmly setting the brand in the history books. After more than eighty years in operation, in 1994 Trifari became part of the Monet Group, and in 2000 it was acquired by Liz Claiborne.

Otumfuo Nana Osei Tutu II

Otumfuo Nana Osei Tutu II,
King of the Asante
b. Kumasi, Ghana, 1950

Otumfuo Nana Osei Tutu II,
16th Asantehene, 2015

Photograph by Eddie Gerald.

Since becoming the sixteenth Asantehene (king of the Asante) in 1999, Otumfuo Nana Osei Tutu II has been praised for his role in championing peace within the Asante kingdom and Ghana at large, as well as preserving the cultural heritage of his realm. Central to the Asante identity is the *Sika 'dwa*, or Golden Stool, upon which the Asantehene is enthroned, and which is regularly seen in ceremonies where the ruler is adorned in layers of finely worked gold jewels. Initially part of the Akan people, who have been making gold jewelry since the twelfth century, the Asante broke away in the seventeenth century. Their land was close to the Akan goldfields, and Asante goldsmiths developed sophisticated techniques for working the metal, including lost-wax casting, engraving, and filigree. The gold became highly valued globally, dominating the trade along trans-Saharan routes. The gold jewelry eventually made its way to the Mediterranean and Europe, establishing the Asante as a major economic and political player in West Africa. In 1874, and again in 1900, the British plundered many gold artifacts from the Asante capital, but the Golden Stool and other royal jewels were preserved. Today, Osei Tutu II continues to follow tradition, appearing at official functions wearing elaborate Asante gold jewels, and tirelessly advocates for the return of his people's treasures from Western institutions.

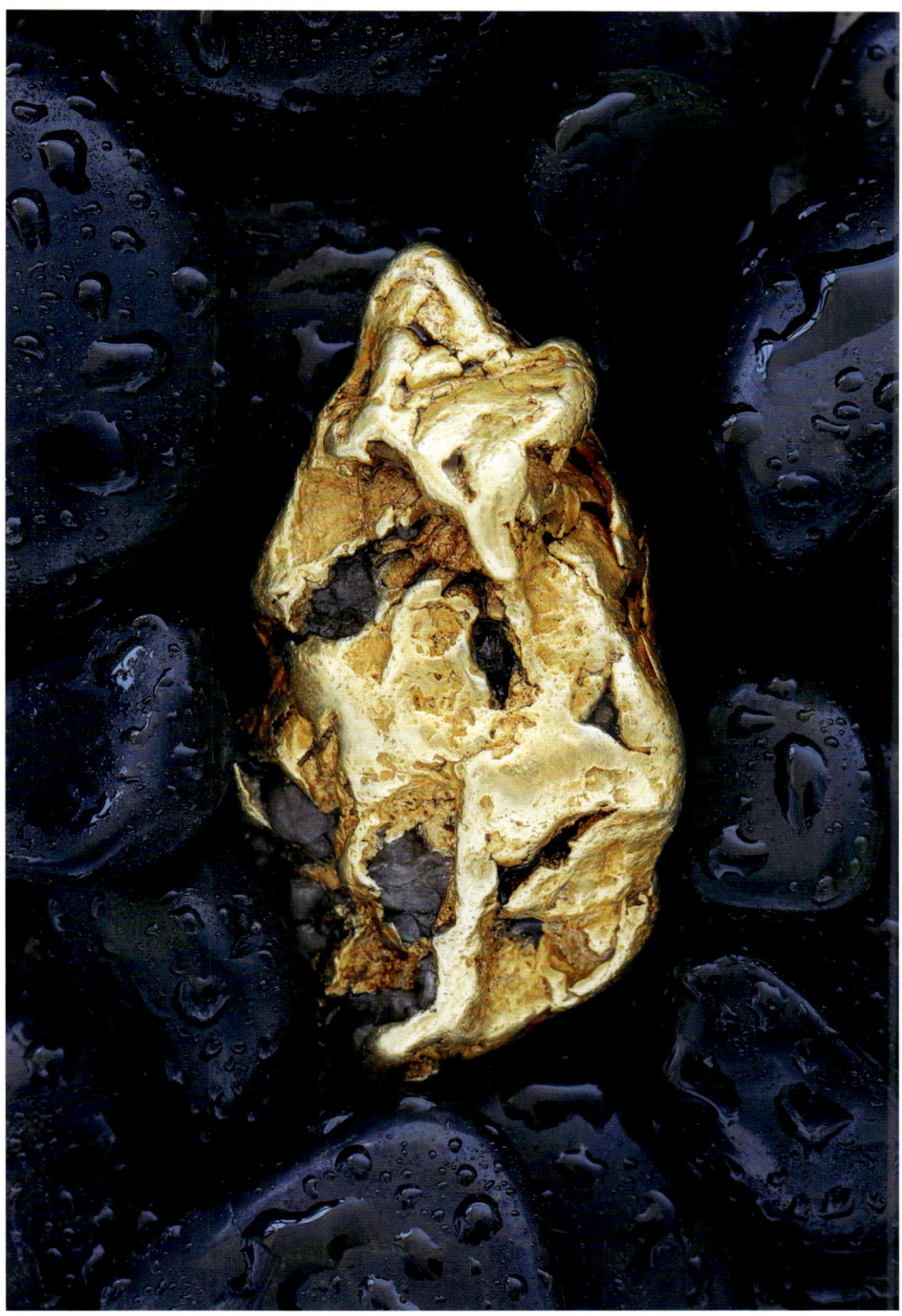

Greg Valerio

Greg Valerio
b. Toronto, Ontario, Canada, 1967

A large gold nugget of similar form to those emerging from PeaceGold cooperative partners, 2007.

Photograph by David Muir.

A maverick and pioneering activist behind the Fairtrade Gold movement, Greg Valerio was appalled as a young jeweler by the conditions endured by garnet miners in Rajasthan, India, galvanizing him to seek transparency and traceability in the jewelry supply chain. Scouring the world for sources of ethical gold, he founded CRED Jewellery in 1996 at the beginning of the fledgling ethical jewelry movement. In 2004 Valerio became a founding member of the Alliance for Responsible Mining (ARM), headquartered in Colombia. Valerio led the campaign on behalf of ARM and Fairtrade International to create the framework for the world's first Fairtrade and Fairmined gold, designed to help the poorest and most marginalized miners create safer working conditions and receive fair pay for their work. PeaceGold is Valerio's latest social enterprise in the Democratic Republic of the Congo. It addresses conflict resolution and fosters collaboration by working with decommissioned ex-militia to integrate them into small-scale gold-mining cooperatives, proliferate mercury-free mining, and offer an export platform in a shared-ownership model. In 2016 Valerio was awarded an MBE by the British Crown for his groundbreaking work, and he has received numerous awards for his humanitarian endeavors and landmark contributions to sustainable sourcing.

Vamgard

Vamgard
est. Rome, Italy, 2015

Le Rêve de Carpe Koi bracelet with micromosaic and diamonds on carbon fiber and gold, 2017.

In 2015 Maurizio Fioravanti, a self-taught micromosaicist and jewelry designer from Rome, envisioned Vamgard as a metaphorical "garden of delights." For him, each Vamgard jewel is a work of art that fuses centuries of knowledge with the technologies of the future and the rarest gems. Fioravanti's ingeniously constructed jewels feature micromosaics of exceptional finesse and painterly quality. He personally crafts his minute glass tesserae—as small as one-tenth of a millimeter—using rare minerals to replicate the effects of eighteenth-century micromosaic masters. Working with Virginie Torroni, a Geneva-based expert gem dealer, to source precious and rare stones, each piece is so intricate and labor-intensive that Fioravanti produces up to only ten each year. For the mounts, he blends traditional jewelry-making techniques with unconventional materials such as titanium, zirconium, and carbon fibers layered with thin bronze sheets. In a 2019 bracelet, Fioravanti used pleated medical-grade steel studded with eight-cut diamonds and diamond-set concentric ripple motifs that encircle a micromosaic of frogs, dragonflies, lotus flowers, and lily pads. Extending well beyond the traditional Roman micromosaic repertoire, Vamgard's creations are primarily inspired by the natural world, especially as interpreted through traditional Japanese aesthetics.

Van Cleef & Arpels

Van Cleef & Arpels
est. Paris, France, 1906

Diamond and platinum necklace commissioned by the Egyptian royal family and worn by Queen Nazli, with a matching tiara, to the wedding of Princess Fawzia of Egypt and the Crown Prince of Iran, Mohammad Reza Pahlavi, in 1939.

From the marriage of Alfred Van Cleef, the son of a lapidary and diamond broker, to Estelle Arpels, the daughter of precious stone dealer Salomon Arpels, in 1895, one of the most storied jewelry houses was born. Van Cleef and his father-in-law founded Van Cleef & Arpels in Paris in 1896, but it wasn't until 1906 that the company officially opened its first boutique at 22 Place Vendôme. In the 1920s and '30s, Van Cleef & Arpels became renowned for its exuberant commissions from Maharajas, as well as for royal wedding parures, and established a reputation for supplying Egyptian revival and Orientalist jewels to the international elite. In 1933 the house patented the "mystery set" technique, in which gold settings disappear to highlight specially cut rubies, emeralds, or sapphires that are inserted one by one. Another trademark, the innovative *Zip* necklace, was an idea suggested by Wallis Simpson, the Duchess of Windsor, who was fascinated by the zipper, which had begun to appear more widely in women's clothing (see p.260). In the 1940s Van Cleef & Arpels created ballerina clips at the behest of Louis Arpels that soon became a signature. It was in 1968, however, that Van Cleef & Arpels introduced what is perhaps the maison's most iconic and enduring design: the *Alhambra* collection, inspired by the four-leaf clover, a symbol of luck and elegance for a global audience of enthusiasts.

Bibi van der Velden

Bibi van der Velden
b. New York, New York,
United States, 1980

The *Scarab Malachite Ring* in 18-karat yellow gold with green tourmaline, white diamonds, and tsavorites.

Photograph by Mafalda Boavida.

Fantastical, surrealist, and often maximalist, the dreamlike jewels of Dutch designer Bibi van der Velden are informed by her background in the fine arts. A childhood spent in the studio of her mother, the sculptor Michèle Deiters, proved formative for van der Velden, who began by creating sculpture before launching her eponymous jewelry line in 2006. This approach is evident in the voluminous silhouettes and intricate details that characterize her creations. Inspirations such as Egyptian mythology and the work of fifteenth-century painter Hieronymus Bosch are translated into extravagant, tactile jewels that combine a cacophony of gemstones with textured gold and silver. Hidden details reveal themselves the more you look. Nature is a recurring theme in her oeuvre for both motifs and materials: from playful monkeys grasping carved-gemstone bananas and alligators that bite down on an earlobe or wrist to scarabs adorned with iridescent beetle shells and fantastical beasts carved from sixty-thousand-year-old mammoth tusk. Moving elements are another frequent feature, such as the wriggling tentacles of a jellyfish or a tiny mermaid hidden behind a golden wave that crashes around an opal rock pool. "I like to tell a story and tickle the imagination," she says. "I want to create jewelry that is not just beautiful but also lively and fun."

Sophia Vari

Sophia Vari (Sophia Canellopoulos)
b. Vari, Greece, 1940
d. Monte Carlo, Monaco, 2023

Sousta earrings in marante wood and yellow gold, 2022.

Photograph by Ali Emre Göloğlu.

Displaying a modern sculptural sensibility, the graceful jewelry of Sophia Vari was a natural evolution of her acclaimed practice as an artist. Born Sophia Canellopoulos and raised in the Greek village of Vari, from which she took her adopted name, she initially worked as a figurative painter. Turning to sculpture in the 1970s, Vari developed a distinct visual language of abstraction through which she strove to express a harmony of volume and proportion, eventually producing monumental sculptures in bronze and marble. In the late 1980s, she began using modeling clay to create small maquettes and quickly realized these forms had the potential to become wearable art. Characterized by their fusion of geometric and organic lines, Vari's limited-edition jewelry combines precious materials such as gold, silver, and sapphire, with wood, ebony, and leather, among others. Resin, in particular, was an oft-used medium, prized for its transparent, marblelike qualities and lightness, which enabled her to increase the size of her rings and earrings without adding extra weight. Amaranth wood (also known as purpleheart) was another favorite, chosen for its ability to create dramatic and sensuous curves. Imbuing each piece with a unique sculptural form, Vari's statement that she wished her jewelry to "embellish and reassure the woman who wears it" was soundly accomplished.

Nicholas Varney

Nicholas Varney
b. New York, New York,
United States, 1971

Vear pendants in 24-karat gold with diamonds and carved hardstone and ebony, 2024.

Photograph by Ed Parrinello.

Nature, in forms majestic and humble, fuels Nicholas Varney's sophisticated design aesthetic. Equally awestruck by light glinting off the surface of a pond as he is by the vivid primary colors of a macaw's feathers, Varney assembles painterly, unconventional color combinations using gemstones as his medium. Clients often seek out his collection of one-of-a-kind pieces for their sensitive balance between scale, form, texture, and tone. A pair of snake earrings with white mother-of-pearl and reverse-set diamonds has a subdued shimmer and intriguing shape that invite closer examination, while his work with banded agate deploys the material as a graphic striped accent to surround diamonds, tourmalines, and sapphires in a subtle play of color. The rare pearls Varney favors come in eye-catching hues too, with natural conch, clam, and cassis among them. He often sets them together in a piece, such as pendant earrings, to create an unexpectedly harmonious blending of pink, purple, orange, and gray hues. Varney's work is a lesson in seeking inspiration everywhere, including in his own backyard, where he finds another of his preferred materials—eggshells from the chickens in the coop of his Upstate New York farm.

Ara Vartanian

Ara Vartanian
b. Beirut, Lebanon, 1975

Brooch in 18-karat white gold with inverted black diamonds and white diamonds.

Photograph by Gabriel Cabral.

Inverted diamonds, two- and three-finger rings, and earrings that hook around the lobe are all signatures of Ara Vartanian's subversive style. "I'm known for blending elegance with a rebellious spirit," says the Beirut-born, São Paulo–based designer, who left a career as a trader on Wall Street to join his father's diamond-dealing business in 2000 and established his eponymous brand five years later. Vartanian's designs are a departure from the classical styles created by his parents, influenced by his love for vintage cars and motorcycles, modernist design, and rock 'n' roll. Vibrant colored gemstones—Paraíba tourmalines, tanzanites, rubies, emeralds—are the starting point for jewelry that plays with scale and placement of stones. Unconventional, asymmetrical forms exude an offbeat glamour, executed with meticulous handcraftsmanship in Vartanian's atelier. In 2017 he collaborated with supermodel Kate Moss on a collection inspired by Vartanian's personal talismanic mandala. The following year, he launched his The Future Is Brilliant program, including the Conscious Mining project, to champion responsible gemstone mines and raise standards across the industry. "I always challenge myself not to do the obvious," says the designer, who likens his role to that of a chef—creating something extraordinary from the finest natural ingredients.

Vendôme

Vendôme
est. New York, New York,
United States, 1944

Veruschka wears large, square earrings by Vendôme, *Vogue*, June 1968.

Photograph by Franco Rubartelli.

Named after Paris's historic jewelry square, Vendôme was founded in New York in 1944 as a high-end division of Coro jewels, which grew to become the largest manufacturer of costume jewelry in the United States. Vendôme captured the French sophistication and energy of "bon chic, bon genre" luxury with daring lines crafted from top-quality materials such as cut-glass beads and rhinestones sourced from Australia and Czechoslovakia, hammered gold-plated brass, hand-painted enamel inserts, and faux baroque pearls. In 1958 actor Natalie Wood wore a dramatic Vendôme parure crafted from blue and translucent rhinestones for a magazine advertisement. With individual pieces then priced between five and thirty-five dollars, the floral-inspired three-piece set was an affordable adaptation of a suite worn by Wood in the film *Marjorie Morningstar*. The label reached the peak of its success in the 1960s thanks to lead designer Helen Marion, whose playful collections captured the cultural zeitgeist of the moment. Under Marion's tenure, the label introduced a patented adjustable ring shank on cocktail rings, as well as a series of brooches inspired by Cubist artist Georges Braque (see p.43). Although the company ceased operations in 1979, Vendôme vintage pieces are highly sought after for their statement silhouettes, immaculate craftsmanship, and exuberant motifs.

Diane Venet

Diane Venet
b. Paris, France, 1944

Joana Vasconcelos's *Extravaganza (rose)* necklace in sterling silver, pink ceramic lacquer, and rubber, part of Diane Venet's collection, 2022.

Photograph by Nikolaï Saoulski.

French art patron Diane Venet is one of the foremost champions of artist-made jewelry from the late twentieth century to today. A former broadcast journalist raised by a family of art collectors, she turned her focus to jewelry in 1985 after her husband-to-be, conceptual artist Bernar Venet, rolled a bar of silver around her finger and offered it as an engagement ring. Since then, her collection has grown to include more than 220 pieces of sculptural jewelry from celebrated photographers, sculptors, and painters, including Giacomo Balla, Jenny Holzer, Yayoi Kusama, Frank Stella, Louise Bourgeois, Salvador Dalí, Max Ernst, and Pablo Picasso (see pp.40, 77, 98, 223). She often collaborates with artists directly to realize their visions as distinctive wearable sculpture, however over-the-top or outside the norms of jewelry they might be. French body artist Orlan was commissioned by Venet to create her 2010 *Tête de fou* brooch, a silver and gold rendering of a woman's head in profile, to emulate Orlan's famed *Self-Hybridization* series. In 2008 Venet curated the exhibition *Bijoux Sculptures* at La Piscine museum in Roubaix, France, which highlighted 170 pieces of jewelry by 75 artists, including many works from her own collection. The success of the show led to expanded stagings titled *From Picasso to Koons: The Artist as Jeweler* at museums in New York; Athens; Paris; Riga, Latvia; and beyond.

Fulco di Verdura

Fulco di Verdura
b. Palermo, Italy, 1898
d. London, England, 1978

Original gouache renderings by Fulco di Verdura, including iconic designs such as the *Beehive Pendant Watch* (top left), *Lion's Paw Brooch* (center left), *Wrapped Heart Brooch* (center), and an emerald scarf necklace made for Dorothy Paley in 1941.

Growing up in an aristocratic household in Palermo, Sicily, Fulco di Verdura inherited his father's title and became the last Duke of Verdura. As a young man, Verdura had artistic talents and strong connections among artists, designers, and entertainers. His jewelry career began when he met Gabrielle "Coco" Chanel in the late 1920s and went on to become the head designer of Chanel jewelry, where he created his iconic *Maltese Cross Cuffs*, famously worn by Chanel herself (see p.60). Verdura moved to New York in 1934 and five years later opened his own store on Fifth Avenue, financed by longtime friends, composer Cole Porter and his wife, Linda (see p.228), and American businessman Vincent Astor. Verdura's designs were in demand by the elite of American society, and he created one-of-a-kind pieces for the likes of Millicent Rogers, Tallulah Bankhead, Betsey Whitney, Minnie Astor, and Babe Paley. His collaborations with Surrealist Salvador Dalí are among his most famous pieces (see p.77). One creation, the *Medusa* brooch, features thirteen intertwined snakes made of 14-karat yellow gold and cabochon ruby eyes framing a miniature painting of Dalí's *Medusa*, set with a 73-carat morganite. Ward Landrigan, the former head of Sotheby's jewelry who acquired the Verdura brand in 1985, called the piece the world's greatest Surrealist artwork.

Henri Vever

Henri Vever
b. Metz, France, 1854
d. Noyers, France, 1942

Sylvia pendant in gold with agate, rubies, diamonds, and plique-à-jour enamel, c. 1900.

At the turn of the twentieth century, French designer Henri Vever led his family's namesake jewelry house to the forefront of Art Nouveau. Born in Metz, France, in 1854, Vever studied at École des Arts Décoratifs and apprenticed in Louguet's and Hallet's studios, eventually taking over management of Maison Vever from his father in 1881. Working alongside his brother Paul, Vever was the creative force that drove the company's success, drawing acclaim for gem-forward pieces that incorporated motifs from nature and mythology. Epitomizing the Vever aesthetic is the *Sylvia* pendant, which garnered the maison a Grand Prix for high jewelry at the 1900 Exposition Universelle in Paris. In addition to his work as a designer of fine jewelry, Vever was the author of *La Bijouterie Française au XIXe Siècle*, published in 1908, one of the era's best chronicles of French jewelry production. He retired in 1921, and Maison Vever became dormant in 1982. But in 2021 Camille and Damien Vever—the seventh generation of the family—reestablished the house with a focus on environmentally conscious and ethically sourced materials. By upholding the brand's signature motifs such as flowers and nymphs, but producing its designs with recycled gold and lab-grown diamonds, the siblings honor Vever's mission to celebrate the natural world through jewelry.

Vhernier

Vhernier
est. Valenza, Italy, 1984

Verso earclips in rose gold with diamonds, 2008.

Photograph by Isabelle Bonjean.

In 1984, in Valenza, one of Italy's premier high-jewelry hubs, entrepreneur Carlo Ciarli, designer Roberto Boldi, and gem specialist Angela Camurati founded Vhernier. Their goal was to create artisanal yet modernist jewelry that would bring fresh innovation to Valenza's then-stagnant scene. The house's designs are sculptural, minimalist, and rounded, with a sensual feel, influenced by the sculptures of Constantin Brâncuși and Jean Arp. Their polished gold features a warm yellow hue with a tinge of rose, while the white gold is notably unplated; they also use ebony and titanium to striking effect. Rounded pavé surfaces are set with stones of varying sizes, held by two prongs rather than the conventional four to allow for a smooth, uninterrupted reflection of light across the jewel. To expand their palette, Vhernier pioneered *Trasparenze*, a technique of layering gem materials to create surprising new colors. In 2001 Vhernier was acquired by the Traglio family, with Carlo Traglio as president and Camurati remaining in her design role as production director. Together, they developed new collections and made *Calla*, *Abbraccio*, *Pirouette*, and *Palloncino* iconic. Under Traglio's leadership, Vhernier established itself as an internationally renowned contemporary Italian jeweler, and in 2024, Vhernier was acquired by the Swiss luxury group Richemont.

Victoria

Victoria, Queen of the
United Kingdom
b. London, England, 1819
d. Isle of Wight, England, 1901

A portrait of Queen Victoria by
Franz Xaver Winterhalter, 1847.

For Queen Victoria, jewelry was inextricably intertwined with emotion: more than an adornment, it was also a signifier of love and promise, becoming a marker of personally significant milestones throughout her sixty-three-year reign. As a young woman, she favored bold colors and elaborate forms, later appreciating a jewel's ability to indicate power and status. Throughout her marriage to Prince Albert, he had pieces designed for her, including an emerald and diamond diadem—part of a matching suite she wore at many public events—and a gold and porcelain orange blossom brooch, which was a nod to the orange blossoms she wore in her hair on her wedding day. At odds with such extravagance was the glass heart-shaped pendant she wore constantly, containing a lock of her husband's hair. Victoria loved jewelry for its own sake, often regardless of value, discovering a fascination with unexpected materials upon the couple's purchase of the Balmoral Estate in Scotland in 1848. As well as the family's tartan colors depicted in enamel, she acquired pieces in moss agate and jasper, and wore local pebbles framed in precious metals. Upon Albert's untimely death, Victoria wore only colorless jewelry to complement her lifelong all-black mourning attire, culminating with the spectacular 22.48-carat Lahore diamond she wore suspended on a pendant at her Golden Jubilee in 1887.

Giorgio Vigna

Giorgio Vigna
b. Verona, Italy, 1955

Geodi necklace in oxidized silver with elements in yellow gold, 2022.

Exploring the transformation of matter into wearable forms, Italian artist and designer Giorgio Vigna makes work that brings fresh possibilities to jewelry. Born in Verona, Italy, in 1955, he has worked for more than four decades to push creative limits through his art, favoring slow procedures and handmade techniques. He makes no distinction of scale in his creative practice and views the jewelry he designs as sculpture for the body, intended as a way of engaging with the physicality of gesture and touch. The dialogue between his larger-scale sculpture and jewelry reflects the connection between the micro and the macro that runs through his work. Nature, the four elements, and the cosmos are ongoing inspirations, as Vigna moves between reality and imagination in his work. The sizeable chunks of gold rock in a necklace are revealed to be featherlight hollow copper, while a central stone in one of his signature magnetic brooches turns out to be a limpid pool of Murano glass—earth passed through fire to become solidified water. Swaying with aquatic grace, his gold and pearl *Floralia* earrings reflect the movement of marine life and ocean inflorescence. And while nature provides the foundation, Vigna says his jewels are meant to be evocative rather than representative—equally impactful and alive when exhibited as art or worn on the body.

Daniela Villegas

Daniela Villegas
b. Mexico City, Mexico, 1981

From right to left: *Koala Rings* in lapis and malachite with 18-karat yellow gold, opal, rose-cut white diamonds, and multicolor sapphires and emeralds; *Sisters Rings* in 18-karat yellow gold with tourmalines and sapphires; Daniela Viellegas's earthworm wedding band in 18-karat pink gold and diamonds; *Cosquilleo Ring* in 18-karat yellow gold and sapphires.

Nature is not so much a muse for Daniela Villegas as the oxygen without which her creativity could not flourish. The designer founded her namesake label in 2008, bringing to life a fantastical universe. Born and raised in Mexico City, Villegas developed a passion for jewelry thanks to her great-grandmother Dolores, whom she describes as someone "who believed every day to be a special occasion." This sense of optimism and joy is embedded in her work, which draws on folkloric beliefs about the spirituality of animals—from beetles, crabs, and scorpions to koalas, coyotes, and sloths. "I believe in the power of storytelling and symbolism that brings talismanic energy to the jewels," she says.

Crafted by artisans in her L.A. atelier, her work combines gemstones that she "connects with"—zircons, emeralds, opals, sphenes, rubies, and tourmalines—and organic materials, such as beetle shells, porcupine quills, feathers, pebbles, and wood. From fashion to film, Villegas has expanded her reach: in 2016 she collaborated with Salvatore Ferragamo on a capsule collection inspired by tropical birds, and in 2018 she created a range of bejeweled dinosaurs with Universal Pictures to celebrate *Jurassic Park*'s twenty-fifth anniversary. Eschewing trends, Villegas aims to "dig deeper into the fantastic layers of life and nature, to keep embedding joy and inspiration in every piece of jewelry."

Patricia von Musulin

Patricia von Musulin
b. Johnstown, Pennsylvania,
United States, 1947

A model wears Patricia von Musulin hand-carved Lucite bracelets and rings, 1992.

Photograph by Roberto Rabanne.

Bringing an artistic fervor to her work, Patricia von Musulin considers shape, composition, and materials as much as the wearability of her designs, each sculpted piece contoured to the body. Von Musulin's first bracelet, inspired by the pleating of French couturier Madame Grès's gowns, was indelibly captured by Richard Avedon in a 1981 image for *Vogue*: actor Nastassja Kinski naked but for a serpent slithering across her body and the carved ivory cuff on her wrist. Von Musulin's venerated pieces are timeless and organic, using sterling silver, ebony, and particularly Lucite for its transparency and ability to evoke the rippling flow of water. The palette is mostly monochromatic, incorporating onyx and pearl, but occasionally punctuated with large colorful pieces of amber, coral, and jade. Born in 1947 and originally trained as an industrial designer, von Musulin began her jewelry career in 1976 and has worked with such legendary American fashion figures as Geoffrey Beene, Ralph Lauren, Perry Ellis, Michael Kors, and, more recently, Rihanna for her Savage and Fenty shows (see p.236) and LaQuan Smith, creating bold jewelry with scale and presence. With an openness to experimentation and honed artistic vision, von Musulin has made it her mission to dismantle the traditional definition of "accessories," offering her powerfully original work in its stead.

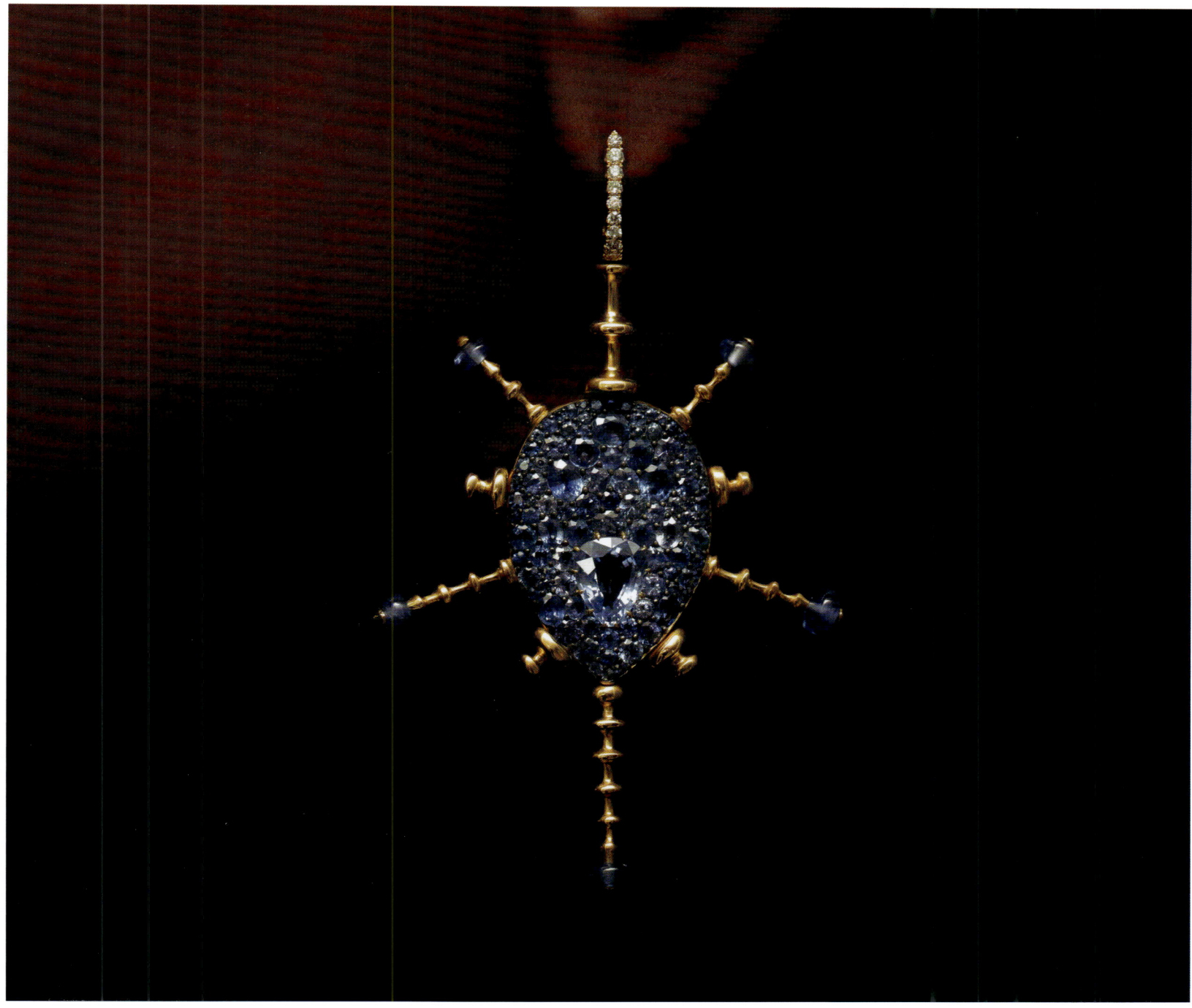

VRAM

VRAM
est. Los Angeles, California,
United States, 1985

Chrona Disco Earrings in 18-karat yellow gold and sterling silver with pear-cut blue sapphire center stones, oval and round brilliant-cut blue sapphires, round brilliant-cut diamonds, and blue sapphire beads.

"I can't remember a life before jewelry," says Vram Minassian, whose "first classroom" was his father's jewelry and watch store in Beirut. This below-the-radar Lebanese designer-maker spent thirty years producing high jewelry for private clients before quietly launching his eponymous label's debut creative collection in 2016. Limelight-averse, he has nevertheless built a fan base of collectors who appreciate VRAM's distinctive aesthetic and exceptional craftsmanship. Naturalism runs throughout his abstract, organic creations: it's there in the gently upturned profile of the *Chrona Butterfly Ring*, in the wavelike undulations of the *Caryn* collection, and in the concave leaf of the *Split Super Sine Earrings*. These designs share an air of timelessness, with gently bold silhouettes that could have been plucked from any era. Some are sculpted in brushed gold, others are blanketed in a masterful pavé of gemstones that are the result of numerous hours of meticulous application by nuanced shade and size. In his Los Angeles atelier, Minassian combines the traditional goldsmithing techniques employed by his father with more modern advances. His priority, he asserts, is that the resulting jewel is appreciated for its sensual qualities first and foremost: "Perhaps the more explanation it requires, the less it succeeds as an object," he says.

Diana Vreeland

Diana Vreeland
b. Paris, France, 1903
d. New York, New York, United States, 1989

Diana Vreeland wearing her signature warrior-style cuffs, 1982.

Photograph by Priscilla Rattazzi.

Diana Vreeland left an indelible mark on fashion not only as a visionary editor but as a connoisseur of jewelry. Born in Paris but primarily based in New York, she had a career in magazines that spanned five decades, first as a columnist at *Harper's Bazaar* from 1936 until 1962 and then as editor in chief at *Vogue* from 1963 to 1971, where she shaped the aesthetics of fashion with fearless creativity. From oversize Lucite bangles and pendants of enameled tusks to glittering brooches and giant pearls, the transformative power of statement jewelry was central to her personal style and editorial vision. Vreeland championed designers who matched her flair for the dramatic, including Fulco di Verdura, whose *Maltese Cross* cuffs became iconic beyond the 1930s through her influence (see p.298). She treasured the diamond- and amethyst-encrusted *Trophée de Vaillance* brooch—designed for her in 1941 by Jean Schlumberger of Tiffany & Co.—so much that she displayed it on her bedside table as art (see pp.251, 283). David Webb's animal motifs and vibrant enamel work, Kenneth Jay Lane's high-impact costume jewelry, and sleek, modern silver pieces by Elsa Peretti also featured prominently in her wardrobe (see pp.78, 162, 221). Vreeland's influence elevated jewelry designers to new heights, further cementing her legacy as a style arbiter with an unerring eye for the extraordinary.

Andy Warhol

Andy Warhol
b. Pittsburgh, Pennsylvania,
United States, 1928
d. New York, New York,
United States, 1987

Boivin *Beribboned Heart* bangle bracelet in gold and blue enamel with old- and single-cut diamonds, commissioned for Millicent Rogers in 1939, part of the Andy Warhol collection sold by Sotheby's in 1988.

American artist, film director, and producer Andy Warhol led the Pop art movement with a series of iconic works that skewered contemporary culture. His most famous works, including the silkscreen painted *Campbell's Soup Cans* and brightly printed portraits of Marilyn Monroe and others, questioned the role of capitalism and consumerism in the American Dream. As well as his ability to tap into the zeitgeist, Warhol was celebrated as a harbinger of good taste in his refusal to distinguish between high and low culture, a mindset that fed into his status as an eclectic and avid collector of art, furniture, knickknacks, and jewelry. His extensive collection of jewels went largely under the radar until after his death, when his estate went under the hammer at Sotheby's in 1988. So vast was his collection, found hidden around his New York townhouse, it required a second auction later in the year. Particularly drawn to Art Deco and mid-century pieces, Warhol favored jewelry houses including Bulgari, Cartier, Seaman Schepps, and Van Cleef & Arpels, as well as Elsa Peretti and Jean Schlumberger designs for Tiffany & Co. (see pp.46, 54, 221, 251, 253, 283, 291). Toward the end of his career, Warhol explored jewelry in art, creating the *Gems* print series in 1978, which depicted unset rubies, diamonds, and emeralds—his idiosyncratic tribute to the ultimate status symbol.

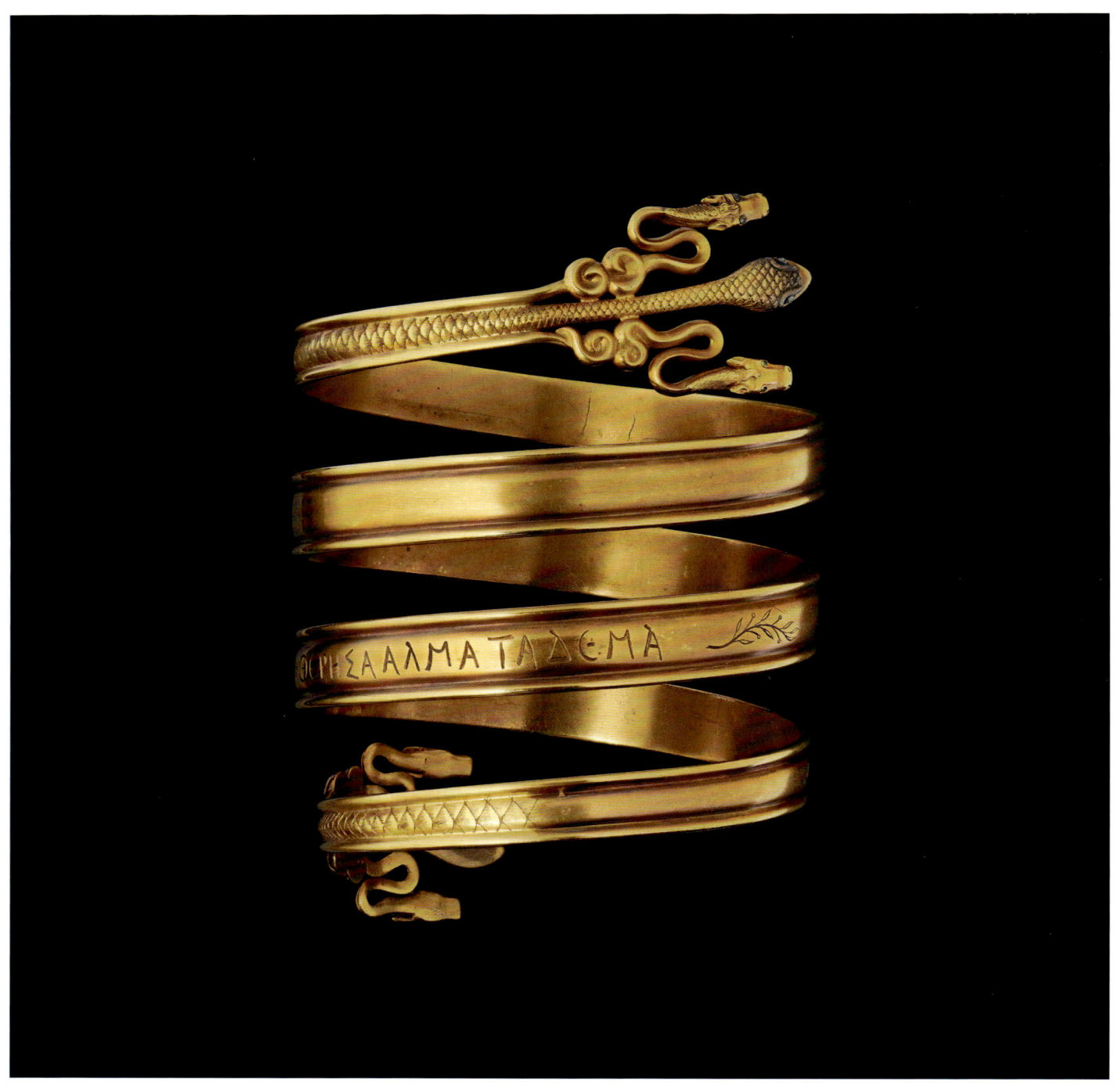

Wartski

Wartski
est. Bangor, Wales, 1865

Part of the Wartski collection, the ancient Greece–inspired Tadema Armlet takes the shape of a coiled gold serpent with diamond-set eyes flanked by stylized horse heads with eyes of turquoise, ruby, sapphire, and emerald. The armlet was commissioned by artist Lawrence Alma-Tadema as a gift to his wife, Laura Theresa, c. 1871–74 and features in many of his famous paintings.

Wartski, now the world authority on jewelry and objets d'art by Peter Carl Fabergé (see p.101), began with somewhat unlikely origins as a jeweler in Bangor, Wales. Founded by Polish refugee Morris Wartski in 1865, the firm sold silver and porcelain to Victorian industrialists holidaying on the Welsh coast and subsequently received the patronage of King Edward VII. In 1913 Morris's daughter, Harriette, and her husband, Emanuel Snowman, expanded the business and opened on London's New Bond Street. It was Snowman and later his son Kenneth who, following the Russian Revolution in 1917, facilitated the acquisition of the vast treasures made by Russian goldsmiths, including Fabergé's Imperial Easter Eggs. The finest masterpieces of Fabergé and his peers drew collectors, including six generations of the British Royal Family, European royals, and Hollywood stars. In 2014 Wartski unveiled one of the eight missing Imperial Easter Eggs—only three were believed to have survived the revolution—confirming the historic identity of the small gold egg found by a scrap metal dealer in America. Today, as continuing specialists in antique jewelry, alongside Fabergé creations, Wartski offers a range of treasures from enameled Falize bracelets and a micromosaic brooch from Castellani to sixteenth-century posy rings and the earliest known surviving Cartier jewel (see p.54).

Lorraine West

Lorraine West
b. Islip, New York,
United States, 1976

Suki Waterhouse wears Lorraine West *Abstract Palette Earrings* in brass and 14-karat gold, 2023.

Photograph by Caleb & Gladys.

Twenty years into her jewelry-making career, Lorraine West experienced overnight success. When the legendary singer-songwriter Beyoncé (see p.29) wore a pair of the designer's earrings—polished brass hoops shaped like a painter's palette—in her 2020 film *Black Is King*, West thought to herself, "These earrings are going to change my life." Her supposition was correct, and a stampede of requests flooded in for her newly recognizable jewel. Until then, she had established a steady stream of commissions as her name spread by word of mouth among New York City's creative set. However, with a higher profile, opportunities to stretch creatively arrived too. New work inflected with her personal influences—hip-hop, fashion, the Caribbean culture of her parents—emerged through playful pieces such as a gold necklace with a hot comb pendant and a collection of heart-shaped jewels based on her own handwriting. Now, West is at the top of the list when legacy brands want to inject a fresh outlook into their work. She created capsules for De Beers (see p.80) and Muzo Emerald Colombia and exhibited at Sotheby's historic 2021 exhibition *Brilliant & Black*, the first time an auction house devoted a sale to the work of Black jewelers. With one big break, West became part of a vanguard of designers who continue to define the direction of fine jewelry.

Thelma West

Thelma West
b. Lagos, Nigeria, 1983

Rebel Black ring with a Botswana pear-shaped diamond set in black ceramic.

Photograph by Simon Martner.

Growing up in Lagos, Nigeria, jewelry was all around Thelma West. She knew from an early age that she had found a medium that bridges the ancient and the modern, the personal and the universal, and would allow her to craft pieces that resonated on deeply emotional levels. When West packed up and moved to Antwerp at seventeen, she had one goal in mind: to further her education and pursue a career in the world of diamonds and design. As a diamond grader, she amassed the technical expertise and understanding of precious stones that now infuses her creations. In 2012 West founded her namesake company, establishing a commitment to both ethical sourcing and sustainability. The process of transforming raw materials into jewelry is almost alchemical to her. Unafraid to experiment, she devises novel ways to work with titanium and ceramic, and employs recycled gold and repurposed gems within the mix. Her heritage is deeply ingrained in her designs, such as pieces inspired by sugarcane, "a staple treat in Lagos that captures the essence of resilience and beauty found in nature." Her predilection for brushed finishes results in bold and textured jewels, glowing in warm hues of rose and yellow gold. At her London studio, West's jewels become a repository of memories and aspirations, each piece building toward a legacy that is equal parts luxury and responsibility.

Zendaya

Zendaya (Zendaya Stoermer Coleman) b. Oakland, California, United States, 1996

Zendaya wears Bulgari's *Magnifica Hypnotic* high jewelry necklace in platinum with a 93.83-carat emerald, 57 carats of diamonds, and 233 buff-cut emeralds, at the Venice International Film Festival, 2021.

Photograph by Vittorio Zunino Celotto.

American actor Zendaya has established a playful and eclectic sense of style during her meteoric rise to fame, making her a magnet for the high jewelry world. In 2020 she became an ambassador for Italian luxury house Bulgari, a collaboration she kicked off by wearing a necklace featuring a large blue sapphire and strands of diamonds for the launch of the house's *B.zero1 Rock* jewelry collection that same year (see p.46). It marked the start of a string of red-carpet appearances featuring an array of spectacular precious stones, most notably at the 2021 Academy Awards, which saw Zendaya pair a yellow Valentino gown with platinum necklaces and rings studded with white and yellow diamonds, a suite of jewelry totaling more than 238 carats. Sartorially astute, Zendaya's jewelry style at film premieres is tailored to the film's theme. For *Challengers* in 2024, Zendaya offered a sensual rethink of the classic tennis bracelet with a Bulgari *Serpenti Viper* bracelet to complement tennis ball-spiked Loewe shoes and a Thom Browne dress. At the *Dune: Part Two* premiere that same year, Zendaya layered a Bulgari sapphire-and-diamond necklace over a vintage Thierry Mugler futuristic suit of armor. High jewelry is part of Zendaya's personal style as well, and the star splashed out with a large Bulgari yellow diamond ring in 2021, a precious addition to her own collection.

Directory

This directory provides a selected list of galleries, institutions, and other jewelry organizations and destinations that can be visited by prior arrangement or on regular open days. While every care has been taken to ensure accuracy, please check individual websites for opening hours and visiting information in advance of making travel arrangements.

Albion Art

Tokyo, Japan
www.albionart.com

Alice and Louis Koch Collection

Swiss National Museum
Zürich, Switzerland
www.nationalmuseum.ch

The Al Thani Collection

Hôtel de la Marine
Paris, France
www.thealthanicollection.com

American Museum of Natural History

New York, New York,
United States
www.amnh.org

Ashmolean Museum

Oxford, England
www.ashmolean.org

Bharat Diamond Bourse

Mumbai, India
bdbindia.org

Boghossian Foundation

Villa Empain
Brussels, Belgium
villaempain.com

Carpenters Workshop Gallery

London, England
Paris, France
carpentersworkshopgallery.com

Cooper-Hewitt, Smithsonian Design Museum

New York, New York,
United States
www.cooperhewitt.org

Dallas Museum of Art

Dallas, Texas, United States
dma.org

The Diamond District

47th Street, New York,
New York, United States
diamonddistrict.org

Didier Ltd

London, England
www.didierltd.com

Domvs

The Bulgari Heritage Collection
Rome, Italy
www.bulgari.com/en-int/the-heritage-domvs

Dubai Gold Souk

Deira, Dubai, United Arab Emirates

Elisabetta Cipriani Gallery

London, England
www.elisabettacipriani.com

Faerber Collection

Geneva, Switzerland
www.faerber-collection.com

FD Gallery

New York, New York,
United States
fd-gallery.com

Galerie Marzee

Nijmegen, the Netherlands
www.marzee.nl

Galerie MiniMasterpiece

Paris, France
www.galerieminimasterpiece.com

Gemological Institute of America (GIA)

Carlsbad, California,
United States
www.gia.edu

The Goldsmiths' Company

London, England
www.thegoldsmiths.co.uk

Grand Bazaar

Istanbul, Turkey

Hancocks

London, England
hancockslondon.com

Hatton Garden

London, England
www.hatton-garden.london

Heard Museum

Phoenix, Arizona, United States
heard.org

Hillwood Estate, Museum & Gardens

Washington, DC, United States
hillwoodmuseum.org

Houston Museum of Natural Science

Houston, Texas, United States
www.hmns.org/exhibits/faberge

Ilias Lalaounis Jewelry Museum

Athens, Greece
www.lalaounis-jewelrymuseum.gr

Imperial Treasury Vienna

Vienna, Austria
www.kaiserliche-schatzkammer.at

Los Angeles County Museum of Art

Los Angeles, California, United States
www.lacma.org

Louisa Guinness Gallery

London, England
www.louisaguinnessgallery.com

The Louvre

Paris, France
www.louvre.fr

Mahnaz Collection

New York, New York, United States
mahnazcollection.com

Metropolitan Museum of Art

New York, New York, United States
www.metmuseum.org

Le Monde des Arts de la Parure

Marrakech, Morocco
www.lemapmarrakech.com

Montreal Museum of Fine Arts

Montreal, Quebec, Canada
www.mbam.qc.ca

Musée des Arts Décoratifs

Paris, France
madparis.fr

Museo del Gioiello

Vicenza, Italy
www.museodelgioiello.it

Museum of Arts and Design (MAD)

New York, New York, United States
madmuseum.org

Museum of Fine Arts, Boston

Massachusetts, United States
www.mfa.org

Museum of Meenakari Heritage

Jaipur, India
www.momhindia.org

National Museum of Western Art

Taito City, Tokyo, Japan
www.nmwa.go.jp

Petit Palais

Musée des Beaux Arts de la Ville de Paris, France
www.petitpalais.paris.fr

La Piscine

Roubaix, France
www.roubaix-lapiscine.com

Place Vendôme

Paris, France

Responsible Jewellery Council

London, England
www.responsiblejewellery.com

Rijksmuseum

Amsterdam, the Netherlands
www.rijksmuseum.nl

Schmuckmuseum

Pforzheim, Germany
www.schmuckmuseum.de

Shanghai Gold Exchange

Shanghai, China
en.sge.com.cn

Smithsonian National Museum of Natural History

Washington, DC, United States
naturalhistory.si.edu

Swarovski Crystal Worlds

Wattens, Austria
kristallwelten.swarovski.com

Symbolic & Chase

London, England
s-c.com

Tower of London

London, England
www.hrp.org.uk/tower-of-london

Treasury of the Grand Dukes

Pitti Palace
Florence, Italy
www.uffizi.it/en/pitti-palace

Victoria and Albert Museum

London, England
www.vam.ac.uk

Virginia Museum of Fine Arts

Richmond, Virginia, United States
vmfa.museum

The Walters Art Museum

Baltimore, Maryland, United States
thewalters.org

Wartski

London, England
wartski.com

World Jewelry Museum

Seoul, South Korea
www.wjm.or.kr

Index

A

A$AP Rocky 11, 112
Abit, Amam 33
Academy Awards 9, 148, 165, 174, 227, 311
Accademia di Belle Arti di Venezia 25
Aderemi, Adesoji Tadeniawo 172
Adler 12, 164
Adler, Allen 12
Adler, Daisy 12
Adler, Jacques 12
Adler, Karen 12
Adrian, Gilbert 116
Aga Khan, Salimah (Sarah Frances Croker-Poole) 13
Aga Khan IV 13
agate 91
Akan people 288
Akers, Zerina 29
Akkad, Walid 14
Al Qusaiby, Ibtisam 213
Al Thani Collection 15
Alaïa, Azzedine 142
Albert, Prince 117, 301
Albert "Bertie" Edward, Prince of Wales 18
Albion Art 16
Albright, Madeleine 17
Alexander II, Tsar 131
Alexander III, Tsar 101
Alexandra of Denmark 18, 187
Alexandra of Mecklenburg-Schwerin, Grand Duchess 101
Alexis Mdivani, Prince of Georgia 140
Allen, DeMarcus 94, 248, 259
Alliance for Responsible Mining (ARM) 289
Almasika 214, 248
Amado, Stephany 172
American Gem Society 69
Amfitheatrof, Francesca 19, 170
Anderson, Leomie 188
Anderson, Ron 281
Anderson, Wes 276
Angostura 26
Angoulême, Duchesse d' 100
Anthony, Aurora 208
Apfel, Carl 20
Apfel, Iris 20
Applied Art Forms 185
Arad, Ron 49, 175
Arikawa, Kazumi 16
Armani, Giorgio 19
armlets 282, 308
Arp, Jean 23, 50, 154, 300
Arpels, Estelle 291
Arpels, Jacques 113
Arpels, Louis 238, 291
Arpels, Pierre 8
Arpels, Salomon 291
Arrowsmith, Clive 13
Art Deco 9, 204
   Alexis Bittar 33
   Andy Warhol 307
   Asscher cut 22
   Bhagat 30
   Bulgari 46
   Cartier 54
   Dusausoy 93
   Elie Top 285
   Erté 99
   Fabio Salini 246
   Fred Leighton 165
   Hancocks 131
   Hedy Martinelli 186
   Jackie Onassis 150
   Kenneth Jay Lane 162
   Lacloche Frères 159
   Lily Safra 244
   Louis Boucheron 261
   Maison Fouquet 179
   Marlene Dietrich 88
   Michelle Ong 216
   Mikimoto 195
   Nikos Koulis 155
   Paul Flato 107
   René Lalique 161
   Satta Matturi 189
   Suzanne Belperron 28
   Trifari 287
Art Nouveau
   Alexis Bittar 33
   Anna Hu 138
   Boodles 38
   Faerber Collection 102
   Fred Leighton 165
   Georg Jensen 120
   Henri Vever 299
   Maison Fouquet 179
   René Lalique 161
   Tiffany & Co. 283
Artcurial 160
Arte Povera 36, 220
Artwear 202
Asante people 288
Ashmolean Museum 70, 95
Ashoka diamond 38
Asprey 97, 151, 213
Asprey & Garrard 19
Assael 21, 76
Assael, Christina Lang 21
Assael, Salvador 21
Asscher, Joseph 22
Asscher cut 22
Assemi, Mona 29
Astley Clarke 49
Astor, Minnie 298
Astor, Vincent 298
Atamian, Philippe 102
Atawhai, Makau Ariki 184
Ateliers Hugo 23
Athena 36
Aubert, Ange-Joseph 63
Aurangzeb 279
Avedon, Richard 13, 135, 304
Ayoko, Rebecca 245
Azagury-Partridge, Solange 24
Aztecs 6

B

Babetto, Giampaolo 25
Badu, Erykah 26
Bailey, David 174
Baker, Josephine 9, 27
Baker, Samuel 267
Balenciaga, Cristóbal 135, 236
   Gloria Guinness 130
   Goossens 126
   Mellerio dits Meller collaboration 193
Balla, Giacomo 297
Ballets Russes 9
Balmain, Pierre 129, 193, 241
Ban, Lynn 176
Bankhead, Tallulah 298
Bapst, Georges-Michel 110
Barnum, P. T. 156
Baroda, Maharani of 270
Baselitz, Georg 141
Bauhaus 33, 64
Beaton, Cecil 13, 51, 97, 140, 159, 262
Beaucé, Esther de 114
Beckham, Victoria 190
Beene, Geoffrey 202, 304
Begum Aga Khan 270
Belle Époque
   Cartier 92
   Faerber Collection 102
   Lily Safra 244
   Maison Fouquet 179
   Moussaieff 203
   Paul-Jules Dusausoy 93
Bellini, Mario 196
Belperron, Jean 28
Belperron, Suzanne 28
   Boivin 35, 204
   Fred Leighton 165
   Symbolic & Chase 277
Benin 8
Bergdorf Goodman 76
Bergé, Pierre 245
Berlin iron jewelry 8
Bernhardt, Sarah 129, 161, 179
Beth, Jehnny 185
Beyoncé 29, 148
   Dries Criel 75
   Fernando Jorge 143
   Lorraine Schwartz 252
   Lorraine West 309
   Lydia Courteille 74
Bhagat 30
Bhagat, Viren 30
Bhupinder Singh, Maharaja 261
Biçakçi, Sevan 31
bijoux de couture 129
Binns, Tom 214
Bird, Gail 32
Bischofberger, Bruno 256
Bischofberger, Yoyo 256
Bittar, Alexis 9, 33, 214
Black Panther Party 208
Black Starr & Frost 55
Blanchett, Cate 31, 165
Blass, Bill 162
Bleu de France 110
Bloomingdale's 76
Boekhoudt, Onnno 136
Boghossian 34, 37
Boghossian, Albert 34
Boivin 35, 307
Boivin, Jeanne Poiret 35, 204
Boivin, René 35
   Fred Leighton 165
   Suzanne Belperron 28, 204
   Symbolic & Chase 277
Bonfield, Michael 36
Bonfield-Colombara, Joy 36
Bonjean, Isabelle 37, 194, 300
Boodle and Dunthorne 38
Boodles 38
Bosch, Hieronymus 274, 292
Boucheron 10, 39
   Eugénie de Montijo 100
   Faerber Collection 102
   Georges Lenfant 166
   Lily Safra 244
   Mahnaz Collection 177
   Pierre Sterlé 270
   René Lalique 161
   Reza 235
   Salimah Aga Khan 13
   Solange Azagury-Partridge 24
Boucheron, Frédéric 39
Boucheron, Louis 261
Bourgeois, Louise 40, 297
Boutron, Martine 245
Bowles, Hamish 41
Bown, Jane 262
Boyd, Latoya 42

bracelets
- Aldo Cipullo 69
- Andy Warhol 307
- Arthur King 152
- Boghossian 34
- Boivin 35
- Buccellati 45
- Charles Loloma 173
- Diana Vreeland 306
- Dries Criel 75
- Elsa Peretti 221
- Fritz Maierhofer 178
- Georges Lenfant 166
- Glenn Spiro 269
- Hedy Martinelli 186
- Hemmerle 133
- Latoya Boyd 42
- Lucio Fontana 109
- Méret Oppenheim 217
- Monies 196
- Moussaieff 203
- Patricia von Musulin 304
- Paul Flato 107
- Pol Bury 48
- Reza 235
- Sam Kramer 156
- Sharon Khazzam 151
- Studio Renn 272
- Theodoros 282
- Tiffany & Co. 221
- Trifari 287
- Vamgard 290
- Winifred Mason Chenet 65
- Lydia Courteille 74
- Mahnaz Collection 177
- Maison Fouquet 179
- Marguerite Stix 271
- Michele Ong 216
- Nevin Holmes 137
- Paul Flato 107
- Pierre Sterlé 270
- Prince Dimitri 230
- Salvador Dalí 77, 87
- Seaman Schepps 253
- Symbolic & Chase 277
- Tiffany & Co. 251
- Wallace Chan 59

Brâncuşi, Constantin 154, 185, 300
Braque, Georges 43, 296
brass 7
Breakfast at Tiffany's (1961) 162
Breton, André 77
Bright Young Things 262
Brodovitch, Alexey 135
Bronfman, Clarissa 49
brooches
- Alberto Giacometti 122
- Andrew Grima 128
- Anna Hu 138
- Ara Vartanian 295
- Arnaldo Pomodoro 226
- Boivin 35
- Boucheron 39
- Capucine Huguet 139
- Cindy Chao 61
- Dusausoy 93
- Fred Leighton 276
- Fulco di Verdura 298
- Georg Jensen 120
- Giovanni Corvaja 73
- Joy Bonfield-Colombara 36
- Judy Geib 118
- Kevin Coates 70
- Luz Camino 52

Brooks Brothers 33
Brunei, Sultan of 158
Brush, Daniel 44
Buccellati 45
Buccellati, Andrea 45
Buccellati, Mario 45
Bulgari 46
- Andy Warhol 307
- Desiree Mattsson 188
- Di Portanova collection 86
- Fabio Salini 246
- Georges Lenfant 166
- Hancocks 131
- Lily Safra 244
- Madonna 176
- Mahnaz Collection 177
- Moza bint Nasser 205
- Zendaya 311
Bulgari, Constantino 46
Bulgari, Gianni 30
Bulgari, Giorgio 46
Bulgari, Marina 46
Bulgari, Sotirio 46
Bülow-Hübe, Vivianna Torun 286
Burberry 33
Burés, Chus 40
Burle Marx, Haroldo 47
Burle Marx, Roberto 47
Burton, Richard 22, 132, 280
Bury, Pol 48, 199
Busquets, Carmen 49
ByChari 214

C

C & C Jewelers 56
Caicedo, Tito 171
Caillol 245
Calder, Alexander 50, 175, 202
- Art Smith 265
- Didier Ltd 87
- Louisa Guinness Gallery 175
Callas, Maria 51
Calvin Klein 281
Camilla, Queen 242
Camino, Luz 52
Campbell-Walter, Fiona 250
Camurati, Angela 300
Cannes Film Festival 66, 148, 174, 239
Capote, Truman 130
Carnet 216, 243
Carponcy, Serge 55
Carrington, Leonora 98
Carson, Susannah 53
Cartier 54
- Alfred Philippe 287
- Andy Warhol 307
- Barbara Hutton 140
- Bhupinder Singh necklace 261
- Cartier jewel 308
- Cartier London 15
- Cartier New York 69
- Carvin French 55
- Cole and Linda Porter 228
- Desiree Mattsson 188
- Di Portanova collection 86
- Doris Duke 92
- English Art Works 269
- Eugénie de Montijo 100
- Fabio Salini 246
- Faerber Collection 102
- Farah Diba Pahlavi 218
- Georges Lenfant 166
- Gloria Guinness 130
- Grace Kelly 148
- Hannah Martin 185
- Irving Penn portrait 219
- Isabelle Bonjean 37
- Jackie Onassis 150
- Juliette Moutard 204
- Lily Safra 244
- Luz Mila Patiño Rodríguez 238
- Madonna 176
- Maria Callas 51
- María Félix 105
- Marilyn Monroe 198
- Marjorie Merriweather Post 229
- Marlene Dietrich 88
- Moza bint Nasser 205
- platinum jewelry 8–9
- Pol Bury 48
- René Lalique 161
- Reza 235
- Sabba 243
- Salimah Aga Khan 13
- Taylor-Burton diamond 54, 132
- Wallis Simpson 260
Cartier, Jacques 54
Cartier, Louis 54
Cartier, Louis-François 54
Cartier, Pierre 54, 192
Cartier-Bresson, Henri 113

Carvin French 55
Cassandre 179
Castellane, Victoire de 81, 89
Castellani, Enrico 96
Castro, Terry 56
Castro NYC 49, 56
Catherine, Princess of Wales 54
Catherine the Great 57
Cellini, Benvenuto 58, 141
Centenary Diamond 80, 284
Central Saint Martins 94, 137, 139, 143, 185, 274
Chalme, Rose 194
Champagnat, Jean-Claude 89
Chan, Wallace 59, 67, 243
Chanel 60
- Ateliers Hugo 23
- Francesca Amfitheatrof 19
- Man Ray 180
- Métiers d'Art 126, 139
- Nan Kempner 149
- Rihanna 236
- Victoire de Castellane 81
Chanel, Gabrielle "Coco" 60, 250
- Ballets Russes 9
- Codognato 71
- Cole Porter 228
- Fulco di Verdura 298
- Goossens 126
- Gripoix 129
- Swarovski 275
Changkou, Akon 239
Chao, Cindy 61
Charles I, King 11
Charles III, King 242
Charles VII, King 6
Charlotte of Mecklenburg-Strelitz 62
Chaumet 11, 63
- Faerber Collection 102
- Lily Safra 244
- Luz Mila Patiño Rodríguez 238
- Mahnaz Collection 177
- Moza bint Nasser 205
- Pierre Sterlé 270
Chaumet, Joseph 63
Chavez, Jared 64
Chavez, Richard 64
Chenet, Winifred Mason 65, 265
Chervin, André 55
Chevalier de l'Ordre des Arts et des Lettres 61
Chin, Edmond 34
Chiuri, Maria Grazia 160
Chloe 264
Choisne, Claire 10, 39
chokers
- De Beers 80
- House of Malakai 29
- Louise Bourgeois 40

Mary of Teck 187
Paul Flato 107
Chopard 37, 66, 236
Chopard, Louis-Ulysse 66
Chow Tai Fook 59, 67, 170
Christensen, Helena 60
Christian IX of Denmark 18
Christie's 13, 68, 277
    Catherine the Great 57
    Christie's New York 86
    Elizabeth Taylor 68, 280
    Fabergé 101
    Glenn Spiro 269
    Jewels for Hope 244
    María Félix 105
    Salimah Aga Khan 13
Cipriani, Elisabetta 96, 220
Cipullo, Aldo 69
Circle Fine Art 99
Claiborne, Barron 212
Claiborne, Liz 287
Clement VII, Pope 58
Cleveland, Pat 245
Clinton, Hillary 17
Coates, Kevin 70
Cocteau, Jean 239, 250
Codognato 19, 71, 276
Codognato, Attilio 71
Codognato, Simeone 71
Colbert, Claudette 204
Collins, Joan 33, 86
Colombara, Annalisa 36
Conant, Howell 148
Condé Nast 41
Consagra, Pietro 199
Conscious Mining 295
Constructivism 25
consumerism 6
Cooper, Wilhelmina 135
coral 8
Corbelin, Sylvie 72
Coro jewels 296
Coronation Regalia 187, 242
corsages 267
    Paulding Farnham 104
    René Lalique 161
Corticelli, Alberto 102
Corvaja, Giovanni 19, 73, 136
Cosmopolitan 132
Côte de Bretagne 110
Council of Fashion Designers of America (CFDA) 26, 33
Courteille, Lydia 49, 74
CoutureLab 49
Crawford, Joan 107
CRED Jewellery 289
Creole hoops 7, 10, 171
Criel, Dries 75
Croker-Poole, Sarah Frances (Salimah Aga Khan) 13
Crown Jewels 119
    "alternative" Crown jewels 267
    British Crown Jewels 8, 117
    Catherine the Great 57
    French Crown Jewels 8, 100, 110
    Iranian National Jewels 8, 218
    Italian Crown Jewels 249
Cruz, Rosa de la 49
CTF Pink Star 267
Cubism 43, 179, 223
Cullen family 86
Cullinan Diamond Mine 38
Cullinan I diamond 67, 187
Cullinan II diamond 22, 187
Cullinan III diamond 97
Cullinan IV diamond 97
Cullinan VIII diamond 187
Cult Beauty 49
Cummings, Angela 76, 149
Cummings, Bruce 76
Curiel, François 280

D

Dada 180
Dalí, Salvador 77, 98
    Ateliers Hugo 23
    Daniel Roseberry 239
    Diane Venet 297
    Didier Ltd 87, 200
    Elsa Schiaparelli 250
    Fulco di Verdura 298
    Louisa Guinness Gallery 175
    Sam Kramer 156
Dalits 7–8
Damiani 276
D'Annunzio, Gabriele 45
David 167
David Webb *see* Webb, David
Davies, Joseph E. 229
De Beers 80
    De Beers Diamonds International Awards 128
    De Beers Sightholder 278
    De Beers yellow diamond 261
    Golden Jubilee Diamond 284
    Lorraine West 309
    Satta Matturi 189
de Syllas, Charlotte 83
Decker, Ute 10, 84
Degen, Joel 247
Deiters, Michèle 292
de La Falaise, Loulou 82, 245, 285
Delettrez, Bernard 85
Delettrez Fendi, Delfina 85, 276
Delevingne, Cara 24
del Verrocchio, Andrea 167
Democratic Republic of the Congo 10, 289
Deneuve, Catherine 74, 180
Design Miami 96
Devonshire, sixth Duke of 131
di Portanova, Enrico (Ricky) 86
di Portanova, Sandra 86
di Sant'Angelo, Giorgio 221
diamonds
    Ashoka diamond 38
    Asscher cut 22
    Bleu de France 110
    Centenary Diamond 80, 284
    Côte de Bretagne 110
    Cullinan I diamond 67, 187
    Cullinan II diamond 187
    Cullinan III diamond 97
    Cullinan IV diamond 97
    Cullinan VIII 187
    De Beers 80
    De Beers yellow diamond 261
    Diamond Diadem 242
    English Dresden 113
    French Blue 279
    Golconda diamond 57
    Golden Jubilee Diamond 284
    Great Mogul Diamond 279
    Harry Winston 132
    Hope Diamond 132, 192, 279
    Koh-i-Noor diamond 117
    Krupp diamond 22
    lab-grown 10, 275
    Lahore diamond 301
    Lesedi La Rona diamond 127
    Louis IX 6
    Mazarin diamonds 110
    Millennium Star 80
    Moussaieff Red 203
    Oppenheimer Blue diamond 68
    Orlov Diamond 279
    Regent diamond 110
    Royal Cullinan diamond 22
    Sotheby's Diamonds 170
    Star of the East diamond 192
    Star of the South diamond 113
    Taylor-Burton diamond 54, 132
    Tiffany diamond 29, 251
    Tiffany Yellow Diamond 157
    Wittelsbach diamond 68
    Wittelsbach-Graff blue diamond 127
Diana, Princess of Wales 117, 119, 158
Didier Ltd 87
Dietrich, Marlene 9, 35, 88, 107
DiMaggio, Joe 198
Dine, Jim 178
Diné culture 173
Dior 81, 89, 160, 245
Dior, Christian 89
    Gloria Guinness 130
    Goossens 126
    Gripoix 129
    Kenneth Jay Lane 162
    Swarovski 275
    Victoire de Castellane 81
Dior Joaillerie 81
Diringer, Alexander 182
Dolce & Gabbana 275
Donald, John 90, 137, 177
Douglass, Frederick 208
Doutreleau, Victoire 89
Dreher, Gerd 91
Dreher, Patrick 91
Dreher Carvings 91
du Barry, Madame 68
du Boisrouvray, Comte Guy de Jacquelot 238
Du Pont family 253
Duchamp, Marcel 50
Duke, Doris 92, 107
Duke, James Buchanan 92
Dumas, Robert 134
Dunand, Jean 27
Durst, André 35
Dusausoy 93
Dusausoy, Justin 93
Dusausoy, Paul-Jules 93

E

earrings
    Adler 12
    Albion Art 16
    Alexander Calder 175
    Alexandra Mor 201
    Angela Cummings 76
    Arthur King 152
    Asprey Nuun Jewels 213
    Assael 21
    Azza Fahmy 103
    Bhagat 30
    Bina Goenka 125
    Boodles 38
    Buccellati 45
    Catherine Sarr 248
    Chopard 66
    Cora Sheibani 256
    Creole hoops 7, 10, 171
    Delfina Delettrez Fendi 85
    Erté 99
    Fabio Salini 246
    Fernando Jorge 143
    Gail Bird and Yazzie Johnson 32
    Gearry Suen 274
    John Donald 90

Lorraine West 309
Melanie Eddy 94
Messika 194
Nicholas Varney 294
Otto Jakob 141
Piaget 222
Sabba 243
Satta Matturi 189
Schiaparelli 239
Silvia Furmanovich 111
Sophia Vari 293
Tasaki 278
Vendôme 296
Vhernier 300
VRAM 305
East India Company 62
Ebihara, Yuto 195
École de la Chambre Syndicale de Bijouterie et de Horlogerie 14
École des Arts Industriels 122
École des Arts Décoratifs 299
Edaakie, Dennis 197
Eddy, Melanie 94
Edward VII, King 54, 308
Edward VIII, King 260
Egyptians, Ancient 5, 7, 10, 75, 78, 189
Ehrmann, Gilles 286
Einaudi, Luigi 249
Eisenhower, Mamie 287
Ekart, George Friedrich 57
Ekubia, Ndidi 95
El-Ain Gallery 103
El Yacoubi, Ansar 103
Elbaz, Alber 285
Eleanor, Queen of France 110
Elena of Montenegro, Queen 230, 249
Elisabetta Cipriani Gallery 96
Elizabeth II, Queen 8, 90, 97
   coronation 131, 242
     Haroldo Burle Marx 47
     Mary of Teck 187
     Millennium Star 80
     Pippa Small 264
     Sophia Loren 174
Ellies, Aji 191
Ellington, Duke 265
Ellis, Perry 304
Elson, Karen 163
Engelbert, Giovanna 275
English Art Works 269
English Dresden 113
Enners, Carol 156
Enninful, Edward 188
Erivo, Cynthia 112, 124
Ernst, Max 23, 98, 297
Erté (Romain de Tirtoff) 99
Escuela Sindical de Joyería 52
ethical credentials 10

Etruscan women 11
Eugénie de Montijo, Empress 100, 193
Exposition Internationale des Arts Décoratifs et Industriels Modernes (1925) 93
Exposition Universelle, Paris 39, 104, 299

Fabergé 91, 101, 158, 182
Fabergé, Peter Carl 101, 308
Faerber, Thomas 102
Faerber Collection 102
Fahmy, Azza 103
Fahmy, Randa 103
Fairmined gold 10, 49, 84, 289
Fairtrade Gold 289
Fairtrade International 289
Falize 110
Farnham, Paulding 104
Farouk, King of Egypt 270
Fashion Institute of Design & Merchandising 42
Fawzia, Princess 291
Fazioli, Livia Mimosa 186
Feldmeier, Johanna 127
Félix, María (La Doña) 105
Fellowes, Daisy 28, 35
Fendi 85
Feng J 106
Fenty 236
Féron, Louis 55
Ferragamo, Salvatore 303
Field, Patricia 33
Fioravanti, Maurizio 290
Fisher, Jennifer 214
Flato, Paul 107, 228
Flöckinger, Gerda 83
Folies Bergère 27
Fonssagrives, Fernand 108
Fonssagrives, Lisa 107, 108
Fonssagrives Solow, Mia 108
Fontana, Lucio 109, 199, 226
Ford, Tom 24, 264
Fossin, Jean-Baptiste 63
Fossin, Jules 63
Fouquet, Alphonse 179
Fouquet, Georges 179
Fouquet, Jean 179
Franchina, Nino 87
Francis I, King 58, 110
Frank, Jean-Michel 122
Frederick, Prince of Wales 117
French Blue diamond 279
Fresh, Doug E. 263

Freud, Sigmund 35
Frissell, Toni 130
Furmanovich, Silvia 49, 111, 205
The Future Is Brilliant project 295
Futurism 56, 179

G

Gabby Elan Jewelry 112
Gaga, Lady 31, 75, 239
Gaekwad, Maharaja Pratap Singh 113
Galerie MiniMasterpiece 114
Gallé, Émile 161
Galliano, John 89
Gallone, Marlène 115
Gallone, Paolo 115
Ganesha 247
Garbo, Greta 9, 107, 116, 251
Garrard 18, 117
   see also Asprey & Garrard
Garrard, Robert 117
Garvey, Marcus 265
Gaultier, Jean Paul 275
Geib, Judy 118
Gem Cellar 94
GEM Montebello 48, 109, 199, 226
Gem Palace 119
Gemological Institute of America 42, 138, 257
Georg Jensen 120, 177, 233, 286
Georgacopoulos, Melanie 121, 175, 278
George III, King 62, 159, 242
George IV, King 62, 242, 279
George V, King 38, 187
George VI, King 97
Ghali, Amina 103
Ghali, Fatma 103
Ghana Empire 6
Giacometti, Alberto 87, 122, 250
Giacometti Foundation 122
Gilot, Françoise 224
Gilson, Sean 21
Giorgio B 46
Givenchy 129, 163
Givenchy, Hubert de 123, 130
Givenchy, James de 123
Godfrey, Lauren Harwell 124
Goenka, Avanti 125
Goenka, Bina 125
Golconda diamond 57
gold 6
   Edo Japan 7
   Fairmined gold 10, 49, 84, 289
   Fairtrade Gold 289
   gold granulation technique 44

gold hoops 7, 10, 171
mining of 10, 289
Goldberg family 38
Golden Jubilee Diamond 284
Goldsmiths' Company 83, 90, 137, 266
   Goldsmiths' Company Award 200
Goossens 9, 60, 82, 89, 126
Goossens, Robert 126, 245
Gorgoni, Gianfranco 109
Goude, Jean-Paul 142
Graff 127, 188, 205
Graff, Francois 127
Graff, Laurence 127
Grande, Ariana 275
Granville, Countess of 131
Great Exhibition (1851) 117
Great Mogul Diamond 279
Greece, ancient 6, 7
Grès, Madame 126, 304
Grillz 26, 112
Grima, Andrew 128, 137, 177, 178
Gripoix 9, 129
   Chanel 60, 129
   Dior 89
   Loulou de La Falaise 82
   Yves Saint Laurent 245
Gripoix, Augustine 129
Gripoix, Suzanne 129
Guadagnino, Luca 276
Gucci 11, 264
Gucci Museo 19
Guggenheim, Peggy 50
Guinness, Daphne 74
Guinness, Gloria 130
Guinness, Louisa 175
Gurung, Prabal 278

Habana, Chris 26
Hadid, Bella 112, 239
Hadid, Zaha 96, 120, 177
Hallet 299
Halsman, Philippe 280
Halston 221
Hamel, Veronica 78
Hammer, Armand 57
Hancocks 131
Hannah Martin Pierced 185
Hardy, Pierre 134
Harpers & Queen 41
Harper's Bazaar 99, 135, 180, 188, 262, 265, 306
Harrah, William 168
Harris, Kamala 124

Harry Winston 9, 132
    Ambaji Shinde 257
    Anna Hu 138
    Carvin French 55
    Farah Diba Pahlavi, Empress 218
    Hiro 135
    Irving Penn 219
    Madonna 176
    Marilyn Monroe 198
    Reza 235
    Salimah Aga Khan 13
    Symbolic & Chase 277
    Wallis Simpson 260
Harwell Godfrey 124
Haspeslagh, Didier 87
Haspeslagh, Martine 87
Haute École d'Art et de Design 12
Haute École de Joaillerie 139
Hawkins, Rebecca 38
Hayworth, Rita 107
Hecate 43
hei tiki 184
Hemmerle 8, 133, 243
Hemmerle, Christian 133
Hemmerle, Yasmin 133
Henriques, Bob 198
Hepburn, Audrey 162
Hepburn, Katharine 107
Hepworth, Barbara 190
Hermès 134, 148, 166, 240
Herz, Bernard 28
Herz, Jean 28
Hiro 135, 221
Hjartarson, Ragnar 120
Hofer, Evelyn 50
Hoffmann, Josef 271
Hogg, Dorothy 136
Holiday, Billie 65
Holmes, Nevin 137
Holmes, William Frederick 137
Holzer, Jenny 297
Hooper, Elizabeth 214
Hope Diamond 132, 192, 279
Hope Ruby 244
Hopenhajm, Anthony 253
Hopi culture 173, 177, 197
Horne, Lena 265
Hornsey College of Art 83
Horst, Horst P. 92, 107
Hôtel de la Marine, Paris 15
House of Emmanuele 176
House of Malakai 29
Hovas, Sandra 86
Hozier, Lady Clementine 159
HStern 210
Hu, Anna 138
Hugo, François 23, 98, 223
Hugo, Nicolas 23
Hugo, Pierre 23, 223

Huguet, Capucine 139
Huguier, Françoise 245
Hussein, Saddam 17
Huston, Angelica 50
Hutton, Barbara 54, 140, 152
Hutton, Edward Francis 229
Hypatia 36

I

Iman 135, 245
IMG 20
Impressionism 138, 182
India 7–8
Industrial Revolution 6
Inez & Vinoodh 132
Institute for Afghan Arts and Architecture 94
Instituto Statale d'Arte Pietro Selvatico 25
International Exhibition of Modern Jewellery (1961) 90
Io, Kenji 266
Iranian Central Bank 8, 218
Iranian National Jewels 8, 218
iron 6, 7, 8, 9
Ispahani Bartos, Mahnaz 177
Istituto Statale d'Arte Pietro Selvatico 25

J

Jackson, Sophie 277
Jacob & Co. 176
Jacobs, Marc 112
Jacobsen, Arne 120
Jakob, Otto 141
James, Louisa 50
JAR *see* Rosenthal, Joel Arthur
Jeannet, Pierre 240
Jensen, Georg 120, 154
Jhaveri, Nanubhai 257
Jhaveri, Rahul 272
Jhaveri, Roshni 272
Johnson, Yazzie 32
Jolie, Angelina 119, 231, 252
Jones, Grace 142
Jones, Stephen 29
Jorge, Fernando 49, 143
Joseff of Hollywood 116, 198
Joseph Saidian & Sons 236
Josephine, Empress 63, 193
Judicael Sacred Skulls 144
Juzu, Kaori 145

K

Kahlo, Frida 146
Kamal, Dina 147
Kapoor, Anish 49, 175
Karan, Donna 202
Karim Al-Husseini, Prince 13
Kasliwal, Munnu 119
Kasliwal, Sanjay 119
Kasliwal family 119
Katz, Alex 199
Kelly, Grace 148, 159
Kempner, Nan 149
Kennedy, Jacqueline (Kennedy Onassis) 9–10, 150
    Andrew Grima 128
    David Webb 78
    Jean Schlumberger 251
    Kenneth Jay Lane 162
    Marguerite Stix 271
Kennedy, John F. 150
Kering 225
Khazzam, Sharon 151
Khouri, Ana 49
Kidman, Nicole 165
Kihry 214
kinetic art 25
King, Arthur 152
King, Martin Luther Jr. 208, 258
King, Phillip 114
Kinski, Nastassja 304
Kiss, Gabriella 153
Kissing technique 34
Knight, Nick 24
Knowles-Carter, Beyoncé *see* Beyoncé
Koh-i-Noor diamond 117
Koons, Jeff 175
Koppel, Henning 120, 154
Koppel, Nina 120
Kors, Michael 33, 202, 304
Koulis, Nikos 155
Kounellis, Jannis 96
Kramer 89
Kramer, François 100
Kramer, Sam 156
Kravitz, Zoë 190
Krupp diamond 22
Kubitschek, Juscelino 210
kundan jewelry 119
Kunz, George Frederick 157, 283
Kusama, Yayoi 297
Kutchinsky 158
Kutchinsky, Hirsch 158
Kutchinsky, Paul 158

L

LaChapelle, David 254
Lacloche, Jacques Jr. 159
Lacloche Frères 159
Lacroix, Christian 129
Lafferty, Bernard 92
Lagerfeld, Karl 60, 129
    Francesca Amfitheatrof 19
    Lydia Courteille 74
    Robert Lee Morris 202
    Swarovski 275
    Victoire de Castellane 81
Lahore diamond 301
Lalanne, Claude 49, 160, 175, 199, 245
Lalanne, François-Xavier 160
Lalaounis 86, 150
Lalique, René 161
La Maison de Loulou 82
Landrigan, Nico 28
Landrigan, Ward 28, 298
Lane, Kenneth Jay 149, 162, 306
Lanvin 27
Larsson, Emil 79
Lauren, Ralph 304
Le Monde des Arts de la Parure 115
Leane, Shaun 163
Lee, Austy 164
Lee, Grace 214
Lee Sung-kyung 45
Lee Ufan 114
Léger, Fernand 50
Léger, Hervé 188
Leguéreau, Patrice 60
Leighton, Fred 165, 244, 276
Lemonnier, Alexandre-Gabriel 100
L'Enchanteur 29
Lenfant, Georges 134, 166
Leonardo da Vinci 167
les Diamants de la Couronne de France 110
Lesedi La Rona diamond 127
Lewis, Mark 247
Liberace 168
Lichtenstein, Roy 169
Lichtenstein, Stella 178
Lieou, Nicholas 67, 170
Life 132, 280
Lindbergh, Peter 79, 188
Lipa, Dua 75
Lively, Blake 252
LL Cool J 171
Loggia dei Lanzi 58
Lola Fenhirst 172
Loloma, Charles 173, 197
Loren, Sophia 165, 174
Loring, John 224

Louguet 299
Louis IX, King 6
Louis XIII, King 193
Louis XIV, King 6, 110, 279
Louis XV, King 68, 110, 183
Louis Vuitton 19, 188
Louisa Guinness Gallery 175
Louise Nevelson Foundation 209
Louvre 15, 100, 102
Löwenfeld, Heger de 43
Lowit, Roxanne 224
Luce, Clare Boothe 152
Lucite 33, 304
Ludwig II, King of Bavaria 158
Lumley, Joanna 33
LVMH 46, 63, 283

M

Maar, Dora 217, 223
McCormack, Jessica 190
McGrath, Pat 188
McKinney, Margot 191
McLean, Edward Beale 192
McLean, Evalyn Walsh 192
McQueen, Alexander 163, 275
MACRO 96
Madame Figaro 37
Madonna 24, 138, 176
Mahnaz Collection 177
Maierhofer, Fritz 178
Maison Fouquet 179
Majeng, Mamuor 241
Malakai 26
Malcolm X 258
Man Ray 180, 202
    Didier Ltd 87
    GianCarlo Montebello 199, 226
    Louisa Guinness Gallery 175
    Hannah Martin 185
    Surrealism 98
Māori 184, 255
Mapplethorpe, Robert 181
Marchak 182
Marchak, Alexander 182
Marchak, Joseph 182
Margaret, Princess
    Andrew Grima 128
    Cartier 131
    Christie's auction 68
    John Donald 90
Margherita, Queen 249
Margrethe of Denmark, Queen 47
Maria Feodorovna, Empress 18
Maria Theresa, Archduchess 267

Marie Antoinette 8, 104, 140, 183, 229
    Affair of the Diamond Necklace scandal 62, 183
    Ange-Joseph Aubert 63
    Empress Marie-Louise 68, 100
    Mellerio dits Meller 193
    pearl pendant 267
Marie de Médici, Queen 193
Marie Louise, Empress 68, 100, 102, 219
Marina B 46, 86
Marineau, Guy 82
Marion, Helen 296
Maripiol 142
Markle, Meghan 190
Marshall, Brian 247
Marsters, Joel 184
Martin, Hannah 175, 185
Martin, Thierry 213
Martinelli, Francesca 186
Martinelli, Hedy 186
Martinelli, Vincenzo 186
Mary, Queen 8, 97, 117
Mary of Teck 187
Mattsson, Desiree 74, 188
Matturi, Satta 189
Matturi Fine Jewellery 189
Mauboussin 204
Maya 11
Mazarin, Cardinal 110
Mazarin diamonds 110
MC Lyte 7
Médici, Marie de 193
Medici family 167
Medusa 36, 58
Mellerio dits Meller 100, 193
Mellon family 253
Melrose, Ventura 75
Memphis group 268
Meneghini, Giovanni Battista 51
Mert and Marcus, 275
Merveilles technique 34
Messika 37, 194
Messika, André 194
Messika, Valérie 194
Metacom 7
Metropolitan Museum of Art 15, 20, 44
    Met Gala 11, 41, 165, 236, 252
Mikimoto 195, 198
Mikimoto, Kokichi 7, 195
Millennium Dome 80
Millennium Star 80
Minassian, Vram 305
Minimalism 25
Miranda, Carmen 107
Miró, Joan 77, 169
Misfit Diamonds 259
Mr. Lieou 170

Mr. T 206
Moda Operandi 49
Modernism
    Alberto Giacometti 122
    Andrew Grima 128
    Bhagat 30
    Ettore Sottsass 268
    Joy Bonfield-Colombara 36
    Richard Chavez 64
Mondrian, Piet 50
Monet, Claude 106
Monet Group 287
Monies 196
Monies, Gerda 196
Monies, Karl 196
Monies, Nikolai 196
Monongya, Jesse 197
Monongye, Preston 197
Monroe, Marilyn 198, 307
Montebello, GianCarlo 109, 160, 180, 199, 226
Moore, Gene 69
Moore, John 10–11, 200
Moore, Julianne 281
Moore, Roger 86
Mor, Alexandra 201
Morgan, J. P. 157
Morphit 10–11, 200
Morris, Robert Lee 202
Moss, Kate 194, 281, 295
Moussaieff 203
Moussaieff, Remo 203
Moussaieff, Shlomo 203
Moussaieff Red 203
Moutard, Juliette 35, 204
Moza bint Nasser, Sheikha 205
Mucha, Alphonse 179
Muehling, Ted 153
Mugler, Thierry 311
Mulas, Ugo 109, 199, 209
Multiples Inc. 169
Munari, Cleto 268
Muray, Nickolas 146
Muse, Arizona 132
Musée des Arts Décoratifs 43, 61, 96
Museum of Fine Arts Boston 70, 207
Musy Padre e Figli 249
Muzo Emerald Colombia 124, 211, 309

N

Nagar, Avi 216
Nakaba, Shinji 207
Napoleon I 8, 63, 100, 102, 219

Native Americans 7, 32, 64, 173, 197
Navajo 197
Nazli, Queen 291
necklaces
    Alexander Calder 50
    Alexis Bittar 33
    Ambaji Shinde 257
    Angela Cummings 76
    Art Smith 265
    Azza Fahmy 103
    Bina Goenka 125
    Bulgari 46
    Cartier 54
    Carvin French 55
    Castro NYC 56
    Charlotte de Syllas 83
    Chaumet 63
    Codognato 71
    David Yurman 79
    De Beers 80
    Diane Venet 297
    Dorothy Hogg 136
    Francesca Amfitheatrof 19
    Fred Leighton 165
    Fulco di Verdura 298
    Gem Palace 119
    Georges Braque 43
    Giorgio Vigna 302
    Giuseppe Penone 220
    Goossens 126
    Harry Winston 132
    Harwell Godfrey 124
    Henning Koppel 154
    Hermès 134
    Jacqueline Rabun 233
    Lily Safra 244
    Lola Fenhirst 172
    Louise Bourgeois 40
    Marchak 182
    Margot McKinney 191
    María Félix 105
    Max Ernst 98
    Melanie Georgacopolous 121
    Messika 194
    Mia Fonssagrives Solow 108
    Michele Oka Doner 96
    Ndidi Ekubia 95
    Nikos Koulis 155
    NN by NGHI 211
    Paul Flato 107
    Pomellato 225
    Robert Mapplethorpe 181
    Roy Lichtenstein 169
    Studio Renn 272
    Tasaki 278
    Ten Thousand Things 281
    Ute Decker 84
    Van Cleef & Arpels 291
    Victoire de Castellane 81
Neiman Marcus 76

Nelson, Johnny 208
Net-a-Porter 49
Nevelson, Louise 209
Nga, Nghi 211
Nicholas II, Tsar 66
Niedermair, Brigitte 222
Niemeyer, Oscar 210
Nita Mukesh Ambani Cultural Centre 41
Nitot, François-Regnault 63
Nitot, Marie-Étienne 63
Nizam Ali Khan 159
NN by NGHI 211
Noni, Julia 239
the Notorious B.I.G. 212
Nourah Al Faisal 213
Nuun Jewels 213
Nyong'o, Lupita 165, 201

Obama, Barack 252
Obama, Michelle 10, 143, 214
O'Keeffe, Georgia 281
O'Keiff, Natalie Kane 99
Okura Tokyo 16
Oladunjoye, Lola 172
Old World Weavers 20
Oloyé, Jariet 215
Omega 128, 178
Onassis, Aristotle 51, 150
Onassis, Jacqueline Kennedy *see* Kennedy, Jacqueline
Ong, Michelle 216
op art 25
Oppenheim, Méret 77, 217, 250
Oppenheimer Blue diamond 68
Orlan 297
Orlov, Count Grigory 57
Orlov Diamond 279
Orosemane, Mounia 245

Padua School 36, 87
Page, Russell 14
Pahlavi, Farah Diba, Empress 8, 47, 218
Paley, Babe 162, 298
Palme d'Or 66
Paltrow, Gwyneth 119
Panichgul, Thakoon 278
Parallel 26
Paris Fashion Week 124, 194, 241

Parker, Sarah 165
Parkinson, Norman 13, 86
Parsons School of Design 138
Patcharavipa 236
pâte de verre 129
Patiala, Maharaja of 54
Patiño, Simón 238
Pauzié, Jérémie 57
Pavilion of Art and Design (PAD) 96
PeaceGold 289
pearls 5, 9–10
   Assael 21
   Josephine Baker 27
   Melanie Georgacopolous 121
   Mikimoto 195
pectorals
   Azza Fahmy 103
   Benvenuto Cellini 58
   John Moore 200
pendants
   Castro NYC 56
   Elisabetta Cipriani Gallery 96
   Fulco di Verdura 298
   Henri Vever 299
   Maison Fouquet 179
   Max Ernst 98
   Mia Fonssagrives Solow 108
   Paul Flato 107
   Roy Lichtenstein 169
Penn, Irving 78, 108, 219
Penone, Giuseppe 96, 220
Peretti, Elsa 221
   Andy Warhol 307
   Beyoncé 29
   Diana Vreeland 306
   Tiffany & Co. 76, 135, 149, 221, 283
Perry, Grayson 175
Perseus 58
Peter III 57
Petochi 246
Philipp, the Duke of Württemberg 267
Philippe, Alfred 287
Philippe II, Duke of Orléans 110
the Phillips Collection 44
Philo, Phoebe 264
Piaget 222
Piaget, Georges-Édouard 222
Piaget, Yves 222
Picasso, Pablo 202, 223, 224
   Ateliers Hugo 23, 223
   Ballets Russes 9
   Cubism 43
   Diane Venet 297
   Didier Ltd. 87, 200
   Frida Kahlo 146
   Louisa Guinness Gallery 175
   Max Ernst 98

   Méret Oppenheim 217
   Roy Lichtenstein 169
   Tiffany & Co. 149
Picasso, Paloma 76, 224, 245, 283
Pinhasov, Elan 112
Pinhasov, Gabby 112
Pittman, Ashley 214
platinum 8–9
Platt, Harry 149
Pliny the Elder 141
Poiret 27
Poiret, Paul 99, 129
Pomellato 225
Pomodoro, Arnaldo 226
Pomodoro, Giò 226
Pomodoro, Teresa 109, 199
Pond, Toby McFarlan 69, 134
Ponsonby, Loelia, Duchess of Westminster 159
Pop art 169, 234
Portanuova Gioielli 86
Porter, Billy 227
Porter, Cole 192, 228, 298
Porter, Linda 228, 298
Portman, Natalie 138, 165
Post, Marjorie Merriweather 57, 229
pounamu 184
Prada, Miuccia 165
Prince Dimitri 230
Procop, Robert 231
Prussia 8
Pueblo culture 32, 64, 173
Pulsar 128
Putnam Art Works 79
Pyer Moss 208

Q

Queen Elizabeth Scholarship Trust 83
Quinn, Marc 175, 232

R

Rabolini, Pino 225
Rabun, Jacqueline 120, 233
Rainier III, Prince 148
Ramshaw, Wendy 234
Rawlings, John 260
Rees, David 281
Regent diamond 110
Reinoso, Pablo 114
Repossi 276

Repossi, Gaia 181
Reza 235
Reza, Alexandre 235
Reza, Olivier 235
Rhodes, Cecil John 80
Ricci, Nina 129
Richemont 300
Richter, Hans 199, 226
Rick, Slick 263
Rihanna 112, 124, 236
rings
   Arman Suciyan 273
   Austy Lee 164
   Bibi van der Velden 292
   Buccellati 45
   Castro Smith 266
   Daniela Villegas 303
   David Webb 78
   Dina Kamal 147
   Elie Top 285
   Elsa Sarantidou 247
   Ettore Sottsass 268
   Faerber Collection 102
   Garrard 117
   Giampaolo Babetto 25
   Graff 127, 188
   Hannah Martin 185
   Haroldo Burle Marx 47
   James de Givenchy 123
   Jariet Oloyé 215
   Johnny Nelson 208
   Kutchinsky 158
   LL Cool J 171
   Lola Fenhirst 172
   Lydia Courteille 74
   Marc Quinn 232
   Messika 194
   Monies 196
   Nicholas Lieou 170
   Oscar Niemeyer by HStern 210
   Pablo Picasso 223
   Pippa Small 264
   Richard Chavez 64
   Robert Procop 231
   Sevan Biçakçi 31
   Shinji Nakaba 207
   Solange Azagury-Partridge 24
   Suzanne Belperron 28
   Sylvie Corbelin 72
   Thelma West 310
   Walid Akkad 14
   Wendy Ramshaw 234
   Winifred Mason Chenet 65
Rivers, Joan 165
Robbie, Margot 252
Robert Mapplethorpe Foundation 181
Robinson, Michael 237
Rockefeller family 253
Rodkin, Loree 176, 214

Rodríguez, Luz Mila Patiño 238, 244
Rogers, Ginger 9, 107
Rogers, Millicent 262, 298, 307
Romans 5–6, 7
Roosevelt, Eleanor 265
Roosevelt, Franklin D. 253
Roseberry, Daniel 239
Rosenthal, Joel Arthur 240, 243
    Faerber Collection 102
    Lily Safra 244
    Nan Kempner 149
Rosenwald Fund 65
Rousteing, Olivier 241
Roversi, Paolo 61
Royal Asscher Diamond Company 22
Royal College of Art 36, 90, 121, 274
Royal Cullinan diamond 22
Royal House of Savoy 249
Royal Prussian Iron Foundry 8
RS&A 19
Rubartelli, Franco 296
ruby, Hope Ruby 244
Rundell, Bridge & Rundell 97, 242

S

Saadi, Aouatif 74
Sabatie, Eveli 173, 177
Sabba 243
Sabbatini, Alessandro 243
Sacador de Fuego 52
Safra, Lily 238, 244
Saint Laurent, Yves 245
    Claude Lalanne 160
    Elie Top 285
    Goossens 126
    Gripoix 129
    Loulou de La Falaise 82
    Nan Kempner 149
    Paloma Picasso 224
Saint Laurent Haute Joaillerie 245
St. Maarten 7
Saint Phalle, Niki de 199, 226
Saks Fifth Avenue 76
Salini, Fabio 246
Salon Art + Design 87
Salt-N-Pepa 7
samurai 7
Sánchez, Fernando 82
Sanchez, Violeta 245
Sarandon, Susan 281
Sarantidou, Elsa 247
Sarr, Catherine 248
Sarr, Mamadou-Abou 248
Sarr Collection 248

Saunders, Jennifer 33
Savopoulos, Theodoros 282
Savoy, Royal House of 249
Sayed, Hajj 103
Scemama, Roger 245
Schepps, Seaman *see* Seaman Schepps
Scheufele, Caroline 66, 236
Schiaparelli 23, 239
Schiaparelli, Elsa 239, 250
    Alberto Giacometti 122
    Jean Schlumberger 250, 251
    Lacloche Frères 159
    Méret Oppenheim 217
Schlumberger, Jean 150
    Elsa Schiaparelli 250, 251
    Kenneth Jay Lane 162
    Tiffany & Co. 19, 76, 135, 150, 250, 251, 283, 306, 307
School of Modern Photography 135
School of Visual Arts, New York 69
Schwartz, Lorraine 29, 227, 252
Seaman Schepps 253, 307
Selfridges 232
Seliti by Hedy Martinelli 186
Shakur, Tupac 254
Shalom, Lillian 26
Sheehan, Joe 255
Sheibani, Cora 49, 256
Shimoyama, Vivian 17
Shinde, Ambaji 257
Shrimpton, Jean 128
Simone, Nina 258
Simpkins, Maggi 259
Simpson, Wallis (Duchess of Windsor) 260
    Cartier 54
    David Webb 78
    Harry Winston 132
    Seaman Schepps 253
    Sotheby's auction 267
    Suzanne Belperron 28
    Van Cleef & Arpels 291
Singh, Sumit 119
Siriano, Christian 227
Sita Devi, Maharani 113
Sitwell, Edith 262
slavery 7, 8, 94
Slimane, Hedi 209
Sloane, Jenna 42
Small, Pippa 264
Smith, Adam 11
Smith, Art 65, 265
Smith, Castro 266
Smith, LaQuan 304
Smith, Patti 181
the Smithsonian 44, 61
Snowman, Emanuel 308
Solomon, Jack 99
Sonnabend, Joan 202

Sonwai (Verma Nequatewa) 173
Sorel, Agnès 6
Sotheby's 267, 277
    Andy Warhol 307
    Anna Hu 138
    Barbara Hutton 140
    Brilliant & Black (2022) 42, 95, 172, 259, 309
    hip-hop memorabilia 212
    Jackie Onassis 150
    Luz Mila Patiño Rodríguez 238
    Maria Callas collection 51
    Marie Antoinette 183
    online jewelry sales 9
    Sotheby's Diamonds 170
    Sotheby's New York 163
    Tupac Shakur 254
Sottsass, Ettore 196, 199, 268
Spada, David 142
Spartans 6
Spatialism 109
Sperling, Josh 23
Spiro, Glenn 269
Star of the East diamond 192
Star of the South diamond 113
Stella, Frank 297
Sterlé, Pierre 270
Stern, Bert 287
Stittgen, Karl 177
Stix, Hugh 271
Stix, Marguerite 271
Storr, Paul 242
Streep, Meryl 165
Streisand, Barbra 252
Studio Renn 272
Styles, Harry 11
Suciyan, Arman 273
Suen, Gearry 274
sumptuary laws 6, 7, 8
Suntum, Per 145
Surrealism
    Alberto Giacometti 122
    Art Smith 265
    Elsa Schiaparelli 250
    Fulco di Verdura 298
    Irving Penn portrait 219
    Joy Bonfield-Colombara 36
    Man Ray 180
    Max Ernst 98
    Méret Oppenheim 217
    Salvador Dalí 77, 298
    Schiaparelli 239
    Sylvie Corbelin 72
    Victoire de Castellane 81
Suzuki, Hiroshi 266
Svenskt Tenn 154
Swarovski 89, 275
Swift, Taylor 252
Swinton, Tilda 276
Symbolic & Chase 93, 277

T

Taffin 123, 243
Tajima, Toshikazu 278
Tanning, Dorothea 23
Tarpin, Emmanuel 37
Tasaki 121, 278
Tate, Sharon 128
Tavernier, Jean-Baptiste 110, 279
Taylor, Elizabeth 148
    Arthur King 152
    Bulgari 46
    Christie's sale 68, 280
    David Webb 78
    Jean Schlumberger 251
    My Love Affair with Jewelry 10
    Taylor-Burton diamond 22, 54, 132
TEFAF Maastricht 87
Teller, Juergen 112
Ten Thousand Things 281
Tethys 139
Theodoros 277, 282
Theron, Charlize 165, 190
Thom Browne 239
Thurman, Uma 138
tiaras 11
    Alexandra of Denmark 18
    Barbara Hutton 140
    Chaumet 63
    Elizabeth II 97
    Fabergé 101
    Farah Diba Pahlavi 218
    Feng J 106
    Garrard 97, 117
    Hamish Bowles 41
    Hancocks 131
    Lacloche Frères 159
    Lorraine Schwartz 252
    Mary of Teck 187
    Princess of Wales 54
    Queen Mary 187
    Royal House of Savoy 249
    Sophia Loren 174
Tiffany, Charles Lewis 283
Tiffany, Louis Comfort 104, 283
Tiffany & Co. 283
    Aldo Cipullo 69
    Angela Cummings 76
    Beyoncé 29
    Billy Porter 227
    Carvin French 55
    Doris Duke 92
    Elsa Peretti 221
    Eugénie de Montijo 100
    Francesca Amfitheatrof 19
    George Frederick Kunz 157
    Georges Lenfant 166

Jackie Onassis 150
Jean Schlumberger 19, 76, 135, 150, 250, 251, 283, 306, 307
Marilyn Monroe 198
Nan Kempner 149
Nicholas Lieou 170
Paloma Picasso 224
Paulding Farnham 104
Tiffany Diamond 251
Tiffany Yellow Diamond 157
Todd, Mike 280
Tolkowsky, Gabriel "Gabi" 284
Tom of Finland 185
Top, Elie 285
Toros, Misak 273
Torroni, Virginie 290
Torun (Vivianna Torun Bülow-Hübe) 286
Toussaint, Jeanne 54
Trabert & Hoeffer-Mauboussin 88, 116
Traglio, Carlo 300
Traglio family 300
Trapani, Francesco 46
Travis, Martin 277
Treasury of National Jewels 8
Trifari 9, 287
Trifari, Gustavo 287
Triolet, Elsa 250
Tritoff, Romain de (Erté) 99
Trott, Chet 94
Trova, Ernest 178
Truth, Sojourner 208
Tubman, Harriet 208
Tucson Gem Fair 124
Tuheitia, Kiingi 184
Tukoji Rao Holkar III, Maharaja 63
Turlington, Christy 129
Turquoise Mountain 94, 264
Tutu, Otumfuo Nana Osei, II 288
Twiggy 287
Tyler 112

U

Umberto I, King 249
Umberto II, King 249
Universal Pictures 303
Urquiola, Patricia 120

V

Vaccarello, Anthony 82
Vairelli, Amalia 245

Valentino 240, 311
Valerio, Greg 10, 289
Vales, Judicael 144
Vamgard 277, 290
Van Cleef, Alfred 291
Van Cleef & Arpels 291
  Alfred Philippe 287
  Andy Warhol 307
  Anna Hu 138
  Carvin French 55
  Faerber Collection 102
  Farah Diba Pahlavi, Empress, 8, 218
  Georges Lenfant 166
  Grace Kelly 148
  Hancocks 131
  Jackie Onassis 150, 162
  Juliette Moutard 204
  Lily Safra 244
  Luz Mila Patiño Rodríguez 238
  Madonna 176
  Maria Callas 51
  Marlene Dietrich 88
  Moza bint Nasser 205
  Salimah Aga Khan 13
  Sita Devi 113
  Sophia Loren 174
  Symbolic & Chase 277
  Wallis Simpson 260
Vanderbilt, Gloria 107
van der Velden, Bibi 292
Vari, Sophia 293
Varney, Nicholas 294
Vartanian, Ara 295
Vendôme 296
Venet, Bernar 297
Venet, Diane 96, 114, 297
Venice Biennale 96
Verdeille, Nathalie 283
Verdura 55, 149, 298
Verdura, Fulco di 298
  Chanel 60, 298
  Cole and Linda Porter 228, 298
  Diana Vreeland 306
  Greta Garbo 116
  Hamish Bowles 41
  Salvador Dalí 77, 298
Verger, Jacques 182
Verger Frères 204
Versace 232, 275
Versailles 63, 193, 230
Vertès, Marcel 250
Veruschka 296
Vever, Camille 299
Vever, Damien 299
Vever, Henri 299
Vever, Paul 299
Vhernier 300
Victor Emmanuel II, King 249

Victoria, Queen 18, 117, 131, 187, 242, 301
Victoria and Albert Museum 16, 70, 83, 95, 255
Vigié, Sophie 37
Vigna, Giorgio 302
Villegas, Daniela 49, 303
Virgin Mary 6
Vladimir, Grand Duchess of Russia 140, 230
von Musulin, Patricia 304
Vonnegut, Kurt 273
VRAM 305
Vreeland, Diana 306
David Webb 78
  Jean Schlumberger 251
  Kenneth Jay Lane 162
  Suzanne Belperron 28

W

Wainwright, Henry 38
Wales, Prince of 213
Wallace Chan Porcelain 59
Wallace Collection 70
Wallace Cut technique 59
Wallajah, Muhammad Ali 62
Wallerstedt, Sara Grace 61
Warhol, Andy 71, 307
Wartski 308
Wartski, Harriette 308
Wartski, Morris 308
Waterhouse, Suki 309
Watson, Gordon 24
Watts, Naomi 201
Waugh, Evelyn 262
Webb, David 78
  Aldo Cipullo 69
  Diana Vreeland 306
  Doris Duke 92
  Fred Leighton 165
  Jacqueline Kennedy Onassis 150
  Kenneth Jay Lane 162
  Nan Kempner 149
Webster, Stephen 273
Weckström, Björn 177
Wedgwood 19
Weil, George 177
Wendy Yue 164
West, Lorraine 29, 309
West, Mae 107
West, Thelma 310
Wheeler, Emily P. 214
White Cube, London 19
Whiting & Davis 196
Whitney, Betsey Cushing 41, 298

Wickes, George 117
Wilkins, RH 266
William, Prince of Wales 54
Williams, Pharrell 252
Windsor, Duchess of see Simpson, Wallis
Windsor, Duke of 54
Winfrey, Oprah 201
Winslet, Kate 165
Winston, Harry see Harry Winston
the Winter Show 87
Witherspoon, Reese 281
Wittelsbach diamond 68
Wittelsbach-Graff blue diamond 127
Wood, Natalie 296
Woolworth, Frank W. 140
World Gold Council 10
Worth, Charles Frederick 129

X

Xinyue, Chen 126
XIV Karats 236

Y

Yamaguchi, Sayoko 245
Yamamoto, Kansai 202
Yard, Raymond 55
Yazzie, Lee 197
Yewn, Dickson 214
Yoruba culture 172, 215
Young, J. B. 283
Yurman, David 79
Yurman, Sybil 79
Yusupov, Felix 229

Z

Zendaya 190, 311
Zolotas 160, 224
Zschaler, Othmar 102

Acknowledgments

They say you should never take advice, but, really, I have found advice is only as good as the inspirational nature of those who give it. In that vein, I would like to dedicate this book to my mother, Maudie, who taught me the meaning of freedom. When I was a child, she advised me that I could be and do anything, and I believed her, which is why I'm here today within the pages of this book. When writing my first book, *Coveted*, for Phaidon, jeweler Nicholas Varney advised me never to give my power away for money, and that profound piece of advice has stood me in good stead as a writer over the years. Wallace Chan advised me to empty my cup so that better things could come, and they did. I pass on these morsels in the hope that you follow your own jewelry dreams and as a thanks to those who have helped me follow mine. To the writers whom we commissioned to create this book, I thank you. To the photographers, designers, artists, brands, illustrators, collectors, and institutions who gave us permission to use their imagery, and to the advisory committee who gave their thoughts on who should be included—a world of thanks to you, too. Much love goes to Lynne, my fabulous commissioning editor; Deb for saying yes to a jewelry book of this magnitude at Phaidon; and Siobhan for her crack marketing skills. Freedom, I realized quite some time ago, is everything, and every piece of good advice will point you, as it did me, in that direction.

The publisher would also like to thank Rosie Pickles, Annalaura Palma, Sarah Massey, Laine Morreau, Amélie Cherlin, Vanessa Bird, Victoria Clarke, Olivia Clark, Deb Monti, and João Mota.

Advisory Panel

Catherine Cariou
Elisabetta Cipriani
Richard Edgcumbe
Frank Everett
Didier and Martine Haspeslagh
Mahnaz Ispahani Bartos
Amin Jaffer
Daphne Lingon
Caroline Morrissey
Valeria Napoleone
Katherine Purcell
Adrianne Sanogo
Daisy Shaw-Ellis
Emily Stoehrer
Antonello Trifelli
Diane Venet
Trino Verkade

Text Credits

Felix Bischof: 13, 40, 60, 69, 135, 210, 224, 239, 245
Charlie Boyd: 72, 75, 215
Annabel Davidson: 28, 83, 95, 123, 183–84, 190, 202, 207, 255
Anthony DeMarco: 21, 44, 59, 76, 87, 107, 133, 141, 177, 222, 231, 253, 267, 280, 298
Maria Doulton: 31, 70, 86, 96, 105, 115, 136, 146, 152, 158, 175, 200, 230, 235, 242–43, 274, 281, 288–89
Tanya Dukes: 27, 104, 118, 151, 153, 258, 265, 276, 294, 309
Francesca Fearon: 18, 34, 49, 82, 92, 113, 163–64, 194, 204, 216, 250, 261, 272, 279, 285, 287, 304, 308
Melanie Grant: 36–37, 39, 56, 137, 188, 213, 237, 240, 247
William Grant: 128
Avril Groom: 12, 19, 24, 38, 74, 89, 90, 193, 264, 266, 269
Amin Jaffer: 16, 30, 57, 62, 100, 110, 218
Sebastian Kaufmann: 41, 78, 106, 126, 142, 170, 203, 219, 244, 252, 277, 291, 306
Milena Lazazzera: 15, 35, 51, 54, 71, 73, 84, 88, 101, 121, 134, 174, 182, 229, 249, 270, 282
Ming Liu: 61, 68, 80, 132, 278
Kate Matthams: 26, 32, 64, 67, 150, 176, 214, 233, 241, 302
Kim Parker: 29, 33, 53, 63, 66, 97, 117, 124, 140, 187, 189, 192, 195, 221, 251, 283
Elizabeth Peng: 17, 20, 22, 91, 119–20, 138, 145, 162, 165, 178–79, 196–97, 234, 275
Coco Romack: 98, 168, 180–81, 199, 212, 227, 263, 268, 297, 299
Sarah Royce-Greensill: 23, 45, 81, 85, 94, 103, 111, 127, 143, 147, 155, 185, 248, 292, 295, 303, 305
Smitha Sadanandan: 14, 52, 79, 125, 172, 191, 211, 256, 259, 273, 310
Adrianne Sanogo: 157, 171, 257, 284
Hannah Silver: 50, 77, 205, 223, 236, 238, 254, 260, 262, 286, 301, 307, 311
Emily Stoehrer: 55, 116, 129, 148, 156, 173, 228
David Trigg: 25, 43, 47–48, 93, 99, 108–9, 122, 154, 160, 217, 220, 232, 293
Amanda Triossi: 46, 186, 225, 246, 290, 300
Ranyechi Udemezue: 42, 65, 112, 139, 208
Alexandra Zagalsky: 58, 102, 114, 130–31, 144, 149, 159, 161, 166–67, 169, 198, 201, 206, 209, 226, 271, 296

Image Credits

Every reasonable effort has been made to identify owners of copyright. Errors and omissions will be corrected in subsequent editions.

© ADAGP, Paris and DACS, London 2025: 43, 220; Photo: Greg Adamski/Art director & stylist: Ahmed Rashwan -1602 studio/Makeup: Manuel Losada/Hair: Deena Alawaid/Model: Ansar Elyacoubi: 103; Adler: 12; Pedro Aguilar: 34; Courtesy Albion Art: 16; DeMarcus Allen: 94, 248, 259; © The Al Thani Collection/Photo by Laziz Hamani: 15; Photo by Scott Archibald: 49; Image from Archive.org/Contributed by the GIA: 157; © Arkivi UG All Rights Reserved/Bridgeman Images: 101; Simon B Armitt/@simonbarmitt: 83, 215; Clive Arrowsmith/Camera Press/Redux: 13; © Les Arts Décoratifs/Jean Tholance: 299; Courtesy Assael: 21; Atelier Mai 98/Jeremy Zenou: 14; Photo: Baker & Evans/www.fernandojorge.co.uk: 143; Courtesy Barrett Barrera Projects: 163; Carlo Bavagnoli/The LIFE Picture Collection/Shutterstock: 218; Oliver Beamish Photography: 233; Cecil Beaton/Camera Press/Redux: 51, 140; Cecil Beaton/Condé Nast Collection via Getty Images: 159; © Cecil Beaton/Victoria and Albert Museum, London: 97; © Richard Bellia: 171; Steve Benisty: 108; Photo Danita Bethea/Johnny Nelson: 208; Bettmann via Getty Images: 88, 168; Bettmann via Getty Images/© Salvador Dalí, Fundació Gala-Salvador Dalí, DACS 2025: 77; BHAGAT Images: 30; Bibliothèque nationale de France: 35; Image by Leo Bieber: 277; Clemens Bilan/AFP via Getty Images: 205; Photo: Alexis Bittar & KRONUS/Courtesy Alexis Bittar/Model Amam at Marilyn NY: 33; Photo by Jillian Boardman/Designed by Pippa Small: 264; Bonhams: 173, 271; Isabelle Bonjean: 300; Isabelle Bonjean for *Citizen K* magazine: 37; Adrian Boot/Urbanimage.tv/Camera Press/Redux: 142; Boucheron: 39; Latoya Boyd, GIA GG: 42; Bridgeman Images: 58, 100; Private Collection/Bridgeman Images: 152; Photo by Jane Bown/Camera Press London: 262; Clarissa Bruce: 70; Photo: Anthony Byrne/Courtesy Hannah Martin Ltd: 185; Caleb & Gladys/Trunk Archive: 309; Calouste Gulbenkian Museum, inv. 1197/Photo: Catarina Gomes Ferreira: 161; Capucine H/Photo: Di Messina: 139; Stephane Cardinale/Corbis via Getty Images: 241; Courtesy Carnet Jewellery: 216; Gilbert Carrasquillo/GC Images via Getty Images: 252; Courtesy Susannah Carson: 53; Photo by Tom Carter/Courtesy Louisa Guinness Gallery/© Marc Quinn, 2025: 232; © Fondation Henri Cartier-Bresson/Magnum Photos: 113; Castro NYC, all rights reserved/The Castro Family: 56; Vittorio Zunino Celotto via Getty Images: 311; Courtesy Wallace Chan: 59; Chopard: 66; Chow Tai Fook Jewellery Group Limited: 67; Christie's Images, London/Scala, Florence: 68, 76, 182, 240, 244, 257, 307; Christie's Images/Bridgeman Images: 55; Liz Collins/Trunk Archive: 85; © Howell Conant/Adelman Images, LP: 148; Mike Coppola/Staff/Getty Images Entertainment: 41; © Sylvie Corbelin: 72; Richard Corkery/New York Daily News Archive via Getty Images: 176; © Giovanni Corvaja/Victoria and Albert Museum, London: 73; Dries Criel Jewelry: 75; © DACS 2025: 286; David Michael Jewels: 237; De Beers Group: 80, 284; Artist Ute Decker/Photo by Xavier Young: 84; Thomas Deschamps: 63; Didier Ltd, London: 137; Didier Ltd, London/Artwork © Salvador Dalí, Fundació Gala-Salvador Dalí, DACS 2025: 87; © Dior Joaillerie: 81; Kevork Djansezian/Stringer/Getty Images Entertainment: 29; John and Cynthia Donald Archive: 90; Photo: Jordan Doner/Artwork © Erede Ettore Sottsass DACS, London 2025: 268; Photo: Jordan Doner/Stylist: Tiffany Dubin/Model: Zara Black/Artwork © The Easton Foundation/VAGA at ARS, NY and DACS, London 2025: 40; Iga Drobisz: 121; Ndidi Ekubia: 95; Collection Angel Elechiguerra © Ignacio Castillo: 105; Courtesy Elisabetta Cipriani Gallery and Giorgio Vigna: 302; Courtesy Elisabetta Cipriani Gallery and Sophia Vari: 293; Photo: Alexander English/Louisa Guinness Gallery/Artwork © 2025 Calder Foundation, New York/DACS, London: 175; Courtesy Everett Collection: 162; Everett Collection/Bridgeman Images: 150; From the Faerber-Collection/Photo © Katharina Faerber: 102; Courtesy FD Gallery, New York: 243; Deborah Feingold/Corbis Premium Historical via Getty Images: 17; Santiago Felipe/FilmMagic via Getty Images: 227; Fine Art Images/Heritage Images via Getty Images: 249, 279; Courtesy Silvia Furmanovich: 111; Noam Galai/Stringer/Getty Images Entertainment: 20; Galerie MiniMasterpiece/Sophia Vari/Photo by Yann Delacour: 114; Garrard: 117; Alan Gelati/Contour RA via Getty Images: 165; Georg Jensen Archives: 120, 154; Eddie Gerald/Alamy Stock Photo: 288; © Succession Alberto Giacometti/DACS 2025/Photo © James Dunn: 122; Photo by Cho Gi-Seok: 46; Courtesy Bina Goenka: 125; Photo © Nathaniel Goldberg: 19; Photo Ali Emre Göloğlu/Courtesy Elisabetta Cipriani Gallery: 96; Photo: Ali Emre Göloğlu/Courtesy Giampaolo Babetto and Elisabetta Cipriani Gallery: 25; Photo by Álvaro Gracia: 126; Grima Archives: 128; © Philippe Halsman/Magnum Photos: 280; Hancocks London: 131; Photo: James Hart, Santa Fe, New Mexico, USA/Courtesy the Owings Gallery, Santa Fe, New Mexico, USA: 32; Courtesy Hemmerle, Maximilianstrasse 30, 80539, Munich, +49 89 24 22 600, hemmerle.com: 133; © Bob Henriques/Magnum Photos: 198; Heritage Art/Heritage Images via Getty Images: 62; Heritage Images/Hulton Archive via Getty Images: 183; Hillwood Estate, Museum & Gardens/Photo by Edward Owen: 229; Estate of Evelyn Hofer/Premium Archive via Getty Images/Artwork © 2025 Calder Foundation, New York/DACS, London: 50; Maarten Holl, Te Papa: 184; Horst P. Horst, *Vogue* © Condé Nast: 92; Horst P. Horst/Condé Nast Collection via Getty Images: 107; Courtesy HSTERN/Artwork © Oscar Niemeyer/DACS 2025: 210; Françoise Huguier/Agence VU: 245; Anna Hu Haute Joaillerie: 138; Hulton Archive/Hulton Royals Collection via Getty Images: 187; Inez and Vinoodh/Trunk Archive: 132; © Otto Jakob/Photo: Volker Kirschner: 141; Kate Jackling © Cartier: 54; J.N.Luc: 106; Chris W Johnson for Stephanie Windsor: 158; J. T. Vintage/Bridgeman Images: 27; Courtesy Judicael Sacred Skulls: 144; Kaori Juzu: 145; Stylist: Yoko Kageyama/Realization: Yumiko Akita: 278; Dina Kamal/dinakamal.com: 147; Photo by Hee Jin Kang for Mahnaz Collection: 197; Sharon Khazzam Studio: 151; Photo: Turi Lovik Kirknes/Matturi Limited UK/Nomoli Totem Design: 189; Photo: Kevin Kish/Courtesy Mahnaz Collection: 177; Thomas Kletecka: 281; Courtesey Nick Knight & SHOWstudio, 2012: 24; Courtesy Nikos Koulis: 155; Deniz Köylü: 273; © Estate of Sam Kramer/Photo © 2025 Museum of Fine Arts, Boston: 156; David LaChapelle/Contour RA via Getty Images: 254; Karl Lagerfeld: 60; Karl Lagerfeld/Retro AdArchives/Alamy Stock Photo: 129; © Emil Larsson: 79; Photo: Matthieu Lavanchy/Artwork © ADAGP, Paris and DACS, London 2025/ © Yves Saint Laurent: 160; Austy Lee: 164; Leon Production Limited Hong Kong: 170; Library of Congress, Prints & Photographs Division, photo by Harris & Ewing, LC-DIG-hec-16763: 192; Library of Congress, Prints & Photographs Division, Toni Frissell Photograph Collection, LC-DIG-tofr-01445: 130; © Estate of Roy Lichtenstein/DACS 2025/Artimage 2024: 169; Josephine Löchen: 124; Photo: Louisa Guinness Gallery/Alexander English/Artwork © Man Ray 2015 Trust/DACS, London: 180; © Roxanne

Lowit: 224; Baard Lunde/Trunk Archive: 127; Jack MacMillan/New York Daily News Archive via Getty Images: 228; Courtesy Mahnaz Collection: 64; Fritz Maierhofer: 178; *Untitled (Necklace)*, c. 1974 © Robert Mapplethorpe Foundation. Used by permission: 181; Guy Marineau/WWD/Penske Media via Getty Images: 82; © le MAP Marrakech: 115; Courtesy Hedy Martinelli: 186; Eugénie Martinez: 213; Courtesy Margot McKinney: 191; Photo © Takaaki Matsumoto: 44; Photo by Desiree Mattsson: 74, 188; Zoë Kravitz for Jessica McCormack by Campbell Hooper: 190; Mellerio dits Meller Collection: 193; Messika Paris, Fiery Collection/© Isabelle Bonjean: 194; Image copyright the Metropolitan Museum of Art/Art Resource/Scala, Florence/Artwork © ARS, NY and DACS, London 2025: 99; Mikimoto: 195; James Mollison/Contour RA via Getty Images: 71; Necklace by John Moore, modeled by the artist/Photo: David Myers: 200; Image Courtesy Alexandra Mor/Photo by Russell Starr: 201; Martin Morrell: 246; Morten Bjarnhof & Monies: 196; Photo by Shawn Mortensen: 212; Moussaieff Jewellers: 203; David Muir via Getty Images: 289; Photo Ugo Mulas © Ugo Mulas Heirs. All rights reserved: 199, 209; Photo Ugo Mulas © Ugo Mulas Heirs. All rights reserved/Christie's Images, London/Scala, Florence/Artwork © Lucio Fontana/SIAE/DACS, London 2025: 109; Photo by Nickolas Muray/© Nickolas Muray Photo Archives: 146; Museum of Fine Arts, Boston. All rights reserved/Scala, Florence: 204; Courtesy Shinji Nakaba: 207; NN by NGHI: 211; Photo: Brigitte Niedermair: 222; Julia Noni/Trunk Archive: 239; Michael Oldford for SquareMoose: 230; François Pagès/Paris Match via Getty Images: 174; Norman Parkinson/Iconic Images: 86; Irving Penn, *Vogue* © Condé Nast: 78; Irving Penn/Condé Nast Collection via Getty Images: 219; Al Pereira/Michael Ochs Archives via Getty Images: 263; Mark Peterson/Redux: 149; Pictures from History/Bridgeman Images: 261; Courtesy Richard Pierce: 235; Christian Poite © de Laszlo Foundation: 238; Courtesy Pomellato: 225; Toby McFarlan Pond/Trunk Archive: 69, 134; Robert Procop Exceptional Jewels: 231; Menelik Puryear: 172; @rachell_photo: 38; Courtesy Ragc/Wright: 265; Robert Randall/Condé Nast Collection via Getty Images: 250; Priscilla Rattazzi: 306; John Rawlings/Condé Nast Collection via Getty Images: 260; David Redfern/Redferns via Getty Images: 258; Luisa Ricciarini/Bridgeman Images: 57; Jeff Riedel/Contour RA via Getty Images: 214; RM/Trunk Archive: 276; Eric Robert/Sygma via Getty Images: 206; Ann Ronan Pictures/Print Collector via Getty Images: 18; Photo by Olivia Rose: 36; © Paolo Roversi/Art+Commerce: 61; © Royal Collection Enterprises Limited 2024/Royal Collection Trust: 242; Royal Collection Trust/© His Majesty King Charles III, 2024/Bridgeman Images: 110, 301; Franco Rubartelli/Condé Nast Collection via Getty Images: 296; Javier Salas for Classpaper: 52; Photo: Serdan Salman/© Sevan Bıçakçı, 2022: 31; Photo: Nikolaï Saoulski/J. Vasconcelos/Galerie MiniMasterpiece/Courtesy the artist and Diane Venet/Artwork © Joana Vasconcelos, SPA/ DACS 2025: 297; Photo courtesy the Scottish Gallery: 136, 234; Courtesy Seaman Schepps: 253; © Mark Shaw/mptvimages.com: 89; Courtesy Joe Sheehan and Tim Melville Gallery: 255; Cora Sheibani: 256; Courtesy Silverhorn Jewelers/Photo: Robert Weldon/© GIA: 91; Castro Smith: 266; Photo Courtesy Sotheby's: 267; Photo: Sotheby's/Artwork © Succession Picasso/DACS, London 2025: 223; Photo Courtesy Sotheby's/Bridgeman Images: 270; Photo © Sotheby's/Bridgeman Images: 28; Photo © Sotheby's/Bridgeman Images/Artwork © ADAGP, Paris and DACS, London 2025: 179; Photo: Sotheby's/Courtesy Fondazione Arnaldo Pomodoro: 226; Photo: Sotheby's/Private collection/Artwork © ADAGP, Paris and DACS, London 2025: 48; Photo Maxime Souyri: 23; Courtesy Sperlich Jewelry: 47; Courtesy Glen Spiro/www.glennspiro.com: 269; Square Moose Photography: 294; Photo: Joel Stans/Artwork © ADAGP, Paris and DACS, London 2025: 98; Bert Stern/Condé Nast Collection via Getty Images: 287; Studio Renn: 272; Courtesy Gearry Suen: 274; Courtesy Swarovski: 275; Courtesy Symbolic & Chase: 93, 282; Taffin: 123; © Juergen Teller, All Rights Reserved: 112; Photo by Hormis Antony Tharakan/Image from the Tarun Tahiliani Summer 2020 Bridal campaign: 119; Courtesy Tiffany & Co.: 221, 251, 283; Courtesy Elie Top: 285; Ullstein bild via Getty Images: 116; VAMGARD Roma/Fioravanti: 290; © Van Cleef & Arpels SA: 291; © Dirk Vandenberk: 118, 153; Bibi van der Velden: 292; Ara Vartanian/Photo by Gabriel Cabral: 295; © Veneranda Biblioteca Ambrosiana/Metis e Mida Informatica/Mondadori Portfolio/Bridgeman Images: 167; Daniele Venturelli/WireImage via Getty Images: 236; © Verdura: 298; Daniela Villegas: 303; Photo: Giorgios Vitsaropoulos/Jewelry by Elsa Sarantidou: 247; Patricia von Musulin: 304; Vram: 305; © 2025 Estate of Y. Hiro Wakabayashi: 135; Photo: Hans-Jörg Walter/Courtesy Gems and Ladders/Artwork © DACS 2025: 217; The Walters Art Museum, Baltimore: 104; Wartski, London: 308; Thelma West: 310; Susan Wood/Archive Images via Getty Images: 202; JP Yim/Stringer/Getty Images Entertainment: 26; © Kim Young-Jun/Buccellati/Courtesy *Vogue* Korea: 45.

Phaidon Press Limited
2 Cooperage Yard
London E15 2QR

Phaidon Press Inc.
111 Broadway
New York, NY 10006

Phaidon SARL
55, rue Traversière
75012 Paris

phaidon.com

First published 2025
© 2025 Phaidon Press Limited

ISBN 978 1 83866 778 8

A CIP catalogue record for this book is available from the British Library and the Library of Congress.

All rights reserved. No part of this publication may be reproduced, stored in a retrieval system or transmitted, in any form or by any means, electronic, mechanical, photocopying, recording, or otherwise, without the written permission of Phaidon Press Limited.

Commissioning Editor: Lynne Ciccaglione
Production Controller: Zuzana Cimalova
Design: Flávia Nalon/ps.2

Printed in China

phaidon.com

978 1 83866 778 8